REVOLUTION IS THE CHOICE OF THE PEOPLE

Revolution is the Choice of the People

Anne Alexander

Revolution is the Choice of the People
by Anne Alexander

First edition published by Bookmarks in 2022
© Bookmarks Publications Ltd
c/o 1 Bloomsbury Street, London WC1B 3QE
bookmarksbookshop.co.uk

ISBN 978-1-914143-10-6 paperback
ISBN 978-1-914143-11-3 Kindle
ISBN 978-1-914143-12-0 epub
ISBN 978-1-914143-13-7 pdf

Typeset by Kev Kiernan for Bookmarks Publications
Cover design by Simon Assaf
Printed by Halstan & Co, Amersham, England

Contents

Acknowledgements		7
Introduction		13

Section 1: The cycle of revolution and counter-revolution

Chapter 1	What makes a revolution?	21
Chapter 2	The deluge: 2011-12	37
Chapter 3	The ebb and the flow: 2013-22	71

Section 2: The roots of revolution

Chapter 4	States, capitals and markets: the making of the Middle East	109
Chapter 5	The short state capitalist era and its long legacy	137
Chapter 6	Neoliberalism: a realignment of the state and capital	155
Chapter 7	Politics in the neoliberal era	177

Section 3: Agents of change

Chapter 8	'Neither bread nor freedom': the conditions for popular revolt	207
Chapter 9	The revival of the workers' movement	237
Chapter 10	Partners in revolution? Women and the uprisings	265

Section 4: The crisis of the state and the permanent revolution

Chapter 11	Faust's bargain: the failure of reformist strategies	299
Chapter 12	'You became a whip in the hands of the powerful'	323
Chapter 13	'The permanent revolution' and the conditions for dual power	345
Chapter 14	Egypt, Syria, Sudan: Results and prospects	373
Conclusion	The revolutionary party	411

Acknowledgments

The first person who deserves credit for this book reaching publication is Colm Bryce of Bookmarks, who suggested the idea to me that I should write something "for the anniversary of the Arab revolutions." That was in 2020, and at the time we both thought it would all be wrapped up in time for January 2021. To his credit, Colm has stuck with the project throughout, despite numerous detours and a delay of a year and a half after the original planned publication date. Without his dogged persistence it would never have been finished and I am very grateful for that.

Yet in many ways the longer time has not been wasted, as the book would have been much poorer without reflection on the development of the revolutionary process in Sudan, where following the military coup in October 2021 the Resistance Committees took the lead in re-igniting the popular movement. This is one of the dilemmas of writing about revolutions while they are happening, instead of safely relegated to history: the creativity and sheer invention of the people who have chosen revolution will always surprise you. The difficulty is knowing when to stop, when to close the pages.

I have learnt a great deal from Sudanese activists over the past three years, and many of those conversations have fed into this book, especially those with Muzan Alneel, Mohamed Abelrahman, Marwa Kessinger and Rania Obead, Fatima Rushwan and colleagues from the Sudanese Uprising Support Group in Edinburgh. Some of those discussions have also been part of work to build solidarity with the Sudanese Revolution through MENA Solidarity the network of trade unionists and activists I helped to found in 2011. Miriam Scharf, Donny Gluckstein and

Louise Regan have all played a crucial role in this process and which has formed part of the bedrock on which this book as an intellectual project is based.

MENA Solidarity and the wider networks it connects to have been an essential element in the process of writing. Unlike an academic research project, this book has grown out of attempts to build practical solidarity with some of the movements discussed here. I want to thank Alice Finden, Luke Bhatia, Irang Bak, Andy Reid and the many other people who keep MENA Solidarity going. Sheila Amrouche made a huge contribution to our coverage of Algeria which helped me understand much better the dynamics of the uprising there in 2019, and also read through the manuscript of this book, making careful comments (and reminding me not to forget the North African dimensions of the regional revolution).

Jad Bouharoun was also one of several generous readers, and someone who has shaped the final outcome through many years of discussions. Other comrades who gave their time to read the whole or part included Gianni Del Panta, Sheila McGregor, Charlie Kimber, Martin Empson, Muzan Alneel and Hossam el-Hamalawy.

The impact of the Egyptian revolution and counter-revolution is a thread which runs throughout this project and the ideas articulated here are forever indebted to the many Egyptian comrades I have been lucky enough to know and work with over the last 30 years. In particular, books and articles I have co-authored with Mostafa Bassiouny and Sameh Naguib played a key role in developing some of the ideas here. I would also like to thank Ahmed Ezzat for sharing his recollections of the development of the Popular Committees for the Defence of Revolution. There are many other comrades in Egypt whose experiences and ideas have fed into this project, and I am sorry not to be able to acknowledge that in full.

Much of the theoretical framework for the book was tested out in the reading group I set up on Crisis, Resistance and Revolution in the Middle East during 2020. Oisin Challen Flynn, Nadia Sayed, Naima Omar, Irang Bak, Ethan Pratt, Richard Donnelly and Hared Abdullah joined the group and their contributions to the discussions we had helped shaped the arguments outlined here. Thanks are also due to Alex Callinicos and Joseph Choonara as editors of *International Socialism* for publishing many of the articles which allowed me to develop the foundations of the book's arguments, and to comrades on the editorial board and beyond whose comments enriched both the content and the writing.

Discussions with John Rose on the questions of dual power and the failures (and occasional victories) of communist movements in the 20th century helped to clarify my thoughts and stimulated new sets of questions. In particular I have learnt from him that the questions which might be unanswerable or even unknowable are the most important to keep asking.

It is customary at this point to move on to personal thanks, especially to harassed and exasperated family members for forbearance. Like everyone who writes anything, I am aware that the space and time to create is all too often a privilege, and I am immensely grateful to my sons and partner for putting up with all the emotional baggage and late nights working which came with writing this book.

D.N, you know who you are—thank you for reading it and for believing in me even when I didn't believe in myself.

Thanks too to Simon Assaf for designing a very striking cover and to Kev Kiernan for all his work on the layout of the book.

Finally, it is also customary to also to add the caveat that none of the above can be held responsible for errors and omissions in the text. One person who can certainly be absolved of that responsibility is Phil Marfleet, who quite sensibly read part of the draft and suggested strongly that I should take an extra few months before finishing it. I have on this occasion ignored his advice, but in many ways he is partially responsible for the project itself, since he was one of the people who first showed me that it is possible to write with rigour and commitment without giving up on acting in the world to change it.

Anne Alexander
19 June 2022

Revolution is the choice of the people

Freedom, peace and justice
Revolution is the choice of the people

Sudanese protesters' chant, April 2019

Revolution is the choice of the people

Introduction

The theoretical framework which underpins this book draws especially on the work of major figures from the classical revolutionary Marxist tradition, including Karl Marx and Friedrich Engels, Vladimir Lenin and his fellow Russian revolutionary Leon Trotsky, and Polish revolutionary Rosa Luxemburg who was a leader of the German revolution of 1918-9. The idea that writers who lived more than a century ago, when the global capitalist system was at a very different stage of development, have anything important to say about the revolutions in the Middle East and North Africa during the last ten years is not something I take for granted.[1] Yet, one of the goals of this book is to make a renewed case for Marxism as critical to both theory and practice for revolutionaries, by showing how the fundamental building blocks of the revolutionary Marxist tradition are essential for understanding why and how revolutions happen, how they succeed and fail, and what we can do to influence their outcomes.

One major reason to take seriously the views of the thinkers in the classical Marxist tradition whose work forms the bedrock of the theoretical framework developed here, is that they were all active revolutionaries who paid a heavy cost in their personal lives, enduring exile, prison and even

---

1 It is worth noting that case studies from the violent integration of Egypt and Algeria to the empires of Europe form a substantial part of Rosa Luxemburg's work, *The Accumulation of Capital*—see especially p429-439 on Egypt and p377-385 on Algeria (Luxemburg, 1913). Marx spent some of the final months of his life in Algiers for health reasons. Thanks to Gianni Del Panta for drawing my attention to this and Luxemburg's writings on Algeria.

death for their commitment. Another set of reasons to be interested in the potential application of theories of revolution developed by Lenin, Trotsky and Luxemburg to the experience of the contemporary Middle East lies in the fact that all of them were concerned with the specific problems faced by countries outside the centre of the capitalist system. They devoted close attention to grappling with the challenges of revolution in contexts where the immediate antagonists of popular insurrectionary movements were usually ruling classes which were themselves under pressure in multiple ways from the predatory major powers, whose internecine struggles for supremacy fundamentally shaped the terrain on which the drama of revolution played out.

Yet clearly this tradition cannot be the sole source of insights for understanding the Middle East and North Africa's revolutionary decade. There are plenty of ways in which the Marxist thinkers of the classical period could not adequately prepare an analysis fit for the 21st century because of the ways the world has changed since their time. Nor should everything they wrote about their own times be taken as unquestioned truth. Lenin's argument that there was a privileged layer of workers in advanced capitalist countries, a 'labour aristocracy', bribed by the superprofits of imperialism which could never be won to the revolutionary cause arguably didn't stand the test of real working class struggles during and after the First World War.[2]

Therefore, this book also builds on the work of many later Marxist theorists who have grappled with how capitalism has matured. In particular, I have drawn on the writings of Tony Cliff, Mike Kidron, Nigel Harris, Chris Harman, Colin Barker and Alex Callinicos in mapping out how the dynamics of economic and military competition between states and capitals at the core of the capitalist system changed during the 20th century. From the US Trotskyist tradition I have found Hal Draper's monumental five-volume work, *Karl Marx's Theory of Revolution* an enormously fruitful way to engage with Marx's thought,[3] and the chapters on the role played by fossil fuels in shaping the destiny of the Middle East have benefitted from the work

---

2 See Cliff, 1957.

3 See, in particular, Draper, 1977 & 1978.

of John Bellamy Foster, Ian Angus and Andreas Malm.[4] Gilbert Achcar and Adam Hanieh, other writers whose work is rooted in the broader Trotskyist tradition, have also been important in shaping the arguments advanced in this book.[5]

Just as importantly, this book has been formed in long-term dialogue with the ideas of revolutionaries from the Middle East. Some of those writers mentioned above would also fall into this category. Tony Cliff, for example, was the pen name of Ygael Gluckstein, a Jewish anti-Zionist socialist whose revolutionary politics first developed in Palestine between the First and Second World Wars. However, there is a younger generation of activists, most of whom have been engaged not simply in writing about revolution, but also deeply involved in various forms of revolutionary practice to whom this book owes a major intellectual debt. The writings of Sameh Naguib, Mostafa Bassiouny, Hossam el-Hamalawy, Rabab el-Mahdi, Magdi el-Gizouli, Hèla Yousfi, Rima Majed, Muzan Alneel, Jad Bouharoun, Ghayath Naisse, Joseph Daher, Miriyam Aouragh, Peyman Jaafari and Hamza Hamouchene are some of those whose work has been a particularly important intellectual stimulus for this project, even (or maybe especially) where they would profoundly disagree with some of the arguments I am making here.

There are also of course much wider numbers of comrades from the region from whom and with whom I have learnt an incalculable amount over the more than two and a half decades since I first arrived there as a nineteen-year-old in 1994 for an overland journey from Antalya in Turkey to Alexandria in Egypt where I was to spend a year learning Arabic. Where possible I have mentioned them by name, except where such public acknowledgement might put them at risk of repression.

Middle of where? East of what? The ideology of a region

The very idea of a 'Near' or 'Middle' East is an imperialist construct, rooted deep in the psyche of generations of British and French colonial administrators (and later US State Department officials) for whom the area and its peoples only made sense

---

4 Malm, 2017.
5 See Hanieh, 2011, 2013 & 2018 and Achcar, 2013.

in relation to the European or US centres of economic and political power on the one hand, and the Far East on the other. Yet there would be obvious problems with using other terms. Geographical labels such as 'North Africa and Western Asia' (NAWA) to replace the more common 'Middle East and North Africa' (MENA) are not widely-known beyond activist circles.

Names related to the assumed ethnicity, culture and languages of the peoples of the area are also problematic for different reasons. The term 'Arab revolutions' has been widely used (including by myself), but as will become clear in later chapters, to restrict the scope of this book to the countries which are majority Arabic-speaking would obscure the structural role played in the political economy of the region by states such as Turkey and Iran. It would also gloss over the significant part played by people who are not 'Arab' or 'Arabic-speaking' in these revolutionary processes, for example, the role of the Amazigh people of North Africa, or the Kurds in Syria, or the many and varied sections of Sudanese society (Nubians, Darfuris etc) who are not Arab, and moreover have been on the receiving end of official, state-sanctioned racism because of that fact.

These three revolutions were partially revolutions *against* the 'Arabism' of the existing authoritarian regimes. It should be noted here as well, that although the idea that these were 'Muslim' revolutions has been less widely proposed, it would be equally problematic and obscure also the way in which the popular revolt mobilised non-Muslim minorities alongside Muslim majorities in societies such as Egypt where there is a large Christian population, and provided a platform for common struggle for Syrians and Lebanese of all different religious sects. So I have stuck with 'Middle East and North Africa', or 'Middle East' for short. This does not mean that the experiences of countries across this large area can be collapsed into one. Part of the argument of this book is that unevenness and inequality within the region, as well as within individual countries, are factors in preparing the ground for revolution.

Before going further, it is worth adding a few caveats about what this book is *not*. It is not an academic study—there are plenty of fine examples of these, some of which will be referenced here—and there is also plenty of dross. It is also *not* an attempt to write a general history of the revolutionary movements and popular protests in fifteen or sixteen countries

Introduction

over the span of ten years. So there will inevitably be gaps and omissions. If you want to delve deeper into the history of any one country you will need to read further. Data and additional resources which could not be included in the book for lack of space will be published on the accompanying website which can be found at *revolutionisthepeopleschoice.wordpress.com*

This leads on to a final note on what this book *is*, which is a *comparative* study. It attempts to make patterns of protest and the choices of protagonists in the revolutionary dramas hinted at here more visible and open to critique by comparing and contrasting across space and time. It is informed above all by the issue of agency in circumstances 'not of our choosing', of the multiple potentials in each moment (one of the definitions of revolution, after all), using comparison as a method to ask questions about roads not taken and possibilities not realized. This is why the last part of the book also starts to make a case for the kind of revolution which *hasn't* happened in the Middle East (or anywhere else since October 1917)—a social revolution against capitalism, and not simply a political revolution against dictatorship—and why building revolutionary socialist organisation is an essential part of preparing for it.

Revolution is the choice of the people

Section one

The cycle of revolution and counter-revolution

Revolution is the choice of the people

Chapter 1
What makes a revolution?

Writing on 8 February 2011 as the 18-day popular uprising in Egypt neared its climax, Dina Hashmat described Midan al-Tahrir (Liberation Square) in central Cairo as a "republic of possible dreams".[1] More than a decade later, revolutions have created numerous other spaces for people to think differently about every aspect of social, cultural and personal life, not only to imagine radically altered futures, but to start creating them. For the Russian revolutionary Vladimir Lenin the active intervention of ordinary people in shaping the revolutionary process was what unleashed this potential. Rather than measuring a revolution's success or failure solely against changes in government, Lenin insisted on analysing the degree to which:

> ...the mass of the people, their majority, the very lowest social groups, crushed by oppression and exploitation, rose independently and stamped on the entire course of the revolution the imprint of their own demands, their attempt to build in their own way a new society in place of the old society that was being destroyed.[2]

The idea that revolutions open up possibilities to build something radically new in the midst of the destruction of the old, resonates with our own times. After all, we live in an age of crises—economic, ecological and health—but it is also an age of

---
1 Hashmat, 2011.
2 Lenin, 1917c, Ch 3.

Revolution is the choice of the people

popular uprisings which have mobilised millions of people in an active effort to change the world through mass protests, strikes and other forms of direct action. Although many of these mass mobilisations have declared their nonviolence, they have often triggered repressive reactions from the state. In other cases, anger and frustration from below has boiled over into violent challenges to those in power, including pitched battles with the police, burning down buildings and destroying symbols of wealth and authority.

Over the last decade, the Middle East and North Africa as a region has experienced one of the greatest concentrations of both popular revolts and revolutions in the world. The examples discussed in this book include Tunisia, Egypt, Libya, Syria, Bahrain, Yemen, Sudan, Algeria, Lebanon and Iraq. In other countries where mass mobilisation has not been on the same scale as these cases, governments have endured major storms of protests and strikes: Morocco and Jordan are some prominent examples. The long-running struggle of the Palestinian people for justice against the racist Israeli state has also witnessed a new recent peak of activity with the general strike which took place across historic Palestine in May 2021. Even the Gulf States, the authoritarian monarchies have not been immune, particularly in Saudi Arabia and Kuwait both of which have experienced waves of mass protests during the last ten years.

Such cycles of popular rebellion are more common than is sometimes presented in the history we learn at school. The histories of the countries discussed in this book are full of revolutionary experience. Egypt, for example experienced a popular revolution against British control in 1919, another major wave of mass protests and strikes against colonialism between 1945 and the overthrow of the monarchy in 1952, and an explosion of protests and riots in January 1977 over president Sadat's attempts to impose huge cuts in ordinary people's living standards at the behest of the World Bank. Algerians fought a successful revolutionary war of national liberation against French rule between 1954 and 1962. Sudan saw mass movements from below topple dictators in 1964 and 1985. Nor are regional waves of revolutions and popular revolts unprecedented. The revolutions which swept Eastern Europe in 1989 are one example, and the so-called 'Pink Tide' of popular revolts which engulfed Latin America in the 2000s are another.[3]

The decade of revolutionary experience in the Middle East is also worth considering from another perspective. The revolutions and uprisings discussed in this book are notable not just because they represented the direct intervention by millions of ordinary people in *political affairs*—even though this in itself was deeply significant in a region where the political systems of most countries were republican or monarchical authoritarian regimes. They all raised hopes of much wider kinds of social and cultural transformation: the promise of liberation from violence and harassment for women, an end to state racism against non-Arab citizens and discrimination against Christians or other religious minorities, for example. In the waves of strikes, social protests and occupations of workplaces which were woven into the revolutionary process, visions of economic justice also began to take shape: the return of privatised companies to public control, an end to casualised contracts, jobs for the unemployed, the removal of corrupt and bullying bosses, increases in the minimum wage and the imposition of a maximum wage.

Yet this still begs the question—what is a revolution? And does it matter who makes it and how they bring about the fall of the regime? The issue of the outcomes of these processes also urgently needs to be answered. Why do some mass mobilisations from below succeed in not only toppling tyrants but in effecting longer-lasting political change? Is it enough to alter the political system without touching the sources of the ruling class's economic power? The question of defeat looms large over the experience of revolution in the Middle East in particular. In Syria, Libya and Yemen the hopes of peaceful change were quickly dashed and all three countries have gone through searing experiences of civil war and foreign military intervention, killing hundreds of thousands, forcing millions to flee their homes and leaving large parts of the country in ruins. The Egyptian counter-revolution was likewise a cruel and violent process, characterised by large numbers of state-backed murders, an epidemic of torture, tens of thousands of arrests and detention without trial. Bahrain's revolutionary moment ended early, in March 2011, when Saudi tanks rolled in to crush the mass protests by force. The second

---

3 See Barker, Dale & Davidson, 2021 for analysis for some of those revolts from below.

wave of popular uprisings and revolutions which began in late 2018 in Sudan, followed by Algeria, Lebanon and Iraq in 2019 only saw a partial breakthrough to make changes to the state in Sudan, where a mixed civilian and military Transitional Government took power on 17 August 2019. A military coup by the generals who signed this deal, against their own civilian "partners" in October 2021 underscored how the failure to drive the revolutionary process deeper into the state in order to fracture the military-bureaucratic machine at its core, opens the road to counter-revolution.

The question of how crisis leads to popular revolt, and when revolts become revolutions is the central concern of this book. It presents a theoretical toolkit for understanding these processes which is rooted in the revolutionary Marxist tradition. It also asks the question: if we want to see revolution's promise of a different and better world for ordinary people realised in practice, what attitude should revolutionaries take towards the existing state? Is it enough to stop with a rearrangement of the personnel at the top, or does the whole system need to go? And what forms of political and social organization are best suited to the task?

Defining revolution

While a proper discussion of the concept of 'revolution' in the Marxist tradition would obviously be a lengthy affair, for the purposes of this book, I want to highlight a few key ideas drawn from Lenin's writings as a good place to begin.

Firstly, what Lenin calls a "revolutionary situation" needs to develop for a revolution to take place, although as Colin Barker points out "not every revolutionary situation ends with a successful revolution".[4] This is not something which can simply be 'willed' into being by revolutionaries. There are objective factors at play, conditions which need to be met before revolution comes onto the agenda of history. The symptoms of the revolutionary situation include crisis at the top, but also crisis at the bottom. Both rulers and ruled can no longer live in the old way.

Secondly there has to be "a considerable increase in the activity of the masses, who uncomplainingly allow themselves to be robbed in 'peace time', but, in turbulent times, are drawn

---

4 Barker, 1987, p220.

What makes a revolution?

both by all the circumstances of the crisis *and by the 'upper classes' themselves* into independent historical action".[5]

Thirdly, these objective changes must be accompanied by a *subjective* change if the revolutionary situation is to be transformed into a revolution "namely, the ability of the revolutionary *class* to take revolutionary mass action *strong* enough to break (or dislocate) the old government, which never, not even in a period of crisis, 'falls', if it is not toppled over".[6]

Leon Trotsky shared with Lenin an unshakeable belief in the agency of ordinary people. In his magisterial *History of the Russian Revolution* Trotsky argued:

> At those crucial moments when the old order becomes no longer endurable to the masses, they break over the barriers excluding them from the political arena, sweep aside their traditional representatives, and create by their own interference the initial groundwork for a new regime. Whether this is good or bad we leave to the judgement of moralists. We ourselves will take the facts as they are given by the objective course of development. The history of a revolution is for us first of all a history of the forcible entrance of the masses into the realm of rulership over their own destiny.[7]

Here is a brilliant presentation of the way in which revolution is not just shaped by ordinary people, but that their eruption into history is *part* of the revolution. They interfere, they batter down the door, they "break over the barriers". This echoes Lenin's point about how revolution is not just a crisis at the top, but also a huge rise in agency at the bottom of society. Trotsky was also well aware that such momentous events would bring about enormous changes in the way that people thought as well as acted:

> The dynamic of revolutionary events is *directly* determined by swift, intense and passionate changes in the psychology of classes which have already formed themselves before the revolution.

---
5   Lenin, 1915, Ch 2.
6   Lenin, 1915, Ch 2.
7   Trotsky, 1930, Preface.

The swift changes of mass views and moods in an epoch of revolution thus derive, not from the flexibility and mobility of man's mind, but just the opposite, from its deep conservatism. The chronic lag of ideas and relations behind new objective conditions, right up to the moment when the latter crash over people in the form of a catastrophe, is what creates in a period of revolution that leaping movement of ideas and passions which seems to the police mind a mere result of the activities of 'demagogues'".[8]

Political and social revolutions

Both Lenin and Trotsky were clear that revolutions could not be made solely at the level of political ideas. Rather they had to result in concrete political and social change or at least involve mass struggles to bring about such changes. However, the exact nature of the relationship between political and social revolutions and indeed to what extent it is possible or desirable to distinguish between revolutions in this way, has been the subject of constant debate since Marx's time. In the first volume of *Karl Marx's Theory of Revolution*, Hal Draper argues that Marx painted a broad brush picture of two basic types of revolution. Political revolutions are transfers of governmental power, although Draper points out that what is usually labelled as a political revolution involves the shift not just between different personnel at the top, but between types of political system, for example, a move from democratic forms of government to a dictatorship, or the other way round. On the other hand, there are social revolutions. Draper argues that Marx uses the term 'social revolution' in two ways. Firstly, he uses it in the sense of a long-term transformation in society to indicate the rise and fall of whole social systems. Draper suggests it makes sense to call this a 'societal revolution', to distinguish it from Marx's other usage of the term. The other kind of 'social revolution' in Marx's writings that Draper wants to explore is:

...a political revolution that expresses a social-revolutionising drive towards the transference of

8 Trotsky, 1930, Preface.

state power to a new class. It is, he says, 'a political revolution with a social soul,' in Marx's earliest (1844) formulation. By the same token it points in the direction of a societal revolution, regardless of when changes in the social system actually begin to take place. It does this by establishing a new constellation of sociopolitical forces, with new historic potentialities. The societal revolution is the realisation of these potentialities. 'Every real revolution', wrote Engels, 'is a social one, in that it brings a new class to power and allows it to remodel society in its own image.'[9]

Draper's final point in this passage is to emphasize that the mingling of political and social revolutions, or the potential for political revolutions to discover that they have a 'social soul' and turning into more than a clash over "governmental power", is a feature of modern life. Containing a political revolution, within the bounds of a palace coup is increasingly difficult in modern capitalist societies.

From a combined crisis to permanent revolution

There is another aspect of the relationship between political and social revolutions in the Marxist tradition which are especially relevant to this book. The revolutionary path from social to political power followed by the bourgeoisie in Britain and France was not repeated in exactly the same form in countries where capitalism took root later. In the introductory chapter to his *History of the Russian Revolution*, Trotsky provides a brilliant and succinct overview of how the dynamics of economic growth at the centre of the emerging capitalist system affected society and culture in the Russian Empire, which was located on the edge of Europe and shaped by a radically different natural environment, in a highly uneven fashion. There are several key insights that underpin Trotsky's theorisation of the relationship between what he called 'uneven and combined development' and revolution which we will draw on to build a theoretical framework for understanding the nature of the *combined crises* of capitalism which create the conditions for revolution. In later

---

9   Draper, 1978, p19.

chapters we will return to the implications of the other, essential counterpart to Trotsky's argument: this uneven layering of social relations with cultural and political forms, created the possibility of *combining* different kinds of revolutions. The revolution which would bring the bourgeoisie into political power, dispensing with the Tsarist autocracy, could immediately 'grow over' into a *permanent revolution* under the leadership of the organised working class.

Vast reams of academic literature have been written about Trotsky's theory of uneven and combined development. Here we will rely on five key points to build our theoretical framework. The first of these is his insight that unevenness at the beginning of capitalism's development replicates itself and even intensifies over time. Societies like Russia, which started becoming capitalist in a world where other capitalist societies already existed, did not simply repeat the same trajectories of development as their forerunners. The second point therefore is that capitalist development doesn't always proceed through a linear succession of stages. Late adopters of capitalism can borrow and adapt technologies and institutions from their predecessors, leading to rapid leaps and advances, holding out the tantalising prospect of even potentially overtaking their more developed rivals in the future.

The third crucial element of Trotsky's theory for our argument here concerns the state. The Russian absolutist state assumes a pivotal role in his outline of the history of capitalist development. It 'hothouses' economic growth of a particular kind in a desperate attempt to preserve military parity with its more advanced capitalist neighbours—building railways, creating steel foundries and armament factories. In the process it encroaches on the role of the bourgeoisie which ought to be the social class pushing open the doors of a new mode of production. The implications of this process for class structure form Trotsky's fourth point, that the overbearing role of the state as the midwife of capitalist development leads to a shrunken and politically impotent bourgeoisie, but an enlarged and politically advanced working class, concentrated in big workplaces of strategic importance to the state and its apparatus of repression, in the midst of a peasantry which has only recently emerged from pre-capitalist agricultural social relations.

Finally, this produced what Trotsky labelled an 'explosive

amalgam' of combined social relations and political institutions from different phases of economic development—think of the Tsarist monarchy with its penchant for palaces modelled on the French court at Versailles in the 18th century, and its fondness for religious rituals derived from the Medieval Russian orthodox church, ordering Cossack soldiers to shoot down striking workers from gigantic factories where industrial production methods rivalled those of the most advanced capitalist countries. The underlying instability of the social and political compounds which formed the building blocks of Russian society was, he argued, a fundamental cause of the revolutionary crises which ripped through the country in the early years of the 20th century.

Revolutionaries in the Middle East have long faced comparable problems to those experienced by their Russian counterparts at the beginning of the 20th century. In contrast to Russia, which was not directly colonised, across large parts of the Middle East it was not local states which shaped the trajectory of capitalist development, but the imperial powers at the core of the world system. The bourgeoisie did indeed develop late and was by and large just as craven as Trotsky had predicted, but it was not the organised working class which led political revolutions against the colonial powers and their local allies among a landowning and merchant ruling class, but sections of the modern middle class.[10] These political revolutions which rolled across the region between the 1940s and the late 1960s did establish a new social class in power in many places, creating in most cases conditions for the domination of a bourgeoisie which derived its wealth and political influence directly from the state.

Half a century later, the limitations of the "social-revolutionising drive" of the anti-colonial revolutions is clearly visible. While the overthrow of the colonial order did lead to a transfer of class power, this took place within the confines of a global capitalist system, where wealth and power remained highly polarised, and where very few of the ruling classes of the Middle East were able to create much space to make genuinely independent decisions about how to develop their economies or pursue their own political goals. From the point of view of the majority of ordinary people in the region, the situation is much worse. The last half century has seen multiple countries

---

10 Cliff, 1963.

devastated by war, millions have swapped poverty in the countryside for poverty in the city, while worsening ecological crisis adds to the strains of everyday existence.

Class and revolutionary agency

Such discussions of the agency of particular classes in revolutions need some further elaboration. It is worth starting by distinguishing the use of 'class' in the Marxist tradition from more mainstream academic and popular approaches, which often use 'class' in the sense of 'income', 'status' or more loosely in the sense of a group of people (or things) with common features. By contrast, although Marx does use the term 'class' in the second sense quite frequently in his writings, as Hal Draper notes, "in the context of Marx's theory, a socio-economic class is a class of people playing a common role as a structural component of a given society".[11] Marx does not stop here, because the "structures" of society are formed by *processes*, and the most basic of these is the process of production. Social classes form in relation to the historically concrete ways in which production is organised, which in turn underpin the broader processes of the *reproduction* of human life. This encompasses both questions of how human beings meet their immediate physical needs—such as for food and shelter—and also the relations with other humans which are inseparable from those processes. Moreover, a fundamental feature of classes in Marxist analysis is that they are formed in *antagonistic* relationships with other classes, and thus cannot be separated from the class struggle.[12]

A further important idea which flows from this last point is that in any given mode of production, there will be 'polar' classes, whose interests are so directly counterposed, and between whom the struggle over the surplus from the production process is so intense, that their antagonism shapes the whole of society. This idea, which Marx and Engels articulated so vividly in *The Communist Manifesto*, does not require either of the polar classes to be a majority in society, nor for all other classes to have disappeared, in order to be a useful analytical tool.[13]

11 Draper, 1977, p14.
12 Callinicos & Harman, 1987, p6.
13 Choonara, 2018.

What makes a revolution?

The key point here is that classes are both 'real' and 'abstract' at the same time. They are real in the sense that there is objective evidence for their existence, independently of people's consciousness and while individuals may self-identify with one class or other as they choose, their objective relationship with production is subject to factors outside their will. In Britain today, a train driver may be on an annual wage which is higher than the owner of a small business, for example, but this does not mean that she stops being a worker (even if she considers herself to be middle-class).

Classes are abstractions because a class analysis provides a simplified vision of society, and it is all too easy to forget that the brutally clear image of the two polar classes of capitalist society confronting each other across a battlefield, which Marx and Engels popularised, is rarely what revolutions look like in real life.

Lenin, for one, was acutely aware of this problem. In a blistering polemic written in response to dismissive accounts of the 1916 Easter Rising in Ireland written by left and liberal activists in Germany and Russia, he argued forcefully that failure to grasp "social revolution as a living phenomenon" in all its complexities and contradictions could leave so-called revolutionaries on the sidelines of history:

> To imagine that social revolution is conceivable without revolts by small nations in the colonies and in Europe, without revolutionary outbursts by a section of the petty bourgeoisie with all its prejudices, without a movement of the politically non-conscious proletarian and semi-proletarian masses against oppression by the landowners, the church, and the monarchy, against national oppression, etc. to imagine all this is to repudiate social revolution. So one army lines up in one place and says, 'We are for socialism', and another, somewhere else and says, 'We are for imperialism', and that will be a social revolution! Only those who hold such a ridiculously pedantic view could vilify the Irish rebellion by calling it a 'putsch'. Whoever expects a 'pure' social revolution will never live to see it. Such a person pays lip-service to revolution without understanding what revolution is.[14]

---

14 Lenin, 1916.

Revolution is the choice of the people

Rosa Luxemburg was another Marxist whose writings on revolution provide an exceptionally clear picture of the overall dynamics of the struggle, without losing sight of the complex way in which the actions of specific groups and even individuals combine in dynamic and uneven ways to 'move' as a class during revolutions.

The mass strikes which gripped the Russian Empire in the early 1900s and rose to a crescendo in the revolution of 1905, involved strikes and protests by workers in a huge variety of professions—bakers, printers, steelworkers, railway workers, shop workers—and many people who may well not have even considered themselves as workers until they started taking action, such as actors, commercial employees, members of the liberal professions, technicians and even policemen.

> This is a gigantic, many-coloured picture of a general arrangement of labour and capital which reflects all the complexity of social organisation and of the political consciousness of every section and of every district; and the whole long scale runs from the regular trade-union struggle of a picked and tested troop of the proletariat drawn from large-scale industry, to the formless protest of a handful of rural proletarians, and to the first slight stirrings of an agitated military garrison, from the well-educated and elegant revolt in cuffs and white collars in the counting house of a bank to the shy-bold murmurings of a clumsy meeting of dissatisfied policemen in a smoke-grimed dark and dirty guardroom.[15]

Driven from below by the masses themselves and not conforming to the preconceived plans of party leaders about the order, forms or timing of action, nevertheless, what Luxemburg calls "the sultry air" of revolution, begins to create the alchemy of a moment when these disparate struggles can take on a collective power and forge the kind of unity which turns class into a weapon for change.

---

15 Luxemburg, 1906, Ch3.

Events, moments and processes

A final set of theoretical questions about the nature of revolution concerns the relationship between events, moments and processes in revolutions. The idea that revolutions are about change and dynamism is central to Trotsky's writing.

> The fundamental political process of the revolution thus consists in the gradual comprehension by a class of the problems arising from the social crisis—the active orientation of the masses by a method of successive approximations. The different stages of a revolutionary process, certified by a change of parties in which the more extreme always supersedes the less, express the growing pressure to the left of the masses—so long as the swing of the movement does not run into objective obstacles. When it does, there begins a reaction: disappointments of the different layers of the revolutionary class, growth of indifferentism, and therewith a strengthening of the position of the counter-revolutionary forces. Such, at least, is the general outline of the old revolutions.[16]

The first, and perhaps the most basic point to grasp is that the revolution is not just a *single* event, however spectacular. This is important because the common sense view of revolutions usually does reduce them if not to single *events*, at least to very concentrated periods of time, often those which involve some dramatic or symbolic *moment* where the old order visibly breaks.

This begs the important question of what is a *process*—another useful but slippery abstraction. One way to think about this is by returning to events and moments and daisy-chaining them together into a series. Yet there are problems with this approach as well, including arguments about where to mark beginnings and endings. For some activists, the revolution sometimes appears as a kind of philosophical abstraction, disassociated from actual events and moments in history.

I think this is the wrong way of looking at revolution for two main reasons. Firstly it makes it appear as if revolutions can just

---

16 Trotsky, 1930, Preface.

be willed into existence by revolutionaries. The need for objective conditions to be met in order for a revolution to be possible was one of Lenin's key points in the 1915 article discussed above. Secondly, this kind of abstract, almost timeless way of thinking about revolution tends to obscure the way in which the outcomes of individual and collective actions in revolutionary crises make a difference. And while it is rarely the case that any single event on its own determines the whole course of a revolutionary process, there are some which constitute turning points, moments when the choices made and the roads taken fundamentally shape the trajectory of what comes after. This is why the 'bounded' nature of revolutionary processes is important. They do have beginnings and ends, outcomes and consequences in terms of defeats and victories for the protagonists.

"We meet at 4pm, revolution time"

Yet what people can accomplish when they get a whiff of what Rosa Luxemburg called "the sultry air of revolution" makes the passing of time feel different to normal life. In April 2019, the Sudanese Professionals Association put out a call for protests on its Facebook page: "We meet at 4pm: revolution time," the appeal ended. For anyone who has never experienced the sense of time accelerating, of days being crammed into hours and years into days during revolutions, this sentence probably made little sense. But "revolution time" can be something that the hundreds of thousands at the heart of popular uprisings win back from history. From one perspective it is an exhilaratingly fast time. Movements grow like weeds in the summer, people change their ideas overnight, old certainties dissolve. What took years of struggle to achieve in the past can be accomplished in weeks, days or even hours. It took four months of protests to oust Umar al-Bashir from the presidency he occupied for 30 years in Sudan. His minister of defence, Ahmed Awad Ibn Auf, lasted only 30 hours as head of the military's Transitional Authority in the face of mass protests demanding the handover of power to a civilian government.

Yet the scale of these processes also can make "revolution time" feel slow. The end of the dictator turns out to be just the beginning of a much larger struggle, as the process continues

What makes a revolution?

of challenging and removing from office those who exercised power on his behalf. Who knows how long "revolution time" will last? Within two and a half years of the fall of Mubarak, the Egyptian military had unleashed a bloody counter-revolution and instituted a new dictatorship. The collective agency of millions of people suddenly awakened to political consciousness can throw the existing rulers into a profound crisis. They will always seek to tip the scales back, to restore their capacity to rule by any means they can. In a very real sense, therefore, "revolution time" is always borrowed time. So the question then arises, if time is short, what can revolutionaries do to make the most of it?

This book is a tentative step towards some possible answers.

Revolution is the choice of the people

Chapter 2
The deluge: 2011-12

During the last ten years, exceptionally large numbers of people across the Middle East have gained first-hand experience of revolution and counter-revolution. The two major waves of popular uprisings in 2011-2013 and 2018-2022 have brought tens of millions into intense political activity, often for the first time in their lives. Yet although the forms of protest have often appeared alike and the slogans of the demonstrators could leap across borders, even within the first heady weeks of the 2011 uprisings, it was clear that the revolutionary processes could take markedly different routes despite the apparent similarities of their starting points.

The following two chapters present an overview of the points of convergence and divergence in the major revolutionary processes and popular uprisings which have unfolded in the Middle East since 2010. While this will only briefly touch on the details of events in any of the countries discussed here, it will flesh out a crucial argument which will be further developed later in the book, that while the choices open to revolutionary activists were constrained by a wide variety of factors, ranging from the local class structure and history of economic development to the political experiences of the pre-revolutionary period including the character of both the existing regime and the opposition, there was nothing preordained about the eventual outcomes.

The horrors of the counter-revolutionary offensives, civil wars and imperialist interventions which followed the uprisings of 2011 were not the inescapable consequence of ordinary people daring to try and remake the world with their own hands. Nor is it correct to see each of these experiences as essentially unique and only explicable by reference to the specific pattern of social, economic and political development within each particular country. On the contrary, there are broad patterns of contestation repeated not only across space, but also across time. One of the striking features of the 2018-2022 wave of popular uprisings discussed in chapter 3, and in particular the experiences of Sudan and Algeria, was the degree to which they shared common ground with the previous wave between 2011-2013 both in terms of the preconditions for the revolt and the forms of protest.

The first important point to clarify here is the rationale for choosing these specific countries for comparison out of a wider set of possible case studies. This chapter discusses three clusters of popular uprisings which between them shaped the trajectory of the revolutionary process at a wider level across the region as a whole. We will first look at the revolutions in Tunisia, Egypt and Libya between 2011 and 2012. Tunisia was the first uprising, but it was the eruption of revolution in Egypt which triggered the deluge of popular protest across the wider region. The influence of the Tunisian revolution on Egypt was clear from the beginning. This was famously illustrated in the way that the revolutionary slogans 'al-sha'ab yurid isqat al-nidham' ('the people want the fall of the regime') and 'irhal' ('Depart'!) were adopted enthusiastically by the swelling crowds in the streets of Egypt despite the fact that their classical Arabic form was not commonly used in Egyptian colloquial Arabic.[17] There were also other factors which made the Tunisian and Egyptian experiences of revolution comparable, including the important role played by the organised working class in both cases.

Libya's revolution exploded in a different social and political context, and its fate reflected both the fact that the organised working class had been unable to develop any degree of independent organisation, but also the rapidity which

---

17 Some protesters helpfully provided a translation of 'irhal' for Hosni Mubarak's benefit, just in case he missed the point. "Irhal, ya'ani imshi, law mish fahim bil araby qulu bil 'ibry" ('Depart means 'get lost'! If he doesn't understand it in Arabic, better tell him in Hebrew'), adding in a reference to the regime's long-standing collaboration with the Israeli state under US auspices.

The deluge: 2011-12

with Western powers intervened militarily in the revolution, prompted mainly by the desire to protect their interests in Libya's huge oil resources. Nevertheless, the geographical proximity of the three countries and the interactions between their societies and economies did also intertwine the fate of their revolutions. In all three cases there was a clear rupture in the political system brought about by mass collective action from below, most deeply in the case of Libya where the pre-revolutionary regime of Mu'ammar al-Qadhafi was destroyed in the process (although some of its leading personnel quickly defected to the rebel side), but also in the cases of Egypt and Tunisia where the changes took the form of political reforms. The fact that in the Egyptian case these were later reversed does not in itself make it inaccurate to talk about a revolution.

The second cluster of revolutions and popular uprisings took place in the Gulf. In the case of Bahrain, although the revolt from below was brutally snuffed out, through the military intervention of the Gulf Cooperation Council (GCC), the fact that the ruling Al Khalifa family was unable to contain the popular uprising on its own, again point to this as an example of a revolution which failed. The containment and eventual destruction of the Yemeni revolution took longer but was eventually achieved through a GCC-sponsored 'national dialogue' which preserved much of the old regime in substance, if not in outward form, and then by military intervention. The Bahraini revolt represented a much more immediate threat to the Saudi ruling class in particular, because it lit flames of hope for change among the oppressed Shi'a population of Eastern Province. Finally, the chapter considers the experience of Syria in 2011-2012, tracing the path from popular revolt, concentrated in the provinces and the suburbs of the major cities, to the beginnings of the counter-revolutionary war launched by the Assad regime as it fought for survival.

Before plunging into the drama of revolution in specific countries, it is worth noting that *waves* of revolutionary upheaval, followed by a cycle of counter-revolutionary retreat, are a feature of the history of the region. We can identify two other major periods since the Second World War, when mass popular protests driven by comparable causes, occurred in a wide range of countries in the region. The first of these was the cycle of anti-colonial revolutions which opened in the late

1940s and continued over the following two decades. Over that time frame, one after another, both European settler colonial regimes and many of the local rulers who had allied themselves to the colonial powers were forcibly ejected by mass movements, many of which engaged in bitter armed struggles. The second wave of uprisings over about a decade between the late 1970s and the late 1980s came as many of the regimes which had emerged out of the struggles against colonialism faced their own moments of crisis as they attempted to shift their economic trajectory from state-led development policies towards the emerging neoliberal consensus.

Unlike the anti-colonial struggles of the previous generation, few of the uprisings of the late 1970s in the Middle East succeeded in toppling existing regimes. The obvious exceptions were Iran, where revolution ended the rule of the Shah (a staunch ally of the US, though not subject to direct colonial rule) and Sudan, where a popular uprising did unseat Jafa'ar al-Numeiri in 1985, only to face a counter-revolution led by Umar al-Bashir four years later and the restoration of some elements of the old regime in a new Islamist guise. These previous waves are important because they help to illustrate an important element in the argument put forward in this book—that the revolutions and uprisings of the last ten years share common features which are related to phases in the economic and social development of the societies concerned. In other words, the arguments for grouping together these revolts from below as part of a broader wave of revolutions is not just about the coincidence of their timings, but about the deeper, structural roots of the crisis.

Tunisia leads the way

The revolts which would convulse the whole region began in the town of Sidi Bouzid in the centre of Tunisia in December 2010. The spark, in both a literal and figurative sense, was the attempted suicide of Mohamed Bouazizi, a young man who was eking out a living selling vegetables in the market. Bouazizi set himself on fire in protest at the confiscation of his cart by municipal officials, touching off angry protests in the town by unemployed youth. Soon the movement broadened beyond the

The deluge: 2011-12

call for justice for Bouazizi himself, who lingered between life and death in hospital having suffered terrible burns, to raise more general demands for justice for Bouazizi's generation, with jobs and economic dignity at the forefront.

Alongside the unemployed and students, a broad coalition of local trade unionists and professionals began to form. Activists from the primary and secondary school teachers' unions affiliated with Tunisia's major trade union federation, the Tunisian General Labour Union (UGTT), played a key role in organising protests which spread the movement from Sidi Bouzid to the nearby towns of Regueb, Menzel Bouzayane, Souk Jedid, Sidi Ali Ben Aoun and Meknassy. Having learnt the lessons from previous rounds of similar protests which had faced harsh repression, they helped to form layers of protection for each other, and for the young people braving daily and sometimes nightly clashes with the riot police.

> They would avoid appearing at the head of demonstrations, try not to be singled out and repressed, but also "establish solid relationships" between union members, lawyers and the population at large in order to break with the geographic isolation which their predecessors foresaw. These different elements, connected by the neighbourhood youth's mastery of urban spaces, encouraged the transmission of know-how deemed to be "strategic" from activists to groups who were just discovering repression: how to mitigate the effects of tear gas, spare public buildings, break apart sidewalks, build barricades and predict the reactions of the forces of law and order.[18]

Yet in order to become a revolution, the protest movement needed a mechanism to draw the coastal cities, wider sections of the working class and the capital into the battle with the regime. One route to national attention came via lawyers' organisations, which called out their members in a national strike on 6 January in protest at the escalating repression.[19] It was the regime's attempts to crush the protests by killing at least six demonstrators in Kasserine and Thala between 8-12

---

18 Hmed and Raillard, 2012, p39.
19 Beinin, 2016, p102.

January which proved a major turning point, as this galvanised mass strikes and solidarity protests in the industrial port city of Sfax and Tunis.

Once again, the UGTT played a key role in this process. As Mohamed Sghaeir Saihi, a regional official for the UGTT-affiliated teachers' union in Kasserine comments, the support of local unions for the protest movement had only been achieved after fierce battles inside the UGTT.

> We broke the control of the bureaucracy by working with the youth groups, the school and college students and the large numbers of unemployed. They didn't have unions of their own, so we opened the union offices to them. This was the opposite of what the bureaucracy wanted. The union leaders were telling us to close the doors of our offices and not to get involved in 'politics' inside the union buildings.[20]

In the industrial port of Sfax, the powerful UGTT regional committee had scheduled a routine meeting on 9 January to discuss issues related to pensions. Activists from local branches demanded that the committee throw out their prepared agenda and discuss the more urgent question of solidarity with the protesters in Kasserine, Thala and the provinces in revolt. "The conclusion of the meeting was historic: the decision to hold a large demonstration and a general regional strike," recalled Moufida, an activist in the Postal Service.[21] Similar arguments were also being debated in the regional committees representing the phosphate mining area of Gafsa and the capital Tunis. Without explicit coordination they all called regional strikes on the same day, 12 January.[22]

By now the pressure on the Executive Board of the UGTT was intense, and the union leadership was finally pushed into calling a two-hour national general strike on 14 January. Meanwhile the numbers in the streets were growing exponentially: 100,000 marched in Sfax, equivalent to a third of the city's population, while 10,000 took to the streets of Sidi Bouzid. Demonstrators surged into the streets of Tunis on 14

---

20 Sghaeir Saihi, 2012
21 Yousfi, 2018, p60.
22 Yousfi, 2018, p63.

The deluge: 2011-12

January, while UGTT activists stretched the 'two-hour' general strike to last the whole day.

The panicked flight of President Ben Ali to Saudi Arabia on 14 January led to the Prime Minister Mohammed Ghannouchi forming an interim government. This was the first test for the movement in the streets. Would the process of change set in motion by the popular uprising stop at the removal of the head of state? The government formed by Ghannouchi was a clear attempt by the ruling party to contain the damage without initiating any serious reforms. The new cabinet included members of the former government from the ruling Democratic Constitutional Rally party (usually referred to by its French initials RCD) along with members of the tame, legal opposition parties and, more importantly, trade unionists from the UGTT. Their hopes that this would suffice to clear the streets were quickly dashed after a furious reaction from both the protest movement in the central provinces where the revolution had begun and the UGTT's rank-and-file which forced the resignation of the UGTT-affiliated ministers after a single day.[23] A major sit-in outside the seat of government in the Kasbah Square kept up the pressure until a cabinet reshuffle on 27 January removed the RCD figures from major ministerial posts.

Shuffling the deckchairs aboard the sinking ship was not enough to save Ghannouchi's government. On 25 February around 100,000 people protested, calling for a new government and elections to a National Constituent Assembly.[24] By now it was clear that more significant reforms would have to be discussed and the new 'technocratic' government under Béji Caïd Essebsi announced the suspension of the 1959 Constitution and elections for a Constituent Assembly in July. National parliamentary elections were scheduled to follow in October 2011.

Mobilisations in the streets continued, with demonstrators marching regularly on Sundays to demand further reforms. Former dictator Ben Ali and his wife Leila Trabelsi were convicted in absentia of theft on 20 June, and were sentenced to 35 years in jail and fined $64 million. The UGTT remained outside the government, instead channelling political energy into shaping the National Council for the Protection of the Revolution

---

23   Yousfi, 2018, p77.
24   Yousfi, 2018, p77.

(known by its French acronym CNPR) which brought together representatives of opposition parties, including the previously banned Islamist party, Ennadha, professional organisations such as the Order of Lawyers, human rights groups and trade unionists. The CNPR contested the government's claim to legitimacy, arguing that it had no democratic mandate and should give up its decision-making powers to the Council.[25] Eventually, the major opposition parties, the UGTT and key civil society organisations agreed on a compromise with the government, giving their support to a new body, the High Authority for the Realisation of the Objectives of the Revolution, Political Reform and Democratic Transition (referred to by its French acronym ISROR). The High Authority had only an advisory role, leading some UGTT activists to argue that its creation represented the "hijacking" of the revolutionary process and a "fatal blow to the revolutionary movement".[26]

The Islamist party Ennadha won the largest bloc of seats in the new parliament and the chance to form a coalition government with two secular opposition parties, the left-wing Ettakatol and the liberal Congress for the Republic in elections held on 23 October. The following months would see deepening conflict over the political character of the state. On the surface, the major axis of debate appeared to be between Islamists (represented not just by reformist currents such as Ennadha, but also by groups demanding more radical political and social reforms bringing Tunisia's political system into line with their conservative vision of Islamic law), and secular parties including liberal and left-wing opposition groups, but also Nidaa Tounes, a new right-wing secular party led by Béji Caïd Essebsi which was formed in June 2012. This split tended to mask another fracture, between those seeking to use the struggles in the streets and workplaces to push for deeper political changes and real steps towards social justice for the millions who continued to face poverty and marginalisation on the one hand, and the reformist politicians on both sides of the Islamist-secular divide, who preferred to reinstate elements of the old regime in a "reformed" political system rather than address the injustices which had led to the revolution in the first place.

---

25   Yousfi, 2018, p89.
26   Yousfi, 2018, p90.

The deluge: 2011-12

Egypt: 'The people want the downfall of the regime'

The fall of Ben Ali in Tunisia on 14 January set in motion a regional revolutionary process of popular uprisings which followed a similar initial trajectory of massive street protests and sit-ins. The next country to be convulsed by a new mass movement from below was Egypt. A loose coalition of opposition activists and some of the admins of prominent Facebook pages which had been amplifying anger over the brutality of the security forces, such as the 'We are all Khaled Said' page—set up in protest at the murder of a young man by the police in Alexandria—agreed to put out a national call for protests on 25 January, celebrated by the regime as 'National Police Day'. At this stage the major opposition forces, such as the Muslim Brotherhood, were not involved directly and the initiative lay with younger and more radical networks of activists from the secular left and liberal Islamists.

The 25 January saw street protests on an unprecedented scale, both in the capital and provincial towns, with thousands attempting to break police control of symbolic public spaces in the city centres. The size of the mobilisations took the regime by surprise. Emboldened by the popularity of the call for demonstrations, and by the way in which the slogans of the Tunisian revolution—including the now famous slogan "the people want the downfall of the regime"—were being echoed in the streets, activists called for major protests on Friday 28 January, with mosques and churches serving as rallying points for marches.

By the end of the day it was clear that the regime had suffered a major defeat, as protesters had forced the hated Interior Ministry to withdraw Central Security Forces troops (the armed riot police relied on as the main vehicle for repression by the Mubarak regime) to their barracks, leaving swelling encampments of demonstrators in city centre squares across the country. Significantly, this included Tahrir Square, a huge junction in the centre of Cairo close to the Nile and overlooked by major government buildings and the ruling National Democratic Party (NDP) headquarters.

Over the next few days, the uprising's centre of gravity shifted to the sit-ins, especially the crowds in Tahrir Square, where a tent city sprang up under the eyes of the international media. Having lost control of the Square, the regime hoped to isolate the protesters from wider society and then physically smash their resistance by forcibly retaking it. Government workplaces were shut down, employers told to send their workers home, internet services were turned off, as ruling party officials tried to mobilise the state-run trade unions to call out their members in support of the regime. Meanwhile, worried that the conscripts of the Central Security Forces' rank-and-file, or even the regular army, might prove unreliable, the security forces hastily assembled a motley army of thugs and paid informers which attacked the Tahrir sit-in on 2 February.[27]

Both these tactics failed. The attacks on the sit-in were repulsed at makeshift barricades by the protesters and workers ignored the regime's trade union leaders' call for 'solidarity' with the dictatorship. The regime then switched tack, hoping instead to draw elements of the opposition into negotiations while letting the protest movement run out of steam until numbers dwindled to an extent where repression was more likely to succeed. Workplaces reopened and internet services were reconnected. However, these attempts to isolate the uprising by confining it to the squares also failed. New waves of protesters replenished the major sit-ins over the weekend of 5-6 February and over the following days an increasing number of workplaces were shut down by mass strikes. These were largely uncoordinated, representing an explosion of pent-up energy by hundreds of thousands of workers who sensed an opportunity for a reckoning with their bosses over a host of issues.

Only in a minority of cases were these strikes over explicitly political demands, but the strike wave marked another turning point in the revolutionary process. With pressure mounting on him, Mubarak promised cosmetic reforms in a speech on 10 February as huge crowds again massed in central Cairo and other cities. The following day he was removed from office by the leadership of the armed forces, who assumed power. Major opposition figures and the Supreme Council of the Armed Forces (SCAF) jointly urged Egyptians to return to work on 12 February and the major sit-ins disbanded.

This did not quell the rising tide of strikes which peaked several weeks later. Many of the strikes now sought to remove ruling party officials from management roles, as well as raising demands for wage increases, job security for those on casualised

27 Naguib, 2011.

The deluge: 2011-12

contracts and union rights. Hundreds of new, independent unions emerged during the first few months of the revolution. Regular Friday demonstrations raising demands for deeper political reforms escalated in size over the following months. Key demands, which continued to mobilise tens and sometimes hundreds of thousands, included calls for the dissolution of the ruling party, the exclusion of regime figures from the government and justice for the hundreds killed by the security forces during the uprising by bringing the Interior Minister, Mubarak and other major regime figures to trial. The generals who had found themselves running the country through SCAF were able to enforce a curfew and ban on overnight encampments in the main squares. They cracked down especially hard on small groups of junior army officers, who appeared in public at major protests in April, some of whom were arrested after attempting to re-establish the Tahrir sit-in on 8 April.

The military's efforts to assert their right to control the streets also took specifically gendered forms, through the sexual abuse of detained women protesters who were forced to undergo 'virginity tests' (a physical examination purporting to discover whether their hymen was still intact). Over the following months a pattern of organised, group sexual assaults on women demonstrators during protests would also emerge. Many activists saw these not simply as expressions of sexism in wider society, but a specific tactic adopted by the security forces in order to reassert their control over public spaces through traumatising women's bodies. The recovery of the state's agency through such oppressive mechanisms was not restricted to women, but also included the targeting of Coptic Christians. During the 18 days of the initial uprising, the character of the Tahrir sit-in had been strongly marked by expressions of unity between Muslims and Christians, most famously on 'Revolution Sunday' (6 February) when joint prayers were held in the square. Yet when Copts and their supporters attempted to challenge the structural forms of discrimination they faced at the hands of the state through peaceful protest on 9 October 2011, they were attacked in the state-run media, while armoured cars rammed into demonstrators, killing dozens.

SCAF's leaders did not only count on repression, but also looked to reformist opposition groups, particularly the largest political organisation in the country, the Muslim

Brotherhood, to help them channel the energies unleashed by the January uprising into more manageable electoral and constitutional channels. A snap referendum on amendments to the constitution in March saw the main Islamist groups back the proposed changes which paved the way for parliamentary and presidential elections. The relationship between the military and the Brotherhood remained rocky. The military's attempts to preserve its leading role in the new political order led to a breakdown in relations in October 2011. This reflected, in part, pressure on the Brotherhood's leadership from the organisation's own activist base. Many younger members had joined the uprising earlier in the year in defiance of their leaders' orders to remain on the sidelines. However, it also demonstrated that the Brotherhood could not risk ignoring the growing anger in the streets where protesters found themselves confronted by military security forces.

Unlike Mubarak before them, the generals of SCAF had a wider range of cards to play. The mass protests and sit-ins of November took place in the context of national parliamentary elections. The major opposition parties, particularly the Brotherhood, hoped that these would open the door to participation in government, following the path of Ennadha in Tunisia. Although the Brotherhood did initially call out its activists to join the Tahrir sit-in, over the following days it became clear that for the Islamists, the ballot box, rather than the streets, held the key to change. Once the scale of the renewed protests had wrung some concessions from SCAF over the degree of direct military oversight of the political system, the Brotherhood shifted focus back to the electoral process.

Debates between activists advocating mass collective action in the streets and workplaces and reformists who argued that securing a majority in parliament was the best chance of achieving the revolution's goals came to a head in early 2012. A call by revolutionary activists from major youth movements, left-wing groups and some figures in the independent trade unions for a general strike on 11 February, the anniversary of Mubarak's fall, did not win over large numbers of workplaces, in part because the Muslim Brotherhood mobilised a major campaign opposing it.[28] Having won the largest bloc of seats in the new parliament, the Brotherhood argued that the prospects

---

28 Alexander & Bassiouny, 2014, p217.

The deluge: 2011-12

for reform would be harmed by continued confrontations with the military.

The Brotherhood's candidate, Mohamed Morsi, emerged as the eventual victor in the presidential elections of June 2012. The result was hardly a triumph for the Islamist camp. Morsi emerged as the narrow victor in the first round, and went on to face Ahmad Shafiq, a former Minister of Civil Aviation in the last Prime Minister of the Mubarak era, in a run-off. Morsi failed to unite the votes of a wider spectrum of pro-revolutionary opinion behind his campaign. In the first round he faced stiff competition from Nasserist Hamdeen Sabahi and former leading Muslim Brotherhood figure Abd-al-Moneim Abu-al-Fotouh, both of whom stood on platforms calling for a continuation and deepening of the process of political and social reform. Even more worryingly, when it came to a straight fight between Morsi and the clear candidate of the counter-revolution, Ahmad Shafiq, a wide range of revolutionary activists abstained. Morsi's narrow victory also appeared to be under threat from ominous moves by SCAF, which ordered the dissolution of parliament by the courts. After a brief power struggle within SCAF a compromise seemed to have been reached: Morsi would take office as president alongside a younger generation of generals such as Abdelfattah al-Sisi, former head of Military Intelligence who became Defence Minister in the new cabinet.

Just over a year later, al-Sisi would overthrow Morsi, instituting an openly counter-revolutionary regime which embarked on a wave of repression far more vicious than any during Mubarak's rule.

Libya: uprising, Nato intervention and civil war

The uprising in Libya was directly inspired by the revolutions in neighbouring Tunisia and Egypt, but similarly drew on years of political and social grievances by the subjects of Mu'ammar al-Qadhafi's brutal but politically eccentric regime. The initial trigger for the eruption of the uprising was the arrest of lawyer Fethi Terbil in Benghazi. Terbil represented families of political dissidents killed in a prison massacre in the notorious Abu Salem detention centre in 1996 and his detention prompted a small-scale demonstration outside the law courts in Benghazi.

Revolution is the choice of the people

Online calls for a 'Day of Rage' similar to the mass mobilisations which had launched the uprisings in Tunisia and Egypt were already beginning to circulate through networks of Libyans abroad and news of the repression of the protest in Benghazi was the final spark needed to set a new mass movement alight.

From the start the regime's response was highly militarised and the battles between protesters on one side and the security forces including several of the regime's feared paramilitary groups on the other over public space saw hundreds of casualties among demonstrators. Benghazi, the country's second city, fell into rebel control relatively quickly and the establishment of local revolutionary councils to direct the protests and take over the rudiments of government in areas freed from regime control seemed to offer hope of radical change. By 27 February, just ten days into the uprising, the National Transitional Council (NTC) had emerged as an alternative government in Benghazi.[29] Meanwhile the regime seemed to be cracking from within, with the rapid defection of some key figures such as the Minister of the Interior and some military units.

But the popular uprising in the capital failed in the face of extremely heavy repression as the regime rallied its forces. The uprising now became a series of battles for control over strategic towns and cities, starting with the fight for Misrata on the coast. Rebel forces also had to contend with the impact of foreign intervention. Days after the beginning of the uprising, on 22 February, the Arab League had suspended Libya's membership. By the 26 February the UN had imposed sanctions on Libya and referred al-Qadhafi to the International Criminal Court. However, it was the US-dominated North Atlantic Treaty Organisation (Nato) which took on itself the job of intervening in an effort to tip the military balance in favour of rebel forces. The question of who would control Libya's enormous oil resources and protecting the interests of Western oil companies was a major factor driving the intervention of the great powers, and by mid-March Nato air strikes were pummelling regime positions. The Nato intervention may have saved the rebellion from military disaster but at the same time, it set in train the processes which lead to the destruction of the revolution and the ripping apart of the country in a civil war a year later.

The character of the NTC shifted in response to external

---

29 Assaf, 2012.

military and diplomatic intervention. It now opened up to include former regime figures in order secure recognition by the UN and to smooth the path towards further military support from Nato. By August 2011, rebel forces were closing in on the capital Tripoli. They were welcomed by the city's residents, who rose in revolt against Qadhafi with mass protests, barricades in neighbourhoods and the disarming of regime forces. The dictator and his son fled to make a last stand in Sirte, where al-Qadhafi was eventually captured and executed in October 2011.

Al-Qadhafi's regime was now disintegrating, but the rebel forces which had replaced it also began to fracture, with tensions and competition along regional lines appearing over the following months. Rebel leaders in Benghazi argued that the oil-rich East of the country had long suffered from marginalisation and oppression and began to agitate for autonomy from the West. By the time parliamentary elections took place in July 2012 the drive towards civil war was unstoppable, deepened by the intervention of the regional and global powers and fuelled by competition over access to oil.

Bahrain: revolution in the heart of the Gulf

In early February 2011, youth activists in Bahrain began circulating calls for a day of protests on 14 February. Inspired the uprisings engulfing Tunisia and Egypt they emulated the model of a social call for a 'Day of Rage' over local political grievances. The date chosen marked the tenth anniversary of a referendum on the adoption of National Action Charter setting out a path to constitutional reforms. The referendum was overwhelming endorsed by voters, including Bahrain's politically marginalised and economically excluded Shia majority, and was the culmination of an officially-endorsed process of discussions between the regime and opposition parties which had come out a previous round of mass protests and civil disobedience between 1994 and 1998. In 2002, the King had adopted a constitution without consultation which departed from the agreement made with opposition parties in 2001.The failure of dialogue with the regime exacerbated a generational split between the leadership of the major reformist currents among the Shia Islamist opposition and layers of younger activists who

Revolution is the choice of the people

by 2011 were becoming increasingly impatient and frustrated by the regime's intransigence.

Poverty and inequality overlap frequently with confessional cleavages in Bahrain, which is ruled by an authoritarian Sunni monarchy, although the majority of the population is Shi'a. A large proportion of the labour force are migrant workers and Shi'a activists have long argued that the regime deliberately encourages migration by Sunnis from outside Bahrain in order shift the demographic balance. This is a particularly contentious issue in relation to recruitment for the security forces and police, which have historically been dominated by British advisers whose relationship with the royal family goes back to the colonial period.

The scale of protests on 14 February surprised not just the organisers, a loose coalition of youth networks, but also the established political parties and the regime. Thousands congregated at Pearl Roundabout, a large traffic intersection in the capital Manama, a highly significant shift in tactics by protest organisers who had previously concentrated on small-scale demonstrations involving young men burning tyres and confronting the police in the Shia villages around the capital. The demonstration at the roundabout was not only a much bigger scale, it was in a strategic central location and attracted a much wider layer of people, not just Shi'a activists but Sunnis as well.

The regime's attempts to crack down on the demonstrations including shooting young protesters quickly escalated the mobilisation as thousands and then tens of thousands joined funeral processions for the victims of the repression. Early on 17 February, security forces battered their way into the protest camp at Pearl Roundabout forcing protesters to withdraw. However, the uprising could no longer be contained in the streets alone: the General Federation of Bahraini Trade Unions (GFBTU) called a general strike. The Crown Prince opened negotiations with al-Wifaq's leaders, partially at the urging of US officials. A compromise was reached whereby the police were withdrawn from the roundabout and protesters returned, setting up an encampment which became a magnet for the whole of the political opposition.

Over the following two weeks Crown Prince and legal opposition leaders attempted to negotiate a deal which would resolve the crisis, but both came under increasing pressure from

The deluge: 2011-12

their own side. The Crown Prince was facing opposition from 'hardliners' within the royal family who favoured crushing the uprising by force. These included the unelected Prime Minister, Sheikh Khalifa, a key target of demands for reform who had been in post since 1971, but also by the Khawalid branch of the royal family. There were also regional forces pushing towards crackdown across the Gulf Cooperation Council, particularly Saudi Arabia. Bahrain's economic dependency on its neighbour was one source of leverage: the two kingdoms share the revenue from the Abu-Safa oil field, and the finance and tourism sectors of the Bahrain economy are also highly dependent on Saudi investment and Saudi tourists who regularly cross bridge linking the mainland to the island. The causeway itself would provide a convenient route for the eventual military intervention, fulfilling the purpose for which it was constructed in the wake of the 1979 revolution in Iran.

For the 'hardliners' in the royal family and the GCC, the issues of 'national security' and sectarian dominance intersected and reinforced each other. Viewing the Shi'a population of the Gulf as a literal 'fifth column' for the Islamic Republic of Iran, they argued that only harsh repression could protect the existing political order in Bahrain. Protests demanding democratic reforms were the cover for a sinister plot to establish an Islamic Republic modelled on the state built by Ayatollah Khomeini in Iran, they claimed. Bahrain is the only Gulf state where Shi'a Muslims form a majority of the population across the country. Saudi Arabia's oil-rich Eastern Province is also majority Shi'a. In comparison to Bahrain, religious discrimination is at a higher pitch and is coupled with even more severe forms of political repression which interact with economic inequality and injustice to marginalise Shi'a within Saudi Arabia. Inspired by the sudden success of the protest movement in Bahrain, Shi'a activists in Eastern Province also began to mobilise their own demonstrations in February 2011. Although small-scale at first, the rallies and marches demanding the release of political prisoners began to swell to hundreds of participants, buoyed by the public support of Sheikh Nimr al-Nimr, an influential cleric who joined the demonstrations.

Meanwhile in Manama, the withdrawal of the police created a breathing space for the protest movement to develop. As the licensed opposition parties like al-Wifaq pursued their dialogue with the Crown Prince, other political currents were also being bolder and more radical in their demands. There was a noticeable convergence between the unlicensed Shi'a opposition parties, such as Al-Haq, whose leader Hussein al-Mushayma, returned to Bahrain in late February, and the young activists now loosely grouped together in the 14 February Coalition a network of youth groups supporting calls for a political revolution. Al-Haq and two other unlicensed Shi'a Islamist parties formed the Coalition for the Republic, a political alliance demanding the abolition of the monarchy, and announced they would work closely with the 14 February youth groups to achieve their aims.

The radicalisation of sections of the protest movement, and in particular the demands for an end to the monarchy, prompted an intensification of sectarian propaganda by the regime. The early stages of the February protests had been characterised by expressions of unity against sectarianism. This appeared to be striking a chord with Sunnis beyond the narrow layers of historic leftist opposition groups such as the Al-Wa'ad party, which maintained a principled rejection of sectarianism and included figures such as Ibrahim al-Sharif. Official media outlets pumped out constant propaganda accusing the protest organisers of hiding a violent sectarian agenda behind their calls for political reform and of being in the pay of Iran.[30]. Pro-regime rallies at the Al-Fatih Mosque began to draw larger crowds and residents in largely Sunni areas began to organise themselves to protect themselves from attack saying they feared violence from protesters. Protesters at Pearl Roundabout attempted to push back at the sectarian narrative using creative protest tactics, such as a massive human chain which physically linked the Al-Fatih Mosque to Pearl Roundabout on 5 March.[31]

As the weekend of 11-12 March approached, tensions built towards a climax. In Bahrain, the Coalition for the Republic and the 14 February youth were pushing for a shift in tactics towards confrontation with the regime, including a blockade of the Bahrain Financial Harbour and the financial district close to Pearl Roundabout and a march on the Royal Court in al-Riffa, an upper class, largely Sunni neighbourhood. Meanwhile in Saudi Arabia, online calls for a 'Day of Rage' on 11 March modelled on the protests, which had launched uprisings elsewhere

---

30 Matthiesen, 2013, p48–49.
31 Richter, 2011.

The deluge: 2011-12

in the region, were gathering thousands of supporters—an unprecedented show of public anger in a context where street protests were not just banned but extremely rare. Sunni Islamist opposition activists in Saudi Arabia, such as prominent cleric Salman al-Awda, began to agitate for political reform, arguing that unless the monarchy granted more freedoms the royal family risked a revolution.

In the event it was only in Eastern Province that protesters took to the streets on 11 March. In Riyadh, a lone activist showed up and was promptly arrested. Emboldened by the failure of the 'Day of Rage', the authorities ratcheted up their sectarian propaganda against the movement in Eastern Province, presenting it as an Iranian-inspired secessionist fifth column. In Manama, the Bahraini opposition parties were deeply divided over the escalation in protest tactics, with al-Wifaq's leaders denouncing the proposed march to al-Riffa on the grounds that it would draw Sunnis closer to the regime and could be presented as a threat to their lives and property. Yet their failure to produce any concrete signs of progress towards reform from the negotiations with the Crown Prince undermined their ability to influence younger activists who argued that escalation was the only way forward.

Having assured themselves that the protest movement in Eastern Province could not link up with dissidents elsewhere in the country, the Saudi authorities now moved against the revolution in Bahrain. Acting in concert with the factions inside the Bahraini royal family who wanted to crush the protests, they dispatched GCC military forces to Bahrain to help the regime there 'restore order'. On 14 March, Saudi armoured cars and troops rolled across the causeway and seized control of key locations in Manama. Despite a call for a general strike in response, the protesters were eventually overwhelmed and repression on a mass scale began with arrests of opposition leaders, sackings and victimisation of striking workers while the security forces beat demonstrators off of the streets. Even the Pearl Roundabout's distinctive architecture did not escape, the monument at the centre—a concrete structure topped with a ball symbolising a pearl—was demolished on 18 March.[32]

The events of mid-March marked a turning point in the revolutionary process: although it took more than a year for

---

32 Chulov, 2011.

the regime to close down the streets entirely as a space for protest, the intervention by GCC forces was crucial in breaking the forward momentum and providing the regime with a breathing space to organise a counter-attack. Under pressure from the Obama administration in the US, the regime agreed to an "independent inquiry" into the events of February-March and the repression during the aftermath. The commission, which reported in November 2011, produced a surprisingly detailed chronicle of human rights abuses on a grand scale (although it also recycled the regime's claims of that the security forces were merely reacting to protester violence), but the recommendations were simply ignored. Meanwhile repression carried on apace, not sparing the licensed opposition parties such as al-Wifaq, whose leaders were jailed and stripped of their Bahraini citizenship. Protests continued but were largely contained once again in the Shi'a villages.

Yemen: "parallel revolution" against the regime

The revolution in Yemen appeared at first an early emulator of the Tunisian and Egyptian model of popular uprisings powered by mass protests and strikes against authoritarian regimes. The revolutionary mobilisation was driven by a generation of young protesters rather than the existing opposition parties (even if one of the best known of the new leaders—the journalist and activist Tawakkul Karman—was a member of the opposition Islamist movement, al-Islah). The first major street demonstrations in the capital Sana'a erupted on 27 January, just two days after the Egyptian uprising began.[33] While the regime mobilised its supporters to seize control of Tahrir Square in Sana'a, young activists set up camp outside the university at a crossroads they named *Taghir* Square 'Change Square'.

> As in Cairo's Tahrir Square, the physical space around the university was transformed into a sociopolitical entity with political festivities, songs, stage plays, poems, exhibitions and dance. For the first time in decades, there was public mixed interaction between men and women... In Taghir Square, women were

33 Abdullah & Ghobari, 2011.

The deluge: 2011-12

among the most energetic participants in the protests. Yemen's social intifada created a new space for women's empowerment, networks, courage and voices.[34]

Street protests continued to escalate over the following two months until the embattled president Ali Abdallah Saleh attempted to crush the movement by force, launching a murderous attack on one of the major protest sites on 18 March, killing around forty people. This assault deepened the crisis in the state, with defections hitting the army which began to split over the president's actions. There were also signs that broader support for the regime beyond Saleh's base in the security apparatus and his own family was beginning to crumble. Leaders of the Hashid tribal confederation and leading religious figures issued a statement calling on the president to leave power.[35] The rapid disintegration of Saleh's control over the army, and the coalescence of a broad anti-Saleh coalition of tribal leaders, mainstream opposition parties and defectors from with the regime's own ranks including several ministers and ambassadors signalled that the relatively powerful opposition political parties whose tacit support had ensured the survival of the political system now felt that Saleh's removal was imperative in order to reassert political control over a movement on the streets led by a younger generation of activists.

The military revolt against Saleh and the eruption of fighting in the capital triggered a desperate scramble by the Gulf Cooperation Council (with Saudi Arabia and the United Arab Emirates in the lead), working in collaboration with the US and EU diplomats, to divert the revolution into negotiated 'transition process'. A fundamental obstacle to this process initially lay in Saleh's stubborn refusal to relinquish power.[36] A bomb attack on the presidential palace on 3 June left Saleh badly injured and temporarily removed him from the political scene for treatment in Saudi Arabia. He returned in September 2011 and finally agreed signed a transition agreement in November. Abd Rabbuh Mansur Hadi, his vice-president, was the single candidate in presidential elections held on 21 February 2012.

The major regional powers, such as neighbouring Saudi

---

34   Fattah, 2011, p81.
35   Al Jazeera, 2011b.
36   Sudam & Ghobari, 2011.

Revolution is the choice of the people

Arabia and the UAE, together with the US and EU states all presented this process, which sought to limit change to a superficial exchange of personnel at the top to the state, as vital to avoid the collapse of the Yemeni state and civil war. The decline of the USSR's geopolitical power in the late 1980s eventually forced the ruling class of the People's Democratic Republic of Yemen (PDRY) into unification on terms which were largely set by its Northern rival and in 1990 a unified Yemeni republic emerged, with Salih as president and the secretary general of the ruling Yemeni Socialist Party in South Ali Salim Al-Beidh as vice president. This did not end the Southern Question in Yemeni politics. Although Abd Rabbuh Mansur Hadi, another Southerner, became vice-president in 1994 after a brief civil war, where Southern political parties announced their secession, Salih's regime put loyalists from the North into key roles governing the South and facilitated land grabs, as formerly state-owned properties were put up for quick sale.[37] This laid the foundations for a resurgence of a mass Southern separatist movement from 2007 onwards, characterised by forms of protest and mass mobilisation which pre-figured the 2011 uprising.

The split between North and South Yemen was only one way in which the dynamics of imperialist competition worked their way into the structures and institutions of the state. Saleh, for example positioned himself and his security forces as junior partners in the US-sponsored 'War on Terror' and was rewarded with increased US military aid.[38] Saudi Arabia doled out stipends to tribal leaders, mirroring Saleh's own efforts to maintain the web of patronage which helped to support his regime.

The revolutionary mobilisation did begin to offer hope that a real alternative could be built from below which would benefit the vast majority of Yemenis excluded from these corrupt structures. The vitality and resilience of the protest movement which continued to mobilise extraordinary mass protests demanding Saleh step down was a formidable obstacle to a quick deal preserving the regime intact. These were accompanied by an escalating "parallel revolution" in the workplaces, where workers took action to remove regime loyalists from management through strikes and occupations. As early as mid-February, dock workers in Aden were taking direct

37 Murray, Rebecca, 2013.
38 Baron, Al-Madhaji & Alharari, 2017.

The deluge: 2011-12

action against their bosses, for example, storming the offices of the Yemen Gulf of Aden Port Corporation, seizing its chairman and other senior corporate figures. "We have had it with corrupt officials and it's time to tell them to leave," Ali Bin Yehya, a port worker, told *Al-Jazeera*. "What happened in Egypt and Tunisia motivated the workers to demand their rights".[39]

In late 2011 and early 2012, strikes targeting Saleh loyalists who expected to keep their jobs under the new president began spread again. Abubakr al-Shamahi describes the scenes as workers ran bullying, corrupt bosses out into the street.

> One protester at a government office in the city of Taiz said his boss had put a gun to his head only the week before. The boss, at first confused, and then angry, was barred from entering the building by the protester and his colleagues. Such scenes have been replicated across the country, and across a wide array of government institutions—any success giving encouragement to other workers tired of their overlords. And they have met with success in many cases now. One video shows Abubakr al-Amoodi, a military man who heads the Civil Status Office, being hounded out of the building. The employees line the path cheering his exit.[40]

The protest movement in the streets, coupled with the pockets of radical action by workers in strategically important industries and services, such as the oil industry and parts of the public sector, had the potential to form the basis for revolutionary unity among the poor majority of Yemenis who had nothing to gain from the survival of the corrupt, repressive old regime and its relatively cosy relationship with the major opposition parties.

Tragically, the tantalising vision of revolutionary unity across sectarian and tribal differences and the divides created by the uneven economic development of the country's different regions, began to unravel. Centrifugal competition between different sections of the Yemeni ruling class to attract external support unleashed a dynamic where workers and the poor from different regions could see no real alternative to localised, often

39   Al Jazeera, 2011a.
40   Al-Shamahi, 2012.

Revolution is the choice of the people

military solutions to their problems over forging unity on a class basis with different parts of the country.

Syria: revenge of the regime[41]

The first call for a "day of rage" by Syrian social media activists went largely unnoticed in early February 2011. On 17 February hundreds staged an improvised protest in the al-Hamidiyah market in Damascus. After a policeman beat up a local shopkeeper they chanted "the Syrian people will not be humiliated" and only dispersed after the Interior Minister came down in person and promised an official inquiry into the incident. While police brutality was a normal occurrence, improvised angry protests of this kind were not, especially in a high-profile area like the al-Hamidiyah market. However small in size and scope, this event hinted that the liberating mood of the Arab uprisings was beginning to challenge the state of fear that had gripped Syrian society for so long. As Syrian activist Razan Ghazzawi put it:

> The main demand in the Souk was: The Syrian people will not be humiliated. That is why the revolution was named by many the 'Dignity revolution'. There were no clear demands at the time, people were wondering what to do, experimenting with the movement. The movement was still 'finding itself' in a way.[42]

On March 6th, young teenagers were kidnapped by security forces for writing the Arab revolutions' slogan "The people want the downfall of the regime" on a wall of their school in the southern city of Deraa. The following days would see protests held in Damascus and Aleppo to demand the liberation of political prisoners who had gone on hunger strike. They were attacked by riot police and several protesters were beaten and arrested. Thousands of Syrian Kurds held protests in al-Hasakah and al-Qamishli, commemorating the 2004 riots that saw 30 Kurds fall victim to the regime's bullets. Back in Deraa, a series of protests on 18 March were met by live bullets from the Syrian army, killing

---

41 Based on part of pamphlet I co-authored with Jad Bouharoun, *Syria: revolution, counter-revolution and war*. Alexander & Bouharoun, 2016.
42 Alexander & Bouharoun, 2016.

The deluge: 2011-12

up to 10 demonstrators. The funerals of the victims—held the following day according to Islamic tradition, turned into larger protests, and the 10,000 strong crowd was again met with teargas and bullets, leaving up to four dead and dozens injured. The next day, the release of the kidnapped boys with their bodies showing clear signs of torture sparked more angry demonstrations with protesters setting fire to the local Baath party headquarters. On 25 March, tens of thousands marched in Deraa alone, and large protests were held in Homs, Hama, Baniyas, Latakia, Aleppo and central Damascus. The state's bloody response left 70 protesters dead and hundreds behind bars. "Repression only hardened the protesters' resolve," explained Razan, "and they kept on protesting in spite of live ammunition being used by the armed forces against them. In the first few weeks, the protesters' demands mainly concerned political and economic reforms. People would demand jobs, better public services, education, healthcare etc. The regime's repression caused the escalation of the demands towards the toppling of the regime".[43]

The movement gained momentum in April, and mass demonstrations became a regular occurrence in the Damascus suburbs of Douma, Zamalka and Moadamiya, as they had in Deraa, Homs, Baniyas and Latakia. In an apparent attempt to defuse the protest movement, Bashar al-Assad repealed the Emergency Law and abolished the state security courts on 20 April. But the following day his soldiers and thugs killed 104 protestors across the country. Around the same time, the army moved to strike a decisive blow at the still defiant people of Deraa. Checkpoints were established around the city to prevent anyone from crossing in or out and water, electricity and phone lines were cut. On 29 April it launched a large-scale military assault on the town using tanks and artillery, killing dozens and arresting hundreds.

The new tactic applied by the regime in Deraa was to be turned into a systematic response to protests and uprisings in multitudes of localities around the country. In 2011 alone, the cities of Baniyas, Latakia, Homs, Rastan and Hama, as well as dozens of other localities were targeted using similar methods. As the conflict developed, millions of Syrians would become familiar with the regime's artillery barrages, barrel bombs and minefields.

---

43 Alexander & Bouharoun, 2016.

Another crucial aspect of the regime's response, unleashed as early as April 2011, was to create or exploit sectarian tensions. The explicitly anti-sectarian nature of the protests and demonstrations threatened the regime, and the division of the movement along sectarian lines became a priority. State media accused all demonstrators of being terrorists with an extremist Islamist agenda in an attempt to portray the Assad regime as the protector of religious minorities and to dissuade their members from joining the growing popular movement. The regime also used more direct means to try and give the crisis an increasingly sectarian character; for instance, it sent members of shabiha criminal gangs alongside, or instead of the regular army to suppress protests in specific parts of the country.

Growing numbers of soldiers refused to take part in the killings of protesters and left the army. Together with locals, they formed the first armed resistance groups. Initially, they would mainly act as an armed escort for demonstrations, in case the regime's security services opened fire. As the repression intensified, their numbers swelled with both defecting soldiers and local people who took up arms to defend their neighbourhoods or towns. Thus they evolved into more effective fighting groups, and by May 2011 were conducting hit-and-run attacks on army checkpoints and positions, and later defending whole neighbourhoods against army incursions. In June 2011 in Jisr Al-Shughour, an armed uprising wiped out the security forces in the town. The army counterattacked with hundreds of armoured vehicles and chased the insurgents all the way to Turkey where they sought refuge along with 5,000 of the town's population.

From July 2011 officers and soldiers began to announcement their defection to the "Free Syrian Army" (FSA). The early armed groups they formed reflected the grassroots, but fragmented nature of the uprising. They were mostly composed of soldiers who had defected as individuals or in small units, not as entire battalions, let alone divisions. There are no known instances of large-scale mutinies with a political character. However, the fate of the FSA groups was not only shaped by local factors. As time passed, the regional and global powers began to see the FSA as potential force to advance their interests. Throughout 2012 FSA groups began to receive funding and arms from of a range of countries. Intervention by these external forces increased competition between the different armed groups

The deluge: 2011-12

and accelerated the slide towards civil war. Later still, the FSA groups found themselves pushed aside by Islamist battalions which attracted more funding from the Gulf.

The mass movement developed throughout May, June and July 2011. The killing and jailing of protesters continued, so much so that by June 2011, over 12,000 activists and demonstrators had been detained without trial. While the siege and bloody assault on Deraa in April greatly reduced the scale of the unrest there, in other cities the movement was on the rise. The first notable demonstrations in Hama had not occurred until May, and in July, profiting from a break in the regime's large-scale military operations the city held the two largest rallies of the Syrian revolution, with several hundreds of thousands of participants each time.

Relatively small protests erupted in Damascus' centre, but the security services were deployed so densely that any gathering of more than a few hundred was impossible. However, the large and sustained protests in the suburbs of the capital certainly brought rural migrants together with impoverished workers and lower middle class clerks who had been driven out of the city centre by soaring rents in the decade leading to the uprising.

Another decisive feature of the Syrian revolution was the absence of the organised working class as an active player. Although workers certainly took active part in the uprising as individuals and as part of their "local communities", they did not exercise their objective collective power through strike action. Millions of workers in the internal or external transport sectors (such as railways, airports and ports), in power or water infrastructure, as well as industrial workers, civil servants, teachers and healthcare workers had the potential to bring the economy and the state to a halt. Collective, class-based action would also have been the most effective deterrent against the sectarian divisions that the regime tried to exacerbate.

In the popular movement itself, local activists set up coordination committees, small grassroots organisations that took care of the logistical aspect of protests and played a crucial role in putting together reports on the demonstrations and the repression. Their extensive presence on social media and their links with international media outlets were essential to keep the world informed of the events in Syria, as the regime had barred foreign journalists from entering the country and all private media outlets belonged to loyalist businessmen who relayed the regime's propaganda. As the state withdrew from certain neighbourhoods or cities, many of the activists participated in the numerous Revolutionary Councils, set up by locals to run essential services and manage the public infrastructure, often with the support from local FSA brigades.

The political groups which claimed to have some kind of overall, coordinating role in directing the uprising also lacked real roots on the ground. The Syrian National Council, which was formed seven months after the beginning of the uprising in 2011 was dominated by exiled opposition figures. They were well-practised in carving out a place for themselves in the endless circuits of diplomacy between the regional powers such as Turkey, Qatar and Egypt (until the military coup of 2013), and the global powers. But they were neither able to offer any coherent direction for the uprising nor act independently of their regional and global sponsors. In November 2012, under pressure from the US, the SNC joined a new, broader alliance of opposition forces, the National Coalition of Syrian Revolutionary and Opposition Forces. This new body suffered many of the same problems as the SNC and was relatively quickly sidelined by the regional and global powers as they looked for other means to influence the outcome of the battle now raging for Syria.

Funding and arms from the Gulf, both from state and private sources, flowed primarily to Islamist armed factions, boosting their influence and military capacity compared to the FSA groups. The latter remained scattered, in spite of attempts to unite under regional commands recognized by the Syrian National Council, which gave them access to some military aid from the Gulf, Turkey and the USA. This made the Free Syrian Army effectively dependent on foreign powers and sponsors whose agendas did not coincide with the values expressed in the Syrian people's uprising; what is more, the aid itself was often irregular and unreliable, and the sudden lack of ammunition forced the FSA to abandon many battles.

The different groups started to compete for resources and donations, only reinforcing their fragmentation and foreign dependency. This created an environment favouring the dominance of the ultra-conservative armed Salafist groups, like Ahrar al-Sham whose fighters were connected to well-organised

The deluge: 2011-12

international networks providing funding and combat expertise. Another important Jihadist group is Jabhat al-Nusra (al-Nusra Front) which was formed in 2012 and pledged allegiance to the Al-Qaeda network led by Ayman al-Zawahiri. Better organised, financed and armed than most rebel groups, it was able to attract many young Syrians eager to fight the regime in more favourable conditions, notably FSA fighters who defected to it in large numbers during 2013. However, Jabhat al-Nusra's politics and actions are completely opposed to the spirit of the 2011 popular uprising.

Around the same time, as the regime was losing territory, it needed new, reliable recruits to fight what began to look like a war of attrition. The National Defence Force was formed in mid-2012 as a pro-regime militia, distinct from the regular army, set up and trained with assistance from Iran's Revolutionary Guards. It has played an important role in assisting the regular army, and numbers tens of thousands of recruits. Perhaps more crucial is the intervention of Hezbollah from 2012; the Lebanese Shi'a armed group sent thousands of well-trained and well-equipped elite combatants into Syria to bolster the ailing regime forces. Finally, Iraqi sectarian militias as well as Iranian Revolutionary Guard brigades came to al-Assad's aid.

Conclusion

As 2012 drew to a close, it was clear that the hopes for democratic reforms and social justice which lit up the region in early 2011, as one after the other dictators tottered and fell in the face of the insurgent people, were not going to be easily fulfilled. In Libya, the rebels had survived their baptism of fire and blood to emerge triumphant over the old dictator, but tensions were building up between competing armed factions within the new state which would soon plunge the country into another, more deadly civil war. Foreign military intervention had played a major role in creating the conditions for this to happen, and the regional and global powers tussling for influence over the fate of Libya's oil would continue to stoke the pressures fracturing the country over the following eight years. Bahrain's revolution had been snuffed out early on by Saudi tanks, although the embers of the mass movement for political and social justice against the sectarian and repressive monarchy continued to flare from time to time. In Yemen, like Libya, the faltering 'transition' process would collapse into open civil war in 2014 and by 2015 Saudi and UAE bombs were raining down on the capital.

The struggle inside Syria was also morphing into a civil war, with jihadi Islamist groups gaining the upper hand militarily over other factions opposed to the regime partly as a result of arms and funding flowing in from Salafist networks in the Gulf. Nevertheless, in some areas, forms of rebel government persisted and the shrinking size of the territory which Assad still controlled appeared to give some grounds for hope that the eventual outcome might be military defeat of the old regime.

Despite different appearances on the surface, in all of these cases a common pattern had emerged: the space for political initiative by the broad masses of ordinary people through collective action such as protests and strikes had almost disappeared. Instead the initiative had either passed to a constellation of armed groups or the old regime was firmly back in charge. The picture in Tunisia and Egypt was different. There, the popular phase of revolutionary mobilisation was still in full swing although with a markedly different political character to the initial months of the revolutions. Now Islamist and secular parties were locked in battle over the shape of the political institutions of the state, each seeking mobilise support on the streets and sometimes in the workplaces. How this struggle paved the way for a military-led counter-revolution in Egypt but was resolved in a longer-lasting reformist compromise in Tunisia, will be discussed in later chapters.

Yet although the experiences of 2011-2012 presaged future defeats, the core features of the revolutions which erupted in these years mapped out a terrain which would also be traversed by the uprisings of the second round of revolt which began six years later. Firstly, these were all genuine popular uprisings. Their genesis lay not in a political crisis caused by ruptures in the elite. The mass protests and strikes which characterised the first phases of the revolution were not orchestrated or led by factions of the existing ruling class. Moreover, in most cases it was independent collective action by the poor majorities of these societies—workers and unemployed—which provided the engine for the uprisings. There were sections of the middle class who also joined the revolts, and often played a

The deluge: 2011-12

disproportionately important role in the leadership of these mobilisations from below, but the fate of the revolutions was shaped in almost every case directly by the outcomes of the struggles against social inequality and injustice and not simply won or lost on the terrain of politics. This was not always well understood by external analysts, and often denied by some of the protagonists. Examples of efforts by both opposition forces and governments to restrict 'the revolution' to addressing questions of political reform, rather than also addressing social inequalities abound.[44]

Specifically, the presence or absence of organised workers as actors in the revolutionary process made a material difference to whether the uprising retained this popular, mass character beyond the initial phase. As we have seen, organised workers played a pivotal role in both the early phases of Tunisian and Egyptian revolutions, but not in Syria or Libya, where they had been unable to accumulate experience of self-organisation because of the intensity of the regime's repression in the pre-revolutionary period. The situation in Yemen was somewhat different—workers' mobilisations were part of the uprising and in some areas continued even in conditions of external military intervention, but the social weight of the working class was not sufficient for this to prevent the slide into civil war.[45] In the case of Bahrain, mass strikes were also important in creating the conditions for a genuine revolutionary crisis, but the trade unions, like the rest of the opposition forces, were overwhelmed by the scale of repression after the Saudi intervention in March 2011.

The question of whether revolution could provide an answer to oppression was woven throughout the revolutionary experience in all the countries discussed here. One way in which this manifested was in the participation of women on a massive

---

44 See Bassiouny & Alexander, 2021 for a discussion of the impact of the media campaign against strikes and workers' social demands under slogans demanding they "restart the wheel of production". Wael Gamal, writing in 2011 pointed out that one of the things "the people demand" was "a different wheel of production" rather than returning to the same patterns of exploitation (Gamal, 2011).

45 Aden in particular had long-established traditions of activism in the workplaces, see reporting in Middle East Solidarity magazine on some of the strikes there. See menasolidaritynetwork.com/?s=aden.

scale in protests and strikes, and in the use of violence against women protesters by the embattled authorities as a mechanism to reassert control over the streets. The issue of religious oppression and freedom was also an important theme in the uprisings. In Syria, protesters posed the idea of revolutionary unity and solidarity between activists from different religious backgrounds as a counterweight to the Assad regime's effort to both mobilise sectarianism on its own behalf (through facilitating sectarian killings by the *shabiha* gangs for example) and to characterise its opponents as motivated by a sectarian Sunni Islamist agenda of their own. The Bahraini monarchy carried out similar manoeuvres, working to drive a wedge between Shi'a and Sunni protesters and mobilising support for repression on a sectarian basis both within the country and at a regional level through the GCC.

The revolutions all posed—but did not answer—the question of what is to be done about the relationship between the *regime* and the *state*. The clash between protesters with the existing rulers was framed as a confrontation with a regime which was corrupt, unjust and repressive, through mobilisation over concrete demands for radical changes in the workings of the institutions of the state. If we look beyond the specific nature of these demands (for the removal of symbolic figures, for new constitutions, for changes to the electoral process) then three broader themes characterise the popular challenge to the existing order: its peaceful (*silmy* in Arabic), civil (*madany*) and national (*watany*) character. While all of these aspects of the uprisings were contested from within, they form common threads across all the examples discussed here. Firstly, the idea that peaceful mass collective action *ought* to be the primary form of contestation with the old order, rather than armed insurrection, a military conspiracy, or guerrilla warfare, was not restricted to the small networks of liberal activists who actually espoused a theory of non-violent civil disobedience. Rather it became a kind of common sense about what 'revolution' meant for hundreds of thousands, and perhaps millions of people. The violence of the of regimes' responses immediately put this tactical choice under unbearable pressure, should also not obscure the point that this aspect of the uprisings posed a profound ideological challenge to the existing political order. It ripped apart the regime's contention that the purpose of

The deluge: 2011-12

the security forces and army was to defend society against 'terrorism' and external threats. It made visible what ordinary people well understood from their day-to-day encounters with the regime and its agents, that the primary function of these apparatuses of violence was to maintain the regimes in power.

The 'civil' nature of the uprisings also constituted a challenge to the regimes at several levels. In Arabic the word '*madany*', has a number of connotations which are not obvious from the English translation. It may be used both in opposition to 'military' (*askari*) and in opposition to 'Islami' (Islamic) or '*ta'ifi*' (sectarian). The implication that the uprising could rework the structures of the state in order to leave civilian politicians, rather than military leaders, the final arbiters of the country's destiny was complicated by the polarisation over the role of Islamist currents in the process of democratic reform. As we will discuss in the next chapter, Islamist opposition parties in Tunisia and Egypt did enjoy periods in government as a direct result of the uprisings of 2011. They both faced hardening opposition from a coalition of non-Islamist forces including some elements close to the old ruling parties, but working in alliance with other 'secular' forces including Arab nationalists and some elements of the Stalinist left. In the Egyptian case, far from working towards deepening civilian control over the state, this 'secular' alliance facilitated the political rehabilitation of the military.

The 'national' (*watany*) character of the uprisings was symbolised by the ubiquitous sight of the national flag on the protests. Acting as a kind of shield against the regime's defensive claims that the protesters were agitators in the pay of foreign powers, it also fostered the idea that the people in revolt truly represented 'the nation' in contrast to the self-serving, narrow clique whose rule they were contesting. As we will discuss in more detail in later chapters, the ideological terrain of nationalism proved much friendlier to the restoration of the old order than to reform. The national flag and its associated ideologies of xenophobia and militarism were easily reappropriated by those fighting to restore the 'prestige of the state' in the face of the challenge from below as the counter-revolutions gathered pace. Yet the rulers who emerged triumphant out of the ruins had themselves all reached far beyond their borders to mobilise the resources and weapons (both material and ideological) needed to defeat the uprisings.

Revolution is the choice of the people

Chapter 3
The ebb and the flow: 2013-22

Counter-revolution is not simply a restoration of the old order, but always involves its transformation. It is a dynamic process in the opposite direction to revolution. Counter-revolution turns weaknesses in revolutionary movements into weapons against them. It worms into every vertical crack and fissure in their ranks—between Sunni and Shi'a, between Muslim and Christian, between men and women, between migrants and locals—creating such gaping holes that the unity of purpose which directed anger against the old rulers is shattered. Nationalism and xenophobia are often its primary tools. In order to escape the spectre of class war which revolutionary uprisings unleash, the leaders of the counter-revolution launch other wars.

The revolutionary wave which swept the Middle East in 2011 showed the potential for a region united horizontally, through the ties of social class which connected the fates of the impoverished majority with each other and pitted them against the kings, generals and big businessmen who rule. It demonstrated the possibility of a future where ordinary people could liberate themselves from all kinds of oppression, whether on grounds of gender or religious belief. This promise was both explicitly written into the demands of popular protests and strikes, which raised anti-sectarian slogans and implicit in the mass participation of women and oppressed religious groups.

As we saw in the previous chapter, within all of the countries where uprisings erupted in 2011, by late 2012 the tide of revolution was on the turn. Over the following years the process of counter-revolution would gather pace, taking different shapes and forms but animated by the same basic goals: to shatter the promise of solidarity between workers and the poor across the region, and instead bind their citizens and subjects to 'their' rulers through appeals to national unity against enemies within and without. Thus, across the Arab world as the hopes of 2011 receded, the phase of counter-revolution turned swiftly into accelerated competition between rival regional powers, pregnant with military adventurism, hot and cold proxy wars and geo-political confrontation.

In Egypt the counter-revolution took the form of a restoration of military dictatorship in an even more brutal form than under Mubarak. The fate of Syria, Libya and Yemen was even worse: lengthy civil wars, fuelled by the intervention of regional and global powers, ripped apart the fabric of these societies. Only in Tunisia did the strength of the workers' movement create the temporary conditions for a reformist compromise brokered by the trade union bureaucracy of the UGTT federation, which preserved some of the democratic gains of the revolution, although none of the elected governments—whether Islamist or secular—were able to offer any alternative to neoliberal austerity.[46] Yet despite these defeats, by early 2019 it was clear that the era of popular revolution was far from over. In Sudan, an uprising was gathering pace against the corrupt rule of Umar al-Bashir while Algeria was also on the brink of an explosion against ailing president Abdelaziz Bouteflika's attempts to secure a fifth term in office. Later the same year would also see uprisings in Lebanon and Iraq force the resignation of their respective Prime Ministers amid paralysing political and financial crises. As this chapter will explore, the pattern of the uprisings in Sudan and Algeria bore a great deal of similarities to the revolutions of 2011: these were revolts from below which mobilised millions of people in mass protests and strikes to demand fundamental democratic reforms and social justice. The slogans from 2011 found a ready echo on the streets once again, or were adapted to fit the local context. In the case of Iraq and

---

46 The temporary nature of this compromise was affirmed in July 2021, when President Kais Saied carried out a 'constitutional coup' sacking the Prime Minister, suspending parliament and granting himself interim executive powers. Sadiki & Saleh, 2021.

The ebb and the flow: 2013-22

Lebanon, these were revolts against a sectarian regime which emerged in the wake of internationally sponsored neoliberal 'reconstruction process' after military occupation and war. Although in neither case did the uprisings result in the kind of crisis which gripped Sudan and Algeria, they were still highly significant interventions by hundreds of thousands of people in politics which raised demands for radical change not just in government, but across the political system as a whole.

Tunisia and Egypt after 2013: diverging trajectories?

As we saw in the previous chapter, by the end of 2012 in both Tunisia and Egypt, the political landscape had been reframed by the clash between 'secular' and 'Islamist' currents over the future shape of the state. The consequences of this polarisation were strikingly different in the two countries. In Tunisia, the UGTT union federation imposed a compromise on both the main Islamist movement, Ennahda and its opponents which paved the way for a reformist route out of the crisis. This included the partial rehabilitation of elements in the old ruling party who were able to return to government through elections, but Ennahda retained its place in national politics and did not suffer the intense repression experienced by its counterpart in Egypt.

The political crisis had been brought to a head by the gunning down of two opposition political figures well-known for their pan-Arab and leftist views in February and July 2013.The killing of Chokri Belaid in February led to the resignation of Prime Minister Jebali amid a general strike and mass protests against the Ennadha-led coalition government. The assassination of Mohammed Brahimi, another leftist politician in July triggered a further general strike and huge demonstrations. Rather than push for the immediate resignation of the Ennadha-led government, the UGTT leadership oversaw the formation of the National Dialogue Quartet, composed of the UGTT itself, the employers' federation UTICA, the Order of Lawyers and the Tunisian Human Rights League. The Quartet brokered negotiations between the major political parties which resulted in Ennadha handing over power to a caretaker government in December 2013. Although the Islamist party retained a substantial bloc of seats at parliamentary elections in 2014, Nidaa Tounes now became the largest party, while Essebsi won the presidential elections in December that year. Ennadha did not find itself shut out of the political system, re-joining a coalition government in early 2015.

The sharp polarisation between secular and Islamist political currents in Egypt over almost the same time scale was resolved through the counter-revolutionary restoration of a military regime led by Abdelfattah al-Sisi, the Minister of Defence appointed by Mohamed Morsi following his narrow victory in the presidential election of 2012. Sisi's regime distinguished itself immediately by massacring hundreds of Muslim Brotherhood supporters, throwing tens of thousands in jail, and instating a dictatorship even more brutal than Mubarak's. That this would be the outcome of the struggles which marked Morsi's year in power was not obvious at the start. During the autumn of 2012 huge protests challenged Islamist efforts to give more powers to the presidency and pass a new constitution. The liberal and even revolutionary framing of protesters' demands, their adoption of some of the same slogans as the uprising against Mubarak, were given greater authority by the fact that once in power the Muslim Brotherhood showed frequent tendencies to behave in an authoritarian manner—using the courts to silence criticism in the press, jailing protesters and strikers. As the year went on, the creation of a broad 'secular' alliance, the National Salvation Front (NSF), which included not only currents which had supported the revolution such as the left-Nasserists led by Hamdeen Sabahi, but also (as in Tunisia) elements of the old ruling party, worked to rebuild the credibility of key elements of the old regime, starting with the judiciary, but ending with the military. The crisis climaxed at the end of June 2013, as enormous protests coordinated by the *Tamarod* (Rebellion) youth movement brought hundreds of thousands on the streets demanding Morsi step down. Al-Sisi was thus able to frame not just his assumption of absolute political power, but also the orgy of counter-revolutionary violence which followed, including the massacre of over 1,000 protesters in August 2013 as the military cleared sit-ins in solidarity with Morsi from the streets of the capital, as mandated by 'the people'.

In both Tunisia and Egypt there was also a crucial social dimension to the crisis of Islamist reformist parties in power. Ennadha and the Muslim Brotherhood alike sought to portray themselves as safe pairs of hands to international investors,

The ebb and the flow: 2013-22

committed to continuing and extending the process of neoliberal economic reforms. In the face of rising unemployment and growing frustration among workers and the poor that the revolution's promise of social justice was turning sour, they faced high levels of strikes and protests over pay, working conditions and job security. Their inability to offer any alternative to the neoliberal policies which had created the conditions for revolution in the first place thus contributed to their political downfall. In Tunisia, the UGTT provided a mechanism for workers to translate their frustrations into organised pressure on the governments which followed the "National Dialogue", whether led by secular or Islamist politicians. While the general strikes organised by the UGTT in 2013 dealt with political questions—and were instrumental in forcing Ennadha to compromise and relinquish power in a negotiated process—the tempo of the economic struggles has accelerated in subsequent years leading to waves of general strikes over primarily social demands in 2018, 2019 and 2020.

By contrast, in Egypt, the counter-revolutionary forces of the military and security apparatus were able to channel workers' frustrations with the Brotherhood's failures over social questions while in power towards providing them with political cover during the coup of July 2013. Al-Sisi appointed Kamal Abu Aita, president of the Egyptian Federation of Independent Trade Unions to his new cabinet after Morsi's overthrow as Minister of Labour. Abu Aita toured TV stations and trade union meetings promising that the new regime would look after workers' interests. In fact, even before the blood had dried from the military's massacres of Islamist protesters, it was locking up striking workers and insisting that the interests of "national security" demanded a pause in the struggle for social justice. This was followed by further assaults on independent trade unions and the right to organise at work, the implementation of a whole panoply of neoliberal reforms targeting subsidies on basic consumer goods and the revival of the privatisation programme which had been halted under pressure from below during 2011-2012. Meanwhile, the regime threw tens of thousands in jail across the full spectrum of the opposition from Islamists to the radical left, carried out forced disappearances and torture on an industrial scale and murdered hundreds in both extrajudicial and judicial executions.[47]

---

47 Reuters, 2019a.

Descent into hell: Syria, Libya, Yemen

In Syria, Libya and Yemen revolutionary uprisings gave way to wars which would tear apart the social fabric of these countries, forcing millions of people from their homes, killing and injuring hundreds of thousands and exposing the survivors to the horrors of famine and disease. In many accounts, this descent into hell is often presented as a simple causal process, either because the revolutions caused 'chaos' which led to war, or because the revolution itself was actually a plot by foreign-funded terrorists to bring down a legitimate government. Before unpicking the real reasons behind the disasters of endless war which overtook Syria, Libya and Yemen, it is worth briefly outlining the scale of destruction involved.

The Assad regime's counter-revolutionary war against the Syrian people began as early as spring 2011. By 2018 the Syrian Observatory for Human Rights estimated that over 500,000 Syrians had been killed during the conflict, largely at the hands of the regime and its allies. Out of a pre-revolutionary population of 21 million, 6.6 million had had been displaced within Syria while a further 5.6 million had fled the country, with 3.6 million seeking refuge in neighbouring Turkey.[48] Poverty rates soared: the World Bank estimated that by 2017 economic activity inside Syria had shrunk by 60 percent compared to 2010.[49] By 2021 according to the UN 90 percent of the Syrian population was living in poverty with 60 percent at risk of hunger.[50]

Libya also saw huge numbers forced to flee their homes and suffering rising levels of poverty and insecurity. The war against al-Qadhafi's regime in 2011 led to just over 20,000 deaths and 435,000 displaced, while the later rounds of civil war after 2014 also saw hundreds of thousands forced to flee.[51] Once the country with the highest per capita income in Africa (although that belied systematic hoarding and corruption by the elite), by 2018 one in three Libyans was living below the international poverty line.[52]

Yemen experienced disaster on an even greater scale. In 2019

---

48 Human Rights Watch, 2018.
49 World Bank, 2020.
50 United Nations, 2021.
51 Daw, El-Bouzedi & Dau, 2015.
52 Armitage, 2018.

The ebb and the flow: 2013-22

after more than five years of war, the UNDP warned that human development had been already set back by over two decades, and that if the war continued to 2030 that would rise to the loss of forty years' worth of progress in health, education, infrastructure and economic development.[53] The same year, Amnesty International reported that around 233,000 Yemenis had died as a result of the fighting and the humanitarian crisis and that 16 million people, equivalent to two-thirds of the pre-2011 population, were waking up hungry every day.[54] Hunger was already turning to famine, UN agencies said in 2018, reporting on the deaths of an estimated 85,000 children from malnutrition. Two years later and the combined impacts of war and the Covid 19 pandemic meant that millions faced the risk of starving to death.[55] None of these catastrophes were straightforward outcomes of *internal* conflict, nor inevitable results of the popular uprisings. Rather, they were all driven by the way in which the process of counter-revolution at a regional level intermeshed with intensifying military competition between both regional and global powers. Yet the wars which ripped apart Syria, Libya and Yemen also fed back into these same processes and deepened them.

With the exception of Bahrain, the regimes of the Gulf proved less vulnerable to the internal challenge of mass opposition movements than most other countries in the region. So, led by Saudi Arabia, after they had crushed the Bahraini revolution they moved on to ally themselves with Egypt's generals as they plotted their bloody comeback in 2013. Meanwhile, the al-Assad regime called in the military and logistical support of regional allies in countries such as Iraq and Lebanon which at the time experienced only a weak echo of the revolutions elsewhere, and Iran, which was largely unaffected by the wave of protest.

The process of counter-revolution in Yemen differed in the initial stages, but led to similarly catastrophic results for ordinary people. As we saw in the last chapter, the scale of the revolutionary mobilisation, and the relative of strength of the mass mobilisations from below, particularly in the South, meant that the kind of military intervention which snuffed out the movement in Bahrain was not practical. Yemen's far greater size than the island kingdom, distance from the power

---

53   UN OCHA, 2019.
54   Amnesty, 2020.
55   Al Jazeera, 2020b.

Revolution is the choice of the people

centres of the Gulf coast and mountainous terrain, also made a significant difference to the strategy of the GCC leaders. So they had attempted to preserve the core of the regime by sacrificing president Ali Abdallah Saleh, its head. The process of "national dialogue" which was meant to develop a new, federal constitution satisfying some of the demands of Southern activists for autonomy from the central government, fell apart in 2014. The Huthis, an armed Shi'a Islamist movement from the far north of Yemen which had already been involved in several local uprisings against the government in Sana'a before the revolution, seized the capital in collaboration with Saleh and the sections of the old armed forces still loyal to him.

Meanwhile, the mood on the streets in the South, frustrated by the failure of the "national dialogue" to even begin to address the underlying roots of the poverty, discrimination and repression which had fired the mass movement for autonomy in the first place shifted towards support for complete independence. In 2015 Saudi Arabia and UAE launched military action against the Huthis and their allies, which has taken the form of devastating air strikes and the blockade of key ports. On the ground, the Huthis were initially more successful than their opponents, and they were able to capture Aden, temporarily driving out Abd-Rabbo al-Mansur Hadi, Saleh's successor as president and head of the internationally-recognised Transitional Government. Saudi Arabia and UAE's intervention ostensibly on behalf of Hadi's government has had catastrophic results for millions of Yemenis. It has been spectacularly destructive of the country's infrastructure and is the major cause of the famine which haunts large areas of the country.

Moreover, military intervention by the two GCC allies has—despite their much greater resources—been relatively unsuccessful. Instead of rapidly pounding the Huthis into submission, the Saudi-UAE intervention morphed into a long drawn-out stalemate where the main losers have been the Yemeni people. This has driven the UAE in particular to attempt to build deeper alliances with some elements of the Southern movement for independence, and to mobilise Southern separatist fighters to support the war aims of the GCC allies.

Libya's collapse into civil war followed a very similar timescale and was driven by many of the same regional processes. The 2011 military victory of anti-Qadhafi forces

The ebb and the flow: 2013-22

supported by Nato did destroy the framework of the old regime and was followed by process meant to map out a new constitution and state institutions through elections to a transitional parliament and constitutional assembly. However, as in Yemen, this masked the fact that many elements of the old order were now ensconced in the new regime, having defected to the revolutionary side at the outbreak of the uprising or shortly afterwards.

Moreover, the character of the victory over al-Qadhafi and his allies, which was enabled by military support from outside, shifted the balance of power within the revolutionary camp away from those who wanted to build democratic institutions or address questions of social inequality and in favour of both new and old military leaders for whom the revolution opened up opportunities to seize control of Libya's resources for their own benefit. This dynamic towards military competition over key assets such as oil facilities was heightened because it mapped onto longstanding tensions between elites in Eastern and Western Libya over the equitable division of the country's resources between them. In addition, the pattern set by Nato military intervention demonstrated the potential for drawing in external powers—and thus military and financial aid—to take sides in the conflict. The civil war which began in 2014 would see Egypt, UAE and eventually Russia, taking the side of Khalifa Haftar, leader of one of the biggest armed factions, the Libyan National Army, as he took control of Eastern Libya and attempted to seize the capital Tripoli and remove the UN-backed Government of National Accord (GNA) from power. Meanwhile, the GNA was saved from military collapse by support from Turkey and Qatar.[56]

A further important destabilising factor in all three of the conflicts has been the emergence of jihadi Salafist armed groups often affiliated either with Al-Qa'ida (formerly led by Osama Bin Laden) or its Iraqi descendent (and rival) ISIS as serious military contenders. Khalifa Haftar's initial military campaign which saw him take control of Benghazi in Eastern Libya in May 2014 was framed as targeting Ansar al-Shari'a, a jihadi Salafist militia. Groups such as Al-Qa'ida had previously mainly targeted the US and its allies, carrying out spectacular terrorist atrocities in Western capitals and waging guerrilla operations against

56 BBC News, 2019b.

US military targets around the globe. Conditions of civil war created opportunities for these groups to shift strategy towards attempts at building their own mini-states, governed under the most reactionary interpretations of Islamic law. This process did not, in fact begin in 2011, but had its roots in the destruction of Iraq through years of war, sanctions and US occupation as that was where the leaders of ISIS (the Islamic State of Iraq and Syria) learnt their trade. ISIS's leaders were trained in the brutal environment of US-occupied Iraq after 2003. The group's predecessor organisation, a small group led by Jordanian Islamist Abu-Mus'ab al-Zarqawi, was distinguished by its extreme sectarianism and its use of mass-casualty bombings, not directed against the US forces, but at Shi'a citizens of Iraq. Their atrocities helped to trigger a vicious cycle of ethnic and sectarian "cleansing".

In Syria, ISIS's fighters enjoyed a number of advantages over other armed groups. They had long experience of combat, including fighting larger and better-equipped opponents in the Iraqi Army and the US forces. They also had access to Iraq as a hinterland for their operations in Syria. Finally, they had different territorial and political goals to almost everyone else and benefited from the fact that their opponents were fighting each other. For the al-Assad regime and its opponents, the ultimate goal was the capital city, Damascus. ISIS by contrast set its sights on first creating a new state somewhere else. This is one reason why the al-Assad regime from time to time pragmatically cooperated with ISIS around the oil industry, for example continuing to pay salaries to oil workers in areas under ISIS control in order to maintain oil and gas supplies to the capital. In Yemen, Al-Qa'ida in the Arabian Peninsula (AQAP) had been fighting Yemeni government forces for years as Saleh's regime sought to gain access to US support by playing a bit part in the "war on terror". As the country spiralled into civil war, AQAP's fighters were able to take over large cities, such as the port of al-Mukallah with a population of 300,000, temporarily creating an "emirate" governed by their repressive interpretation of Islamic law.

Likewise, in Libya, jihadi Salafist "emirates" were proclaimed in Derna, a port city of 150,000 and Sirte, with a population of 80,000 in 2014 and 2015 by groups allied with

The ebb and the flow: 2013-22

ISIS.[57] The spectacular territorial gains made by such groups in all three countries at the height of the civil wars were intimately linked to the retreat of the mass revolutionary movements, the exhaustion of the population, and the devastation caused by the counter-revolutionary repression and war. The fact that small numbers of jihadi Salafist fighters took over large cities with almost no resistance was a symptom of the defeat of the popular revolutions.

The final crucial element of analysis needed to make sense of the relationship between war and counter-revolution is the pattern of polarisation and competition between the strongest military and economic powers in the region. At first two opposing axes of regional powers emerged. One was centred on the Gulf states led by Saudi Arabia, and sought to draw in Turkey. The other was led by Iran with its regional allies in Iraq and Syria and with support from Lebanese organisation Hezbollah. The confrontations between the two axes deepened the sense that a region-wide sectarian battle was taking place, as they pitted 'Sunni' powers against 'Shi'a' states and parties. The two regional poles also related to different competing global powers: with the US standing behind the Gulf states and Russia intervening in Syria to help ensure the Assad regime's survival. This process was not simply an expression of the ideological needs of the various ruling classes to convince the millions in the streets that their erstwhile enemies were really their friends. A simplistic picture of 'eternal' ideological cleavages over religious identity—such as the division between Sunni and Shi'a forms of Islam—can't explain why the contending powers sometimes changed sides and fell out among themselves. The Gulf states, all led by 'Sunni' dynasties, are internally divided with Qatar's foreign alliances and diplomatic strategy diverging sharply from that of Saudi Arabia and the UAE (driven partially by the fact that its rulers cannot afford to simply cut off ties with their counterparts in Iran, with whom they must share the spoils of the major natural gas field off the coast). Likewise Turkey under Recep Tayyip Erdogan has taken an ever more militarily assertive role in the conflicts in Syria and Libya, where its support for the GNA government has brought it into direct conflict with Khalifa Haftar's forces backed by Egypt, the UAE and Russia.

---

57 Human Rights Watch, 2016; International Crisis Group, 2017.

Revolution is the choice of the people

Against the odds: the return of revolution

The deepening repression in Bahrain, restoration of military dictatorship in Egypt and the ravaging of Syria, Libya and Yemen by wars fuelled by the regional and global powers left little space for hope. The agency of popular protest, which had seemed so powerful in 2011, by 2015-6 appeared a distant memory, and those who clung to a strategy of non-violent mass collective action derided as naïve at best, complicit in the later horrors at worst . Yet as we will now discuss, despite the searing experience of counter-revolutionary defeat and war, just a few years later popular revolts resembling the wave of revolutions in 2011 would again be shaking the region, this time setting alight first Sudan, then Algeria, Lebanon and Iraq. As the uprisings escalated in Sudan and Algeria, a commentary in the Egyptian revolutionary socialist publication, *al-Ishtaraki*, noted that once again there were signs that the counter-revolution had not succeeded everywhere.

> At the same time as the Sudanese and Algerians are rising, a strong protest movement is developing in Morocco, with participation of professionals and trade unionists, while Tunisia is witnessing major workers' strikes, and in Lebanon there have been mass protests against deteriorating living conditions. Even in Jordan, last June a mass movement forced the King to reverse the government's economic decisions, and before that we saw the Great Return marches in Palestine. Meanwhile growing popular anger in Egypt and other countries is still looking for a spark to start the fire. Despite the defeats it has suffered, the memory of the region's revolutions remains inspiring, offering lessons and experiences. The spectre of revolution still haunts the region's tyrants. If the uprisings in Sudan and Algeria achieve significant victories in the near future, waves of hope and confidence will spread across the region.[58]

In Sudan, popular revolt led clearly to a political revolution which ousted not just the former dictator, but forced through major changes in the personnel at the top the state, with

---

58 Al-Ishtaraki, 2019

The ebb and the flow: 2013-22

civilian opposition figures and technocrats joining army and paramilitary leaders from the old regime following a negotiated handover of power in August 2019 to a Transitional Government. However, the continued presence of figures such army General Abdelfattah al-Burhan and Mohamed Dagalo, better known as Hemedti, whose Rapid Support Forces militia had risen to prominence under the former regime thanks to the brutal efficiency of its violent campaigns directed at al-Bashir's perceived enemies, recalled the choices made by Islamist reformists in Egypt as they attempted to contain the forces of counter-revolution within the structures of the existing state. In Algeria, Lebanon and Iraq, massive waves of popular protest initially claimed scalps at the highest level, with the fall of the president and prime ministers. As in Sudan, many protesters who took to the streets in all three countries considered themselves to be engaged in making a revolution, not merely agitating for specific reforms. Once again, the similarity between their rejection of not just the figureheads at the top, but the whole political system, and the demands which echoed through the 2011 uprisings was striking.

Yet, the world in which the uprisings of 2018-22 took place was not the same as the one where revolution had erupted in 2011. The quick victories and rapid regional spread of revolt in early 2011 was not likely to be repeated, with the explosions of the second wave detonating in countries often bordering societies still traumatised by the effects of counter-revolution following the first revolutionary wave.

Sudan: the struggle for the civil state

Sudan's revolutionary crisis began with a popular revolt in December 2018 in response to the government's desperate austerity measures which tripled the price of bread overnight. Spontaneous protests erupted in several provincial cities and the capital in the week of 18 December. Within a few days the uprising began to take on more organised forms, with strikes by doctors in Port Sudan and on 1 January a wide spectrum of opposition organisations launched the Declaration of Freedom and Change, a set of principles for the transfer of power to a new civilian government.[59] The political forces which signed onto the Declaration were quite heterogenous, including opposition parties led by figures in the traditional elite, representatives of some of the movements which continue to wage armed struggle against the regime, and newer networks of civil society activists, independent trade unions and professional associations. Crucially they included the Sudanese Professionals Association (SPA), which would become a key organiser of the uprising over the coming months.

Around 1800 Port Sudan workers also walked out 28 January 2019, demanding a halt to the privatisation of the southern port. Videos of the workers bringing a shipping container to blockade the port circulated on social media, as activists mobilising for anti-government protests embraced the port workers' action as part of the generalised rebellion against the regime. The city was one of the first to join the protest movement in December 2018, and picketing workers on 28 January combined their strike with the commemoration of a massacre by government troops of protesters from the Beja ethnic minority in 2005. Striking workers and tribesmen commemorating the massacre reportedly joined forces in a demonstration which chanted "freedom, peace, justice", the main slogan of the anti-government movement.[60] The tempo of protests accelerated significantly in early March with the first attempted general strike and over the following months workers in key agricultural processing industries such as the flour mills and sugar refineries began to mobilise. Workers at the Sayga Flour Mills went on strike on 5 March in response to a general strike call by the Sudanese Professionals Association.

Sudanese activists told Egyptian independent news website *Mada Masr* that participation in the strike was around 60 percent, with more than 30 professional sectors taking action.[61] These included health services, public and private schools, pharmacies. Strike action by lawyers shut the civil courts, while journalists walked out at seven major newspapers. Private sector companies reported to be affected by strike action included telecoms and mobile phone companies such as Zein, MTN and Ericsson. Strikes were also reported at the Sakhr Cement company. Kenana Sugar Company, with its more

---

59 Forces of Freedom and Change, 2019.
60 Amin, 2019.
61 Mada Masr, 2019.

The ebb and the flow: 2013-22

than 6000 workers housed in a "company town," was also hit by a wave of strikes in early May. Posts on social media listed workers' demands for the returned of sacked workers to their jobs, the resignation of the company's human resources director, the dissolution of the pro-government trade union and the formation of a new one, and an end to the security forces' repression of protests.[62]

Strike action by doctors and health professionals has played a key role in developing combative forms of union and strike organisation in the health service. A major strike by doctors in 2016 demanding protection from assault for frontline health staff spread to 65 hospitals across the country by 9 October.[63] The road from 'economic' to 'political' demands was short. In the same month as the Doctors' strike, one of the key coordinating bodies, the Sudan Doctors' Central Committee (SDCC) joined with the Sudanese Journalists' Network and the Alliance of Democratic Lawyers to form the Sudanese Professionals' Association.[64]

Unsurprisingly, doctors and other health professionals formed one of the strongest and most visibly-organised groups spearheading the four-month uprising which led to the fall of El Bashir in April 2019. A few days after the eruption of protests in late December 2018, the SDCC called a strike in solidarity with the demonstrations which quickly spread to dozens of hospitals. Doctors themselves became targets of repression, as the security forces stormed hospitals, arrested doctors and even killed Dr Babiker Abdelhamid while he was treating injured protesters.[65] Data on the protests from December 2018—March 2019 collected by Isra'a Sirag-al-Din shows a wide variety of health professions involved organising through their workplaces and professional networks. In addition to doctors, Sirag-al-Din noted protests and strikes by pharmacists, anaesthetists, radiologists, workers in the Health Ministry, health officials and medical students.[66]

Workers in the banking and financial sector also emerged as important players in the developing revolutionary movement

---

62 Civil Disobedience in Sudan, 2019.
63 Radio Dabanga, 2016.
64 Abbas, 2019; El-Gizouli, 2019.
65 Hummaida & Dousa, 2019.
66 Sirag-al-Din, 2019.

during the first part of 2019. Again, Sirag al-Din's data, which only covers the first 3 months of the uprising, documents a range of actions by different groups of financial sector workers in support of the revolution, including protests, civil disobedience and strikes.[67] This was followed by the initiation of huge popular sit-ins outside army headquarters in Khartoum and provincial capitals on 6 April, the anniversary of the overthrow of Jaafar al-Nimeiri, Sudan's military dictator in 1985. The sit-in outside the Sudanese Armed Forces' General Command in Khartoum rapidly exposed the growing disunity at the top of the state: Umar al-Bashir, who had ruled Sudan since seizing power in 1989, was deposed by his own generals on 11 April. Key figures who emerged out of a brief power struggle at the top of the crumbling regime included General Abdelfattah al-Burhan who became head of the Transitional Military Council (TMC) and Mohamed Dagalo (Hemedti), commander of the Rapid Support Forces militia, an outfit which had already become a byword for murder, rape, extortion and smuggling across Sudan, where they were deployed by Bashir to fight his dirty wars in Darfur and South Kordofan.

The TMC was unable to demobilise the popular movement now in command of the streets. The sit-ins swelled further and key protest leaders including the SPA continued to demand a handover of power to a civilian government, beginning negotiations with the TMC on 13 April. The revolutionary process reached a new turning point in late May, as an effective two-day general strike on 28 and 29 May increased the pressure on the TMC to make concessions to protesters' demands for civilian rule as this report from *MENA Solidarity* illustrates:

> Public sector employees walked out across the country, defying threats by General Hemeti, the deputy head of the transitional military council, and commander of the notorious Rapid Support Forces, a brutal militia formed out of the Janjaweed forces which terrorised Darfur a few years ago. On Tuesday 23 May, Hemeti said he would sack government workers for taking part in the strike. The strike was also strong in Sudan's small industrial sector, with major flour mills shut, cigarette and edible oils manufacturers on strike, and cement workers joining the

67 Sirag-al-Din, 2019.

The ebb and the flow: 2013-22

action. Workers in the military production sector were reported to have walked out, according to independent news station, *Radio Dabanga*. Workers in the financial sector joined the strike in droves: the SPA listed 27 separate banks and financial services companies on its Facebook page which took action on 28 May. Pharmacies were shut across the country, alongside hospitals and clinics. Healthworkers have played a crucial role in the revolutionary movement, with doctors' organisations providing much of the organisational backbone for the first phase of the uprising. Teachers joined the strike and organised street protests. Crucial transport hubs were paralysed by workers' action, including the main ports. Pictures on the SPA's Facebook page showed the docks empty of workers and signs proclaiming 100 percent support for the strike. Airport workers and civil aviation engineers also joined the strike, with large protests taking place at Khartoum airport.[68]

It was of course this general strike which led to the assault on the sit-in out the army headquarters in Khartoum by the full spectrum of the state's "armed bodies of men" (and not just those of the key instigator, Hemedti and his Rapid Support Forces). Significantly, though, the military and militias did not attack organised workers directly, but rather went for the symbolic heart of the uprising, seeking to force the strikers into submission by attacking their allies, mainly the young men and women from impoverished neighbourhoods like Kalakla and Columbia on the barricades defending the sit-in outside the Army General Command in Khartoum. On 3 June they stormed the sit-in killing scores, beating, assaulting and raping demonstrators.[69]

RSF forces occupied the Central Bank, telecoms exchanges and key transport hubs, but they did not have the confidence or the numbers to gun down workers in the ports, flour mills and public services. The massacre at the sit-in, coupled with an internet shutdown, did not stop the movement, and following a further general strike on 9-11 June and mass mobilisation for protest marches on 30 June, a final deal

---

68 MENA Solidarity, 2019.
69 Physicians for Human Rights, 2020.

Revolution is the choice of the people

on the exact composition of a transitional government was signed on 17 August.[70]

Although many Sudanese celebrated the agreement, the leaders of the protest movement had made major concessions. Rather than fight on for a fully civilian-led government for the transitional period envisioned in the Declaration of Freedom and Change, they agreed to share power with the TMC. The highest body in the new governmental structures, the Sovereignty Council would be balanced between military and civilian members, with the chairman's role during the first 21 months going to the military.. Moreover, far from being held to account for their role in the killings of protesters, including the 3 June massacre, Abdelfattah al-Burhan and Hemedti were confirmed in key roles—as chairman and vice-chairman respectively.[71]

The creation of the Sovereignty Council opened a new phase in the revolutionary process, dominated by struggles over the reform of state institutions in a context shaped by a worsening economic crisis. measures to root out some elements of the old regime from financial and media institutions gathered pace. The Transitional Government's Anti-Corruption committee has dissolved the administrative boards of the Central Bank of Sudan and 11 other banks, and frozen accounts in the name of 47 leaders of the Bashir regime.[72] Newspapers and media organisations connected with former regime officials have also been shut down.[73]

The purge of the old regime barely touched the repressive institutions of the state. Senior figures in the security apparatus, such as the National Intelligence Security Service (NISS) chief Salah Gosh were early casualties of the revolution: Gosh resigned on 13 April, two days after Bashir was overthrown, and the Transitional Military Council "retired" 98 other senior NISS officers on 11 June.[74] Nevertheless in January, armed former NISS agents were confident enough to seize control of security buildings near Khartoum Airport, leading to a firefight with the armed forces lasting several hours, while other NISS

70 Al Jazeera, 2019.
71 Reuters, 2019b.
72 Radio Dabanga, 2020a.
73 Amin, 2020.
74 Radio Dabanga, 2019.

The ebb and the flow: 2013-22

agents also shut down oilfields in Darfur, in protest over their dismissal by the Transitional Government.[75]

But the regime's other bodies of armed men, including both the armed forces and the Rapid Support Forces militia led by Hemedti were firmly ensconced in the Transitional Government. Far from reforming itself, the army leadership has cracked down on junior officers and soldiers who risked their lives to defend protestors before Bashir fell from power. Al-Burhan and Hemedti formed an alliance with some of the armed groups which had previously led rebellions against the central government from Sudan's provinces. The Juba Peace Agreement, signed in October 2020, provided a route into office for former Darfurian rebels such as Minni Minawi of the Sudan Liberation Movement / Army and Gibril Ibrahim Mohammed of the Justice and Equality Movement.

Bashir's generals also worked to enhance their international lines of support, as the surprise meeting between Abdelfattah al-Burhan, chairman of the Transitional Government's Sovereignty Council, and Israeli president Binyamin Netanyahu on 3 February illustrates. Acting on direct prompting by US Secretary of State Mike Pompeo, and with the support of UAE, Saudi Arabia and Egypt who arranged the meeting, al-Burhan is clearly looking to tap into the flows of weapons and funding which are the usual price-tag for such public displays of homage to Israel's role as a pillar of US imperial domination in the Middle East.[76]

Such manoeuvres emboldened the generals who seized power from their civilian "partners" in October 2021. They were met with an explosion of popular organising, civil disobedience, mass protests, strikes and stay-aways, led not by the civilian parties ousted from the Transitional Government but by the neighbourhood based Resistance Committees. Over the following months the generals tried and failed repeatedly to consolidate their rule behind a new civilian façade only to face further waves of protest and mobilisation from below.

---

75 Reuters, 2020.
76 El-Gizouli, 2020.

Algeria: 'Get rid of them all!'

The spark for the explosion of a mass protest movement demanding systemic political change in Algeria was the announcement that President Abdelaziz Bouteflika would stand for election again, aiming to take a fifth term in power. The first day that the *hirak* or popular mass mobilisation emerged onto the streets across the country was Friday 22 February 2019, although there are earlier reports of protests in Kherrata and Khenchala in Kabyle. For many who joined the protests, the fact that the ailing president, who had not even been seen in public for years because of ill-health, was being pushed forward once again to lead the country was symbolic of a much deeper political malaise, the product of a corrupt system fronted by the aging leaders of the ruling FLN party, the movement which had led the struggle against French colonial rule to victory in 1962. Behind this political crisis lay a much deeper social one. Algeria's rate of youth unemployment was running at 29 percent, among a population where 70 percent are under the age of 30.

The power of the street protests that exploded on Fridays after 22 February also expressed pent-up fury over crumbling public services, poverty pay, precarious working conditions and resentment over the mafia-like clans of businessmen and generals who loot the country's wealth. As Gianni del Panta points out, there were three main components to the social revolt which heralded the coming storm: public sector workers, in particular teachers and junior doctors; workers in Algeria's remaining citadels of heavy industry with long traditions of militancy such as the SNVI car plant in Rouïba; and the unemployed and marginalised in areas such the South, where grievances over social exclusion and poverty combined with resistance to the threat of environmental devastation as a result of shale gas fracking by the state oil company Sonatrach.[77]

After 22 February 2019, and for much of the following year, the rhythm of regular mass protests on Fridays drove the popular movement forward. The scale of the initial demonstrations in the capital Algiers was particularly significant because the authorities had succeeded for much of the previous two decades in enforcing a ban on street protests there. In addition to the Friday protests, students also began to mobilise weekly

---

77 Del Panta, 2017.

The ebb and the flow: 2013-22

protests, starting from Tuesday 26 February. Tens of thousands of student activists across the country marched in support of the *hirak*. Coordination of the local student demonstrations was organised through mass student assemblies in the universities which also debated and implemented other forms of protest such as student strikes.[78]

A third component of the developing popular movement was the role of organised workers as strikes began to spread. The independent union confederations, composed of unions established outside the official UGTA federation since the early 1990s, were at the forefront of calls for workers to use their power in the workplace in support of the *hirak*. Battles between the rank-and-file and the pro-regime bureaucracy were also starting to shake the UGTA. In several regions UGTA branches, including in key industrial workplaces such as the SNVI vehicles plant in Rouiba, backed the hirak and mobilised their members to join the strikes.

The general strike between 10 and 15 March coincided with a major turning point in the struggle. Bouteflika, feeling the pressure, promised a new constitution if elected, followed by a new presidential election in which he would not stand again. He appointed a new Prime Minister and shuffled the cabinet. These cosmetic changes to the make-up of the government did nothing to appease the anger in the streets and workplaces. On 11 March at the height of the general strike, Bouteflika was forced to go back on his decision to stand again.

If the regime's leaders hoped this would pacify the hirak, they were badly mistaken. By now the slogans on the Friday marches had gone much further, demanding fundamental political change and the removal of Bouteflika from power. As numbers continued to grow, cracks started to appear at the top of the state. On 26 March, Army chief of staff, Gaid Salah openly called on the Constitutional Council to use its powers under article 102 of the Constitution to declare Bouteflika unfit to exercise his duties and remove him from office.[79] Yet the acceleration of the protest movement continued to deepen, with an estimated 1 million taking to the streets of Algiers alone on 29 March. The combined pressure from below and the fractures at the top of the state proved too much for Bouteflika and he resigned on 2 April.

---

78 Larabi, Smith & Hamouchene, 2020.
79 BBC News, 2019a.

Revolution is the choice of the people

Amid their jubilation, *hirak* activists now had to contend with the tactics of a new phase in the struggle, where the central question would be whether the regime could contain and ultimately diffuse the pressure from below within the bounds of the existing constitution. Under article 102 of the Constitution, Ahmed Bensalah, president of the upper chamber of parliament was appointed interim president, on the proviso that a new head of state would be elected within 90 days on 4 July. The immediate answer from the streets in the massive Friday protests of 5 April was that these constitutional manoeuvres would not be enough to satisfy the demands for change. Hoping to conciliate the protesters, the government ordered the detention of senior figures close to Bouteflika and big businessmen on corruption charges. The president's younger brother Said, who had essentially ruled the country from behind the throne, the former head of the feared security apparatus, Mohamed Mediene (better known as Toufik) and two former prime ministers, Ahmed Ouyahia and Abdelmalek Sellal were among those arrested.

Over the next two months, the continued mass mobilisations on Tuesdays and Friday, coupled with further rounds of coordinated strikes supported by the independent unions and rebellious sections of the UGTA, forced the regime to abandon its initial plans for presidential elections on 4 July. Major student protests also took place in the capital, Algiers. Pressure from below also continued to force its way into the higher reaches of the state machine: with thousands of magistrates refusing to supervise the polls. On 2 June, with only two unknown candidates having registered for the vote, the Constitutional Council announced the cancellation of the 4 July elections. The crisis over the presidential elections led to the emergence of a new strategy by the regime as it fought for survival. In a speech on 19 June, Chief of Staff Gaid Salah attacked activists for carrying the Amazigh (Berber) flag, accusing them of undermining national unity. Although protesters defied the order, and the multi-coloured banner continued to mingle with the green and white of the national flag on demonstrations in many places over the weeks that followed, the police started to act on the general's orders. Among the dozens who were seized and detained for carrying Amazigh flags or wearing Amazigh emblems were leading activists such as 25 year old Samira

The ebb and the flow: 2013-22

Messouci, an elected member of the regional parliament in Tizi Ouzou province.

While protests continued to mobilise tens of thousands over the summer, by September the regime felt confident to announce preparations for presidential elections in December 2019. Although the mood on the weekly protests remained defiant, and calls for a boycott of the election began to gather pace over the following month, the regime also struck back at the *hirak*, arresting prominent opposition figures such as social democratic activist Karim Tabbou and veteran of the national liberation struggle Lakhdar Bouregaa, who had become an icon of the protest movement for his rejection of the FLN regime. Protests and calls for a general strike intensified during November 2019 but police repression also increased, with courts now processing sentences against demonstrators rapidly in a bid to derail the movement. The trials of regime figures also continued, with former Prime Ministers Ouyahia and Bensallal receiving 15 and 12 year prison sentences respectively just days before the polls were due to open.[80]

The day of the presidential elections on 12 December was marked by large protests across the country, with tens of thousands taking to the streets despite fierce repression. Abdelmadjid Tebboune, a former prime minister was declared the winner with 58 percent of the vote, on a turnout which even the authorities admitted was strikingly low. Official figures claimed 40 percent of voters took part, but opposition parties argued the real figure was a small fraction of that. The Rally for Culture and Democracy (RCD) which is largely based in Kabylia said that only 8 percent of voters turned out nationally, and media reports suggested a figure of 10 percent.[81] In Kabylia itself, there was an effective general strike which shut down the province in protest at the elections.[82]

Demonstrations in other areas, although still impressive in size, were not on the scale of the mobilisation in Kabylia, and the general strike was not repeated in other provinces. By January 2020 Tebboune had managed to put a new government in place, also offering dialogue with the protesters and creating a commission to amend the constitution and give parliament and the judiciary greater powers. The weekly demonstrations

---

80 BBC News, 2019c.
81 MENA Solidarity Network, 2019.
82 Aissat, 2019.

continued, although with smaller numbers as the anniversary approached in February 2020. It was at this point that the debates dominating Algerian politics were suddenly disrupted by a novel question: how to respond to the Covid 19 pandemic which swept the globe in February and March 2020? Hirak activists reluctantly decided to abandon the streets temporarily to help efforts to slow the spread of the virus, with the major weekly demonstrations ending in March 2020. For its part, the regime took advantage of the pandemic to ratchet up pressure on the popular movement, continuing to arrest activists, handing opposition figures long jail sentences and detaining journalists, a process which accelerated as the pandemic receded during 2021–22.

Lebanon and Iraq: the sectarian regime under siege

Sudan and Algeria were not the only countries rocked by popular uprisings in 2019–20: mass protests in both Lebanon and Iraq erupted almost simultaneously in October 2019. A tax on WhatsApp messages was the trigger for what many activists have labelled Lebanon's "October Revolution".[83] The resignation of prime minister Saad Hariri on 29 October did not slow the pace of popular mobilisation, which expanded its range of tactics by deploying roadblocks which led to violent clashes with the security forces. Leading business organisations even called for a mass shutdown of workplaces and a general strike in order to force the formation of a new government.[84] Over the following months, protests and strikes ebbed and flowed—receding due to the Covid-19 pandemic but swelling again as the economic crisis worsened in June and July with mass layoffs.

Between October 2019 and April 2020 over 200,000 jobs in the private sector evaporated, equivalent to 10 percent of the entire labour force; 20 percent of workers in the hotel industry were laid off. Even before the explosion and the Covid-19 pandemic hit, medical supplies were reported to be running short as importers struggled to find the dollars needed to purchase them.[85] When the rest of the global economy tumbled off a cliff in April 2020 the Lebanese pound was already hurtling

83 Majed, 2019.
84 Bassam & Osseiran, 2019.
85 Knecht & Ellen, 2020.

The ebb and the flow: 2013-22

towards the bottom, dragging a large part of the population with it. The Lebanese central bank had accumulated debts of $44 billion, while the banking system as a whole was estimated to have losses of $83 billion.[86] In February, the government defaulted on its sovereign debt for the first time in Lebanon's history, failing to repay $30 billion in foreign currency bonds.[87] Talks with the International Monetary Fund stalled in the summer with a dispute over the size of the banking system's losses and over the question of reform.

Then on 4 August 2020, a massive explosion shook Beirut port, when a neglected storehouse of ammonium nitrate blew up, catapulting Lebanon onto the front pages of the global media. The volatile chemical was being stored next to the country's main grain silos, which were levelled by the force of the explosion along with much of the port. An estimated $15 billion worth of damage was caused to the highly import-dependent Lebanese economy.[88] Over 180 people were killed directly by the blast, thousands injured and hundreds of thousands made homeless. The scenes from Beirut were apocalyptic as dazed and bloodied survivors sought treatment in shattered hospitals.

The blast on 4 August also brought with it nights of rage, as protesters stormed government ministries and set the Association of Banks headquarters on fire, facing down tear gas and live bullets from the army.[89] There was a growing mood that Lebanon's issues cannot easily be fixed by substituting one or other of its members with less corrupt and violent alternatives. Moreover, at least some of the protestors have clearly understood that this is not an issue of personnel but rather the "old way" in which political and economic power is practised both inside and outside the institutions of the state. One of the chants which caught the imagination of crowds in Lebanon sums this up neatly: "We are the revolution of the people, you are the civil war!"[90]

Iraq's mass protest movement which like in Lebanon exploded in October 2019 followed years of localised demonstrations, particularly in the South. In Baghdad thousands

---

86 Financial Times, 2020.
87 Stubbington & Cornish, 2020.
88 Nur Duz & Geldi, 2020.
89 MENA Solidarity, 2020.
90 Historical Materialism, 2019.

Revolution is the choice of the people

congregated around a sit-in in Tahrir Square in the centre of the capital, overlooked by the famous 'Freedom Monument' a huge slab of modernist sculpture commemorating the 1958 revolution which overthrew the British-backed monarchy. Other cities between Baghdad and Basra, including especially the capital of Dhi Qar governorate Nasiriyyah, and the important Shi'a religious centres Najaf and Kerbala', also emerged as important players in the protest movement.

The boldness of protest tactics and the duration of the mobilisation in the streets signalled an escalation. In Iraq, the movement's repertoire of collective action revolved around the establishment of large, semi-permanent sit-ins with tents in symbolic city centre squares, such as the Tahrir Square sit-in in Baghdad which was first set up in early October 2019 and continued to act as the focal point for large marches (with a brief break for the Shi'a religious festival of Ashura' in mid-October) by the time that the Covid-19 crisis hit Iraq in March 2020. Sit-ins in Basra, Nasiriyyah and other cities also lasted for several months.

It is not just the visible signs of mass mobilisation on a scale not experienced for decades, but the clear signs of stress and fracture at the top which has popularised the idea that these are revolutions, not simply another wave of protest. Prime Minister Adil Abd-al-Mahdi tendered his resignation as Iraq's Prime Minister on 29 November.[91] The Prime Minister's exit ushered protracted process of negotiation between political factions of the existing ruling class, rather than a more radical process of bringing in genuine outsiders or even figures associated with the protest movement on the streets. The formation of Iraq's 'new' government involved intense wrangling between the main political parties blocking agreement on the majority of cabinet posts under Prime Minister designate, intelligence chief Mustafa al-Kadhimi until 7 May.[92] The protesters in Tahrir Square also expressed their opinions on al-Kadhimi's rivals, hoisting a massive banner from the 'Turkish Restaurant' which overlooks the square saying "we reject the candidates of all the corrupt parties".[93]

The Shi'a Islamist parties which have dominated the

---

91 Azhari, 2019.
92 Al Jazeera, 2020a.
93 Haddad, 2020.

The ebb and the flow: 2013-22

political system since the US invasion in 2003 have also faced a revolt in their own backyards, as anger at endemic corruption and poverty boiled over in Najaf (where protesters torched the Iranian consulate), Kerbala', Basra, Hilla and Nasiriyyah as well as Baghdad. The intensification of US pressure on Iran through the tightening of the sanctions regime at the same time as losing political and military influence within Iraq has led some to characterise the Iraqi popular protest movement as a trojan horse for the reassertion of US power.[94] The murder of senior Iranian general Qassem Soleimani alongside Abu Mahdi al-Muhandis, deputy leader of the Popular Mobilisation Forces Shi'a Islamist militia in Baghdad on 6 January 2020 by drone strike was certainly a reminder of the reach of US military technology, although it also re-energised the political confidence of the Shi'a Islamist movements aligned with Iran and created a space for them to mobilise mass demonstrations in the streets for the first time since October denouncing US intervention.

The deadliest blow to the protesters camped in Baghdad's Tahrir Square and other cities across Iraq came from within, as influential Shi'a politician and one-time militia leader Muqtada al-Sadr ordered his supporters to quit the sit-in camps and join security forces in clearing them from the streets.[95] Al-Sadr made his name by launching armed resistance to the US occupation in 2003, founding a movement rooted in the impoverished largely Shi'a suburbs of Baghdad which bear the name of his father, a senior Shi'a cleric murdered by Saddam Hussein. The arrival of the Covid-19 pandemic also dampened protesters' desire to stay in the streets, leading to a temporary lull in the demonstrations. However, in summer and autumn protests resumed, fuelled by anger at assassinations of activists, such as Dr Riham Yaqoob from Basra who was gunned down in the street on 19 August by assailants that local activists say are linked to pro-Iranian paramilitary groups.[96]

The popular uprisings in both Lebanon and Iraq have made spaces for the expression of extraordinary and powerful forms of solidarity between ordinary people, breaking down some of the ideological barriers between men and women, young and old and citizens of different religious beliefs. The scale of the mobilisations,

---

94 Russia Today, 2019.
95 Loveluck & Salim, 2020; Arraf, 2020.
96 BBC News, 2020.

their defiance and their tenacity have helped temporarily to counterbalance the vision of the state as a bargaining table for the elites of various sectarian communities to divide their loot. Yet there are also limits to this process. In the case of Lebanon this is visible in the inability of the popular protests to collectively integrate the demands of the large and oppressed communities of Palestinians, Syrians and other "foreigners" within the struggle for change from below. And in both Lebanon and Iraq the governments which were formed to manage the crises are still just a reshuffling of the existing political elite.

Palestine's 'Unity Intifada'

The general strike across historic Palestine in May 2021 saw unity in action between Palestinians within the borders of Israel, and across the West Bank and Gaza. The target of this mass mobilisation was at one level a regime with a very different appearance to other uprisings between 2018 and 2022: one engaged in systematic racist and national oppression and still shaped by its settler-colonial character long after most other such regimes had vanished from the wider region. For reasons we will discuss in more detail in subsequent chapters, the national oppression of the Palestinians plays a central role in maintaining the imperial architecture of the Middle East and North Africa. However, the specificities of the Palestinian struggle should not obscure the fact that kinship between the latest wave of Palestinian resistance and the other popular struggles discussed here goes beyond coincidences of timing.

While the general strike was officially called by the Higher Follow-up Committee, a body composed of the traditional political leaders of Palestinian citizens of Israel, the mobilisation which ensured the strike's success came from below, argues Riya al-Sanah. "The Higher Follow-up Committee of Arab Citizens in Israel often calls for strikes, but it's strikes for the Palestinian community in Israel only," she points out. "Usually, nothing happens on those days, no politics in the streets, no mobilising."[97] This time, despite only having a couple of days preparation, the situation was very different. Hundreds of thousands of Palestinians stopped work and joined political marches and

---

97 Laura & Charan, 2021

The ebb and the flow: 2013-22

rallies, from Yafa to Haifa and Umm al-Fahm inside the borders of Israel, to Hebron, Jenin and Ramallah in the West Bank.[98]

Across historic Palestine, protesters raised the same slogans: stop the bombardment and siege of Gaza, halt the ethnic cleansing of Palestinian families from East Jerusalem, end the violence and incitement against Palestinians by Zionist settler movements. This alignment of demands and protest tactics represented the temporary fusion of a whole range of localized campaigns challenging the Israeli authorities and the apartheid system. These included escalating (and to a degree successful) mobilisations by Palestinian residents of East Jerusalem to defend their presence in public spaces such as the Damascus Gate, their right to worship at al-Aqsa Mosque, and to defend their homes from racist harassment by settler groups and eviction orders from the courts in neighbourhoods such as Sheikh Jarrah.[99] They built on several years in which young Palestinians had tested themselves against the authorities in street protests and campaigning, with networks of youth activists working alongside the long-standing Popular Committees (which usually bring together activists from different political currents within a local neighbourhood). A wave of demonstrations in 2017 was particularly important in laying the foundations, according to Salhab and al-Ghoul who argue these "were huge civic uprisings involving sustained protest by tens of thousands of people. This civic spirit and infrastructure are the basis upon which the recent uprising was launched".[100]

The sense of confidence this has embedded in Jerusalem's Palestinian youth is palpable not just at the political level but in the music and culture of the streets, imbued with a kind of "up yours" attitude to those in power, summed up by the term "khawa" (which loosely translates as "despite your best efforts").

> And in Jerusalem, *khawa* is a way of life. Palestinians continued their evening demonstrations in Jerusalem *khawa*, undeterred by the machinery of oppression or the closure of the entrances to Sheikh Jarrah. They spoiled the Zionist celebration of Jerusalem Day, which marks the "reunification" of the city, and *khawa* they

---

98 Kingsley & Nazzal, 2021
99 Salhab & Al-Ghoul, 2021
100 Salhab & Al-Ghoul, 2021.

forced the cancellation of the march in the Old City. They barricaded themselves inside Al-Aqsa Mosque and stood up to bullets and tear gas *khawa*.[101]

Among the Palestinian citizens of Israel similar processes have been taking place, as a result of the tightening pressures on their daily lives through increasing political repression and ongoing economic marginalisation. This has intensified at two different scales in recent years, firstly through the passing of the Nation State Law of 2018 which made explicit their unequal status compared to Jewish citizens. While this symbolic change only gave legal form to the lived reality of decades-long oppression, it has further boosted the appeal of joint action with Palestinians elsewhere to confront the same apartheid system. Meanwhile, Palestinians citizens of Israel have also faced increased harassment and violence from 'settler' movements in recent years. Palestinians in the West Bank have long endured racist attacks from armed settlers who destroy their crops, vandalise their property and attack them on a daily basis. Far-right Jewish supremacist movements have expanded in size and grown in confidence in recent years, and are now targeting Palestinians in cities such as Haifa, Lydd and Yafa. There were numerous reports of Telegram and WhatsApp groups of settler organisations mobilising armed mobs to attack Palestinian homes and businesses in May this year.[102] In Lydd, armed settlers patrolled the streets with the Israeli police, while the city was placed under a military curfew.[103] As in Jerusalem, new structures of community mobilisation and self-defence are starting to form in order to resist.

> We found ourselves in a place where we had to self-organise and discovered that we can actually do it. Local committees being developed. Local groups and autonomous kinds of political organising away from established structures that were taking place on the ground. So in Haifa, for example, we had a neighbourhood defence committee, a legal support committee, a medical care committee and a mental health care committee.

101 Hassan, 2021.
102 Maiberg, 2021.
103 Ziv, 2021; Laura & Charan, 2021.

The ebb and the flow: 2013-22

There were different forms of local, independent, and collective committees that were working as part of this uprising and Haifa wasn't the only case.[104]

The majority Palestinian towns in the north, such as Umm al-Fahm have also been the site of massive popular campaigns over the past few years, demanding action over the wave of violent crime which has led to hundreds of murders of Palestinians. Thousands took to the streets of Umm al-Fahm for ten consecutive weeks in February and March 2021. Palestinian activists link the crime wave directly to the establishment of Israeli police stations in the area after the repression of protests in 2000, arguing that the Israeli police tolerate and even encourage the activities of criminal gangs as a way of undermining political resistance. Like Black communities in the US facing the devastating combined effects of police brutality and violent crime, their primary demand is not to strengthen the police but to defund and remove them.[105]

Meanwhile in the West Bank, the decay of the mainstream nationalist movement Fatah, which has dominated the Palestinian Authority (PA) since its creation, has been accelerating. This has created spaces for new activist movements to emerge over a range of questions. Despite the difficult conditions, there is still a culture of protest and self-organisation around mobilisations confronting Israeli settlers and the occupying forces, to defending Palestinian political prisoners, to movements which have raised other issues, such as sexual harassment and violence against women (a rash of demonstrations led mainly by young Palestinian women took on this question in September 2019 and has led to the emergence of a new Palestinian feminist movement, *Tala'at*).[106] The rampant corruption of Fatah's leadership has come under attack even from some of the movement's former members, such as Nizar Banat, whose murder by the PA security forces sparked several days of large protests in June 2021.[107]

---

104 Laura & Charan, 2021.
105 Alsaafin, 2021.
106 Raje, Shukhaidem & Challen-Flynn, 2020.
107 Abu Sneineh, 2021.

A provisional balance sheet of the 'second wave'

All of the rebellions of the second wave are popular revolts driven by mass collective action from below (although in the case of Lebanon and Iraq, political paralysis and fractures at the top were also visible even before the mass movements broke through). On the surface they have taken relatively similar forms: mass mobilisations where the rhythm of regular street protests (often structured by repetition on a specific day of the week, normally Fridays though there have been regular student-led protests on Tuesdays in Algeria and Sundays in Iraq) has provided momentum, while social media platforms provide a loose infrastructure and a space to test out and coordinate slogans and demands. But under the surface there are strikingly different degrees of organisation.

In Sudan, both long-established opposition parties and newer organisations such as the Sudanese Professionals Association (SPA) clearly played a role in leading the uprising, with the SPA emerging as one of the major bodies capable of both speaking for and speaking to wide layers of the protesters—competing with and partially eclipsing the established opposition groups at key moments during the uprising. In Algeria, there was no movement which emerged at a national level to coordinate protests and strikes as had happened in Sudan, but it was not the case that organisation was absent. The general strike in Kabyle in December 2019 for example was built and coordinated between local trade union branches, radical and reformist left organisations, left groups and some of the Berber opposition parties.[108] In Lebanon and Iraq, popular organisation of the *hirak* was more diffuse again at national level, reflecting both sharp rejection of existing political parties and in the Iraqi case especially the need to protect protest organisers from violent attacks by pro-regime and pro-Iranian paramilitary bodies.

A key difference between the uprisings was the level of coordinated participation by organised workers. In Sudan and Algeria general strikes played a significant role in the trajectory of the protests, and the correlation of some of the biggest strikes with turning points such as the struggle over the composition of the transitional government in Sudan and the enforced departure of Bouteflika in Algeria adds weight to the argument

---

108 Aissat, 2019.

The ebb and the flow: 2013-22

outlined in Chapter 2, that workers' collective action was a transformational element in the revolutionary process. Likewise, the fact that collective action within the workplaces was only nascent in the Lebanese uprising, and virtually absent in the Iraqi case, underscores this point from a negative perspective. The Palestinian general strike reflected the challenges imposed by the fractured nature of the Palestinian working class as a result of the Israeli apartheid system. Palestinian withdrawal of labour certainly hurt the Israeli economy, particular in the construction sector, but did not paralyse production sites, transport and services on the same scale as the Sudanese and Algerian general strikes were able to do.[109]

The interwoven nature of the economic and political aspects of the crisis which led to the uprisings and the forms of resistance which flowed through them was just as striking in the 'second wave' as in the 2011 revolutions. Sudan's uprising started with economic demands over lack of access to basic goods, while Algeria's began in the political domain with protests over Bouteflika's candidacy for a fifth presidential term, yet they both ended up in the same place: confronting the question of what kind of regime should control the state. In Lebanon and Iraq, the stresses placed on ordinary people as a result of the economic collapse overseen by the corrupt political establishment were the starting points for the uprisings, taking the initial form of protests over the imposition of taxes on WhatsApp calls in Lebanon and protests by unemployed graduates in Iraq. The continued economic marginalisation of Palestinian citizens of Israel combined with growing poverty in the Occupied West Bank and Gaza (sharpened by the impact of the Covid-19 pandemic) also drove the revival of protest.

The internal unevenness of economic development within each of the countries often played a material role in shaping the movements, as did the deeply-rooted legacies of the colonial era and the post-colonial state capitalist period which preceded the neoliberal turn in the region's political economy during the 1970s. The re-emergence of a new wave of popular organising in Palestine takes place in a context where the colonial *present* rather than the past is still driving resistance. The Zionist movement's attachment to a particular form of settler-colonialism has showed no signs of weakening in recent years, and as we will

---

109 Alexander, 2022.

discuss in later chapters, is sustained by processes of imperialist competition at the heart of the regional and global economy.

And just as in 2011, these uprisings raised the question of how various struggles for liberation from oppression related to the main goals of the popular movement. Women's participation in the mass protests and strikes on very large scale, and sometimes the presence of organised women's movements, such as the feminist collectives in Algeria and women's organisations in Sudan, started to raise this in concrete ways through campaigns over changes to Algeria's repressive family code, and battles to ensure larger numbers of women would be represented in the Transitional Government's institutions.. Iraqi women activists played a prominent role in the uprising there, leading protests in the streets and joining the sit-ins. Issues of religious and national oppression were also crucial themes, for example in Algeria, where the question of solidarity with the Amazigh (Berber) population took centre stage after the Army Commander in chief, Gaid Salah, tried to ban the use of the Amazigh flag on protests.

A highly significant feature of the second wave was that despite the role played by the stronger regional powers, such as Saudi Arabia and UAE in the Gulf; Turkey, and Iran in the victory of counter-revolutions after 2012, this was not enough to pre-empt the emergence of new mass movements or simply snuff them out through external intervention. In the case of Iran, the Islamic Republic's ability to intervene directly against the protest movements in Iraq and Lebanon has been hampered by two things: firstly rising frustrations inside its own borders over the intensifying economic crisis which spilled over into major protests in October and November 2019 at the same time as protests exploded in Iraq and Lebanon. Secondly, and just as importantly, the Lebanese and Iraqi political parties allied with the Iranian ruling class, have faced a degree of revolt from inside their own communities and constituencies which has partially paralysed them, making Iranian intervention a much more obvious act of external intervention and therefore politically more risky. The influence of the Gulf states is clearly a counter-revolutionary factor in Sudan, given the strong ties that Saudi Arabia and UAE have built up with figures such as Al-Burhan and Hemedti, yet this was not enough to prevent a popular revolution from starting.

The ebb and the flow: 2013-22

It is also crucial to note also that the character of the crisis itself has changed since 2011, particularly since the onset of the Covid 19 pandemic. This has posed major challenges to protest organisers who have been faced with the dilemma that the forms of collective action which had succeeded so spectacularly in reasserting the agency of ordinary people could act to spread the virus at terrible cost to lives and health. But it has also intensified the social and economic crisis, shutting down access to foreign investments and disrupting trade, imposing extra burdens on already fragile health systems. In Lebanon's case, the explosion in Beirut on 4 August which left hundreds of thousands homeless, shattered a large part of the capital and destroyed the main port on which the country's import-based economy depends added a further, apocalyptic dimension to the crisis. The direct effects of global and local manifestations of the climate and ecological emergency have also intensified, for example in the rising temperatures in southern Iraq which spark protests every summer, and in the uncontrolled wildfires on Mount Lebanon in October 2019 which many activists saw as symbolic of the criminal negligence of the political establishment.

Finally, as in 2011, all of the uprisings raised, but did not answer, the question of the relationship between 'the regime' and 'the state'. The similarity of the slogans demanding to 'get rid of them all', meaning the whole of the old regime and not just a figurehead or two, was clear. However, the revolts have had mixed success, even in the case of Sudan where the popular movement has made much more progress than the others. When the generals overthrew the Transitional Government in the coup of October 2021, popular organisation in the neighbourhoods and streets expanded to prevent the generals from consolidating their rule, leading to an uneasy stalemate between the people and the regime which at the time of writing in Spring 2022 had not yet been resolved. In Algeria the rolling back of the popular movement's gains involved significant repression but not on the violent scale experienced during the counter-revolutions of the first wave. In Lebanon and Iraq despite early successes in removing the Prime Ministers there has been even less progress in terms of political reforms. The Palestinian popular movement, while scoring significant political victories in the struggle against the apartheid regime, had not seriously or permanently damaged the Israeli state's racist machinery of repression.

Revolution is the choice of the people

All of these point strongly towards deeper structural reasons for both the crisis and the eruption of revolutions, that is to say for the crisis of the ruling class and 'the people's' rediscovery of itself as a political actor in the crisis. The next two sections of this book will thus uncover the longer-term social and political roots of the revolts. In the final section we will return to the problem of the state and why the answer to it remains fundamentally a question of revolutionary organisation.

Section two

The roots of revolution

Revolution is the choice of the people

Chapter 4

States, capitals and markets: making the Middle East

The waves of revolution and counter-revolution experienced by the Middle East and North Africa since 2010 were more than responses to immediate expressions of crisis, rather they had a systemic origin. Even if the majority of people involved in them did not express it explicitly as a rejection of capitalism, the pressures which made them refuse to be "ruled in the old way" any longer had deep roots in the region's history of capitalist development. Likewise, for many of the region's ruling classes, their inability to continue ruling in the old way was an outcome of cumulative failures to claw themselves up the global capitalist hierarchy (or their collapse down it). This also was more than the result of chance, it reflected the irresolvable contradictions at the heart of the capitalist system: underneath the rhetoric of prosperity for all lies the reality of accumulation of wealth at one pole and misery at the other.

The same competitive drive which appears to give capitalism its world-conquering energy is also the source of its tendency towards crisis with the decline in the overall rate of profit.[1] This chapter argues that analysing this long-term tendency and the varying 'fixes' which capitalist ruling classes have adopted in their efforts to solve this problem provides the best framework for understanding the deep roots of the revolutions and uprisings of the last decade. It is not enough to write the history of the revolutions

1 Roberts, 2020.

of the last decade from the standpoint of each individual society. Only through a vantage point which moves between the largest economies and most militarily-powerful states at the 'centre' of the capitalist system, to the smaller and weaker states and capitals further out, allows us to grasp what is really going on.

This is why the history of what Marxists call 'imperialism' is crucial to understanding the history of revolution in the Middle East.[2] The history matters a great deal here because the capitalist system has gone through several periods when patterns of imperialist competition have taken distinctive forms. This chapter focuses on the impact of European colonialism and its role in constructing the 'Middle East'. An important outcome of this phase of imperialism was, I will argue, the domination of a model of agricultural production geared towards the supply of commodities such as cotton, silk, wheat and olive oil destined either as inputs for European manufacturing or for consumption in European households.

Complementing the export of agricultural commodities was a model of the region's societies as consumer markets for certain kinds of European manufactured products, particularly textiles. What was missing from the picture was any mechanism for capitalist industry to take off in the region itself. In general, the political and social institutions fostered by colonial-era capitalism were specifically designed to preclude this happening. It would take a region-wide series of revolutionary uprisings from the 1940s onwards to shake off the old political forms of colonial domination in order to create the conditions for local manufacturing to develop.

This model of 'colonial' capitalist development was not universally experienced across the region. There were some states which did not experience direct colonial rule, such as Turkey (the Anatolian heartland of the Ottoman Empire), Iran (likewise the rump of the pre-capitalist Safavid and Qajar empires) and much of the Gulf. In the case of Turkey and Iran, the residual coherence of these powerful pre-capitalist states, coupled with successful battles from within to lay the political and social basis for capitalist transformation, helps to explain why they were not completely dismembered by the European powers.[3]

In the case of the Gulf it was the fact that the deserts of

---

2 Callinicos, 2009; Bukharin, 1967; Lenin, 1916.

3 Sohrabi, 1995.

States, capitals and markets: making the Middle East

Arabia and the fishing and pearling communities of the coast were initially marginal to the *productive* economy of colonial era capitalism which meant their encounter with the European powers was governed by different practices to that of the richer agricultural domains of North Africa, the Nile Valley and the Levant. How the discovery of oil changed that relationship will be discussed in more detail below.

States, capitals, and markets

The starting point for the discussion which follows is a definition of capitalism as a system based on competition between those who control and own the means of production to accumulate an ever-bigger share of the surplus value they have stolen from the direct producers.[4] 'Capitals' is a short-hand way of referring to these agglomerations of people and the material resources they control, which through their competition with each other, provide the underlying propulsion for the expansion of the system as a whole. Competition between capitals is, however, not the only motive energy here: the collective resistance of the direct producers to their exploitation is embedded into capitalism at molecular level.

The dynamic of competition also makes the capitalist system as a whole unsustainable in the long-term. As Chris Harman puts it "capitalism is doomed by the very forces of production which it itself unleashes".[5] The reason for this lies in the fact that the exploitation of living labour—human beings' mental and manual effort—is the source of capitalist profits. Capitalists steal the surplus value created as a result of the difference between the time required for workers to produce enough for themselves and their families and the total number of hours they work. In contrast to the ruling classes under previous social systems who tended to spend this surplus on their own tastes and desires (or on fighting each other), capitalists then invest it expanding production.

The long-term problem with this system is that the competition to grab a bigger share of surplus value has an in-built tendency to make capitalists invest not in more living labour, but

---
4 Harman, 1991.
5 Harman, 2010, p69.

instead in 'dead labour', especially in the form of time-saving and productivity-boosting technologies which will mean that they can produce more in shorter time scales with fewer workers. However, while this method works well for individual capitalists, over time it has the tendency to drive down the overall rate of profit.[6] That this long-term tendency towards falling profit rates and thus economic crisis is not the same as the more regular 'boom and bust' cycle is illustrated in visual form by Michael Roberts in the graph overleaf which despite major peaks and troughs shows a relentless downward trend.

The correlation between the peaks of profitability in the 20th century and episodes of World War also underlines the impossibility of disentangling the economic and military dimensions of capitalist competition, a point we will return to in the next chapter.

Once capitalism had become entrenched in Western Europe, the rising capitalist powers gained decisive advantages over their neighbours. This helps to explain how it was that Britain and France were able to carve out huge empires for themselves in North Africa, the Gulf and the Levant over the course of the 19th and early 20th century. European colonialism did not emerge into a vacuum but was constructed through the defeat of the Ottoman Empire, a huge state which at its height exercised sovereignty over most of what is called the Middle East today and a large part of Eastern Europe. The instruments of European victory over the Ottomans were varied: the steamship and the Gatling gun, the power loom and the factory system, the account books of the debt collector and the telegraph wires which carried both military orders and commodity prices were some of the most important.

Crucially, capitalist penetration of Ottoman domains was not left up to the impersonal mechanisms of the market but was achieved through the active intervention of European states. This process provides an example of what Chris Harman called "structural interdependence" of capitals and states in the capitalist system.[7] There are long-standing debates among Marxists, and between Marxists and other analysts of capitalist society, about the nature of the relationship between the activities and development of capitals and those of states. One source

---

6 Harman, 2010, pp69–75.
7 Harman, 1991.

States, capitals and markets: making the Middle East

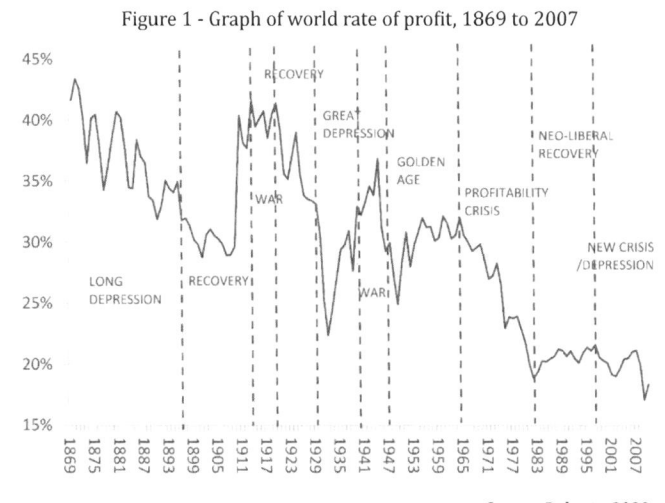

Figure 1 - Graph of world rate of profit, 1869 to 2007

Source: Roberts, 2020

of controversy is the fact that states existed before capitalism, and some of those pre-capitalist states played a significant role in shaping the development of capitalism (both in negative and positive ways).

Another bone of contention is the changing nature of the state as capitalism has developed, a point that was visible during Marx's own lifetime as it evolved from a minimal 'nightwatchman' type entity (memorably labelled as a "but a committee for managing the common affairs of the whole bourgeoisie" in the Communist Manifesto[8] to a gigantic set of institutions which "enmeshes, controls, regulates, superintends" the whole of society).[9] Then there is the question of the plurality of states and capitals. Colin Barker pointed out that Marxists often have a tendency to assume that "capitalism has but one state", while unfortunately "the beast is numerous".[10]

In contrast to the abstractions of neoclassical economics, which present capitalism as a system of self-regulating interactions through the domain of the market, in reality, states perform a whole range of services to the capitalist class, without which the

---

8 Marx & Engels, 1948, Ch 1.
9 Draper, 1977, p393.
10 Barker, 1978.

system would not function. These include directly disciplining and coercing the labour force, intervening in the reproduction of labour power through providing education, health and welfare services (and persuading workers to contribute financially to this process through the payment of taxes), protecting the property and investment of 'their' capitals (or acquiring access to raw materials, technology and markets on their behalf—both by peaceful and warlike means).

Besides the myth of the self-regulating market, the other abstraction which serves the capitalist class particularly well is the idea that the state is an impersonal power which floats above society, mediating all conflicts in the name of some higher 'national' ends. When it comes to conflicts between rich and poor, or between workers and their bosses, this illusion shatters revealing the state as an instrument of ruling class power.[11] In the case of organised workers, the real mediator standing between them and their employers and the state is usually the trade union bureaucracy (or another set of reformists).The mediating role of the state between the interests of different *capitals* is perfectly genuine, however, reflecting the fact that individual capitals are capable of actions which may harm the interests of the ruling capitalist class as a whole. This band of "warring brothers" requires a paternal authority to sort out disputes, allocate resources and adjudicate in quarrels between the siblings.

European colonial powers in their efforts to dominate the region and control its fertile agricultural lands and its mineral reserves adopted two types of strategy. The first strategy involved various forms of direct colonial rule. The most common version involved relatively small numbers of colonial administrators working with a larger layer of indigenous landowners (and sometimes merchants) who formed the bulk of the local ruling class. This landowning elite was often accorded some of the trappings of governmental power in return for helping to contain resistance from below to the escalating demands for taxes and labour power now harnessed to the ruthless cycles of the global agricultural commodity markets and the voracious appetites of the imperial treasuries.

In another variant of the same strategy, a large segment of the landowners were European settlers. Algeria was an example

---

11 Lenin, 1917, Ch 1.

of this of version of colonial rule, but settlers also grabbed prime agricultural land in Tunisia and Libya. The Zionist settlers who seized control of Palestine also initially planned to build an agricultural colony, although as I will discuss later, the reason that the settler-colonial regime survived was the result of its success in capturing military subsidies from the US and much later developing military industries and services through collaboration with its imperial patron.

The other strategy involved enmeshing local ruling classes drawn from landowners and urban merchants in more indirect forms of rule: binding them with treaties, supplying them with 'advisers', plying them with funding and arms in order to win their allegiance. However, in such cases, the local ruling classes sometimes had more latitude to shape the institutions of the state themselves. This margin of independence seems to have played an important role in creating conditions for the emergence of local capitalist classes capable of asserting their will on the wider region.

Three of the four major states which are driving military competition at a regional level in the early 21st century—Turkey, Iran and Saudi Arabia—were not subject to direct colonial rule. The fourth major military power in this system, Israel, of course emerged at the end of the colonial period out of a land-grab by the European settler population in Palestine which destroyed much of the colonial-era state apparatus and built new state institutions which were relatively similar in form and content to those of neighbouring states even if it carried over the overarching ideological justification for Jewish domination from the colonial period.[12]

Landowners, merchants and plantation economies

The fate of Mohamed Ali, Ottoman viceroy of Egypt during the early 19th century provides an illustration of the way in which the rising powers of Europe intervened to obstruct the path of their

---

12 This does not mean that all the institutions and practices of the colonial period, or even the legacy of Ottoman rule which preceded it entirely disappeared. The legal system operating across historic Palestine is a complex amalgam of laws and policies inherited from earlier periods with those created by the Israeli state since its inception.

military and diplomatic rivals towards capitalist development. Confronted by the evidence that European states were militarily overtaking Ottoman forces—most obviously by the shock arrival of Napoleon's troops in Egypt in 1798—Mohamed Ali attempted to combine economic, legal and institutional innovations from Europe with the existing pre-capitalist structures of the state. He imported technology from Europe, sent officials to Europe to study medicine and law, reformed the structures of the army, planted new crops, such as long-staple cotton, and created factories to produce uniforms for his soldiers. While this did not, in itself, add up to the emergence of capitalism in Egypt, because the work on the factories and farms was still carried out by unfree labour, the European powers acted together to break apart this early experiment in hothouse-style industrial development.

Mohamed Ali's descendants, who took oversaw the integration of Egypt into the emerging global capitalist system as a producer of the raw materials to feed the factories of Europe. Debt was a key lever for the establishment of British control: Egypt's rulers were enticed into spending on European technologies and making investments which they were unable to pay back. European creditors took over the bankrupt treasury and bled the peasantry dry with tax demands to ensure that shareholders in London and Paris would not miss out on their dividends. When Egyptian army officers led by Ahmed Urabi were support by a popular revolt, which raised the cry of 'Egypt for the Egyptians', British gunships appeared off the coast of Alexandria to begin a 70-year long occupation.

The First World War saw this British 'residency' transform into a formal 'Mandate' over Egypt and the establishment of the Egyptian monarchy, after an uprising which brought together a portion of the landowning class with elements of the small but politically significant modern middle class and urban working class to demand independence under the leadership of the nationalist Wafd Party. Unsurprisingly, the landowners who backed the Wafd had limited stomach for a serious battle with the British, and the party essentially agreed to form a loyal opposition to the new monarchy in return for seasons in government, while repressing the nascent workers' movement.

French control of the Levant, formally instituted after the defeat of the Ottoman Empire in the First World War, built on long-standing commercial links and cultural intervention in the area. Just as in Egypt, this process was driven by the integration of local agricultural production into the colonial economy, through cash-crop farming for export. Privileging the Christian communities as trading partners and posing as their "protectors" from their Muslim neighbours, the European powers made sure that the integration of the region into the emerging capitalist market wove sectarian ideologies into the emerging class structure.[13]

The Sudanese state and the ruling class that has been formed out of the struggles to control and use the land, its products and its people are still dominated by the persistent inequalities between the centre and periphery. These patterns have deep historical roots in the period of Ottoman rule during the 19th century followed by the Anglo-Egyptian Condominium which created a "central zone of accumulation" at the heart of which lay a "system of big estates that were part of a globally networked, export-oriented cotton and grain agricultural economy". The "peripheral zones of predation" were originally raided to feed the slave trade and later functioned as closed labour reserves for the plantation economy.[14]

Settler colonialism: Algeria, Tunisia, Libya and Palestine

The creation of European settler colonies in the region was mainly concentrated in North Africa, although the late case of the Zionist project in Palestine would turn out to play an exceptionally important role in structuring the architecture of imperialism in the 'post-colonial' era. The settler colonies in Algeria and Tunisia were the result of the French conquest and left deep and bitter legacies, especially in the Algerian case where the presence of a million European colons enjoying the privileges of French citizenship, alongside around 9 million Algerian subjects was one of the driving forces behind the exceptional brutality of French resistance to decolonisation.

The conquest of Algeria was a long-drawn-out process, spanning fifteen years of war between 1832 and 1847, when the Amir Abd-al-Qadir, leader of the Algerian resistance forces

---

13 Makdisi, 2000.
14 Thomas, 2017, p18–19.

finally surrendered to the French. This military victory was only achieved through the adoption of a 'scorched earth' policy by the French forces against the rural communities of Algeria, from among whom Abd-al-Qadir, a leading figure in one of the powerful Sufi Muslim religious orders, drew his support. Destruction of these traditional rural communities and the seizure of the most fertile lands for the settlers to farm was always central to the French colonial project. During the 1840s, French troops burned villages, murdered peasant farmers and harassed local landowners, while the colonial officials tripled taxes for areas under their control.[15] Grants of land to French soldiers accounted for some of the new 'colon' population, while others migrated from France.

The settler community declared its support for the Revolution of 1848 and was rewarded by the formal annexation of Algeria to France. This paved the way for a deeply racist system of government, where the European settler elite controlled the country's resources and exploited its people while Algerians were denied citizenship and subjected to systematic discrimination in every aspect of economic and political life. The economic regime of the colony was the classic model of a resource-extraction hinterland which also functioned as a receptive market for metropolitan imports.[16]

France seized control of Tunisia in 1881, after the traditional ruler, the Bey, was forced into bankruptcy in 1869 after a failed attempt at modernisation which saw the establishment of state-run industries in mechanised olive presses, flour mills, cannon and gunpowder factories in the mid-19th century.[17] During the first decades of colonial control, industrial development stagnated, as the country's new rulers focussed on consolidating control of Tunisia's best farmland to produce agricultural goods for export to Europe, especially olives and vines.

The settlers' land-grab was rapid: by 1892 French colonists controlled 402,000 hectares of fertile land, aided by changes to land ownership laws relating to the existing category of privately-owned land enforced by new land courts headed by French judges. The three decades after 1914, saw a dramatic

15 Drew, 2014, p13–14.
16 Del Panta, 2020.
17 Bellin, 2002, p13; Ayubi, 2006, p119.

shift towards mechanised agriculture, particularly in wheat farming, leading to the expulsion of peasant tenants and major rises in rural unemployment.[18] The same period also saw the beginnings of a new phase of industrialisation. Investment during the colonial period was concentrated in the mining sector and transport, geared towards the extraction of Tunisia's mineral resources such as phosphate, lead and iron ore in order to meet the needs of European industry. This resulted in lop-sided development, with Tunisia largely serving as a source of raw materials (both agricultural products and minerals) and a captive market for European imports.[19]

Libya, by contrast, was colonised relatively late, with Italian troops and settlers arriving after 1911 at the tail-end of the 'Scramble for Africa'. Around 40,000 Italian colonists occupied nearly 400,000 hectares of the better agricultural land in Libya by the end of 1940, largely producing cereal crops.[20] Over the three decades they controlled the country, the Italian colonial authorities faced determined resistance from Libyans, led by Omar al-Mukhtar before he was eventually captured and executed in 1931. The death toll among the local population was a testament to the brutality of the Italian occupation: an estimated 300,000 out of a total of 1 million are estimated to have been killed.[21]

The story of the European settlement in Palestine shared some essential features with that of the French colony in Algeria: the settlers seized agricultural land in order to control its produce for their own benefit and created a deeply racist system of government which denied Palestinians living under their rule full rights as citizens. However, the sequence of events establishing the settler colony took place in a dramatically altered historical context, and the settlers themselves had a different relationship to their European homeland to the French colons.

In this case, the settlement building project was initially a joint affair between a political movement—Zionism—which was supported by a minority of European Jews as providing an escape route from the escalating racist persecution of Jewish

---

18 Bennoune, 1979, p92.
19 Bellin, 2002, p14.
20 Fowler, 1973, p492.
21 Assaf, 2012.

communities in Europe—and the British government. It took root almost a century after the French colonisation of Algeria began, in the wake of the First World War under a British Mandate, and the settler community itself was only able to carry out its 'scorched earth' policy at the very end of British colonial rule.

The purpose of the violent dispossession of Palestinian farming communities was to grab enough land to create an independent state—which the Zionist leaders called Israel. This wave of ethnic cleansing forced around 750,000 Palestinians to flee their homes, for a life in exile, which for many was lived out beyond the borders of historic Palestine. The newly-independent Zionist state hitched its fate not the defence of Britain's declining colonial empire, but to the emerging imperialist power of the USA, sustaining a mutually beneficial partnership long after most settler colonial projects perished.

The rumps of empire and the Gulf sheikhdoms

Not all of the states in the region were subjected to direct colonial rule—two of the important exceptions were Turkey which was born in the Anatolian heartlands of the Ottoman Empire after the First World War, and the Iranian state which emerged out of the rump of the pre-capitalist empires centred on Persia. Political revolutions in both countries in the first decade of the 20th century led to the adoption of constitutional constraints on the power of the monarchy (the 'Young Turk' revolution in 1908 and the Iranian 'Constitutional revolution' between 1905 and 1911).

Undertaking an ambitious programme of capitalist modernisation during the 1920s, Kemal Ataturk laid the foundations for Turkey to develop into an important regional power. Meanwhile in Iran, Reza Shah overthrew the Qajar dynasty and established himself in power in 1925. As in Turkey, the new regime adopted many of the trappings of modernity, backed up by laws mandating 'Western' style dress. Iran's oil wealth had certainly attracted the interest of the old colonial powers—Britain had attempted to establish a protectorate over the country in 1919 in the chaotic aftermath of the First World War, only to be thwarted by a vigorous nationalist campaign

States, capitals and markets: making the Middle East

and the outrage of other European powers and the USA.[22]

Turkey and Iran were the successor states to large, powerful pre-capitalist empires which had remained powerful enough to contest their defeat and dismemberment by the European powers. By contrast, the Gulf and Red Sea coasts and the mainland of the Arabian peninsula were divided between small sheikhdoms when the Europeans arrived. These small, weak statelets were at this stage of interest to the colonial powers because of their strategic importance on the route to India and the Far East. Besides the pearling trade, they appeared to have few natural resources, and little agricultural land. This was a major reason why British officials were largely content with maintaining amicable relationships with the ruling families in a more arms-length fashion than in the rest of the Middle East. They provided guns, gold and advisers, and occasionally intervened to tip the balance in the Gulf's fratricidal wars.

The barren centre of Arabia seemed even less appealing, yet it was from the Najd region that one of the major powers of the Gulf would arise. The Saudi state's genesis began with the alliance which Muhammad ibn Sa'ud, landowner and leader of al-Dir'iyyah, an oasis settlement of around 70 households in the Najd region of Arabia concluded with the preacher Muhammad Ibn 'Abd-al-Wahhab in 1744.[23] The relationship between the descendants of the two men has lasted to the present day, and this ongoing partnership played a critical role in the long process which led to the formation of the modern Saudi state. During the early stages of the state-formation process, Wahhabism acted as a kind of ideological glue, binding together a tri-partite social formation encompassing the Al Saud family, the Wahhabi *'ulama* and their network of ritual specialists, the *mutawwa'a*.

The establishment of the Kingdom of Saudi Arabia in 1932 marked an important transition to a new phase in the development of the state. Ibn Sa'ud's ambitions had reached the territorial limits of Arabia and the Saudi-Wahhabi alliance now had to choose between continuing its wars of conquest (which meant in effect directly challenging its imperial patron, Britain), or seeking acceptance within the existing order of states. Unsurprisingly, since he owed a good part of his success to British rifles and subsidies, Ibn Saud was content to accept his

---

22 Katouzian, 1998.
23 Al-Rasheed, 2010, p14–15.

role in the colonial order, provided he was free to consolidate his grip over Arabia itself. That process was however, deeply enmeshed with the discovery of huge reserves of oil in the Kingdom, transforming Ibn Saud from a relatively cash-poor local dignitary into a gatekeeper for resources which the United States government considered "vital" to its interests.[24]

Towards a new imperial order

As we have seen, the major European powers parcelled out the land and natural resources of the Middle East between them over the course of the 19th and early 20th century. Versions of this process were also underway in Africa and much of Asia over a similar time period. For revolutionary socialists such as Vladimir Lenin and Nicolai Bukharin in Russia and Rosa Luxemburg in Germany, this phase in the development of capitalism did not simply herald the ruin of the societies forcibly incorporated into the global market, it also pointed towards the destructive engine of economic and military competition at the heart of the system. That engine would plunge large parts of the world into war involving all the major capitalist powers in 1914, wreaking havoc on millions of lives.

The underlying problem was that the rapid colonial carve-up had not solved the underlying problem of profitability across the capitalist system, despite periodic booms. Profit rates only recovered temporarily through massive state investment, particularly in military infrastructure and armaments, but also in a shift towards planning the allocation of existing resources and future production to fund the development of welfare systems and public services. Initially, the dominant role of the state in the economy and society was considered an exceptional condition of the war-time economy. However, the severity of the financial crash in 1929 forced all the major capitalist powers, including the US, which had by this time overtaken Britain at the centre of the global economy, to turn to the state to pull themselves out of the Depression which followed. Once again, this process proved impossible to disentangle from the drive to war, in which Germany and Japan were pitted against Britain, France, the USA and the Soviet Union.

---

24 Perkins, Goodwin, Evans & Prescott, 1943.

States, capitals and markets: making the Middle East

The other pressures leading capitalism to rely on the state to play a central role in the economy came not from the centre of the global system, but from its periphery. For ruling classes there, using the state to mobilise the resources and people needed for industrialisation appeared the only viable route away from perpetual economic and political subservience to the great powers. Or as Stalin put it in 1931:

> Such is the law of the exploiters—to beat the backward and the weak. It is the jungle law of capitalism. You are backward, you are weak—therefore you are wrong; hence you can be beaten and enslaved. You are mighty—therefore you are right; hence we must be wary of you. That is why we must no longer lag behind... We are fifty or a hundred years behind the advanced countries. We must make good this distance in ten years. Either we do it, or we shall go under.[25]

The decades which followed appeared at first to vindicate the strategy adopted by Stalin and the bureaucracy he built around him by ruthlessly crushing his opponents and leading a counter-revolution from within to destroy the socialist state which had briefly taken shape in Russia after October 1917. The USSR emerged from the Second World War as a global power, Soviet troops rolled across Eastern Europe, Soviet satellites circled the globe and a Soviet atomic bomb increased military pressure on the USA, launching a new and even more deadly nuclear arms race.

As Alex Callinicos explains, imperialism in the era of superpower competition between the USA and the USSR functioned differently to how it had done at the height of the colonial era. The US ruling class generally did not rely on the creation of colonies, using a variety of other mechanisms to enforce its hegemony over second and third rank powers.[26] These included the creation of military alliances and the siting of US bases, arms and technology transfers, loans, grants and economic aid. Coercion was never far in the background, and the US was sometimes drawn into direct military intervention to prop up its allies (with disastrous consequences for the

---

25 Stalin, 1931.
26 Callinicos, 2009, p166.

whole of South East Asia which was devastated by repeated wars along the frontlines of the Cold War during the 1950s and 1960s). The Middle East saw several instances of smaller-scale military interventions by the US ruling class during the same period. These included the CIA's assistance to the Shah of Iran in organising a coup against popular nationalist Prime Minister Mohamed Mossadegh in 1953, to the expedition by US Marines to Beirut in 1958. In addition, billions of dollars of arms flowed to Israel, Iran and Saudi Arabia from the late 1960s onwards. The Soviet Union also channelled military and economic aid towards its allies in the region, constructed bases, lent technicians and advisors and bought or bartered raw materials and manufactured products.

The logic of capital accumulation meant that "resistance" by the ruling classes of weaker capitalist states to the depredations of the global capitalist powers inevitably reproduced the processes of imperialism at the lower levels of the system. The development of such sub-imperial systems depended on the emergence of centres of capital accumulation outside the historic core of the capitalist system.

Coal and oil: fuel of empire

As we saw at the beginning of this chapter, the violent integration of the Middle East into the world market was already well advanced *before* the discovery of oil. The region's subjugation by Britain and France was largely made possible by the coal-powered warships and the coal-powered textile industries as these two major capitalist powers used their fossil fuel advantage to carve up the region between them. Yet oil changed things in the region and the Middle East's oil changed the world in fundamental ways. The discovery of abundant oil which was relatively easy and cheap to extract at the peak of imperialist competition between the European powers accelerated the carve-up of the region.

It was not the old colonial powers of Britain and France which would reap the greatest rewards, however, but the rising superpower of the United States. Despite both Britain and France maintaining a crucial stake in the international oil industry, the decline of their empires coincided

States, capitals and markets: making the Middle East

Figure 2: Oil production and consumption, USA

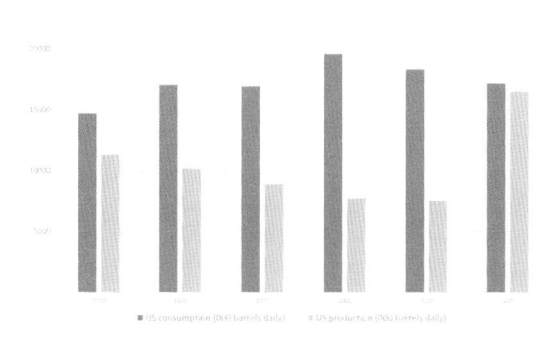

Figure 3: Oil production and consumption, Europe

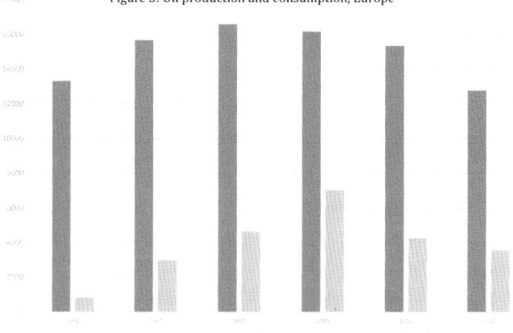

Figure 4: Oil production and consumption, Middle East and North Africa

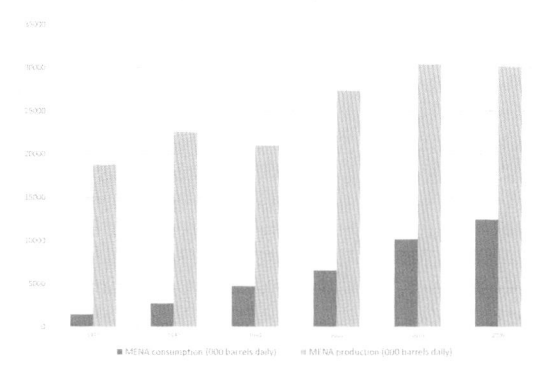

Data source: BP Statistical Review, 2021

broadly with the shift away from coal power in the core of the global economy towards the oil-powered "Great Acceleration" of the Long Boom.[27] It was no accident that both of the superpowers of the era of bipolar imperialist rivalry in the mid-20th century, the USA and the Soviet Union, were oil industry pioneers with large reserves of their own which had already played a crucial role in their economic development. At the outbreak of the First World War the USA dominated global supplies, controlling 70 percent of world oil production. US dominance was entrenched further during the course of the war as Russian production collapsed in the wake of defeat by Germany and revolution in 1917, while US production surged ahead to meet the demands of the Allies.[28]

Just over fifty years later, in 1965, the picture had changed substantially. The US share of world production had dropped to 28 percent of the total, while the Middle East (excluding North Africa) accounted for 26 percent.[29] Over the following decades the Middle East would overtake the US and remain at around double its production levels for most of the next half century.[30] In relation to proven reserves of oil, the Middle East's importance to global supply was even more pronounced.

The US is not only a historic major producer of oil, but consistently the world's greatest single consumer, and until the explosion in shale oil production during the last decade faced a growing gap between production and consumption. For the US's major allies in Western Europe, the production—consumption gap was even bigger. By contrast, the Middle East consistently produces far more than it consumes.

Fossil capitalism

Moreover, oil is of a fundamentally different character to the agricultural commodities, such as cotton, which drove the region's initial integration into the global market. Like the coal which helped to power the initial expansion of capitalism in Britain, oil is a non-renewable resource. It is produced by

27 Angus, 2016.
28 Gliech, 2020.
29 BP, 2020.
30 BP, 2020.

geological processes far beyond the lifetime not just of individual humans but even of the human species. As is becoming ever clearer, this particular form of consumption pose an existential risk to humanity, and countless other species, as it fuels global heating.[31] However, it is the portability of oil, as much as its properties as a store of historic solar energy which shape the role that this commodity plays within the capitalist system., The relative ease with which it can be transported, commoditized and exchanged, is the fundamental quality which underpins the centrality of fossil fuels to capital accumulation. As Andreas Malm has argued, it was not the greater abundance of coal over water in northern England during the industrial revolution which persuaded mill owners to adopt steam power, but their ability to move the energy source to their workforce, rather than the other way around, a fact which gave them an important advantage in their struggle to contain or break workers' resistance.[32]

Compared to coal, oil is relatively less expensive to extract and transport. Once on the surface oil can be transported in bulk by ship or even by pipeline, again at relatively less cost than coal. Vehicles running on liquid, not a solid fuel like coal, are much lighter and adaptable to different terrain. These qualities of oil, combined with a desire to undermine the bargaining power of organised workers in the coal-mining industry help to explain why the British Navy opted to convert from coal-power to oil-power in the run-up to the First World War.[33] In some ways this was a counter-intuitive decision—because in Britain's case it meant switching from a locally-available fuel to one dependent on foreign supplies. As a result, the British state became much more directly involved in the oil industry, taking steps to found and maintain a controlling stake in the company which would become BP.[34]

The very properties which made oil an attractive alternative to coal often magnified problems of chaotic competition leading to glut followed by a price crash. This in turn proved a powerful encouragement towards the creation of monopolies in production and distribution in order to better calibrate

---

31 Angus, 2016.
32 Malm, 2017.
33 Mitchell, 2013.
34 Sampson, 1981.

production and consumption and keep profits flowing.[35] The other significant quality of oil is its finite, non-renewable nature as a resource, and its uneven distribution across the world.

Both abundance and scarcity of oil are frequently framed as if they are either geological or technical questions, when in fact they are fundamentally social. It has become terrifyingly clear that there will now always be *too much* oil from an ecological point of view, so long as the value of oil is determined by the capitalist market. Periods of low prices encourage more consumption, while when the price rises, this shifts the thresholds at which previously "uneconomic" oil reserves become profitable and drive investment in new techniques, and the market once again veers towards a glut. The last forty years in the global oil markets have seen two huge cycles of price oscillations, and the economies of the oil exporters of the Middle East (and most of their non-oil exporting neighbours) have hurtled up and down their switchback curves with increasingly destructive consequences.

Taming the market: oil in the era of state capitalism

The history of Middle Eastern oil and its role in the capitalist system has not only been shaped by the gyrations of the commodity markets, however. In fact, it provides a sharp reminder that states, as well as capitals are actors in the capitalist system. The era of state capitalism began with the huge efforts by the major European states and the US to pull their economies out of depression after the great financial crash of 1929, and Stalin's state-led transformation of agriculture and industrialisation in the Soviet Union. It had as its counterpart the *de facto* suspension of the market in the global oil industry by the major western oil companies through the creation of a price-fixing cartel which lasted until 1970.

The Achnacarry Agreement was thrashed out between representatives of Shell, Exxon, BP and Gulf during a grouse-shooting party in Scotland in August 1928. It preceded the great financial crash by more than a year but was prefigurative of the later trajectory of the global economy as a whole. The "oil lords" made a "gentleman's agreement" between themselves which

---

35 Sampson, 1981.

Figure 5: Global crude oil prices 1861 to 2020 (US$ per barrel in $2020)

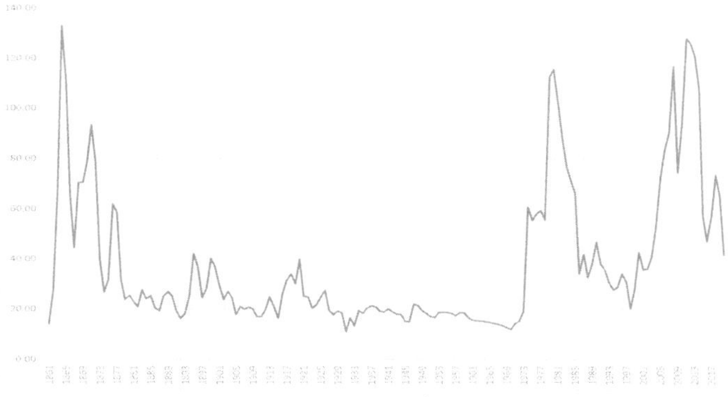

Data source: BP Statistical Review, 2021

would tame the destructiveness of competition between the largest oil capitals for a generation to come through production quotas and collective investment in shared refinery capacity. Further negotiations a few months later agreed to fix prices by controlling output.[36] Its effects can be seen in the decades-long plateau in the global price of crude oil between the 1930s and 1970. Defence of the profits of the US oil industry was its primary aim, faced with the threat of far cheaper supplies from the new fields in Iraq or Venezuela.[37] The two non-US companies (British state-owned BP and the British-Dutch Shell) agreed to come on board in return for a handsome slice of the profits. The mechanism was simply to enforce US prices on non-US supplies, so that oil shipped from Iraq to Italy, for example, would be charged as if it had been pumped in Texas and sailed from the Gulf of Mexico.[38]

The impact was thus to maintain artificially *high* prices for the consumers of Middle Eastern oil, while the domination of production in the region by the so-called "Seven Sisters", as the major Western oil companies were known,[39] ensured that they remained *low* enough to deny the producer states the revenues they craved to fund economic development and

36 Sampson, 1981; Peterkin, 2018.
37 Mitchell, 2013.
38 Sampson, 1981, p90.
39 Sampson, 1981.

Revolution is the choice of the people

make the transition towards becoming independent centres of capital accumulation. The model for how that domination was managed, once again, through a negotiated process rather than the market, was laid out in a deal agreed at almost exactly the same time as the Achnacarry Agreement, on 31 July 1928. The Red-Line Agreement set up a consortium of British, French and US companies to run the newly-discovered oil fields in Iraq, creating the Iraq Petroleum Company (IPC). It also, however, extended far beyond Iraq's borders, including Turkey to the north and much of the Arabian peninsula (with the exception of Kuwait which was reserved for exclusive British influence).

The US oil companies initially had to be cajoled into operations inside Iraq by the State Department, which had imposed the presence of the US firms on the reluctant British and French. The following decade would see the US state and US oil capitals again working in concert to exploit the even larger reserves of Saudi Arabia and cement a political and military alliance with the Al Sa'ud family (this time without British and French involvement through one of the US companies which had not signed up to the Red Line Agreement, Socal). Despite differences of opinion over tactics (and occasional bust-ups over the US anti-trust laws which effectively prohibited the price-fixing cartel), the Second World War would confirm that the US oil companies and the US state were bound together tightly by bonds of mutual interest which could not easily be broken. One of the signs of their structural interdependence was the way in which the US companies involved in ARAMCO, the new, all-American company set up to manage Saudi Arabian oil production, successfully lobbied for the extension of lend-lease aid to the Saudi monarchy (resulting in Roosevelt's famous letter declaring "I hereby find that the defence of Saudi Arabia is vital to the defence of the United States").[40]

Oil managed by the US oil companies collaboratively with the US state, in cooperation with its allies in Britain and France, would thus underpin what Ian Angus terms "the Great Acceleration" of capitalist development during the Long Boom in the West.[41] However, it is important to note that the fundamental principles of the Achnacarry Agreement meant grappling not with the problem of oil scarcity, but of glut, and that the attitude

---

40 Sampson, 1981, p110.
41 Angus, 2016.

of the Seven Sisters and the two states with which they were inextricably linked towards the oil of the Middle East was conditioned by the reflex of controlling production in order to maintain the pricing structure which benefitted the rising imperial power of the US.[42] The sheer scale of the Middle Eastern reserves, and the new discoveries of the 1950s and 1960s multiplied the problem of overabundance. A vast "supergiant" oil field at Rumaila in Southern Iraq was discovered in 1953. French geologists struck oil in Algeria in 1956, while large reserves were also uncovered in Libya in 1959.

Meanwhile, however, the growing economic and political crisis of the model of capitalist development predominating in the former European colonies of the Middle East and North Africa would result eventually in capture of political power across much of the region by sections of the modern middle class impatient for radical social change.

This would prepare the ground for the next phase in the evolution of the global oil industry, as some of the newly independent producer countries would create a new cartel of state-oil-capital complexes and break the Seven Sisters' "gentleman's agreement" by reinstating a global oil market as one of the major mechanisms for managing the flow of oil and its associated profits around the world.

It should be stressed here that what appeared to be a fundamental shift in the circuitry of capital accumulation did not, in fact, alter the underlying order in the hierarchy of states. In fact, the US retained its dominance both of the global oil industry and of the global economy more generally. It triumphed economically over the Soviet Union which finally collapsed in 1991 and continued to impose a neoliberal policy agenda on much of the world for decades afterwards. Nor did the independent initiative of the oil producers in the new cartel, the Organisation of Petroleum Exporting Countries (OPEC), provide a one-way ticket to the club of advanced economies for all its members.

Among the ten countries which had joined OPEC by 1969, eight were in the Middle East: Iran, Iraq, Kuwait, Saudi Arabia, Qatar, Libya, the UAE and Algeria. The remaining two were Venezuela and Indonesia.[43] Half a century later only Kuwait, Saudi Arabia, Qatar and the UAE could be said to have succeeded

---

42   Mitchell, 2013.
43   OPEC, nd.

Revolution is the choice of the people

in making that leap (and that was on the basis of a very specific oil-dependent pathway towards the next phase of capitalist development in the neoliberal era). Iraq and Algeria would all ride a rollercoaster of spending and debt towards disaster in the 1990s. The fragility of Libya's economic development was exposed in the wake of the 2011 revolution which saw the country fragment. Iran experienced a change of personnel at the helm of the state in the wake of the 1979 revolution, and then a devastating war with Iraq and the lasting enmity of the United States, both of which created a mutually reinforcing set of conditions encouraging a pattern of relatively autarchic state-led economic development.

This was not the future that the Arab nationalists who had led the revolutions of the 1950s and 1960s had envisaged. They hoped to use the oil wealth which would be generated by smashing the Seven Sisters' control of production and prices through the creation of national oil companies and resetting the rules of the oil trade to pass back some of the benefits of cheap, abundant oil into their own plans for economic development.

Oil revenues appeared to offer a way out of the problem not just for the oil exporters, but for the wider region. Nasser, for example, took a keen interest in the strategic value of oil. Although Egypt lacked major supplies of its own, he avidly read the reports which were emerging from US experts, some of whom were training the first generation of Arab oil engineers, about the real scale of Middle Eastern reserves. Arab nationalist ideas for a time circulated widely in the Gulf, even penetrating Saudi Arabia and winning unlikely converts among some of the Al Saud princes who defected to Cairo.

More seriously threatening to the stability of the US-Saudi alliance was the role played by the migrant workers who had been recruited from around the Arab world (but especially among the recently dispossessed Palestinians) by the oil industry. Strikes and various forms of agitation inspired by Arab nationalist and left-wing politics were part of "the revolutionary, Arab nationalist tide which inundated the Gulf and Arab peninsula region in the 1950s".[44] Yet the 1960s ended in painful defeat for Nasser both on the military and economic fronts. Israeli forces scored a major victory over Egypt and Syria in 1967 and marched into the West Bank and Gaza Strip, while

---

44 Chalcraft, 2010, p3. Quoting Al-Naqeeb, 1990, p101

the industrialisation drive begun in 1961 ran into financial difficulties after the first Five Year Plan.experiment launched.

Greasing the wheels of war: bases, alliances and partnerships

The emergence of the US's global imperial hegemony was never simply reliant on the markets as a disciplinary mechanism but was fundamentally an exercise in the projection of military power. Oil powered the US battleships, tanks and aircraft carrying troops around the world. This in turn required the military defence of those oil resources from potential competitors, particularly the Soviet Union and its allies. The shift in patterns of imperialist competition at the centre of the capitalist system thus led to the development of a new set of military relations between the two superpowers and the states of the Middle East, which over time came to replace the web of alliances, colonies and military bases created by Britain and France during the colonial era.

The US did not simply begin the process of constructing a similar set of institutions from scratch, but rather interlaced the building blocks of its own 'informal' empire with those of the old colonial powers.[45] There were moments of tension between the old and the new imperial powers, such as the Suez Crisis of 1956, when Britain and France allied with Israel to attack Nasser's regime in Egypt after the nationalisation of the Suez Canal. They faced diplomatic humiliation and political failure as the US and the Soviet Union jointly enforced an end to the war which left Egypt in charge of the Canal, and Nasser triumphant. However, in general, the military relationship between the British and US imperial projects in the Middle East resembled a relatively smooth changing of the guard between the two powers, particularly in the Gulf.

US military dominance of the Middle East, which was explicitly justified as the requirement to appropriate its oil resources for the US and its allies (or at least deny them to its enemies), rested both on the physical presence of US troops on the ground in a string of military bases and navy ports and in the construction of military alliances and partnerships with local ruling classes. The first major milestone in the

---

45 Callinicos, 2009.

'handover' between Britain and the US came with the civil war in Greece in 1947, as the US rushed to intervene and prop up the monarchy after Britain announced the ending of aid to the royalist side. US President Harry Truman's policy of providing military and economic support to "democratic" nations "under threat from external or internal authoritarian forces,"[46] marked a turning point in US "peacetime" foreign policy as it reoriented the US ruling class towards active competition with the Soviet Union in multiple regions of the world in both military and economic spheres.

The impact of the "Truman Doctrine" on the Middle East was first felt in the extension of US aid to Turkey, and the inclusion of Turkey in the new NATO military alliance set up by the US in 1949 to organise the "collective defence" of the Western powers and their allies against the Soviet Union. The US also took an active interest in supporting the Iranian monarchy, intervening covertly in 1953 to help the Shah remove popular nationalist Prime Minister Mohamed Mossadegh from power when his policy of oil nationalisation appeared to threaten the interests of British oil company BP. As with Greece in 1947, the Iranian coup of 1953 saw the rising and declining imperial powers working in concert, but with the US taking over the leading role.

A smooth transition which preserved the existing local regimes proved to be unachievable in the face of the mass mobilisations from below which led directly or indirectly to the downfall of many of the rulers who had been backed by the British and French. US efforts to maintain a degree of political continuity from the colonial era were most successful in Iran, Turkey and the countries of the Gulf. In the case of Iran, the alliance between the monarchy and the US would later be overthrown from within by the revolution of 1979, whereas Turkey and the Gulf remain to this day crucial to the architecture of US military power at both a regional and global level. A major disruption to the imperial transition came with the collapse of the British-backed Hashemite monarchy in Iraq in the face of a revolution in 1958. Baghdad had been chosen by both the British and US government as the anchor of a military security pact designed to extend NATO's reach deep into the Middle East. The success of a coup led by nationalist officers and enabled by a mass popular movement in which the Iraqi Communist Party

---

46 US State Department, nd(b).

played a major role demonstrated the difficulty of attempting to hold on to the political systems of the colonial period.

US military power in the Middle East survived the turbulence of the anti-colonial revolutions, enduring and expanding over the following two decades as a combination of military defeats and economic co-option tamed the nationalist regimes which emerged in the 1950s and 1960s. Significantly, however, the military victory which confirmed US hegemony in the region despite the collapse of the old political order was won its new local military partner, Israel.

In 1967 Israeli forces inflicted humiliating defeats on the Egyptian and Syrian armies, seizing control of Gaza, the West Bank, the Golan Heights and the Sinai Peninsula. Within historic Palestine, this represented a new phase in the process of dispossession of the Palestinians and the colonial occupation of their lands. The regional significance of Israel's victory lay what the military failure of the Egyptian and Syrian regimes told the local ruling classes about risks of confronting rather than cooperating with the allies of the US. Military defeat at the hands of Israel's air force served as a coercive lever forcing open the door to the integration of regimes which appeared to be aligning themselves politically and economically with the Soviet Union back into the "Western" fold from which they had only just escaped.

Revolution is the choice of the people

Chapter 5

The short state capitalist era and its long legacy

How to make the leap from colonial subservience to become an independent capitalist power? This was the challenge which confronted nationalists across the region after the Second World War. The answer seemed to lie in using the state as the driver of economic change. Direct competition from the powers at the centre of the system made it almost impossible to break through otherwise. A second set of reasons was linked with the internal class structure of the late developing capitalist social formations of the 'colonial world'. After the nationalist vanguard had "stormed the ramparts of tyranny" (as the leader of the Egyptian Free Officers' movement, Gamal Abdel Nasser once put it),[47] they discovered the weakness of the local capitalist class which was meant to lead the economic transformation after shaking off the shackles and limitations of colonial rule.

The heyday of the state capitalist era in the Middle East and North Africa is thus characterised by the emergence of large numbers of states which experienced anti-colonial political revolutions and ended up looking to a model of economic development and political institutions associated with the Soviet Union. Many of these would also develop diplomatic and military alliances with the USSR as the tensions of the Cold War rippled through the region, forcing the newly-independent states to choose sides. In Tunisia, Syria, Algeria, Libya, Egypt and

---

47 Alexander, 2005.

Sudan a new ruling class formed around the military, the state bureaucracy and the managers of the nationalised economy, even though the routes travelled to reach this state differed. Algeria went through one of the deepest revolutionary experiences, with an eight-year long armed struggle interlaced with mass urban mobilisations including strikes.

In Tunisia, decolonisation was the outcome of struggle by a nationalist movement with a mass base and a significant working class arm in the UGTT trade union federation, but took place relatively rapidly and peacefully compared to Algeria. Egypt experienced popular upheavals and intermittent guerrilla campaigns against the British military occupation in the dying years of the monarchy, but the masses only played a passive role in the actual coup which brought nationalist junior officers to power in 1952. The Gulf states were an exception to the wave of anti-colonial revolutions, despite the emergence of powerful Arab nationalist currents in some countries such as Bahrain, often connected with the growing social weight of a migrant working class which was concentrated in the expanding oil industry. Yet with the exception of Yemen, the Gulf monarchies survived the end of the colonial era intact.

The paradoxes of the anti-colonial revolutions

In almost all the countries discussed in this book, the colonial period ended in revolutions during the course of which a new ruling class came to power. The uneven and combined processes of capitalist development created pressures and contradictions which were incapable of being resolved within the existing order. In many important ways these pressures reflected histories of economic development and class formation which resembled some of the conditions analysed by Trotsky in Russia in the first half of the 20th century: a highly repressive state apparatus backed up by both the colonial powers and large landowners presided over the immiseration of peasant farmers and an increasingly combative urban working class, which was often concentrated in strategic areas of the economy such as modern transport infrastructures and sometimes in large, modern factories such as Misr Spinning in Egypt which employed over 30,000 workers by the mid-1930s.

The short state capitalist era and its long legacy

Yet in contrast to the process of 'permanent revolution' which Trotsky argued had played out in Russia, the anticolonial revolutions brought a different class to power. A process of what Tony Cliff termed 'deflected permanent revolution' took place, as sections of the lower middle class seized control of the state and used it as a lever to accelerate capitalist development.[48] The anticolonial uprisings in the Middle East were part of a much broader revolutionary wave, including the Chinese Communist Party's takeover of state power in 1949 and the Cuban Revolution of 1959. Despite labelling themselves as 'Communist', the social basis of these movements was an alliance between sections of the lower middle class and the peasantry, who mobilised as guerrilla armies in the countryside to defeat the existing ruling class and win over the political—but largely passive—support of urban workers.

Some of the revolutions which erupted across the Middle East and North Africa during the same period did involve major guerrilla struggles (the Algerian war of national liberation against the French settler-colonial state being a major example). In most, however, urban protest movements, including mass demonstrations and strikes played a more active and important role in destabilising the old order than was the case in China or Cuba. The key point however, is that the *consequences* of the revolutionary wave were directly comparable. During the course of the two decades after the Second World War, the political alignment and social basis of the ruling class across much of the Middle East altered dramatically, with the majority adopting variants of bureaucratic state capitalism modelled to some degree on the economic policies and political institutions of the USSR and its allies.[49] the conversion of these new ruling classes to 'state capitalist policies was often more at the level of rhetoric than substance, however. This facilitated their equally abrupt abandonment of import-substitution industrialisation policies and their swift reorientation towards the new orthodoxy of neoliberalism.

This characterisation of the anti-colonial revolutions as an essential step in the process of *capitalist* development is important for a number of reasons when considering the legacy of the state capitalist era in shaping the trajectories of revolution

48 Cliff, 1963.
49 Cliff, 1996.

since 2010. They formed part of multi-stage bourgeois revolutions which created the potential for independent centres of capital accumulation to emerge. The uprisings loosened the political and military grip of the major imperialist powers and the landed and merchant classes allied with them long enough for a rising local bourgeoisie to at least make an attempt at indigenous capitalist industrialisation. This underscores the point that the 'socialism' espoused by most of these regimes was not an alternative to capitalism. The nationalist leaders who adopted it made a gamble that import-substitution industrialisation would power the ascent of 'their' states (and the ruling class forming around the state bureaucracy) upwards in the global hierarchy of capitalist states.

The problem was that in most cases, neither the state capitalist hopes rapid progress towards an industrialised future, nor the neoliberal policies which followed lived up to their promises. Only a handful of the independent states of the region achieved sufficient levels of sustained growth allowing them to join the select ranks of "developed economies." Tellingly, none of those were among the countries where the ruling class had turned towards the state capitalist model inspired by the Soviet Union.

The social basis of anti-colonial revolution and the state capitalist 'deflection'

The domination of the land and the natural resources by a narrow elite bound to the maintenance of colonial rule was the fundamental social injustice which powered the revolutionary movements of the Middle East in the decades after the Second World War. It was the promise of using the independent power of the state to address this grievance which proved capable of knitting together a diverse spectrum of the social forces which were excluded and marginalised by what Hanna Batatu called 'the old social classes' of colonial era.[50] This spectrum crossed the rural-urban divide, knitting together impoverished peasant farmers and urban workers with restless and ambitious members of the up-and-coming modern middle class—the journalists, lawyers, teachers, doctors and civil servants who raged at the way that the colonial state trapped them in stultifying systems

50 Batatu, 1978.

The short state capitalist era and its long legacy

of deference based on racial and class privilege.[51]

Algeria's revolutionary war for liberation from French rule was conducted by nationalist movement which brought together different sections of society, including both the traditional and modern sections of the middle class, urban workers and the rural poor under the banner of resistance to colonialism.

Despite the mobilisation of thousands of troops to quell the insurgency at enormous cost, the French ruling class was forced to concede defeat in the early 1960s and organise a referendum on Algerian independence. The new Algerian state came into being in March 1962, filling the void left by the precipitate flight of hundreds of thousands of colonial administrators and the colonial bourgeoisie who also withdrew their capital. Not everything which the colonial state had stolen could simply be removed, however, leaving factories and farms abandoned by their French owners. The forces which initially filled this void had been unleashed by the intensity of the liberation struggle, urban workers who took over management of industry and peasants who took control of large tracts of land to farm. This process of *autogestion* (self-management) was initially supported by some sections of the FLN leadership, under Ahmed Ben Bella, the republic's first president. However, rising panic among the propertied classes prompted a coup which installed Houari Boumediène as president in 1965, paving the way for a form of state-led development which was much less threatening to the emerging Algerian bourgeoisie.[52]

In Tunisia, too, colonial rule had left a legacy of intense inequality in land ownership, with small numbers of local landowners or colonists controlling most of the most fertile and productive land. By the 1950s in Tunisia there were around 3000 colonial farmers with an average of 250 hectares each while 480,000 peasant families scratched a living on an average of 6 hectares each of much lower quality land.[53] However, not all Tunisian farmers had suffered equally under colonial rule: a minority from the northern coastal regions prospered and would form an important component of the social base of the ruling party under Bourguiba's rule after independence.[54]

---

51 Fanon et al, 2001.
52 Del Panta, 2020.
53 Bennoune, 1979, p94.
54 Hanieh, 2013, p79.

Revolution is the choice of the people

A growing nationalist movement brought together sections of the urban working class, driven into alliance with the modern middle class, alongside some of the 'traditional classes' such as urban artisans, religious figures and merchants. All of these groups had their reasons to resent continued French rule, from the racist discrimination in working conditions and pay experienced by Tunisians at work, to the appropriation of religiously endowed land by the colonial authorities, to the destructive impact of European imports on traditional manufacturing. The leaders of the nationalist movement oscillated between confrontation with the colonial authorities and attempts to negotiate their way to independence—organising mass protests and strikes but also embarking on guerrilla warfare. The special relationship between the UGTT union federation and the Tunisian nationalist movement dates from this period: the union federation was politically affiliated with the nationalist Neo-Destour party led by Habib Bourguiba.[55]

Habib Bourguiba and the Neo-Destour Party were able to take over the colonial state apparatus in a negotiated transition during 1954-56. Bourguiba emerged as the president of the new Republic of Tunisia in 1957 following the abolition of the monarchy. However, despite Bourguiba's desperate attempts to encourage the French colonial-era bourgeoisie to stay on, the newly-independent state quickly faced massive capital flight, amounting to an estimated 100 million dinars in 1957-8 alone.[56] French colonial administrators and managers also departed *en masse*, creating a vacuum in the state institutions and in some industrial sectors which the new ruling party was able to fill with its own cadres, helping to cement Bourguiba's control over the state. Between 1955 and 1960, the number of Tunisian Muslims employed in the civil service rose from 12,000 to 80,000.[57]

British colonial rule in Egypt had not involved the creation of a large settler colony, but the cotton-dominated rural economy created during the 19th century was just as subordinated to the needs of British capital as Tunisian agriculture was to French capital. It also rested on a structure of landownership which was similarly unequal. The 1930s and 1940s also saw the growth of local industry, including the emergence of Misr

---

55 Ayubi, 2006, p211.
56 Bellin, 2002, p15.
57 Bennoune, 1979, p236.

The short state capitalist era and its long legacy

Spinning, a large spinning and weaving company established by Talaat Harb in the Delta town of al-Mahalla al-Kubra which employed around 30,000 workers by the mid-1930s. However, in general industrial growth was stunted by a lack of investment capital and the symbiosis between large landowners and British capital lurched towards a terminal crisis as the 1940s drew to a close.[58] An increasing tempo of mass protests and strikes after the Second World War was partially spurred on by the economic and social crisis on the ending of war-time conditions which had created large numbers of jobs servicing the British war effort and in local industries built up to compensate for the disruption to international trade. The junior army officers who seized power in 1952 immediately took steps towards land reform, which aimed both to break the political power of the old landowning class and create a social base for a new regime. Over the following decade, under the increasingly confident leadership of Gamal Abd-al-Nasser, the new regime moved towards a state capitalist experiment in import-substitution industrialisation after failed attempts to stop foreign capital flight and cajole local private capital into investment.

Arab nationalists and Communists alike, were fixated on the leaps in development made by Soviet Russia and other countries which had followed a 'socialist' road towards industrialisation and had apparently made enormous gains in lifting their societies out of rural poverty and towards capitalist modernity. In the case of both the Ba'thists and the Nasserist Arab Nationalists this did not initially translate into uncritical support for either Soviet foreign policy or the local Communist parties. In fact, the Ba'th Party supported the idea of unifying Syria and Egypt under the leadership of Gamal Abd-al-Nasser in 1958 in order to undermine the rising popularity of their Communist rivals who were facing severe repression from the regime in Egypt. The resulting United Arab Republic (UAR) came undone only 3 years later following an army revolt which found temporary backing from large parts of the Syrian political spectrum against the increasingly radical turn in Nasser's economic strategy, with the implementation of the 'Socialist Decrees' nationalising large sections of industry and the banks in 1961.

---

58 Wahdat al-Dirasat, 1999.

'Socialist revolution' from above?

The men who took over from the 'old social classes' were rarely ideologically committed to the 'socialism' they increasingly started to reference in their speeches and economic policies. In fact, many of them hoped fervently that American, rather than Soviet advisors, arms and loans would start to flow in their direction once they had levered the old landowners and merchants out of power. Perhaps they took at face value the promises made by Truman in 1952 when he spoke about the US

> "shirt-sleeve diplomats... carrying the American revolution to the villages and farms of the world. They are providing farmers with better seed and better fertilizer, better methods of plowing and sowing and better means of harvesting and saving the crops. They are helping to fight malaria and dysentery, trachoma and rinderpest. They are providing training in the techniques of modern government. They are helping to build roads and canals and dams, schools and hospitals".[59]

In the first years after taking power, Habib Bourguiba in Tunisia sought to position Neo-Destour as a liberal, secular and anti-communist force. The UGTT had already, even before independence, left the Soviet-inclined World Federation of Trade Unions and joined the International Confederation of Trade Unions, establishing friendly links with the USA's AFL-CIO. This dovetailed with efforts to reassure private investors. As Eva Bellin notes, in the first years after independence, "according to official rhetoric, the driving force behind industrialization and economic development was to come from the private sector, not from the state".[60]

The problem was that while French capital flowed out of the country, neither in agriculture or industry was there an energetic class of emerging Tunisian capitalists, straining to raise production and powering high rates of economic growth. Private sector buyers appeared more interested in becoming absentee landlords rather than investing in raising agricultural productivity, or taking over existing French enterprises rather

---

59 Truman, 1952.
60 Bellin, 2002, p15.

The short state capitalist era and its long legacy

than striking out and creating new industries.[61] The answer appeared to be clear: substitute the state for the non-existent industrial bourgeoisie, and use its power to simultaneously raise agricultural production by pushing private farmers towards working in co-operatives while nationalising large areas of previously foreign-owned land. In 1961 a Ten Year Plan was drawn up and the UGTT general secretary, Ahmed Ben Salah put in charge of achieving its ambitious targets for growth—projected at 6 percent per annum.[62] State-run industries sprang up, and by 1969 more than 80 public sector manufacturing works had been established, producing paper, steel, cement, chemicals, dairy foods, cigarettes, ovens, and clothing.[63] Combined with the state's takeover of the major industries of the colonial period, such as the phosphate mining sector which was progressively nationalised after 1956, the new regime had now established itself in a commanding position in the economy.

In Egypt, since 1958 part of the United Arab Republic with Syria, 1961 too marked the adoption of a set of 'Socialist Decrees' establishing state control over banking and major industries, while in agriculture the small peasant farmers who had received ownership of their land during the agrarian reforms of 1952 were re-organised into state-run cooperatives. In contrast to the experience of state capitalism in the Soviet Union in the 1930s, where the 'leap' made by the Stalinist bureaucracy involved the driving down of workers' living standards in the context of a huge rise in the rate of exploitation, the urban working class was one of the beneficiaries of the redistributive effect of the state-led growth.[64] The nationalisation of foreign and local private capital was supplemented by foreign loans, including funding from the USSR. Between 1960 and 1966, overall industrial production doubled in value, while annual rates of GDP growth soared to 6 percent and a million new jobs were created.[65]

However, weaknesses in the import-substitution model of industrialisation became apparent during the second Five Year Plan which launched in 1965. Unable to earn enough foreign

61 Bennoune, 1979; Bellin, 2002.
62 Bennoune, 1979, p237.
63 Bellin, 2002, p21.
64 Alexander & Bassiouny, 2014; Mabro & Radwan, 1976, p144; Cliff, 1996.
65 Beinin, 2010, p12.

Revolution is the choice of the people

exchange to prevent a balance of payments crisis and failing to raise capital for further investment from internal sources, the regime found itself negotiating with international lenders for loans, while implementing an austerity programme which forced down workers' wages and lengthened working hours.[66] Calamitous military defeat at the hands of Israel in 1967 broke the regime's resolve and after Nasser's early death in 1970, his successor Anwar al-Sadat embarked on a process of *infitah* "opening" to the West which initiated the turn towards neoliberalism and geopolitical realignment with the USA. Over the following years, Sadat liberalised foreign trade, encouraged private sector imports, reformed the banking sector, reorganised public sector manufacturing and began to encourage private sector growth.[67] These economic changes were intertwined with military realignment from 'East' to 'West'. War against Israel in 1973 had restored some of the battered reputation of the Egyptian armed forces after 1967, which Sadat sought to use to strengthen his bargaining position as he prepared to negotiate entry into the ranks of US military allies.

Bourguiba and the now rebranded "Socialist" ruling party in Tunisia essentially abandoned the state capitalist experiment in 1969. Strong resistance to the regime's agricultural policies from the stratum of prosperous farmers in the coastal regions who were now a key element of the regime's social base was a major factor.[68] And the import-substitution policies in industry also ran into difficulties: following a pattern familiar across the region the leap into state-capitalism was accompanied by a worsening balance of trade (imports of industrial inputs and machinery grew faster than exports), a fiscal crisis reflecting the imbalance between a small tax base and ambitious development plans, and a general lack of investment capital.[69] Bourguiba appointed Hedi Nouira as Prime Minister to oversee another dramatic shift in economic policy, this time focussing on the development of an export-oriented manufacturing and agricultural strategy with private capital at its heart.[70]

This pattern of a relatively brief turn towards state

---

66 Wahdat al-Dirasat, 1999; Richards & Waterbury, 2008, p189.
67 Waterbury, 1985, p70.
68 Bennoune, 1979, p237–39.
69 Bellin, 2002, p23; Richards and Waterbury, 2008.
70 Bellin, 2002, p26–27.

capitalist import-substitution policies was repeated in other countries in the region which went through a further wave of military coups led by 'revolutionary' colonels in Syria, Libya, Iraq and Sudan. In Syria the ejection of the colonial power—France—was accomplished relatively early but dislodging the 'old social classes' proved more difficult to achieve. Following the breakdown of the union with Egypt in 1961, the Ba'ath Party took power for the first time in 1963. Yet another coup in 1966 brought a more radical faction of the Ba'th to power. Led by Salah Jadid, the new regime pushed quickly ahead with a programme of deepening state capitalist intervention, including reforms to the education system and massive state investment in infrastructure and industry. However, the catastrophe of military defeat by the Israelis in 1967, which saw Syria lose control of the Golan Heights, opened the door to a counter-attack by the party's right wing. Defence Minister Hafez al-Assad deposed Jadid and his supporters in 1970.

The Ba'th Party was also firmly ensconced in power in Iraq by the end of the 1960s, a position it would not relinquish until the US invasion of 2003. The 1970s was a period of rapid industrialisation powered by the sharp rise in state oil revenues following the nationalisation of the oil industry and the success of OPEC in breaking the international price-setting cartel's monopoly in 1972-3. This increased government oil revenue from $1 billion in 1972 to $8.2 billion in 1975 provided the financial means to invest in infrastructure, industry and services, modernise and expand the military and build up foreign reserves.[71]

Oil also powered the "socialist revolution" from above launched by Houari Boumediène in Algeria, another member of OPEC. Through the development of an import-substitution industrialisation strategy the state became the primary vehicle for investment in industry, creating large, vertically-integrated manufacturing combines in capital intensive sectors such as steel, heavy machinery, iron metallurgy, organic and inorganic chemicals.[72] The transformation of the Algerian economy was startling, economic growth rates were high and the urban working class expanded rapidly, however it was underpinned by the enormous boost to the state's revenues from the

---

71 Alnasrawi, 1992, p335.
72 Del Panta, 2020.

Revolution is the choice of the people

nationalised hydrocarbon industry following the "oil shock" price rises of the early 1970s.

The transformation of Algerian industry was meant to be complemented by a parallel process in agriculture, through policies of nationalisation and the creation of state cooperatives. However, by the end of the 1970s, increasingly serious problems were beginning to emerge. The huge industrial combines persistently made losses, and unbalanced growth with the regime's penchant for spending on iconic heavy industries exacerbating the problem.[73] Despite the windfall of hydrocarbon revenues, the national debt had soared reaching over 70 percent of GDP in 1978.[74] Boumediène died suddenly in 1978, leaving the man chosen by the military establishment to succeed him as president, Chadli Benjedid, free to initiate a process of realignment with the emerging global orthodoxy of neoliberalism.

In Libya and Sudan too, revolutionary colonels seized power at the very end of the 1960s. Mu'ammar al-Qadhafi led a coterie of junior army officers in overthrowing King Idris of Libya in September 1969. Libya's monarchy was weaker and more recent than the others in the region, having been installed in 1951 following the dismantling of the Italian colony in the wake of the defeat of the fascist government in the Second World War. For the first few years of his reign, King Idris had presided as absolute monarch over an impoverished society, which had been deeply scarred by the experience of colonial rule. The discovery of oil in the 1960s changed the fortunes of the country overnight. In 1961 oil revenues were $6 million, but by 1968 the state budget had swelled to over $1 billion.[75] In 1973, as al-Qadhafi surfaced as the undisputed leader of the Revolutionary Command Council governing Libya, the new regime embarked on another "revolution from above".

Rather than follow the text-book state capitalist approach, al-Qadhafi coined a new set of terms for his idiosyncratic brand of "socialism", renaming Libya as a "Jamahiriyya", or state of the masses, where ordinary people would rule directly. Over the next few years the new regime, its coffers overflowing with oil revenues, embarked on an ambitious programme of "popular" management in industry, nationalisation of large parts of the

---

73 Del Panta, 2020.
74 IMF, 2106.
75 US Department of State, 1969.

country's housing stock, trading and commercial establishments and agricultural land.[76]

Meanwhile in Sudan, although there was no oil to power this kind of rapid transformation, nevertheless, the junior army officers led by Ja'afar al-Nimeiri who took power in 1969 brought in Soviet experts to develop a Five Year Plan which launched in 1970 following decrees nationalising banks, industries producing "strategic commodities", manufacturing and import-export companies.[77]

Despite significant ideological differences between the Zionist and Arab nationalist state-building projects, it is important to note that the overall shape of the state institutions which emerged in Israel and their relationship both to capital accumulation and the delivery of public services was in many ways very similar. With its growing military-industrial-service complex evolving side-by-side with a nationalist, state-operated "trade union" movement (the Histadrut) which was also a huge provider of basic welfare to the Jewish population and one of the country's largest employers, Israel in the state capitalist era had more in common with the "Arab Socialist" regimes which surrounded it than many cared to admit. As we will see in the next chapter, one of the key differences, however, was that the Israeli ruling class was much more successful in using its privileged military relationship with the US in order to leap economically ahead of its rivals and embed itself higher up the international economic hierarchy of states.

Political and ideological legacy of the state capitalist era

The uneven, but intense, process of economic and social transformation experienced during the state capitalist era in the countries which attempted to make a 'leap' towards import-substitution industrialisation was accompanied by political changes which left an even deeper legacy. In fact, most of the regimes discussed here clung onto the political institutions created at the height of the state capitalist experiment in some form or other deep into the process of neoliberal 'reform'. The

---

76 Vandewalle, 2012, p108–9.
77 Niblock, 1987, p244.

persistence of political institutions from the state capitalist era into a period when the ruling class had aligned its strategies of capital accumulation with the neoliberal orthodoxy became an important element adding to the combustibility of the amalgam of social and political forms which exploded in revolutionary uprisings. This was an important contradiction. The ruling classes of the USSR's allies in Eastern Europe had faced a similarly unpleasant set of political choices as the decline of the Soviet Union and the terminal crisis of the bureaucratic state capitalist model of development became more apparent in the late 1980s and 1990s, forcing them to adopt neoliberal economic policies. Unlike them however, most of the ruling parties of the state capitalist regimes of the Middle East avoided anything but the most superficial political reforms, exposing as hollow the claim by apologists for 'structural adjustment' that the free market would necessarily bring other kinds of 'freedom' in its wake.[78]

However, it is also important to acknowledge that these regimes did not simply rely on coercion in order to rule. The ideological legacy of the bargains they struck with parts of the workers' movement and the Stalinist Communist Parties in order to stabilise their rule had long-lasting effects not just inside the institutions of the state but also outside them, shaping the terrain on which opposition from below reconstituted itself both before and during the revolutions.

One of the first tasks of the new regimes after taking power was usually to demobilise, often by force, the insurgent and angry masses of ordinary people whose own actions had raised their hopes that revolution would lead to greater political freedoms and a serious redistribution of wealth. The new regimes were faced with a difficult choice: should they attempt to coerce the old ruling class and sections of foreign capital into ceding some of their economic power through policies of land reform and nationalisation of their assets in the hope that this would create enough wealth to satisfy the demands for social change from

---

78 This should not be taken as a suggestion that liberal democratic regimes emerged from the Eastern European revolutions of 1989—clearly this did not happen—but that the old ruling parties agreed a process of political transition with opposition forces. In Poland, for example, negotiations with the trade union Solidarity in early 1989 led to the formation of a new government and presidential elections which were won by Lech Walesa, Solidarity's leader in 1990.

below? How could they contain that process without unleashing social forces they could not control?

Adopting an ideology and institutions which could be labelled as 'socialist' often proved to be an effective way to square this circle for many of the regimes discussed here. Workers, peasants and the poor could be mobilised politically against the old ruling classes and exploited more effectively in the factories and fields under the banner of a 'transition to socialism'. The creation of mass ruling parties, bureaucratic trade unions and peasant cooperatives could contain grievances and frustrations within safe limits, and also act as conduits for the redistribution of some of the growing national wealth back downwards. Meanwhile, the regimes deployed intense repression against anyone who attempted to organise politically or socially outside these new frameworks. The enthusiasm of the new regimes for 'socialism' was driven by a conjuncture of external and internal pressures on them to solve fundamental obstacles to independent capital accumulation. Sometimes this propelled them into actual conflict with the major imperialist powers. At other times their language of 'Third World' radicalism and 'anti-imperialism' was useful camouflage for internal repression and shoddy compromises with external powers. This was a variant of what Hal Draper called 'socialism from above', which had nothing to do with 'socialism from below',[79] as a strategy by the exploited and oppressed to build a fairer and more equal society for all.

A crucial role in this process was played by the Communist movement. Some of the Communist Parties of the region had become significant organisations with genuine roots in the mass movements of the era. They had survived years of repression by the colonial authorities, including jail and torture, and traumas such as the public execution of Iraqi Communist Party General Secretary Fahd in Baghdad in 1948 in revenge for the party's role in the popular uprising of the same year. In many of the countries discussed here, Communist groups had succeeded in putting down some roots in the most combative and strategically important sections of the working class. These included rail, port and oil workers in Iraq, where party activists played key roles in leading major strikes.

The Sudanese Communist Party was central to the first strike in Sudanese history, the epic battle by railworkers in 1946

---

79 Draper, 1966.

against the British-controlled railway administration. In Bahrain, the Communist Party recruited among oil workers. In Syria too, the Communist Party's industrial base was concentrated among textile workers. Egypt, with the largest population and largest working class in the region had a long history of Communist activism, and several competing Communist organisations emerged in the 1940s, before uniting in the mid-1950s. As elsewhere in the region, the Egyptian communist movement did attract some of the most impressive working-class militants of the day, and it had gained experience in leading and supporting the mass strikes of the turbulent years in the run-up to the Free Officers' coup in 1952.

However, the outcomes of the anti-colonial revolutions posed a severe political test for the Communist movement. There were two major problems. The first was their broad acceptance of a theoretical framework which assumed that the level of social development in the Middle East, and the small size of the working class in particular, limited the character of the revolution to a struggle to establish independent, capitalist republics against the colonial powers and what Communist activists often termed the 'feudal' landowning classes.

According to one version of this perspective, such revolutions could not expand into social revolts against capitalism. This meant in effect deferring leadership of the mass movements against the colonial state to other social and political forces—specifically the nationalists—and retreating at the moment of victory into the role of a loyal opposition to the new regimes. Somewhat paradoxically, however, the geostrategic needs of the Soviet Union for allies in the Cold War, then precipitated a volte-face by local Communists. Having said that a socialist revolution was impossible in the short or medium term, they then somersaulted to claim that in fact it had *already happened*, and that the nationalist regimes were in fact building socialist societies.

The second problem was that all of the Communist organisations of the region were bound ideologically and organisationally to the Communist Party of the Soviet Union, and the larger and more important ones subjected to direct intervention by the Soviet leadership in their decision-making processes. These two problems had common roots, of course. The theoretical framework which separated the democratic

The short state capitalist era and its long legacy

and socialist stages played a key role in preparing the ground for Stalin's rise to power in the mid-1920s, leading the Chinese Communist Party to disaster in the failed revolution of 1925-7. The consolidation of the Stalinist state bureaucracy during the 1930s and 1940s naturally affected Communist Parties around the world. They came under inescapable pressure to align their actions not with the actual needs of building revolutionary movements in their own countries, but with the best interests of the Soviet ruling class.

For Communists in the Middle East, this led to political and organisational contortions which had tragic and long-lasting results. The first instinct of the new nationalist regimes on coming into power was often to repress Communist organisations, however, at they moved closer into the orbit of the Soviet Union on the geopolitical stage, the Soviet leadership began to exert increasing pressure on local Communist activists to throw themselves uncritically behind the new ruling parties' drive towards a 'socialist' economy, even from the prison cells where they had been tortured and imprisoned.

The co-option of the Communist movement took an even deeper turn in several of the countries discussed here with the consummation of formal 'national front' agreements (again generally at the urging of Moscow) between the ruling nationalist parties (by now usually having attached 'socialist' to their names) and the Communist Party. These arrangements usually gave the CP the status of a junior partner in the regime, giving it a legal presence and its members access to privileged positions in the state bureaucracy, including in some cases posts in government. The turn towards overt collaboration with the nationalist regimes did provoke debates inside the Communist movement, with a minority of activists rejecting Moscow's orders and continuing to maintain the need for independent (and therefore illegal) organisation. However, the wider damage to the prestige of Communism as a voice for the exploited and oppressed was long-lasting and helps to explain why when the state capitalist regimes themselves entered new rounds of social and political crisis, it was Islamist organisations rather than the left which appeared to represent the authentic voice of popular opposition and resistance.

153

Conclusion

Despite their rhetorical commitment to 'socialism' ruling classes which formed around the state bureaucracies of the region were capitalist ruling classes. Moreover, , even this rhetorical commitment was always conditioned by their balancing act between the superpowers. However, the changes wrought by the leap towards import-substitution industrialisation were real, even if the commitment to it at the top was short-lived. One of the long-term legacies in some of the countries discussed here was the creation of an industrial working class concentrated in the large public-sector manufacturing plants which were often the jewel-in-the-crown of the state-led industrialisation projects. Other persistent legacies included the long-lasting political impact of the alliance between the Stalinist Communist Parties and the ruling nationalist elites, which left the field clear for Islamist organisations to position themselves as the authentic voice of popular discontent once the crisis hit. In the event, the re-emergence of that crisis was brutally swift. The 'socialist' experiments of the states without significant oil revenues to bolster their spending generally lasted little more than one Five Year Plan, before the regimes lost their nerve and began to look for ways to signal their desire to align themselves with the emerging global orthodoxy of neoliberalism.

Chapter 6
Neoliberalism: a realignment of the state and capital

The crisis which brought the 'Long Boom' of Western capitalism to a shuddering halt during the 1970s led to huge changes both at the centre of the global economy and in the regions of the periphery. These policies would eventually be labelled 'neoliberalism': the shifts in economic policy and practice subsumed under this convenient label included both successes and failures from the point of view of the ruling classes of the Middle East and North Africa. On the positive side of the balance sheet, with the exception of Iran, where the crisis at the end of the 1970s resulted in a political revolution leading to the creation of a new ruling class they all rode out the storms of popular protest against the first round of economic reforms designed to pass on the costs of the crisis to the poor. This paved the way for deeper changes, in most cases carried out through the framework of the "structural adjustment programmes" demanded by the World Bank and the International Monetary Fund, using the leverage of the massive debts accumulated to the international lenders during the 1970s and early 1980s.

Unlike the Soviet Union and allied regimes in Eastern Europe, the state capitalist regimes of the Middle East and North Africa did face major political restructuring, but generally were able to manage the introduction of neoliberal reforms through the existing ruling parties and state institutions.[80] This led to the development of a hybrid model of what Sameh Naguib has called "real-existing neoliberalism."[81] The state bourgeoisie of the previous era opened space in the economy and inside the regime and state institutions to the private sector bourgeoisie. Sometimes this consisted of a younger generation of the 'old' landlord and merchant ruling class from the colonial era, but more often it involved new layers of private capitalists whose businesses were incubated inside the state. In quite a few cases, this was literally a family affair, with the sons and daughters of senior figures in the state bourgeoisie (senior officials and top generals in the army and secret police) launching lucrative careers in the private sector thanks to their parent's contacts. Even those ruling classes which oversaw the tearing apart of the countries they ruled through civil war benefitted—creaming off huge fortunes from the desolations they created through seizing control of extractive industries, the import-export trade, and the 'reconstruction' of bombed and blasted urban centres.

Looked at from the perspective of their position in the global hierarchy of capitalist development, the region's encounter with neoliberalism produced few "winners" or even "contenders." Abandoning import-substitution industrialisation in favour of the export-led manufacturing strategies promoted by the advocates of neoliberalism did not lead to the replication of the success associated with East Asian capitalist economies such as South Korea and Taiwan. Instead, it subjected key industries such as textiles to ruthless competition and drove them further down the global production chain. Another key tenet of neoliberal development strategy involved opening 'closed' markets to foreign trade. However, most of the countries discussed here experienced a flood of imported foreign goods which further weakened local industries.

Agricultural reforms pushed small farmers off the land, and locked export-oriented agribusinesses into relationships with richer states bearing uncanny similarities to the extractive,

---

80 This does not mean that the old ruling classes of the Soviet Union and its satellite were overthrown, or that entirely new political regimes emerged—but the degree of political change was much more significant than in the Middle East and North Africa
81 Naguib, 2011b.

plantation economy model of the colonial era, while food security and ecological sustainability were dramatically weakened. By the end of four decades of neoliberal reform, the weaker links in the regional economy had become even more vulnerable to revolt from below. Meanwhile the backwash from the shocks at the centre of the global economy was intensified by the intense oscillations in the global price of oil which followed the breaking up of the state capitalist oil cartel of the major Western powers.

This chapter will explore what the turn towards neoliberalism meant for the ruling classes of the region from two different perspectives. Firstly, we will look at neoliberalism as a process of reconfiguration *within* the ruling class driven by the varying levels of success with which they attempted to find their niche in the shifting global circuits of capital accumulation. Secondly, we will consider how neoliberalism affected processes of differentiation *between* the ruling classes of the region. We will look specifically at the rise of a new, independent centre of capital accumulation in the Gulf which was one the outcomes of the shift to oil-powered fossil capitalism mapped out in Chapter 4. The Gulf states were not the region's only rising economic power of the neoliberal era however, and we will also analyse the economic trajectories of Turkey and Israel, as well as looking at how the ruling class of the Islamic Republic of Iran survived multiple crises to re-emerge as an important military and economic contender in the race to dominate the region.

Defining neoliberalism

At heart of the neoliberal turn lay a transformation in the role of the state in the economy and society. Broadly speaking, this involved a shift towards a focus on its role as facilitation and organisation of capital accumulation and a relative reduction in direct production or provision of services. This was never about the retreat or downgrading of the state's power, however. As Sameh Naguib notes:

> The policies of neoliberalism were never about dismantling or even reducing the role of the state in the economy but rather about increasing the role of the state as facilitator of capitalist profit-making at

the expense of the working class. This created an even more intimate relation between state and capital.[82]

The state's role in creating laws and coercive policies to enact this process remained just as important as ever, , particularly in relation to overcoming resistance from the working class and the poor to the devastating changes wreaked in welfare systems and employment as a result of neoliberal policies. However, it would be a mistake to see the state under neoliberalism as simply managing the overall conditions aimed at restoring profitability after the crisis. Just as during the state capitalist era, individual states continued to intervene actively in the process of accumulation in a host of different ways. These included attempting to woo foreign investors, creating opportunities for profit-making for 'its' private capitalists and foreign capitals by directly commissioning massive infrastructure projects under hire purchase arrangements, organising the sale of public assets through privatisation as well as selling 'intangible' assets such as telecoms licences. Naturally this was (and remains) a highly competitive process, with some states (and some capitals) doing much better than others and using plenty of extra-economic mechanisms to press home their advantage, including military action. Finally, when the neoliberal recipe turned out to be inadequate to save either local or global economies from a resumption of crisis, private capitalists relied on its support to bail them out.

This helps to explain why despite the ideological offensive by the apologists for neoliberalism against the idea of 'big government' and the public sector more generally, there was no return to the minimalist, 'night watchman' type state of the previous 'liberal' era of capitalism during neoliberalism. In economies on the periphery of the global system, private capital had been weak to start with, thanks to the impact of colonialism, and the state was thus even more central in the first phases of independent capitalist development. Unsurprisingly, it remained a 'bloated' presence in society thereafter, and even the most determined and destructive efforts to 'slim down' its institutions through 'shock doctrines' of neoliberal reform imposed from outside generally had the opposite effect to what their proposers intended.

---

82 Naguib, 2011b, p5.

Neoliberalism: a realignment of the state and capital

A new amalgam of state and private capital

The neoliberal era thus saw important changes in the symbiotic relationship between state and private capitals in the Middle East, including a rebalancing of their weights in the ruling class as a whole. This process sometimes involved squabbles over the terms of the transition, which occasionally spilled over into direct conflict. However, there was no fundamental or irresolvable contradiction between the interests of the bourgeoisie which had formed around the state during the previous era and the bourgeoisie of the neoliberal era. Labelling the process of neoliberal reform as a "counter-revolution",[83] is misleading because it obscures the degree to which the private bourgeoisie was incubated by the state bourgeoisie. The history of neoliberalism in the Middle East underscores the fact that the ruling class as a whole, both the parts directly connected to the state, and their private counterparts, were jointly responsible for the misery heaped on ordinary people by their acceptance of Thatcher's mantra: "there is no alternative".

In Tunisia, Prime Minister Hedi Nouira was an early proponent of this strategy after the purging of Ahmed Ben Salah and the abandonment of his "socialist" experiment. The abrupt about-turn in economic policy reflected a combination of pressures from inside and outside Tunisia. The private sector farmers of the coastal regions, who had supported the ruling Neo-Destour Party in its battle for independence from France revolted against the state's intervention in agriculture, providing one of the internal impetuses behind the neoliberal turn. However, it was not the case that the pre-existing private sector bourgeoisie could fulfil the role expected of it in driving forward capitalist economic development in 1970 any more than it could in 1960. After all, it was the chronic weakness of the indigenous private sector bourgeoisie which had prompted the desperate turn towards the state in the first place. Rather the state bourgeoisie worked to nurture private-sector industrial, commercial and agrarian enterprises geared towards finding Tunisia's niche in the changing global market. At first the policy seemed to enjoy remarkable success in stimulating industrial development: growth rates shot up as more than 800 new industrial establishments were created, doubling the country's

---

83 Dumenil & Levy, 2005.

industrial capacity.[84] Yet once again, within ten years, the polarisation of wealth and poverty that these policies created helped to touch off a major revolt by the working class, propelling the ruling party into confrontation with the UGTT which called a general strike in January 1978.[85] There were also major episodes of urban protest such as the "bread riots" of December 1983-4. Fierce repression ensured that the regime survived into the 1980s, but the collapse of global oil prices in the mid-1980s prompted a major debt crisis towards the end of the decade.

The debt crisis, and the removal from power of "president-for-life" Bourguiba in a "medical coup" by Zein-al-Din Ben Ali in 1987 paved the way for intensification of neoliberal policies. The textile sector, an important component of the country's industrial base, accounting for 55 percent of manufactured exports and 47 percent of industrial labour in the late 1990s, was forced to compete on the global market, after signing bilateral agreements with the European Community in 1995 which effectively removed the preferential access to European markets that Tunisian textile products had enjoyed since the 1970s.[86] The insertion of Tunisian textile production into the new global division of labour put severe pressure on the industry , pulling apart the spinning, weaving and garment production sectors, as local thread producers could not compete with much cheaper spinners in East Asia.

Over almost exactly the same period, Egypt's ruling class went through a comparable process of restructuring from within. The sudden death of Nasser in 1970 was followed by a brief power struggle within the regime and the consolidation of the rule of the man who succeeded him: Anwar al-Sadat. Under Sadat, Egypt partially lifted restrictions on trade, liberalised some aspects of the banking system and allowed the growth of networks of private sector companies in parasitical relationships with public-sector enterprises. The last of these provided some of the most visible signs of the growing power of the *infitah bourgeoisie*, typified by the spectacular rise of figures such as Osman Ahmed Osman, who built a business empire which had expanded to 200 companies and 26 banks by 1986. At the heart of this network was the public-sector Arab

---

84 Bellin, 2002, p26–27.
85 Disney, 1978.
86 Cammett, 1999/2000, p34.

Neoliberalism: a realignment of the state and capital

Contractors Company, which had been nationalised between 1961-64 but the expanded Osman group had interests in food-processing, agro-industry, banking, insurance, real estate, building materials, construction and engineering.[87]

Unlike Tunisia, the Egyptian military as an institution played a significant role in this process of reconfiguration of the ruling class. Managers in khaki had inserted themselves into senior positions across public sector industry during the state capitalist period, but the relative decline of that part of the economy prompted the adoption of a new strategy. Muhammad Abdel-Halim Abu-Ghazala, Minister of Defence under Sadat's successor Hosni Mubarak was one of the architects of the transformation of the top ranks of the military from managers of state capitals on behalf of the whole bourgeoisie into a role which combined the direction of private-sector businesses of their own, with a kind of corporate interest in managing the economic affairs of the military institution itself, quite often in direct competition with other state and private capitals. Under Abu-Ghazala, the Armed Forces expanded its business empire in manufacturing, food production, agriculture and land reclamation, construction and services.[88] By 1986 the military-owned National Service Projects Organisation accounted for 18 percent of the total value of food production in Egypt.[89] Abu-Ghazala also played a key role in attracting foreign investment in manufacturing sectors, such as car production, with the aim of inserting Egyptian industries into the new internationalised production chains emerging in the neoliberal era.[90] During later decades, Abu-Ghazala's successors would continue to offer themselves as partners to international investors, through joint ventures in strategic sectors such as energy, transport and communications.

By the 2000s that increasingly meant partnering with Gulf-based capitalists.[91] The Economic Reform and Structural Adjustment Programme (ERSAP) agreed between the Mubarak regime and the international financial institutions in return for a partial debt write-off launched a new phase in the neoliberal transformation of the economy. It created a legal framework

---

87 Vitalis, 1986.
88 Springborg, 1989, p107.
89 Springborg, 1989, p113.
90 Springborg, 1989, p110.
91 Marshall and Stacher, 2012.

for privatisation and saw the setting up of public "holding companies". The overall strategy was to break down the integration between public sector firms and create opportunities for new partnerships between state and private capital at local, regional and transnational levels.

The year 1970 also marked the moment when Syria's state bourgeoisie, under the leadership of Hafez al-Assad embarked on the decades-long process of rebuilding the private sector and re-opening the ranks of the ruling class to a broader coalition. The catastrophe of military defeat by the Israelis in 1967, which saw Syria lose control of the Golan Heights, had opened the door to a coup against the architects of Syria's state socialist experiment. The stability of the Assad regime before the revolution of 2011 was rooted in a long-term compromise between the old and new exploiters: the urban commercial and landowning elite which had prospered under the Mandate and the first years of independence and the bourgeoisie which owed its wealth and power to control of the state apparatus. In making his "Corrective Revolution" of 1970 against Salah Jadid, Al-Assad created a route back to wealth and power for a significant section of the Sunni bourgeoisie and this represented a crucial stabilising feature of his regime, which withstood the pressure of a Sunni Islamist revolt in the late 1970s and early 1980s. The foundations of Assad's economic strategy were laid in the 1970s: the state would take the lead in creating new industries with bought-in expertise and equipment but the aim was to also create spaces in which the private sector would grow. High oil prices and external subsidies initially spurred industrial growth and the development of a range of industries from fertiliser production to paper milling. Many of the major industrial projects suffered from inefficiency and corruption, with the main beneficiaries being the sections of the state bourgeoisie which oversaw their construction.

The rise of new regional powers

Neoliberalism provided opportunities for the ruling classes of every country to reconfigure themselves around changes in the circuitry of accumulation at both regional and global levels. However, it is crucial to recognise that not all of them benefitted equally from this process and that it is also possible to indicate

Neoliberalism: a realignment of the state and capital

'winners' and 'losers' in the brutal competition *between* the states and capitals of the region. But before doing that we will provide a brief sketch of three ruling classes which emerged from the neoliberal period as relatively stronger in both economic and military terms than the vast majority of their rivals: those of the Gulf states, Turkey and Israel. We will also look at the surprising recovery of the Iranian ruling class to a position of regional influence after the catastrophic defeat in the war with Iraq in 1988 despite the continued hostility of the United States.

Such periods of confidence and growth in the ability of any ruling class to project its power beyond its borders are more than not short-lived, and Iran and Turkey are no exception to this. The economic growth which underpinned the reassertion of Iranian military and diplomatic authority on a regional scale went into reverse in 2012. By 2020, Iran's GDP had fallen to around a third of 2012 levels as a result of the combined pressures of tightened US sanctions and the impact of the Covid 19 pandemic. Turkey's GDP has also contracted significantly since 2013. Meanwhile, Egypt's economic growth trends after a period of comparatively weaker and sluggish development in the 2000s have accelerated again. Egypt's total GDP overtook Iran's for the first time in over 50 years in 2019.

The rising and falling fortunes of the regional powers cannot of course simply be read from crude measures such as total GDP. At the time of writing in 2022, Iran remains a much more influential regional power in the military sense than Egypt (despite the Egyptian army's access to lavish funding from its US patron). Yet the trends these figures show do matter. The more the gap between Iran's military capability and the underlying health of the country's economy widens, the greater the risks of being overtaken by a competitor.

One of the features of the neoliberal period has been the 'coming-of-age' of the regional powers as effective agents in the process of counter-revolution. By and large, their effectiveness in this respect is a reflection of their ability to create favourable conditions for capital accumulation within and beyond their own borders. As we will see, in three out of four cases discussed here, this has been achieved in economic and military partnership with powers at the heart of the global economy, specifically with the United States and the major EU states.

The Iranian ruling class, for its part, forged a military

alliance with Russia and developed significant economic ties with China. A further point is worth mentioning here: none of the regional powers discussed here therefore exactly followed the prescriptions in the neoliberal reform agenda which were imposed on the weaker states of the region through the process of structural adjustment. Moreover, two of them—the Gulf States and Israel—have relied for decades on systems of labour control which involve systematic denial of citizenship rights to a very large proportion of their workforces. The spectacular rise of a powerful new centre of capital accumulation in the Gulf is predicated on the systematic abuse of migrant workers while Israel's economic success over the last three decades is rooted in an exclusionary system to first control, and then dispossess, Palestinian workers, followed by the importation of a new migrant labour force from South and East Asia.

As Adam Hanieh notes, the rise of a tightly-connected group of capitals in the Gulf states has shaped the circuits of capital accumulation across the much wider region.[92] The role and nature of Gulf capital in the Gulf itself and beyond are shaped by three distinctive processes. The first of these is the formation of a migrant labour force within the Gulf. The initial waves of migrant workers came from elsewhere in the Arab world but have since been systematically replaced largely by workers from India and Bangladesh. The Gulf's magnetic pull on workers from these countries has been enormously strong: by 2002 some 95 percent of Bangladeshi overseas workers were in the Gulf. By 2007, 95 percent of all Indian labour outflows were to the same destination.[93] Lacking basic rights and vulnerable to all kinds of abuses by employers and the state, the sweat of these "disposable" workforces makes the ascent of Gulf capital to the dazzling heights of the global elite possible.

Secondly, as the Gulf's migrant working class began to form, so too did a local capitalist class, Hanieh argues. While the early phases of its development did indeed begin with the kind of royal gift-giving that appeared to belong to a "patrimonial" pre-capitalist era, over time giant capitalist conglomerates emerged spanning different circuits of capital accumulation in production, the circulation of commodities and finance.[94]

92 Hanieh, 2013, p123.
93 Hanieh, 2013, p125.
94 Hanieh, 2013, p132.

Neoliberalism: a realignment of the state and capital

In the Gulf production is centred on oil and petrochemicals, as well as other commodities requiring massive inputs of energy such as aluminium, steel and concrete. The commodity circuit is focused on luxury goods and shopping malls—estimated to generate around $30 billion in sales annually by the late 2000s.[95] The financial circuit has been increasingly dominated by large private equity firms that gather the richest of the rich to gamble on the international markets and buy into profitable firms.

Finally, Gulf capital has been shaped by a rapid process of internationalisation. This process is very closely tied with the deepening of neoliberal economic reforms. Gulf investors were involved in deals representing 37 percent of the total value of all privatisations in Egypt between 2000 and 2008.[96] By the mid-2010s Egyptian agribusiness and agriculture were thoroughly penetrated by Gulf capital through control of the country's largest dairy farm, largest packaged milk business, largest pasta producers, largest publicly-listed flour mill and companies controlling 50 percent of the commercial poultry market. Egyptian and Gulf capital became more intimately intertwined, for example through joint participation in private equity firms such as Citadel Capital, which brought together some of Egypt's biggest private capitalists with representatives of leading Saudi business groups, a UAE sovereign wealth fund, and the Qatari royal family. The nature of the Gulf partners in Capital underscores a general point that emerges forcefully from Hanieh's analysis of Gulf capital: the difficulty in separating "private" from "state" capital, thanks to the interpenetration of the capitalist class with the government bureaucracy.[97]

The interwoven processes of capital accumulation and class formation in the Gulf were shaped by and contributed to the neoliberal turn in the world economy. They helped to cement US hegemony by ensuring oil markets operate in dollars, recycled the same petrodollars through European and US banks allowing their conversion into new forms of debt bondage for the Global South, preparing the ground for a new wave of assaults on the living standards of the majority through privatisation and "structural adjustment' during the 1990s and accelerating trends towards the financialisation of

---

95 Hanieh, 2013, p135.
96 Hanieh, 2013, p138.
97 Hanieh, 2013, p141.

Revolution is the choice of the people

capital across the system.[98]

The Gulf states were not the only powers in the region to emerge as relative 'winners' compared to their neighbours from the period of neoliberal restructuring. For the first two decades of the 21st century, Turkey's economy was the largest in the region in absolute terms, although a steep downward trajectory since 2013 put Saudi Arabia on track to overtake in size in 2020. Turkey's rapid development was all the more striking, given that the country has to import 90 percent of its oil and gas needs. Underlying the economic growth since the year 2000 has been expansion of manufacturing, with smaller industrial producers benefitting most particularly those based in the provinces rather than the traditional 'big business' sector based in Ankara and Istanbul. The expansion of provincial and small-to-medium-sized industrial capital has had significant political effects and is one of the factors which explains the ability of the AKP under Erdogan's leadership to withstand the pressures from sections of the Turkish state and big business which object to the AKP's Islamist politics and have consistently organised to curtail access by those with an Islamist worldview to the levers of power.[99]

The AKP's electoral success during the 2000s is also likely to be related to Turkey's strong economic growth with the percentage of the population living below the national poverty line declining from 28.8 percent in 2003 to 1.6 percent in 2014.[100] While obviously these statistics hide continued social inequality, and growth in manufacturing seems to have been concentrated in lower-wage, more 'informal' enterprises with relatively lower levels of productivity, the sense that an Islamist government has delivered 'prosperity' for a relatively wide section of the population helped to hold thee deeply contradictory social base of the AKP together. The party retained support in working class and poor constituencies while at the same time relating to an increasingly assertive and wealthy section of Turkish capital historically organised through the Independent Industrialists' and Businessmen's Association (MÜSİAD).

The fate of the Turkish "economic miracle" of the last decade and a half remains inextricably linked, however, to the dynamics of geopolitical competition in the region and beyond. Turkey's

---

98 Hanieh, 2011, p 47.
99 Achcar, 2013; Margulies, 2016.
100 OECD, 2018, p18.

position as the gateway to the world for the oil of northern Iraq means that the Turkish ruling class had much at stake in the question of who governs Kirkuk and Mosul (and both cities have become important export markets for Turkish goods). Turkey's eastern border also connects with Iran, which overtook Iraq as the largest crude oil supplier to Turkey during 2018.[101]

The fact that the Kurdish majority population on the Turkish side of the border with Iraq has been subject to severe repression since the foundation of the Turkish state has long been a complicating factor in Turkey's relations with Iraq. During the 2000s the Turkish ruling class balanced these contradictions by pursuing a policy of a long-term peace process designed to end the insurgency led by the Kurdistan Workers' Party (PKK) within Turkey, while at the same time restricting the PKK's ability to use neighbouring countries as either a military hinterland or a source of diplomatic and political support. This was one reason behind the Turkish government's strong relationship with the Assad regime in Syria (the opening of Syrian markets to Turkish exports was of course another), and the surprisingly cordial relations between Turkey and the Kurdistan Regional Government in Erbil (which is led by the Kurdistan Democratic Party, no friend of the PKK).

The persistence of the Islamic Republic

Iran has long been an important player in the political economy of the region—and with the rise of capitalism, desire to control the country's oil and gas reserves spurred intervention by competing imperialist powers. In fact it was the discovery of oil there in 1908 by a British prospector that triggered the race to carve up the Middle East's oil reserves between the European colonial powers, with Britain taking the leading role in staking a claim to Iran's own oil fields.[102] However, in contrast to the Gulf, agriculture has also played a crucial role in integrating Iran into the global capitalist economy, through the production of crops for export such as cotton.[103] As capitalism matured on a global scale, and independent centres of capital accumulation

101 Tiryakioglu, 2018.
102 Roberts, 1981.
103 Osborn, 1971.

Revolution is the choice of the people

began to emerge outside the historic core of the system in Europe, Iran appeared to have many of the elements present which could propel its economy into this stage of development. Measured in terms of total GDP, and in terms of GDP per capita, in 1970 it would have been difficult to predict where Iran, its neighbour Turkey, or South Korea, a country with a comparable size population which was then at a relatively similar stage of economic development would end up in global rankings.

According to the narratives of Western policymakers and mainstream academia, it was the overthrow of the monarchy in the revolution of 1979, and the subsequent shift towards state capitalist policies (in apparent defiance of global trends towards neoliberalism) that explain why Iran failed to follow the same trajectory as South Korea.[104] To a certain extent they are right, in that the abrupt removal from power of one of the US's most important regional allies did fundamentally shape Iran's economic development over subsequent decades. However, it was not ideological conviction which drove the leadership of the Islamic Republic down a road of relatively autarchic state capitalist development in the 1980s, but a desperate struggle to survive, as the US sought to reverse the defeat it had suffered at the hands of a popular revolution by supporting the Iraqi invasion of Iran in 1980.[105] Seen through the relatively crude lenses of GDP growth rates, the moment at which Iran's economic trajectory visibly shifted was 1986, and it was during the following year that Korea's GDP and GDP per capita overtook Iran's for the first time.

Despite this, the economic history of Iran since the mid-1980s should not be read as one of stagnation and decline. Rather, there has been a slow recovery across different phases of state policy directed by the new bourgeoisie which developed in the intense, hot-house period of relative autarchy imposed by the war with Iraq and US hostility.[106] As Peyman Jafari has argued, the simplistic image of internal competition within the new bourgeoisie as a duel between "neoliberal" Reformist and "statist" Conservative factions hides a much more complex reality.[107] The state capitalist war economy of the immediate

---

104 See for example Maloney, 2015.
105 See Harman 1994; Jafari, 2009; Callinicos, 1988.
106 Jafari, 2009.
107 Jafari, 2009.

Neoliberalism: a realignment of the state and capital

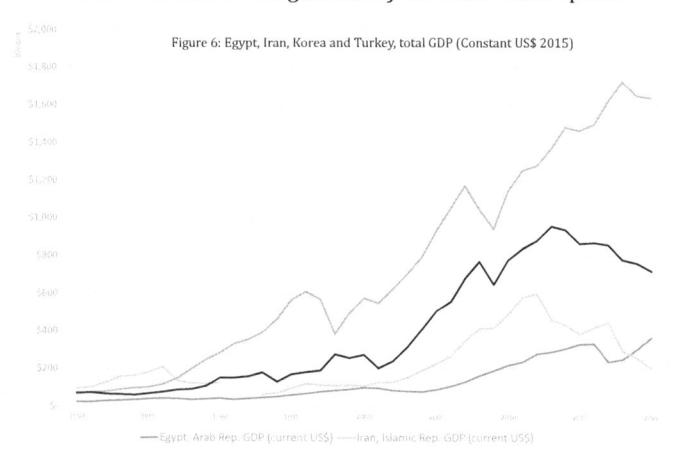

Figure 6: Egypt, Iran, Korea and Turkey, total GDP (Constant US$ 2015)

Data source: World Bank

post-revolutionary era gave birth to the *bonyads*, the massive state "foundations" that organised the distribution of resources and services to the urban and rural poor. They helped to build a social base for the new regime and contributed to the ideological mobilisation necessary for the war effort.

Subsequent periods of neoliberal reforms have not lessened the importance of the *bonyads* to the economy, nor to the state. Instead, they have been integrated into another hybrid form of "real-existing neoliberalism" that combines features of both neoliberalism and state capitalism.[108] The longer-term trajectory of economic development underlying the revival of Iran's role as a sub-imperial power is therefore characterised by the underlying contradictions between the Iranian economy's potential strength and the geopolitical reality of the isolation and vulnerability of the Iranian ruling class. Time and again over the past forty years, Iran's rulers have been reminded of this by geopolitical shocks which have temporarily reshaped the economy. The most recent of these was the rapid reversal in the strong growth of the 2000s following the imposition of sanctions in 2011-2: GDP collapsed from $599 billion in 2012 to $385 billion in 2015 after Iran lost its export markets in Europe[109]

Yet, the fortunes of war in neighbouring Iraq's contest with the US have also brought significant geopolitical benefits to the

---

108 Jafari, 2009.
109 World Bank, 2021.

Iranian ruling class, which was the unintended beneficiary of both the success and failure of US policy. The military defeat of Saddam Hussein in 1991, followed by sanctions and finally the overthrow of his regime by US forces in 2003 removed the threat posed by Iran's belligerent and powerful neighbour. The Iranian regime also benefitted from the failure of US officials to build a viable client state in place of the one they had destroyed. Through its long-standing relations the former Shi'a Islamist opposition groups Iranian influence within Iraq began to grow during the late 2000s.US failures on the battlefield also opened the door to the expansion of Iranian military influence. The much-vaunted troop "surge" of 2006-2008 (which essentially saw US forces reconquering a country they had subdued in a few weeks during the invasion of 2003), prepared the ground for the rise of ISIS and the catastrophic loss of Mosul and much of north-western Iraq in 2014. Iran's military influence in Iraq has largely been channelled through the development of the various sectarian paramilitary forces associated with the Shi'a Islamist political parties which came to dominate the political system set up by the US in the wake of the 2003 invasion. These, rather than the Iraqi army on which the US spent vast sums of money to little effect, proved to be the most effective military forces in confronting ISIS.[110]

Israel in the neoliberal era

Israel's alliance with the US was sealed in the wake of the 1967 war with a massive surge in aid. Direct economic support, which played a crucial role in keeping the Israeli economy afloat in the face of hyperinflation and soaring military spending after near defeat in the 1973 war with Egypt and Syria, was eventually phased out. Meanwhile, Israel's GDP and GDP per capita grew significantly, and the emergence of a new high-tech sector which attracts around 15 percent of the world's venture capital investment in cyber-security has encouraged the rebranding of Israel as a "start-up nation", which can jack straight into the booming global "digital economy".[111] What this picture of plucky entrepreneurialism powering economic growth misses out of

---

110   Watling, 2016.
111   Economist, 2017.

Neoliberalism: a realignment of the state and capital

course is the underlying nexus of connections between rapidly expanding military investment by the US and Israel's militarised state and public sector during the same period. The Israeli army has played a direct role in developing many of the tech start-ups. In 2010 *The Economist* gushed: "The army is more than a high-tech incubator. It sifts the entire population for talent, giving the most promising techies intensive training in elite units, and inculcates an ethic of self-reliance and problem-solving".[112]

This has all taken place in the context of intensifying US-Israeli military cooperation. US military aid is designed to maintain Israel's "Qualitative Military Edge" (QME), over its regional rivals. Since 2008, US arms sales to other countries in the region cannot be agreed on unless the government can prove they will not adversely affect Israel.[113] The framework which governs the transfer of military aid to Israel from the US is a series of ten-year Memoranda of Understanding (MoU), the first of which was signed by the Clinton administration in 1999. As the table below illustrates, the total value of these huge, long-term grants has been rising steadily over the course of several alternations between Democrat and Republican incumbents in the White House.

A significant portion of this military aid has been provided in the form of co-production agreements, such as the 2014 deal which saw US manufacturers and Israeli military industries agree to work together to development the Iron Dome rocket defence system. Like other recent US investments in Israeli military technology, Iron Dome is potentially of benefit to the US as it combats the "asymmetric threat" of lightly-armed resistance groups in other areas.

The huge influx of immigrants from the former Soviet Union starting in the late 1980s and continuing through the 1990s also played a significant role. This was the largest wave of migration to date under the "Law of Return", a policy which essentially allowed anyone with a Jewish parent, grandparent or spouse to immigrate to Israel and immediately claim Israeli nationality, regardless of whether their Jewish relative had immigrated themselves or was even still living.[114] By 2018 there would be 1.2 million immigrants from the Former Soviet Union living in

---

112 Economist, 2010.
113 Sharp, 2018.
114 Ministry of Foreign Affairs, 1950.

Israel, most of whom had arrived since 1990.[115] The percentage of scientists, academics and other related professions among the FSU immigrant labour force in Israel was 69.4 percent as opposed to 26.9 percent for the Israeli Jewish labour force. [116]

Within two decades the economic gap between FSU immigrants and the non-Orthodox Jewish Israeli population narrowed dramatically with their average wage closely approaching the average for the Jewish working population.[117] This contrasted strongly with the experience of Palestinians citizens of Israel who largely remained trapped in poverty and facing systematic discrimination in access to education and better-paid, more qualified jobs.[118] The huge investment by the US ruling class in the active maintenance of Israeli forces' "qualitative military edge" over other military forces in the Middle East had several direct feedback mechanisms specifically into the hi-tech sector. One of these was the role of the Israeli military itself as both consumer and developer of ICT products, services and demanded by its dual missions of maintenance of the apartheid system which governs the lives of Palestinians living under Israeli occupation, and its position as a regional enforcer for the military and diplomatic interests of its imperial patron, the US. Unlike other purchasers of US arms and military technologies, the Israeli military has enjoyed high levels of collaborative access to the research and development component of the US military-industrial-services complex, including first regional access to US military technology, and options to customize US weapons systems.[119]

The Israeli military is not just a consumer and adapter of US weapons. Israeli military products and services also flow back in the opposite direction, these include the Iron Dome missile defence system and the Trophy active defence system for armoured vehicles.[120] A recent article in the *US Joint Force Quarterly* praises the long-term strategies adopted by the Israeli military and academic establishments to create a cadre of technologically-proficient officers through offering intensive education in STEM (science, technology, engineering and maths)

---

115 Israel Central Bureau of Statistics, nd.
116 Sabella, 1993.
117 Lieberman, 2018; Swirski et al. 2020, p18.
118 Sultany, 2012.
119 Sharp, 2018, p3.
120 Dougherty, 2020.

Neoliberalism: a realignment of the state and capital

subjects as part of military service, building in close linkages with the "private" tech sector. The Talpiot programme, which launched in 1979 and recruits high-school graduates for a 9-year long stint in military service combined with advanced STEM training, "is perceived as a breeding ground for Israel's tech industry CEOs.[121] "More than a third of the world's cybersecurity 'unicorns' (private companies valued at over $1 billion) are Israeli, and in the first six months of 2021 Israeli cybersecurity companies raised 41 percent of the total global funds raised by firms in the sector worldwide", according to the Israeli National Cyber Directorate.[122]

The relationship between Palestinian dispossession and the cybersecurity sector in Israel is well illustrated by the Gav-Yam cybersecurity-focussed technology park in Beersheva. Tenants include major international and Israeli IT and military companies (including Deutsche Telekom, IBM, Oracle, Lockheed Martin, EMC and PayPal) whose offices are located in close proximity to Ben Gurion University's Cyber Security Research Centre, and the Israeli military's "ICT campus".[123] The "technology park" is a joint venture between the university, the private sector and the government. It is located in the heart of al-Naqab (the Negev in Hebrew) in a context where forced demolitions of Palestinian villages and homes are intensifying.[124]

The process of mutual reinforcement between the Zionist settler colonial project and Israel's militarised economy thus operates at multiple levels of state, society and economy across historic Palestine and beyond. Palestinians, including the Palestinian minority which remained within the borders of the new Israeli state, have been systematically excluded for reasons of "national security" from what would the most strategically important centres of capital accumulation in the military industries and services (which for obvious reasons were tightly bound up with the military establishment and compulsory military service for Jewish citizens). The combat doctrines, management techniques and technologies on which underpin Israeli military power in the region have been more frequently tested on Palestinians than anyone else.

121 Dougherty, 2020.
122 Solomon, 2021.
123 Hirschauge 2015.
124 Masarwa & Abu Sneineh, 2020.

The re-wiring of the Israeli economy since the 1990s has taken place in conjunction with another dramatic shift, the intensified exclusion of Palestinian labour from the Occupied Territories and the economic marginalisation of Palestinians with Israeli citizenship. New labour migration policies in place since the early 1990s, following the 1987 Palestinian *Intifada*, partially replaced Palestinian day labourers from the Occupied Territories with foreign workers from developing countries in sectors such as agriculture, construction and care-giving services. During the 1990s the number of non-Palestinian non-citizen workers overtook the total number of Palestinians who had ever worked in Israel put together.[125] However, during the following decade the numbers of Palestinians crossing the "Green Line" to work in sectors such as construction rose again. These ebbs and flows fed into the contribution that workers' resistance was able to bring to the popular mobilisations against Israeli apartheid. Israeli construction bosses complained vociferously that they had lost $40 million during the general strike of May 2021 after only 150 out of 65,000 Palestinian workers who cross the "Green Line" to work in Israel daily on construction sites showed up to work. Meanwhile, the Oslo "peace process" and the creation of the Palestinian Authority under the leadership of Yasser Arafat, created a new apparatus of Palestinian officials in direct collaboration with the Israeli state, who in return for the right to fly the Palestinian flag and run their own police force, colluded in the emergence of a shrunken Palestinian entity, entirely dominated by Israel both economically and militarily.[126]

Conclusion

Neoliberalism was an attempt to rescue capitalism from its underlying long-term crisis of profitability. However, unlike the state capitalist 'turn' which took place simultaneously in the centre and the periphery of the global system, neoliberalism was driven from the centre. Its adoption was conditional on defeats for the organised working class and the poor on a global scale, but its policies also served a disciplinary function in relation to the ruling classes of the former colonial world,

---

125 CIMI & PIBA, 2016.
126 Alexander, Rose, Hickey & Marfleet, 2018.

Neoliberalism: a realignment of the state and capital

ensuring they knew their place in the hierarchy of states and capitals. Only a very select few would buck the trend, riding the switchback curves of the global commodity markets towards the mirage of the prosperous future that so many had dreamed of a generation before.

The attempts to impose neoliberal policies as the state capitalist experiments careened into economic crisis did trigger significant episodes of popular mobilisation from below, some of which reached insurrectionary proportions and showed potential for a revolutionary crisis to develop (Egypt in 1977, Tunisia 1978 and 1984, Syria 1976-82 are just some examples). However, the only successfulpolitical revolution in this era took place in Iran, where the popular frustrations with the social inequality and repression embodied in the Shah's regime unleashed a mobilisation from below which had dramatic consequences for the region as whole. Despite the importance of the Iranian exception, however, the most important outcome of the convulsions at the dawn of the neoliberal era was the absence of a revolutionary challenge emerging through the mobilisations from below and the relative success of the ruling classes in the 'socialist' regimes at avoiding paying the full political costs of the failure of their gamble on state capitalism.

Revolution is the choice of the people

Chapter 7
Politics in the neoliberal era

As Daniel Ben Said points out, Lenin, who regarded politics as "concentrated economics", was nevertheless firmly opposed to reducing the political realm to a mere mechanical expression of the economy. "Politics, on the contrary, has its own language, grammar and syntax. It has its latencies and its slips," Ben Said noted.[127] This chapter, therefore will explore how politics changed during the neoliberal era. But it will also discuss what persisted and why these continuities were an essential element in the unstable amalgam of political and social forms which would explode so spectacularly in the decade after 2010. As with previous chapters in this section I will focus on this question initially from the perspective of the ruling classes of the region, asking by what means they sought to persuade and coerce ordinary people to submit to their rule despite the material worsening of their lives. However, the neoliberal era also saw the opening of spaces up for new strands of reformism to emerge. These included significant experiments by Islamist organisations seeking office through electoral means and using the tools of liberal civil society, such as campaigning within the professional associations, to bring about political change. Understanding both the shape of the political space for reformism and the character of the movements and ideological currents which filled them during the pre-revolutionary period will be crucial to analysing the role played by reformists during the drama of revolution and counter-revolution.

---

127 Bensaïd, 2002.

This chapter concentrates on four strategies adopted by the ruling classes of the region for managing the political domain. It is important to remember that most of the institutions and processes discussed here had a dual function—they simultaneously served to manage relations between different elements within the ruling class, *and* their relations with other classes. It is also vital to grasp that in most countries elements of all these were present and that the hybrid, combined nature of the political strategies adopted by the elite which was enriching itself at the expense of the rest of society was a persistent feature of politics in the neoliberal era.

Firstly, I will look at the phenomenon of the persistence of the 'zombie parties' of the 'state socialist' experiments. Secondly, I will analyse how many of these supposedly 'secular' parties turned at the same time towards encouraging conservative expressions of Islamic piety ranging from gigantic mosque construction schemes, funding and support for Qu'ranic memorisation schools, facilitation of the growth of Islamic charities and backing for reactionary laws curtailing women's rights in the name of conforming to the teachings of the Shari'a. These manoeuvres were often designed to stave off the unpalatable third strategy which presented itself to the ruling classes of the region: opening up their ranks to accommodate Islamist reformists. The fourth ruling class strategy for managing politics in the neoliberal period—a form of sectarianism—was adopted in Lebanon, Iraq and Bahrain but nevertheless was firmly anchored in the processes of neoliberal transformation of the economy, society and politics and its echoes reverberated much more widely. In conclusion I will look at how these manoeuvres at the top of society changed the terrain on which all reformist movements and ideological currents—not just their Islamist versions—operated.

The zombie parties

In a large number of countries which would experience revolutions or major popular uprisings in the post-2010 period, protesters confronted ruling parties which displayed a huge degree of continuity from the state capitalist era in terms of their leading personnel and their internal organisation. This was despite in some cases undergoing considerable mutations in their external appearance—for example by shedding the word 'socialist' from their names. Economic liberalisation in the Middle East was a case of 'neither bread nor freedom', where freedoms for businesses were introduced by authoritarian regimes which showed no sign of ever intending to concede reforms, such as allowing the media to operate without government interference or even political pluralism at an elite level, let along more basic democratic rights such as freedom of association, organisation and expression for ordinary citizens.[128]

There were many reasons why despite rhetorical claims to the contrary, an extension of liberal democracy as an outcome of the process of neoliberal reform was never in the interests of the major imperialist powers. At a very basic level, the need to rupture the state capitalist regimes of the Middle East from their military alliances with the Soviet Union was much less pressing than in Eastern Europe. This was because some of the most important of them such as Egypt, were making the switch from East to West of their own volition anyway, thanks to the combined leverage of Israel's military capacity as demonstrated ably in 1967 and the relentless pressures of the global commodity and financial markets which had plunged even the beneficiaries of the early 1970s surge in oil prices into catastrophic levels of debt by the mid-1980s.

In Egypt, the ruling party of the Nasserist era, the Arab Socialist Union was one of the first to change in 1978 after Anwar al-Sadat instituted a very limited form of political pluralism by transforming various 'political platforms' within the ASU into political parties. The rebranded ruling party which emerged out of this process, the National Democratic Party (NDP) remained the party of the state bureaucracy and attracted into its leading bodies representatives of the newly-enriched *infitah* bourgeoisie. The minority left Nasserist and Stalinist Communist loyal opposition within the ASU was allowed to set up as a political party, Al-Tagammu', while the historic liberal nationalist Wafd Party was also re-established. These and other small political parties were permitted to publish newspapers and stand candidates in parliamentary elections provided they did not transgress their role as providing a veneer of pluralistic cover for what was in essence the continuation of the old ruling party under another name.

128 George, 2003.

Revolution is the choice of the people

In Tunisia, the transformation of the old ruling party into a more effective vehicle for neoliberal reform was achieved by Zein al-Din Ben Ali, who shuffled Habib Bourguiba off into retirement via a "medical coup" in 1987. The following year Ben Ali rebranded the ruling Destourian Socialist Party as the Democratic Constitutional Rally (RCD). At first Ben Ali claimed that his seizure of power was setting Tunisia on a path towards a more politically as well as economically liberal future: he abolished the presidency-for-life, recognised new political parties and appeared to have cleared out some of the "dead wood" among the cadres of the ruling party. But within a few years the trend had reversed, back towards elections with impossibly high turnouts and votes for the RCD, back towards repression of opponents as the suffocating embrace of the monolithic ruling party closed in once again.[129] The trajectory of the Ba'th Party in Syria during the neoliberal period resembled that of the Neo-Destour and the Arab Socialist Union more content than in form. There was no phoney shift towards a kind of "authoritarianism lite" pluralism. Nevertheless, the regime did open up the electoral arena to "independent" candidates from the neoliberal bourgeoisie during the 1990s and builtup cordial relations with the Sunni bourgeoisie of Damascus in particular. Iraq's Ba'th Party emerged victorious from the war with Iran in the 1980s only to precipitate disaster by annexing Kuwait in 1990 and triggering US intervention and devastating sanctions. As we will discuss in more detail below, the sanctions era hollowed out the Ba'th Party paving the way for its collapse in the face of the US invasion and occupation of 2003, and the emergence of a new political order based on sectarian and ethnic "power-sharing" among the local allies of the occupying forces. Algeria's ruling party, the FLN, survived political challenge from the Islamist opposition and mass movements in the streets at the end of the 1980s, to oversee both the process of neoliberal reform in the 1990s and a brutal counter-insurgency campaign in the context of a civil war which left around 150,000 Algerians dead.[130] The longevity of

---

129 King, 2003, p137.
130 There are conflicting figures for the numbers of deaths during the civil war. Ghanem-Yazbeck gives a figure of 150,000, citing Algerian President Abdelaziz Bouteflika as the source (Ghanem-Yazbeck, 2017), whereas Kristianasen gives an even higher death toll

the FLN, and its role in knitting together different elements at the top of the state bureaucracy, the state bourgeoisie and the private sector and the army was a major theme in the popular uprising of 2019.[131]

'Crony capitalists' inside the state party machine

The ruling parties which managed the neoliberal transition in the state capitalist regimes found ways to work with, rather than against, those sections of the bourgeoisie who benefitted from the economic changes. This primarily reflected the fact that the state bourgeoisie *itself* was a major beneficiary of neoliberal reform as mapped out in the previous chapter. There was no need to change or disrupt the political establishment because the basic processes of neoliberal transformation could be managed perfectly well among the ruling class using the mechanisms to hand in the existing ruling parties.

The previous chapter already introduced Osman Ahmed Osman, whose business empire spanned multiple sectors of the Egyptian economy. In the mid-1980s, Osman's networks within the wider political system were equally broad. As Robert Vitalis noted: "his influence extends to the Egyptian parliament (he has packed the housing committee with his clients); the ruling National Democratic Party; and the Engineering Syndicate, which he has turned into an economic force tied to the Arab Contractors".[132] Fast forward a generation and a similar convergence of economic and political power could be seen around the person of steel manufacturer Ahmed Ezz, who enjoyed a near-monopoly over iron and steel production in Egypt. As the president of the Planning and Budgetary Committee of the People's Assembly, which was responsible for allocating government investment in construction and public infrastructure, Ezz was essentially able to manage the scale of demand for his own companies' products. Ezz also played

---

of 200,000. (Kristianasen, 2006).
131 The regime has not relied on the FLN alone to rule since 1997, when the Democratic National Rally (Rassemblement National Démocratique, RND) was formed. The RND has become an important element in the regime, complementing rather than replacing the FLN.
132 Vitalis, 1986.

a key role in the National Democratic Party: as Organisational Secretary he was considered the architect of plans to ensure a smooth hereditary succession in power of aging president Hosni Mubarak by his son, Gamal. Overall, as Soliman notes, the NDP underwent a significant process of "bourgeoisification" becoming a party dominated by "business magnates".[133]

In Algeria during the 1990s foreign investors hoping to pick up a bargain through the privatisation of state enterprises as the government implemented neo-liberal reforms found they were expected to budget for clandestine payments to the "submarines", "the hidden body of patrons, often linked to the army, who control decisions about the futures of individual EPEs (state enterprises).[134] The withdrawal of the state from trade also created opportunity for the rise of military "import barons", as generals from particular military factions parcelled up import sectors between them. The election of Abdelaziz Bouteflika in 1999 took place in the context of widespread exhaustion after eight years of civil war. Bouteflika's rebalancing of networks of power and patronage behind the façade of the state reinvigorated the role of the presidency and created greater space for a new layer of private-sector businessmen to join the elite but did not fundamentally weaken the grip of leading generals over the import trade.[135] Moreover, some of the private businessmen and women who have emerged in recent decades are the sons and daughters of key figures in the army. The pharmaceutical industry, which was until 1995 largely controlled by public sector companies, is now dominated by private companies many of whose owners are relatives of senior figures in the military, such as Apotex which is owned by relatives of the former secretary-general of the Ministry of Defence, and Pharmalliance, owned by the daughter of the former head of the Department of Counterespionage and Internal Security.[136]

Sudan provided some of the most grotesque examples of how the ruling class which creamed off profits from the very neoliberal economic conditions which caused misery and hardship for millions was knitted together through webs of

---

133 Soliman, 2011, p148. Thanks to Gianni del Panta for this point.
134 ICG, 2001
135 ICG, 2018.
136 Ghanem-Yazbeck, 2018, p18.

Politics in the neoliberal era

family and party networks deeply embedded in the coercive apparatus of the state. The deep connections between the regime of Umar al-Bashir regime and the major players in the food-processing industry was illustrated by an exchange between Bashir himself and the judge in his trial for corruption. A central exhibit in the prosecution's case was the discovery of millions of dollars in Bashir's residence which the ex-President confessed were a personal gift from Saudi Crown Prince, Mohamed Bin Salman.[137]

The ruling parties' embrace of neoliberalism and their efforts to pass on wealth and power to their own offspring did, it is important to note, create some contradictions. There were always those who were excluded from the new arrangements because although they "made it" in terms of acquiring wealth, lacked the right family or party connections. There were also some whose political convictions kept them firmly outside the regime's ruling circles, despite their strong support for neoliberal reforms. In Egypt these included a minority section of the neoliberal bourgeoisie affiliated with the Muslim Brotherhood, such as the organisation's Deputy Guide, Khairat al-Shater. The Brotherhood's "devout bourgeosie" was concentrated in trade and small and medium-sized manufacturing but shut out of heavy industry. Al-Shater's businesses included a luxury furniture supplier, while Hassan Malek, another important Brotherhood supporter made his money in textiles.[138]

Mobilising workers and the poor to perpetuate dictatorship

The ruling parties with their emerging hereditary elites and family networks of power were not simply mechanisms for managing relations between different sections of the ruling class.

---

137 El-Gizouli, 2020a, p3.
138 Awad, 2012; Al-Anani, 2020 The Islamist segment of the Egyptian bourgeoisie was never more than a minority current during Mubarak's rule, however. Comparisons between the "hidden business empires" of the Brotherhood and the armed forces have not always been clear about the very different scales of networks involved, or their respective influence over and within the state. See Abul-Magd, 2012 for example.

They also influenced other classes to support the continuation of the existing political system and undermined any efforts by opposition currents to mobilise workers and the poor for change. Elections served a purpose here, not as means to alternate power in any meaningful sense between sections of the ruling class, but as a means to bind poor and working-class voters to patrons in the ruling party. In Egypt, both state and private enterprises would routinely bus workers to election rallies for NDP candidates, and the state-run trade union federation ETUF acted as a gatekeeper to the electoral arena for the ruling party thanks to a clause in the 1964 constitution adopted at the height of Egypt's 'socialist' phase which reserved 50 percent of the seats in parliament for 'workers and farmers'.[139] ETUF's role in the electoral process included the formal validation of "worker" credentials via membership in one of its affiliated trade unions, and the ETUF bureaucracy actively intervened to obstruct trade union members who might wish to stand for election as an independent or for one of the legal opposition parties.

The persistence of the ETUF bureaucracy "in the heart of the party," as Minister of Labour Ai'sha Abd-al-Hadi put it in 2010 was no accident.[140] In Egypt, Algeria, Syria and Iraq, the state did not rely on the bureaucracy of independent trade unions to tame workers' frustrations of its own accord. Rather, it integrated workers' organisations into the apparatus of the state, in the process transforming trade union officials into the ruling party's functionaries. 'Trade unions' of this type, such as the Egyptian Trade Union Federation (ETUF) or the Syrian General Federation of Trade Unions (GFTU)served functions in their respective societies which differed from genuine trade unions. Their primary role. was to mobilise workers in the process of production and to mobilise political support for the regime among workers.

At first the regimes' labour bodies did offer something in return: slightly more secure jobs, pensions and social insurance schemes and a host of benefits associated with the workplaces including subsidised housing and health services. Yet as neoliberal reforms deepened, the state-run trade unions could no longer offer this trade-off for workers' social and political acquiescence. The removal of the material benefits on offer

---

139 Al-Mahkama al-Dusturiyya al-Uliya, 2012.
140 Ali, 2010.

through this unequal contract was a key factor in the emergence of independent workers' organisations, born in the context of reviving strike and protest activity from below, which began challenge the ruling party's machines inside the workplaces.

The model outlined above was not the only one present in the region, however. Tunisia was the one country in the region where the trade union bureaucracy retained a much bigger degree of independence of the state, reflecting the fact that the UGTT had emerged as a serious organised force inside the nationalist movement before the end of French colonial rule. This did not mean it completely escaped the pressures from the ruling party, and the leadership of the UGTT union repeatedly compromised with the regime of Zein-al-Din Ben Ali during the two decades before the revolution of 2011. The ruling RCD party had a network of activists inside the UGTT, and some of its MPs were UGTT members.[141] Under the pressure of the mass protests and strikes driven from the base of the UGTT's membership and supported by the bottom and middle layers of officials in the UGTT hierarchy, the hold of the ruling party over the trade union federation disintegrated in Tunisia in a way it did not in the other countries. Meanwhile, in Lebanon and Iraq, the confessional political parties of the ruling class also served as vehicles to mobilise other classes behind the perpetuation of the political status quo, as we will discuss in more detail below in discussing the relationship between neoliberalism and sectarianism.

The pious state and its religious 'subcontractors'

The accelerating process of neoliberal reform posed a dilemma for the former state capitalist ruling parties in terms of how they related to the poor in general and organised workers in particular. The public sector, once a source of national pride and the core of the state's economic strategy was now pilloried as inefficient, wasteful and corrupt. Yet political promises to introduce more pluralistic societies and loosen the grip of authoritarianism remained unfulfilled. One of the ways in which ruling classes across the region attempted to deal with the political consequences of this emerging contradiction was through a visible shift towards encouraging religiosity in society

---

141   Yousfi, 2018.

and encouraging certain kinds of religious institutions to take on expanded social and political roles. This strategy consisted of a number of different components, and not all were present in every country, however there were common threads and experiences across the whole region.

In most of the countries under discussion here, this meant in practice that the state bourgeoisie expressed its sudden rediscovery of the importance of religion through ostentatious acts of Muslim piety. These ranged from grandiose mosque construction projects, to state support for Qur'anic memorisation competitions (for example in Syria), to legal reforms strengthening the relationship between Shar'ia law and state law. In the case of Egypt, Anwar al-Sadat, who styled himself the "Believer President", pushed through an amendment to the 1971 constitution in 1980 changing Shari'a law from "a source of legislation" to "the principal source of legislation". In Algeria, the regime of Chadli Benjedid, who became president after the death of Houari Boumediene in 1978, adopted a reactionary Family Code restricting women's rights in the early 1980s. According to the code women were obliged by law to obey their husbands, polygamy was institutionalised, women were unable to apply for divorce and denied any rights to pass on their name, nationality or religion to their children.[142] At exactly the same time as Algeria's "socialist" ruling party was stripping women of their rights in the name of Islam, the regime in Sudan under Jafa'ar al-Nimeiri was carrying out similar reforms institutionalising some of the most reactionary elements and interpretations of Shari'a law in partnership with the Islamist movement led by Hassan al-Turabi.

Alongside asserting the pious and "believing" nature of the state itself, the state bourgeoisie invited religious institutions to take up expanded ideological, political and social roles. Thomas Pierret suggestively notes that from the 1970s onwards the Ba'thist state in Syria, for example, instituted a system of religious 'sub-contractors', whereby the traditionalist *ulama* were encouraged to revive their networks and institutions with the blessing of the state.[143] This process was aided by the fact that in Syria, during its more radical phase, the Ba'th Party had shied away from the kind of 'nationalisation' of religious institutions

---

142 Salhi, 2003.
143 Pierret, 2013.

carried out by the Nasserist regime in Egypt, for example. The Alawite faith of the ruling family after 1970 provided a different set of reasons for continuing with an arms-length relationship with the traditionalist *'ulama*. Over the decades, shifts in the global regime of accumulation amplified and intensified these tendencies, investing them with material force as religious 'sub-contractors' filled the spaces in social provision vacated by the state through charitable works in the fields of education, health care and welfare. A similar process took place in Iraq after the US-led military onslaught of 1991 wrecked large parts of the country's social and economic infrastructure and the punitive sanctions regime prevented reconstruction.

Some of these changes were masked by the overbearing presence of the authoritarian ruling party. The grotesque forms of personality cult around the dictators themselves, complete with bizarre and extravagant ceremonies and iconographies which unashamedly borrowed from religious traditions, could be seen therefore as an ideological performance which retained the outward façade of the state form built by the previous generation concealing a profound shift towards a sub-contracting model for managing religious belief 'underneath'.[144] In the case of Iraq, this model did not only involve the state looking for sub-contractors among the *'ulama*: the Ba'thist regime also rediscovered the 'tribal sheikh' as a suitable candidate for this intermediary role of managing relations between state and society The direct application of neoliberal 'shock doctrines' after the US invasion of 2003 complemented the work done by US bombers, triggering the rapid collapse of state institutions and their cannibalisation by a host of local political and social actors, including religious movements.[145]

The Islamist alternative?

Attempts to impose neoliberal policies in response to the global economic crisis led to major revolts and protests across the region. Egypt's "Bread Intifada" of January 1977, the Tunisian workers' revolt in 1977-8 and the surge of protests in northern and central Syria from 1978-82 were all linked to worsening

144 See Wedeen, 1999 & al-Khalil, 1990.
145 Herring & Rangwala, 2006; Alexander & Assaf, 2005.

social inequality which was in turn the result of the partial liberalisation of the economy. However, in general it was not the left which reaped the political benefits of disillusion with the regimes, but Islamist opposition groups. The association between Islamism and popular rejection of the existing political and economic system grew infinitely stronger in the wake of the Iranian revolution of 1979. Although the popular revolution there brought down not a "socialist" regime, but a corrupt client of the USA, the overthrow of the Shah boosted the status of Islamism in the minds of a generation.

The relationship between the Islamist current which was ultimately victorious in the contest for state power, the faction around Ruhollah Khomeini which would emerge as the Islamic Republican Party, and the mass movement in the streets and workplaces of Iran was highly contradictory. In similar fashion to the Arab nationalists elsewhere in the region during the 1950s and 1960s, Khomeini and his supporters rode to power on the back of mass movements they were part of, but did not control, and then used the coercive apparatus of the state to halt the process of revolution and restore conditions for capital accumulation to resume, with a new ruling class clustered around the state in charge.[146] Yet this was not how Khomeini's victory appeared to many in Iran and beyond at the time. Rather, the explosive birth of the Islamic Republic, seemed to confirm 'Islam' as an ideology supporting profound social and political change. It appeared to act as a potential alternative to both the discredited 'socialism' of the one-party states, and to the bleak neoliberal world where the wealth of the few was a visible result of the immiseration of the majority.

In his path-breaking analysis published in 1994, Chris Harman identified how sections of four different social classes tended to coalesce in Islamist movements: the "old exploiters" (sections of the traditional pre-capitalist landowning and merchant classes), the "new exploiters" (capitalists who had succeeded despite the hostility of the state bourgeoisie), the poor (especially recent migrants from the countryside to the cities), and "the new middle class" (products of modern education systems who aspired to professional and managerial roles in the state).[147] As we have already seen, most of the former

---

146 Harman, 1994.
147 Harman, 1994, p11–13.

state capitalist regimes were also attempting to attract the support of these classes. The degree to which they succeeded related broadly as to how big a contradiction there was between the material conditions faced by these classes as a result of the reconfiguration of the ruling class and the neoliberal policy regime, and the historic legacy of the social and political struggles which had marked the state capitalist period.

In Syria, Islamist opposition organisations emerged as the regime's major challengers by the late 1970s. This was primarily a reflection of the growing material contradiction between the regime's promises to the poor and the new middle classes and the reality of increasing social inequality and declining opportunities for the graduates of the modern education system to find work which matched their skills in the service of the state. But it also reflected the regional unevenness of the regime's success in building a new ruling-class coalition: sections of the "old" merchant and landowning bourgeoisie in Damascus had done much better from this arrangement compared to their counterparts in Aleppo and Hama for example.[148] The revolt of the late 1970s in Syria ended in catastrophe for the Islamist movement with a failed insurrection in Hama in 1982 which was crushed by the regime at the cost of tens of thousands of lives in a terrifying precursor of the counter-revolutionary military strategy adopted by Hafez's son, Bashar after 2011.[149]

The Islamist advance in Algeria also ended in disaster in the early 1990s. The initial beneficiaries of the political opening which followed the crisis of October 1988 as mass popular protests and riots rocked Algeria were the Islamist movement, principally the Front Islamique du Salut (FIS) which formed in 1989. The FIS was a highly contradictory organisation, led by sections of the middle class but with an appeal which reached into wide layers of the urban poor and working class, despite its tacit endorsement of the neoliberal trajectory of the economic reform, and its condemnation of strikes by public sector workers such as dustmen when it local government.[150] The electoral appeal of the FIS, which swept into local government and looked set to win the general election of 1992, threatening the FLN's decades-long dominance of the state, prompted

148 Lawson, 1982; Batatu, 1982.
149 Batatu, 1982"; Lawson, 1982.
150 Roberts, 2020; Harman, 1994.

panic within the ruling class, leading to a military coup and the installation of a revived dictatorship. The process of neoliberal reform henceforward intensified under the generals' direction, with the signing of an agreement with the IMF in 1994. This involved deindustrialisation rather than simply privatisation, with the closure of many industries which failed to find private sector buyers.[151] There were huge attacks on public sector employment with the loss of 500,000 jobs by 1998, pushing unemployment up to 35 percent, while poverty and inequality increased.[152] All this took place in the context of vicious military repression which triggered a civil war between armed Islamist groups and the state.

In both Syria and Algeria, the experience of repression and the failure of Islamist currents to win political changes through relatively peaceful means such as mass protests or through the ballot box made the option of armed struggle appear an attractive alternative. Armed Islamist organisations such as the "Fighting Vanguard" in Syria and the "Armed Islamic Group" (usually known by its French acronym, GIA) in Algeria attracted new and larger layers of supporters in the wake of repression of peaceful protests or the cancellation of elections by the state. In Egypt, too, small armed groups emerged at the end of the 1970s, including *Takfir wal Higra* which started as a revivalist conservative movement preaching withdrawal from "sinful" secular society but turned to kidnappings and armed resistance to the state. More important was the armed group formed by Khaled al-Islambouli, a young officer in the Egyptian army, which succeeded in assassinating Anwar al-Sadat at a military parade on 6 October 1981. Again, in the Egyptian case there is a relationship between the prominence of the armed groups and the closing down of mass-based and peaceful methods of protest by the government. Al-Islambouli's strike at the man he called "Pharaoh" came in the midst of a huge crackdown against Sadat's opponents, and following the spontaneous popular uprising of 1977 known as the "Bread Intifada". The most famous armed Islamist group of them all, Al-Qa'idah (the Base) had its roots partially in the failure of the movement by Islamist scholars and activists in Saudi Arabia during the early 1990s (known as the "Awakening" (*al-sahwa*

---

151 Del Panta, 2020.
152 Layachi, 2019, p313.

Politics in the neoliberal era

in Arabic) to win political change through petitions and peaceful agitation.

The creation of armed vanguards was not the only route taken by Islamists during the 1980s and 1990s, however. In countries where the opportunity arose to embark on electoral projects, major Islamist organisations embraced this strategy. In the case of Egypt, efforts by the regime to close down the narrow electoral space into which a generation of Islamist reformists had projected their hopes of change proved to be one of the final factors pushing large sections of the base of the Muslim Brotherhood into the streets at the eruption of the revolutionary uprising in January 2011. During the 1980s, 1990s and 2000s the Brotherhood's leadership had made a conscious 'turn' towards reformist political activity which contrasted with the organisation's practice during the 1960s and 1970s when repression forced the movement underground and into exile. The Brotherhood stood candidates for parliament and progressively increased its presence in parliament (although these gains were wiped out in the 2010 elections). Meanwhile a new generation of middle-ranking Brotherhood leaders composed of former activists with the Islamic student associations of the 1970s won elections to the national executive of the professional associations representing doctors, engineers and lawyers, turning these organisations which were previously dominated by the ruling party into spaces where opposition ideas could be discussed and political challenges to the regime formulated.[153]

The Brotherhood's activity in parliament and the professional associations was a reflection of the opening of political opportunities in these areas which resulted from the inconclusive outcome of the wave of social mobilisation and protest which culminated in the popular uprising of January 1977. The opening of a narrow space in which the Brotherhood's reformism could operate was thus clearly the result of a 'push up' by a mass movement from below although the narrowness of the space and slow and cautious way in which the regime opened it were reflections of the relative success of the regime's success in avoiding the development of a genuine revolutionary crisis on the scale it would face in 2011.

It was also the outcome of calculated 'reaching down' by

---

153   Wickham, 2015.

the ruling class as it sought new ways to contain the political and social pressures generated by the undoing of the Nasserist social contract. For relatively long periods of time, the regime was largely successful in calibrating the relationship between pressure from below and opening from above so as to retain the ruling party's dominance of institutions such as parliament and the official trade unions and maintain its suffocating grip on civil society. It conceded ideological and organisational territory in the professional syndicates to the Brotherhood, with the caveat that it would tolerate a degree of criticism and the venting of political frustrations over 'external' political issues such as Palestine provided that its opponents avoided breaching 'red lines' over domestic questions, such as challenges to the authority of the president or raised the question of social resistance to neo-liberalism (rather than attempting to mitigate its effects through charitable work).

The fact that the Brotherhood acquiesced in this compromise is a confirmation of the strength of reformism within the organisation during the period. Moreover, as Carrie Rosefsky-Wickham argues convincingly, the practice of reformism affected not only the wing of the movement led by the former student activists of the 1970s who led the Brotherhood's successful campaign to capture the leadership of the professional associations, but also conservative sections of the leadership who remained committed to engagement with parliament throughout the period. Muhammad Sa'd al-Katatni, a conservative member of the Brotherhood's Guidance Bureau and a leading member of its parliamentary bloc, summed up the achievements of the Brotherhood's MPs in 2010 like this:

> "The biggest achievement has been training a large number of Brotherhood deputies in parliamentary practices, and the second is the Brotherhood's opening to society through the activities of the deputies' offices in their respective districts. The regime treats us as an illegal organisation but having offices in our districts enables us to interact with the mass public in an official capacity. When a person wants to move to another place, it is very difficult, because he faces a lot of bureaucratic red tape. We have an opportunity to help him. We can

Politics in the neoliberal era

also help people find jobs and provide support to the poor by collecting donations from the rich".[154]

The narrow character of the regime's reformist 'offer' would later play a significant role in creating the conditions for the Brotherhood to emerge as the largest and best-organised reformist force following the uprising in January 2011. Toleration of the Brotherhood's forays into parliamentary politics, or winning elections in the professional associations or official trade unions was interspersed with bouts of severe repression, which while not on the scale of the crackdown of the 1950s, included the repeated arrest and jailing of leading members. Compared to the parties of the 'official opposition', who were tainted by association with regime, the Brotherhood was a much more credible 'outsider' force in 2011. The Brotherhood also did not entirely restrict its activities to parliamentary politics, it was highly visible on the university campuses and occasionally mobilised its members in rallies, although its leaders were reluctant to provoke a confrontation with the regime and thus left the streets relatively open for the much smaller forces of the left, the Nasserists and liberals to take the initiative.

The ideological content and the practice of the Brotherhood's reformism differed from the form these took during the 1940s as a result of both internal and external factors. In comparison to the 1940s the Brotherhood's programme was more conservative on questions of social and economic reform. For example, despite having advocated the redistribution of land and curbing the power of large landowners in the 1940s, the Brotherhood did not oppose the neoliberal agrarian reform implemented in 1997 which removed restrictions on land ownership.[155] A number of factors can explain this change: firstly, the social composition of the Brotherhood had altered since the 1940s, with the migration of a layer of its supporters to the Gulf during the 1970s and their subsequent success in business there. Although as Naguib notes, the new middle class elements of the Brotherhood were also refreshed during the same period, the fact that a section of the 'pious bourgeoisie' now supported the organisation was a source of conservatism both in relation

---

154 Wickham, 2015, p136.
155 The law was passed in 1992 but only implemented 5 years later.

to economic and social policies and over 'moral' questions of personal behaviour and gender and sexual relations.[156]

So to what extent was Islamism a project of the neoliberal bourgeoisie? This is an important question which has been sharply debated on the left. For writers such as Gilbert Achcar, Joseph Daher and Adam Hanieh, the class character of the Islamist parties which came to power in Egypt and Tunisia after the revolutions of 2011 was determined above all by the presence of major businessmen among their key supporters, and in some cases their political leadership.[157] Daher has also written extensively on the development of Shi'a Islamist party Hezbollah as a political and military vehicle for the rise of the Shi'a bourgeoisie in Lebanon.[158] In most of the countries discussed here, the implantation of Islamist ideas among sections of the bourgeoisie was real, but there were few examples where this kind of politics became dominant. Moreover, the organisational weight of Islamist movements even those which attracted successful businessmen was usually lower down the social scale among the modern middle class. It is important to be clear about what we are looking for here: ostentatious expressions of piety and a predilection for Islamic charity were perfectly compatible with loyalty to the regimes in power and active engagement with the old ruling parties. One of the features marked out the Islamist project was a sustained political critique of the existing regimes and another was a willingness to either challenge them directly.

In Sudan, the partnership between the Islamist movement and firstly the regime of Ja'afar al-Nimeiri and later Umar al-Bashir is an important exception to the experience of Islamist movements in much of the region. At the end of the 1970s, as Nimeiri's state capitalist project of massive investment in agricultural transformation was foundering, he began to look for new allies inside Sudan and ways to reorient his economic policies towards more dynamic hubs of capital accumulation, in particular the powerful regional bloc of capital emerging in the Gulf. He formed a political alliance with the Islamist politician Hassan al-Turabi in the late 1970s which neatly provided the opportunity to do both. Nimeiri and al-Turabi's first joint project

---

156 Naguib, 2006.
157 Achcar, 2013.
158 Daher, 2016.

was the creation of an Islamic banking sector, with the eager support of Gulf capital.[159] Nimeiri was unable to ride out the storms which saw the downfall of his regime in a wave of mass protests in strikes in 1985, but the military-Islamist alliance survived and took power again in 1989 with Umar al-Bashir's successful coup.

Turkey also provides a counter-example to the general picture of the relative marginalisation of Islamist movements by the regimes. As already discussed above, the rise of the AKP party with its roots in a section of small and medium-sized manufacturing capital in the provinces showed that it was possible for an Islamist movement to maintain a strong Islamist political identity and eventually force the state bourgeoisie to accept its presence not just at the ballot box, but actually in government.

Yet the experiences of Sudan and Turkey were anomalous compared to the rest of the region, where Islamist opposition parties, including those whose ranks were refreshed by some sections of the *infitah* bourgeoisie, remained shut out of political power, with those who stayed loyal to their cause often playing a terrible personal price for their decision. In Algeria, despite the FIS's ambivalence on the question of neoliberal reform, and the potential for common cause with sections of the state bourgeoisie over reactionary campaigns against women's rights and the Berber-speaking segment of the population, after a few years of political liberalisation, the door to an Islamist ascension to political power was slammed shut by the military. The disaster of the war which followed the coup did led to a very limited reconciliation with a tolerated Islamist party, the MSP joining governments as a junior partner from the late 1990s. But a government formed on the basis of an Islamist electoral majority remained unthinkable.

In Egypt, the Brotherhood was allowed limited access to the national political arena for a time, but this was interspersed with bouts of intense repression, which did not spare even its leading businessmen, such as Khairat al-Shater who spent years in jail on trumped up charges. In Syria, as we saw above, the Ba'thist regime carried out an exceptionally brutal crackdown on the Islamist opposition at the beginning of the 1980s, killing, imprisoning or exiling most of its active cadres.

---

159 Thomas, 2017, p10–11.

Revolution is the choice of the people

The rise of the Islamist movement in Palestine does not contradict this overall pattern. The fragmenting of Palestinian society under the domination of Israel's apartheid regime created at one level a mosaic of different political contexts and a range of Islamist responses. These included the growth of a reformist Islamist current among Palestinian citizens of Israel which developed a network of charities and social welfare initiatives and successfully elected candidates to local government and later to the Knesset (participating in national elections triggered a split in the movement with the Northern Branch arguing that running for parliament gave too much legitimacy to the Israeli state).[160] In Gaza and the West Bank, the rise of Hamas as both an armed movement and an electoral project was clearly rooted in the decay of the legitimacy of the older generation of nationalist parties such as Fatah, and mirrored similar processes elsewhere in the region where the former vanguards of the national liberation struggle faced Islamist challengers. The refusal of Fatah's leadership to countenance the peaceful alternation of power with Hamas in the wake of the Islamist movement's victory in the legislative elections for the Palestinian Authority which took place in 2006 led to brief civil war and the splitting of the government of the Occupied Territories in two, with Hamas taking power in Gaza. It remains the governing party in the besieged territory today. Conditions of siege and repeated Israeli bombardment, mean that unlike other Islamist movements which have often been damaged by their season in power, Hamas has retained credibility and popularity among wide sections of Palestinians.[161]

In the Gulf States, Islamist activists who fled there during the 1960s and 1970s were at first tolerated by the conservative monarchies. In Saudi Arabia for example, Muslim Brotherhood activists from around the region were encouraged to take up roles in building the education system, filling in for the lack of

---

160 Rubin, 2015.
161 Polls conducted by the Palestinian Center for Policy and Survey Research in December 2021 showed that overall Hamas was more popular than Fatah, and Hamas leader Ismail Haniyyeh would win comfortably in an election against PA President Mahmoud Abbas of Fatah. However, not all Fatah figures were seen in the same light by voters. Jailed Fatah leader Marwan Barghouti would have beaten Haniyyeh in a one-to-one contest. (PCPSR, 2021).

qualified teachers and university lecturers within Saudi society. Over the decades that followed, some of the Saudi students they taught would develop their own critique of the lack of political freedoms in Saudi Arabia and the glaring contradiction between the ostentatious wealth of the royal family and its claims of Islamic virtue. Yet there was no progress towards meaningful reform, while on the geopolitical front, the Saudi regime moved ever closer into the orbit of the United States and its regional ally Israel.

In short, across most of the region, before 2010 Islamist organisations had failed to win over significant sections of either the *infitah* bourgeoisie (which remained generally in the political orbit of the old ruling parties' countries) or persuade sections of the state bourgeoisie to ally with them and open up the door to political power.

Sectarianism and bourgeois political strategy

In Lebanon and Iraq the neoliberal period saw the consolidation of different model of politics from the rest of the region. This was form of sectarian "power-sharing" as a way of both managing disputes between different sections of the ruling class and a method for the ruling class to mobilise the middle and lower classes behind the perpetuation of the status quo. In both cases this model was bound up with the operation of *'dawla al-muhassasa'* the sectarian "allotment state", where roles and resources were distributed by the political leaders of sectarian or ethnic communities in order to maintain the allegiance of their constituencies.[162]

In the case of Lebanon, the origins of the sectarian political system went back to the colonial era. It was reconfirmed during Lebanon's time as the Middle East's exceptional 'Bankers' Republic' during the state capitalist era and reasserted even

---

162 From a Marxist perspective, the state always operates as an instrument of class rule, and the Lebanese and Iraqi states are no exception to this. The 'sects' and 'communities' supposedly represented by elite politicians in the state apparatus remain divided by social class, even if those politicians have been relatively successfully in suppressing the class identity of workers and other layers of the poor behind loyalty to 'their' community leaders.

Revolution is the choice of the people

more strongly in the neoliberal period. The 1989 Ta'if Accords which ended the civil war that had begun in the mid-1970s, were agreed by the major Lebanese military and political factions and overseen by regional states with a stake in the Lebanese conflict and its aftermath (principally Syria and Saudi Arabia) and blessed by the "international community" in the shape of the US and the UN. The agreement reaffirmed and strengthened the pre-existing mechanisms by which the Lebanese ruling class sorted out its internal differences through the sectarian allotment (*muhassasa*) of state functions but altered the method for calculating how the spoils would be divided.[163]

In Iraq's case by contrast it is the much more recent US occupation which created an 'allotment state' (*dawla al-muhassasa*) in the wake of the 2003 invasion and overthrow of Saddam Hussein and the Ba'th Party regime. The opposition political parties which owed their place in the corridors of power to the US were only too happy to play along, carving out fiefdoms for themselves from the carcase of the Ba'athist state while US corporations grabbed vast reconstruction contracts to rebuild the infrastructure which sanctions and US bombing campaigns had destroyed.[164]

In Lebanon, the institutionalisation of the Ta'if Agreement went hand-in-hand with a reconstruction process which intensified the polarisation of wealth and poverty. The peace agreement paved the way for the revival of Lebanon's banks as magnets for regional financial flows and for the fortunes which would be made from the rebuilding of the shattered capital city, Beirut. In the 1990s this process was personified by Rafiq al-Hariri, the Sunni construction billionaire who acted as the envoy of the Saudi royal family and played a central role in laying the groundwork for the Ta'if Accord, becoming Prime Minister in 1992. While investment from Saudi Arabia and the Gulf flowed into companies such as Hariri's Solidere, growing levels of public debt provided the rationale for successive privatisation drives over the following two decades.[165] The emerging Shi'a fraction of the bourgeoisie, which gradually gravitated towards Hizbollah's political leadership, was a partner in the reconstruction process, gaining an important

163 Salloukh, 2019, p44.
164 Marfleet, 2019.
165 Daher, 2016, p37–39.

Politics in the neoliberal era

foothold in the banking system, creating its own booming construction businesses in the southern suburbs of Beirut and investing in agricultural production in the fertile Bekaa Valley.[166]

The accumulation of wealth in the collective hands of the victors of Ta'if, combined with their control of the mechanisms for redistribution to their constituencies is one way in which the logic of neoliberalism reinforced sectarianism in Lebanon. The global neoliberal assault on the public sector and the drive to turn the state into a commissioner of private services was another. The massive growth in Hizbollah's network of health and education services over the last three decades provides an illustration. Historically, the Shi'a communities where Hizbollah emerged had suffered from neglect and lack of investment by the state.[167]

The end of the civil war and the formal entry of the Shi'a fraction of the bourgeoisie into the governing coalition could have offered an opportunity to redress this imbalance by redirecting state investment to make up the gap. Yet in an area when state investment in health and education remained stagnant and global economic orthodoxy was driving towards privatisation of public services, creating its own private infrastructure to serve the interests of the Shi'a community made both political and economic sense.[168] It should be stressed here that Hizbollah's leaders were simply following in the footsteps of their counterparts from other sects who had already created similarly profitable webs of charities, religious foundations and private companies to cover the gaps in state provision of basic services. The delivery of crucial services by these types of private institutions reinforces the ideological appeal of the sectarian system and reduces the opportunities for mixing with people from other religious backgrounds when accessing services.

We can trace a similar process in Iraq both before and after 2003. The logics of neoliberalism and sectarianism reinforced each other in the wake of the US invasion. US officials often decried the problem of "looting" which gathered pace as the armed insurgency took off, but the greatest looters of all were the multinationals they had invited in to pick over the carcass of the

---

166   Daher, 2016.
167   Petran, 1987.
168   Daher, 2016.

Revolution is the choice of the people

Ba'athist state. Electricity generators, hospital equipment, radio transmission towers all found their way into private hands, but by-and-large it wasn't the foreign multinationals, but rather local militias or sectarian political parties which ended up running things. This was only partially because the US multinationals were themselves targets of the armed insurgents,[169] but also because the vast majority of Iraqis rejected the US occupation and the associated corporate takeover of their public services.[170]

There were features of the neoliberal transformation which made the consolidation of a sectarian system much more likely. Both Iraq and Lebanon have experienced the catastrophic effects of repeated cycles of conflict and the displacement of millions of people from their homes. This has perpetuated a kind of "warlord economy" which is in turn reinforced by the regional and global features of the neoliberal regime of capital accumulation. One area of interaction, as Adam Hanieh notes, lies in the twin businesses of destruction and construction, where buildings flattened by barrel bombs and mortars need to be rebuilt, providing opportunities for building firms, cement makers, aluminium and steel manufacturers.[171] The built environment is one of the key sites of capital accumulation in the Gulf, and a driver behind the emergence of a bloc of Gulf capital spanning the Gulf Cooperation Council members.[172] In the case of Lebanon, the resurrection of the banking system and the rebuilding of Beirut with investment from the Gulf were central to Hariri's project.

The growth of cross-border trade in general (both in its 'licit' and 'illicit' forms) is another area of overlap between the warlord economy and neoliberalism.[173] The collapse of agricultural production in Iraq has been particularly devastating for local employment and is directly linked to the war with ISIS in 2014-2017 which was concentrated in the agricultural heartlands. These were already significantly weakened by years of sanctions, previous wars and US neoliberal policies after 2003 (and exacerbated by accelerating climate change) which undermined local food security to the benefit of US agribusinesses.[174]

169 Glanz, 2007: Streitfield, 2006.
170 Alexander & Assaf, 2005; Marfleet, 2019.
171 Hanieh, 2018, p237.
172 Hanieh, 2018.
173 AFP, 2019.
174 Donnelly, 2020.

Politics in the neoliberal era

A final crucial element in the picture is the enhanced role of the paramilitary sector itself as employer. War destroys jobs in productive sectors such as manufacturing and agriculture (already weakened by other trends in the global economy and increasingly by climate change). It also disrupts trade, often making the wages offered by paramilitary entities (whether those associated with the existing state or opposed to it) the only viable route to a regular wage for the young men who make up a large proportion of the labour force. This tendency has been seen strongly operating in Iraq and Syria in recent years, and to a limited extent in Lebanon with Hizbollah's recruitment of fighters for its battles inside Syria at the side of the Syrian regime.[175]

Conclusion: the paralysis of elite politics and the narrowing space for reformism

Out of the variety of different means by which the ruling classes of the region attempted to manage the political domain during the neoliberal era a number of key points emerge. Firstly, elite politics remained relatively stagnant in many countries, with the ruling parties of the previous era essentially remaining in power with cosmetic alterations. Frequently this was coupled with the grotesque spectacle of the transformation of republics in hereditary political systems—creating the novel political category of a 'jumlukiyya' (a mixture of the Arabic words for kingdom and republic coined by Egyptian opposition activist Saad Eddine Ibrahim.)[176] This in turn reflected the way in which the state bourgeoisie had often literally given birth to a private sector bourgeoisie composed of the sons and daughters of party officials and military top brass.

In a few cases where pressure from below caused a temporary rupture and brief interludes of more open political systems, such as Sudan 1985-9 and Algeria 1989-1992, democratic gains were reversed by the military. In the case of Algeria this was very directly a restoration of the old order with the FLN retaining political power on the back of the generals' coup. In Sudan it was elements of the old regime working in partnership with

---

175 Daher, 2016; El Dahan & Raya, 2018; Alexander, 2016.
176 Abelnasser, 2004, p138 fn37.

an Islamist movement which had also developed an alliance with the old dictatorship that took power. Secondly, with the exception of Turkey, neoliberal reforms did not open a path for a peaceful route to political power for Islamist movements. In Sudan, Islamists came to power by allying with a section of the military. In Lebanon and Iraq, the circumstances of war and foreign occupation created opportunities for Islamist parties to get into government. Almost everywhere else they were blocked, often paying a heavy price in terms of repression. There were two major consequences: firstly, in terms of their social composition, in most of the region, the fraction of the bourgeoisie which had benefitted from the neoliberal reforms was less important within the Islamist movement than the modern middle class of highly educated professionals which provided most of their core cadres. Working class and poor voters and supporters also retained their importance for the Islamist project, but only as troops to be mobilised at the ballot box or sometimes in protests.[177] Even the whiff of a political compromise by the regime or the merest crack of an opening in the fortress of the state would send the Islamist leaders back to working class and poor constituencies appealing for patience and calm.

Despite their hybrid, combined nature, the political arrangements cobbled together by the ruling classes of the region lasted a long time. In order to satisfy the second of Lenin's conditions for revolution, in other words for the lower classes to withdraw their collective consent to be ruled "in the old way", something else had to change. However, when it did, the accumulation of several generations of economic failure and the layering of the scars of inequality and uneven development from the colonial period onwards would lead to the explosion of a revolutionary crisis on a scale not seen for generations.

---

[177] There are almost no examples of Islamist movements mobilising for strikes. The one major exception was the FIS in Algeria which attempted to build its own trade union in competition with the UGTA and called for a general strike in May 1991. Alexander, 2000, p467.

Revolution is the choice of the people

Section three

Agents of change

Revolution is the choice of the people

Chapter 8
'Neither bread nor freedom': Conditions for popular revolt

How did these decades of defeats, wars lay the conditions for a new, and bigger wave of uprisings and more intense crisis for the ruling classes of the region? The 'losers' from the neoliberal turn were found across a very large spectrum of social classes below the ruling class. The wealth of the ruling class soared upwards, but gains made by other classes were precarious at best and for the *vast majority* of the population the outcomes of the neo-liberal era were disastrous.

This chapter concentrates on four key processes: firstly, the neoliberal restructuring of the economy placed immense pressure on wide sections of the rural and urban poor. In particular, in several countries discussed here the neoliberal turn in agriculture forced large numbers to leave the countryside for insecure and marginalised lives in the cities or provincial towns. Impoverished urban communities would provide many of the 'shock troops' of the insurrectionary phase of the revolutions, with their young men (and sometimes young women) dying on the barricades and in confrontations with the security forces from Cairo, to Aleppo and Khartoum. This process intersected with a second: the reconstitution of the working class during the neoliberal period.

It was not only the impoverished majority who experienced these kinds of pressures during the neoliberal period. A third process which would have important political repercussions was the renewal of the crisis of the middle class. The anti-colonial revolutions and the state structures which emerged in their aftermath reflected the hopes of sections of the modern middle class that the state could bring prosperity and security to society as a whole. Neoliberalism represented a crisis for large layers of this class: those whose status and livelihoods depended on the state suffered from its relative decline in resources. Meanwhile, the fruits of neoliberal reform were distributed unevenly, benefiting some who profited from the expansion of trade and finance, but passing others by. Finally, we will look at the generational aspect of the popular revolts— the concentration of much of this misery in the lives of young people and how this spurred on organising by students and unemployed graduates.

Did the revolts have rural roots?

Both the state capitalist era and the neoliberal era led to profound changes in the region's agricultural systems. Crucially neither period had provided answers to the deepening structural problems which resulted from the contradiction between human needs and production for the market. Neoliberal prescriptions for agricultural reform which were touted as providing a route to prosperity only benefitted a small minority and resulted in catastrophic environmental degradation. The exclusion of small producers from the land accelerated, while the turn towards capital- and water-intensive forms of agriculture exhausted soil fertility and groundwater supplies. Meanwhile urban populations became ever more dependent on imported food, increasing vulnerability across society from individual households to national governments to the dramatic oscillations in global prices of food. The peaking of prices for key agricultural commodities in 2008, especially wheat which is a staple food across the region, was particularly painful and cost governments dearly as they desperately sought access to international supplies.

The Middle East and North Africa imports more than 50 percent of its grain and cereal consumption, and in the mid-2000s global food prices spiralled upwards: by 2008 they were 83

Conditions for popular revolt

Figure 7: Rural population, percentage of total

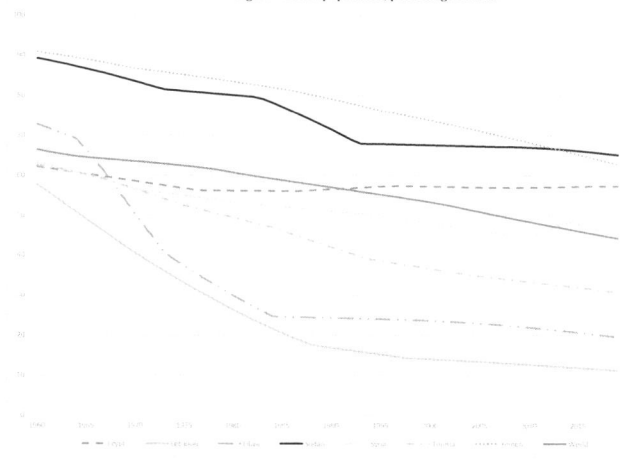

Source: World Bank

percent higher than in 2005.[1] As Ray Bush and Habib Ayeb note, the worsening food insecurity experienced by ordinary people across the Middle East is not a "natural" result of the region's climate, but is the product of policies which have systematically discouraged local and sustainable production of food in order to meet the demands of export markets.[2] The outcomes have been devastating to the poor both in the countryside and in the towns, ranging from the pain of dispossession and exclusion from the land for hundreds of thousands from farming communities, to deaths in the bread queues in the cities.

Yet the connection between changes in the region's agriculture over the past forty years, and the revolts which erupted after 2010 is not straightforward. In order to make sense of how these shifts fed into the patterns of revolution and counter-revolution, it is important to keep in mind both the wide variations in the economies of the region and the huge inequalities within and between them. Of the countries discussed in detail in this book, there is dramatic variation, for example between the percentage of population living in rural areas. Levels of urbanisation have been historically much

---
1 Ayeb & Bush, 2019, p78.
2 Ayeb & Bush, 2019, p80.

higher in the Gulf, where agriculture, as opposed to nomadic pastoralism, is very difficult to sustain. As the graph above shows, less than 20 percent of the Bahraini population lived in the countryside in 1960, compared to between 57 and 90 percent for the other countries in the region at the same date.

The overall trend across most of the region has been downwards, generally considerably faster than the global average, with the exception of Sudan and Egypt. The percentage contributed by agriculture to GDP has also varied widely over time, but the trend (following the global pattern) has also been downwards, Sudan stands out with agriculture accounting for nearly 30 percent of GDP in 2019. Egypt's huge rural population contrasts with the rapid collapse of agriculture's contribution to GDP—in 2019 this was just over 11 percent, compared to 11.9 percent in Algeria, and 10.3 percent in Tunisia the previous year. Under the impact of a devastating war, agriculture had collapsed in Yemen, although its contribution to GDP had already fallen to 8.5 percent by 2011.

Agriculture's declining share of the economy does not mean that employment in agriculture has fallen to comparable percentages—on the contrary, agriculture was still the largest employment sector in all of the countries discussed here until as recently as 2006. By 2011, only in Sudan, Egypt and Iraq was agriculture still the largest sector of the workforce.

These numbers are important for several reasons. Firstly, the timing of sharp, long-term contractions in agricultural employment in some cases seems likely to have fed into rural crises which in turn triggered revolts in the towns. The first of these cases is Tunisia, where the revolution began in the towns of the interior, such as Sidi Bouzid, where the local economy is dominated by agribusinesses generally headquartered on the much wealthier coastal regions, but also by high levels of unemployment and poverty. As Habib Ayeb explains,

> "Because of the unequal competition between investors (agribusiness, tourism, industry, etc.) and local populations, including peasant farmers, access to employment has progressively decreased and has been reduced to low-paid casual day labour. The daily wage in the new irrigated lands is some 5 to 6 euros for men (equivalent to 1 kg of meat), around 3 to 4 euros

for women, and less for children. Incomes are low and inadequate, but, worse than this, are seasonal only. For young people, who typically are educated and usually graduates, the chance to find a job, particularly in Sidi Bouzid, is practically non-existent".[3]

In Syria, a combination of ecological and political factors led to even more catastrophic outcomes for hundreds of thousands living in the country's rural northeastern governorates in the decade before the revolution of 2011. As the graph below shows, the Syrian agricultural labour force went into a steep decline from around 2000, after having risen considerably during the 1990s. The collapse of agricultural employment was driven by a combination of factors. Two severe droughts between 1998-2001 and 2006-2010 played an important role in the process, however the changes in agriculture were also driven by policy shifts at the centre of the state. The Ba'th Party's seizure of power in the 1960s had brought a layer of activists from the provinces, some of whom were of peasant origin, including Hafez al-Assad, president between 1970 and 2000. During the 1970s and 1980s, the Ba'thist state invested heavily in agriculture, especially in wheat and cotton production, and constructed large numbers of dams to expand irrigation systems.[4] Farms were collectivised and the process was overseen by the Ba'th Party, but rural living standards rose, and the party built a solid base for itself among the middle-sized farmers who benefitted from access to subsidised fuel and fertilisers, and from some land redistribution. Yields and acreage increased and rural-urban migration even began to reverse during the 1980s. The turn towards intensive water use from irrigation and pumping came at a cost which was only apparent later: the depletion of groundwater resources by over-pumping.

However, during the 1990s, faced with the demise of its superpower patron, the USSR, the Assad regime began to shift its policies towards greater liberalisation, first instituting decollectivisation, and then after Hafez al-Assad's death, abruptly adopting a "social market" economy in 2005. In practical terms this meant cutting fuel and fertiliser subsidies and reducing the state's role in buying crops. The consequences

---

3   Ayeb, 2011.
4   Daoudy, 2020, p113.

Revolution is the choice of the people

of the sudden shift in state policy after 2005, combined with the onset of drought, was a sharp increase in rural poverty which drove hundreds of thousands, potentially as many as 600,000 to abandon their homes and move elsewhere in Syria. Whole families left the countryside in provinces such as Hassakah, for provincial cities including Deir-ez-Zor, but also further afield including Damascus, Aleppo, Hama, and Raqqa. Some also travelled to the coast and Dera'a in the south.[5]

Egypt had also undergone a major restructuring of agriculture at the insistence of the IMF and World Bank. Law 96 of 1992 which came into force over a five-year period first removed controls on land rents (which surged from 7 times to 22 times the land tax value between 1992 and 1997), and then cancelled land leases allowing the original owners to keep, sell or re-let them at market rates after 1997.[6] The aim of this reform was to drive small cultivators, who were often tenant farmers, off the land, allowing the expansion of large estates geared towards producing for European export markets rather than local food needs. Tenants could no longer inherit leases which were restricted to a maximum of five years.

These attacks on small cultivators whose security of tenure was removed affected millions of people: 904,000 tenants (around 25 percent of farmers) were affected directly by law 96. Women tenant farmers who were heads of household following the death of their husband, or his incapacity to work, suffered disproportionately from the change.[7] However, in contrast to the experience of Syria, the neoliberal reforms to agriculture did not prompt the acceleration of migration to the large cities, which had been slowing down since the mid-1980s.[8] Rather it trapped hundreds of thousands of tenant farmers in even more insecure and seasonal patterns of cultivation, intermingled with agricultural wage labour and poorly paid non-agricultural activities in growing villages and provincial towns.[9] The impact of these changes on rural populations' livelihoods was immense, reversing progress in education as families took children out

---

5 Daoudy, 2020, p160.
6 Ayeb & Bush, 2019, p138.
7 Ayeb & Bush, 2019, p138–39.
8 World Bank, 2008, p10.
9 Ayeb & Bush, 2019; UN Habitat, 2011.

of school so they could earn, and malnutrition rising.[10] There was significant resistance to Law 96 within rural communities. According to the Land Centre for Human Rights (LHCR) "peasants mobilised with demonstrations, roadblocks, sending telegrams to government bodies, organising about 200 'peasant conferences' in 1997 and setting up 'peasant committees'.[11]

However, it was the eruption of revolution in the major cities in 2011 which stimulated a new wave of organising in the countryside, not the other way around, as peasant activists seized control of some farms which had been grabbed by large landowners as repression eased, and efforts to create grassroots 'peasants unions' were re-energised by the revolution.[12]

In Sudan, wars have been the main recent drivers of mass migration out of the countryside, helping to swell the populations of the capital Khartoum and Nyala, the provincial capital of South Darfur. There are intimate connections between the transformation of traditional agricultural and pastoral systems in areas such as Darfur which were geared towards meeting local needs, and the relentless cycles of war which have devastated large areas of Sudan. These conflicts represent a different kind of neoliberal restructuring of the relationship between land and people to the examples discussed above. A central player in this process is Mohamed Dagalo, commander of the Rapid Support Forces militia, who we already encountered in Chapter 3.

The social geography of revolution

The underlying crisis of the countryside in many cases thus forms a major part of the backdrop to the revolutions, and in some significant cases such Tunisia and Syria, the uprisings actually began at the intersections of rural and urban life in the towns of the provinces. Yet the crucial turning points in the revolutionary process, including the transition from localised rebellion to national uprising, took place with the eruption of mass mobilisations in the major urban areas, often in symbolic locations at the heart of the capital city.

10 Ayeb & Bush, 2019.
11 Lellis, 2019.
12 Lellis, 2019; Ahmed, 2019.

Revolution is the choice of the people

So, who were the 'urban masses' whose participation in marches, sit-ins and roadblocks shaped the destiny of the revolutions? And what made them risk arrest, injury and even death to take on the armed might of the state? One way to start to answer this question is to look at the social geographies and organisational histories of the uprisings in order to map their paths onto an analysis of the deeper changes in society during the neoliberal era.

People from a wide spectrum of social classes, from the very poorest to some sections of the middle class which were materially relatively comfortable compared to most of society, joined the revolutionary mobilisations. What rarely happened, however, was that those who were very wealthy or who enjoyed significant power and privilege through the ruling party and state bureaucracies joined the revolutionary side. As we'll discuss in later chapters, there some falling into this category who either defected in the heat of the uprisings (especially in Libya where Gaddafi's regime was rocked by splits at the very top to a greater degree than most of the others), or who tried to position themselves politically as supporting the revolution once it was underway (Naguib Sawiris in Egypt comes to mind here). And some of the larger Islamist opposition parties could count on the support of sections of the bourgeoisie, however these were small minorities and the centre of gravity in organisations such the Muslim Brotherhood remained resolutely further down the social scale, with solidly middle-class, not bourgeois leaderships, and lower-middle class and working-class mass memberships.

Let's look first at the trajectory of the Tunisian revolution from the intersection of rural and provincial urban misery in the interior of the country to the heart of the capital. The protests spread by two routes, firstly reaching areas with similar grievances through a combination of direct solidarity and mimesis[13]—activists in the towns where the uprising began took a conscious decision to try and spread the revolt in order to avoid isolation and defeat. Yet the places where the response was strongest initially were those where the demands of the incipient revolutionary coalition resonated because of similar grievances. This process powered the gathering pace of protests in places such as Kasserine, Thala and Gafsa. It was also one route by which the demonstrations entered the capital

---

13 Del Panta, 2019.

city, after the regime's miscalculated attempt to crush them by force with the shooting of protesters in Kasserine and Thala on 8 January. As Habib Ayeb notes, two days later demonstrations had started in greater Tunis, in neighbourhoods "such as Ettadhamoun, Intilaka and Ibn Khaldoun, where most of the inhabitants, generally of modest means, come from poor or marginalised regions".[14] The following day protests had spread to other neighbourhoods in the capital, such as Zahrouni and Sidi Hssein. On 12 January, it was the turn of:

"Kram, a poor suburb of Tunis situated in the middle of the richest ones. According to a young man in Kram who took part in the movement from the very beginning, young people from upper-class parts of the northern suburb of Tunis (Marsa, Carthage and Sidi Boussaid) used to come to demonstrate in Kram. As it has more working-class residents, Kram becomes the demonstration space for the richest demonstrators".[15]

In the case of Egypt, the uprising in the capital showed a similar dynamic of oscillation between the reservoirs of social anger in the city's working-class and lower-middle class neighbourhoods and the symbolic spaces of the city centre such as Tahrir Square. Radical networks of opposition activists called protests on 25 January, Egypt's 'National Police Day', which brought tens of thousands onto the streets, enough to take and temporarily hold Tahrir Square before the police cleared it. Friday 28 January was decisive in unleashing the revolutionary process: the call for demonstrations after Friday prayers and the state's response pitted the common people against the regime in an epic confrontation.

As in Tunisia, poor, working-class and lower-middle class neighbourhoods were one of the frontlines of the battle, while the other was the major city squares such as Tahrir in central Cairo. The scale of the mobilisation on 25 January prompted the security forces to try and crush protests by force as they arose in residential districts, hoping to stop the surge of demonstrators into the city centre which had temporarily overwhelmed them a few days previously. They badly miscalculated the depth of rage that this repression would trigger. By shooting dead protesters, bystanders who rushed to help the injured, and even people on their balconies, they accelerated demonstrations into localised

14 Ayeb, 2011.
15 Ayeb, 2011.

Revolution is the choice of the people

uprisings across the capital. In district after district local people responded to the killings not by retreating, cowed into their homes, but by sacking the local police station and burning down the local branch of the ruling party. Crucially, tens of thousands also marched on Tahrir Square where they broke the resolve of the riot police late on 28 January, establishing an overnight occupation of the square and humiliating the regime by taking control of the heart of the capital.

Working class, lower-middle class and poor districts gave the majority of dead and injured. Records made by the Society of the Heroes and Victims of the Revolution on 4500 of the injured during the 18 day uprising showed that 70 percent were workers without educational qualifications, and 12 percent workers with intermediate qualifications, 11 percent were school students, and 7 percent with higher qualifications.[16] A list of 120 martyrs compiled by the Journalists' Union which provides occupational data shows that 74 were workers and the rest students or professionals, and the majority came from poor areas. The list of professions of those killed is revealing: they included a welder, a plumber, a mechanic in a cement factory, assistant cook in a hotel, and a laundryman, alongside school and university students, teachers and doctors.[17] The 45 dead from Cairo in this list included a stonemason, a shoemaker, a microbus driver, a glass factory worker, a mechanic, a housewife, cafe workers, chefs, taxi drivers, a worker in the customs administration, an army conscript, a metal worker, and seller of galabiyyas. The occupations of the martyrs who fell in Alexandria included a railworker, an assistant chef, a worker in a glass shop, a carpenter, a printworker, a former barber, a pizza chef, an air conditioner repairman, a furniture-maker, and an army conscript. Most of the dead and injured in these lists were concentrated in working-class or lower-middle class northern and southern suburbs, such as Zawiya al-Hamra, Dar al-Salam and Basatin. Even in wealthier areas, the dead and injured tended to be concentrated among a similar mix of blue and white-collar workers.[18]

What about Syria, which appeared to follow the Tunisian pattern of a revolt at the intersections of rural immiseration, provincial marginalisation and suburban poverty? Accounts

---

16 Alexander & Bassiouny, 2014.
17 ANHRI, 2012.
18 Alexander & Bassiouny, 2014.

Conditions for popular revolt

of the early days of the rebellion in Deraa emphasize the convergence of the first two with the ideological shock of the regime's use of live fire against protesters demanding the release of school children arrested and tortured for writing anti-regime slogans on the walls. The town's resources had been stretched by the arrival of refugees from the severe drought in the northeastern regions,[19] however, it was the densely networked family relationships of the 'old town', Deraa al-Balad, which powered the escalation of protests during the first crucial weeks. It was from mosques in this area that the first public protests started on 18 March, with desperate relatives and neighbours of the detained boys at their heart. They saw two young men shot dead in front of them, and when they set up a makeshift field hospital in the Omari mosque, that too came under attack by the security forces. This set the town on fire, with the epicentre of the emerging mass movement located in Deraa al-Balad, which found itself under siege from Daraa al-Mahatta, the district on the opposite side of the valley, where most of the government buildings were located. A cycle of protests, killings by the security forces and enraged funerals spread the movement further into the surrounding areas, such as Al-Sanamayn, a town of around 30,000 between Daraa and Damascus, where thousands protested and pulled down a statue of Hafez al-Assad on 25 March.[20]

While the issues which drove people in the provinces to revolt were varied, a common pattern was for the regime's declaration of war against whole neighbourhoods and sometimes whole towns to force an unenviable choice between complete submission or rebellion on people from a wide variety of social backgrounds, including some who were relatively wealthy, highly educated or local notables, such as religious figures. By contrast, in the capital, Damascus, the revolutionary mobilisations were concentrated in the impoverished suburbs, districts such as Douma, Zamalka and Moadamiya. These areas, like Deraa and Deir-ez-Zor, had also received many migrants fleeing the drought in the northeast, but were also home to workers and civil servants who had left more expensive areas because of soaring rents. The fringes of the major cities acted as reservoirs of revolutionary anger and mobilisation, as well

---

19 Yassin-Kassab and Al-Shami, 2018.
20 SyriaUntold, 2016.

as points of interchange with their rural hinterlands, with which they retained strong economic and demographic ties.[21] However, as we will discuss in more detail in the next chapter, what was missing in the Syrian case was a mechanism to connect that anger to the strategic capacity to disrupt the workings of state institutions from within. This was to prove the Syrian revolution's Achilles Heel.

If we look at the case of Sudan in 2018-2019, the process whereby protests scaled up into revolution took longer than Tunisia and Egypt, but nevertheless showed strong similarities to events eight years previously. As we discussed in Chapter 3, the touchpaper was lit by huge price rises in basic goods such as bread and fuel, which sparked a wave of spontaneous protests. The 'start' of the revolution is marked by Sudanese activists as being on 18 December, however there were already protests over the price rises in districts across the capital several days before that, according to a database compiled by Egyptian researcher, Isra'a Sirag-al-Din.[22] She logged the first small protest in the neighbourhood of Burri on 12 December. This was followed by 14 more two days later, of which 11 were in the capital and three outside. Besides Burri, other Khartoum neighbourhoods where this first small wave of demonstrations took place included relatively well-off al-Riyadh, and Kalakla, an impoverished neighbourhood in the southwest of Khartoum. Outside the capital the railway town of Atbara, one of the historic centres of working-class organisation in Sudan was one of those where protests were beginning, by 20 December, the dozens of demonstrators in the town had become thousands. By now repression was beginning to bite, with security forces firing on the crowds, beating and arresting demonstrators. With the second week of protests the slogans changed from chants against high prices to calls for the regime to go, thousands were on the streets of Burri, al-Rebek, Gadaref and Atbara. By the end of the month, new areas of the capital were being drawn into the battle, the movement had reached all the major cities from Port Sudan on the Red Sea, to Nyala in Darfur and Dongola in the north.

As Magdi el-Gizouli notes, events in Atbara followed a similar pattern to those elsewhere:

---

21 Alexander & Bassiouny, 2014.
22 Sirag-al-Din, 2019.

Pupils of Atbara Industrial School took to the streets angered by the tripling of bread prices following a long period of bread shortages and were soon joined by day labourers from the town market and students from other schools as well as a local university. Within hours, the headquarters of the ruling National Congress Party (NCP) were on fire, local government officials had disappeared from the scene, their symbols of authority, cars and offices, ablaze.[23]

There was a difference, el-Gizouli argues, however to the dynamics of the uprising in the capital, where the poorest and most marginalised could not even afford the bread which protesters in more middle-class neighbourhoods relied on.

Mapping the social geography of Palestinian resistance reveals how all the peaks of popular mobilisation have expressed the anger of the poor majority of Palestinians at the combination of social injustice and national oppression which blight their lives. From the experience of exile in the wake of the Nakba, to the privatised "McCities" of the West Bank[24] under the Palestinian Authority's rule during the neoliberal era, the impacts of dispossession have not fallen evenly across the different social classes. In exile, middle class and wealthy Palestinians frequently suffered various forms of legal and political discrimination in the countries where they resided, but those lower down the social scale experienced national oppression and social injustice as mutually reinforcing pressures.[25] The majority of those trapped in refugee camps outside historic Palestine faced huge barriers to accessing jobs and services on the same terms as local citizens, compounding the effect of being wrenched from their land and forced into unskilled, precarious wage labour.[26]

A version of the same process took place within the West Bank and Gaza, as 'internally' displaced refugees were transformed into pools of precariously employed or unemployed urban workers, some of whom were treated intermittently as labour reserves for the Israeli hospitality and construction sectors. The refugee

23 El-Gizouli, 2019.
24 Tayeb, 2019.
25 Shiblak, 1996.
26 Shiblak, 1996.

camps transformed into permanently impoverished urban neighbourhoods, while the small rural towns and villages where Palestinians still worked in farming found themselves under siege from the Israeli settlements which stole their land and water, forcing many to abandon making a living from the land.

The fact that Palestine resistance is at the same time a fight against national oppression and a struggle by a large section of the poor against the rich minority who rule them is underscored by the convergence in forms of protest in popular uprisings across the region. Neoliberal reforms reshaped the economy and society through policies which would leave millions living in impoverished urban neighbourhoods, often dependent on relatively precarious waged labour to survive, priced out of access to decent health care, education and housing by the inequalities of the market. The mechanisms which trapped Palestinians in similar conditions may have been different, but the end result was a set of common experiences of social injustice which have the potential to unite the poor majority across the whole region. This is fundamentally why the peaks of the Palestinian popular movement, such as the Intifada of 1987-88 have been both an *example to*, and an *exemplar of* the new type of rebellions by the urban poor and working class which would repeatedly shake the region in the neoliberal era.

The middle class in crisis?

What exactly were the threats which propelled residents of the well-to-do Khartoum neighbourhood al-Riyadh into the streets against the dictatorship in Sudan? And were these repeated in other uprisings? Before we can attempt an answer to this question, we need a brief digression to explore what being 'middle class' means in the societies we are discussing in this book. The Marxist analysis of capitalism is rooted in the idea that it is characterised by the struggle between the two 'polar' classes: the bourgeoisie, who own and control the means of production (and frequently dominate political institutions and steer the direction of the state, although this is not essential), and the working class, whose only way to survive is to sell their labour power. Yet, this abstract model of two armies facing each other across a battlefield frequently appears to bear little resemblance to actual historical development of classes and class struggle. Just as in Marx's day, there are classes and fractions of classes in between the working class and the bourgeoisie, which are sometimes pulled towards accommodation and compromise with the bourgeoisie and at other times pushed by recurrent economic and social crisis into confrontation alongside workers and other layers of the poor. Grasping what defines this 'in-between' position is important: class in the sense that Marx meant it cannot simply be read off from income, level of education or taking home a wage. There are some sections of the middle class who make a living from the ownership of property or trade. Both objective and subjective circumstances could push them into rebellion against the state, and some of this layer of the population of Syria's provincial towns were propelled into revolution in the spring and summer of 2011 by a combination of the encroaching crisis in the countryside and the actions of the regime.

Much more important in terms of the social basis of the revolutions, however, was the crisis of that part of the middle class associated with the state during the neoliberal period. Again, some clarification is important here: working for a government institution does not in itself make you middle-class, even in societies where very large numbers of the poor do not have access to regular work at all. The key test here is whether your role involves controlling the labour of other people, and the degree to which that gives you autonomy in relation to those higher up the managerial food-chain. State employment expanded massively during the state capitalist period, apparently offering a route towards prosperity, influence and power for some of the generation which came of age in the era of anti-colonial revolution. It oversaw a huge growth in the public education system and the institution of a social compact which promised their sons and daughters of a straight path from school to university qualifications in subjects designed to fit them for service in the state as it built a modern society. The onset of crisis and the neoliberal turn by the ruling class threw these plans into disarray. While state employment actually rarely shrank, or at least not for civil servants, health workers and education workers, its status, pay and working conditions were systematically degraded. Moreover, the state's role as a ladder which anyone could apparently climb if they had the motivation to 'better themselves' and make a 'better society' was disrupted. Power and influence in the neoliberal period coalesced in new channels, some of the people who wielded it owed their social rise to business success but frequently they were the sons and daughters of the very top layers of state bureaucracy. While the idea that the state was genuinely an instrument of meritocracy was always a myth, this does not make the rage at corruption and nepotism of those shut out of it any less real.

A further set of pressures which weighed heavily on both the middle class and the poor during the neoliberal period was the systematic downward shift in the burden of services supporting the reproduction of social life as well as the production of capital such as housing, healthcare and education. The state capitalist turn had created welfare, health care and housing systems which redistributed some of the wealth in society downwards through providing basic medical services, public education and subsidising rents. During the neoliberal era this process was partially reversed, not just because less state investment was directed towards these areas, but also because they became once again frontiers for private capital accumulation. The people who suffered the most from this process were workers and the poor, but the burdens of paying more for education and health care also weighed on the middle class.

There were sections of the middle class which did much better during the neoliberal period, some who benefitted from the expansion of trade and the financial sector in particular. The social basis of Umar al-Bashir's regime in Sudan partially rested on the expansion of this layer of society, for example. Migration to the Gulf during the 1970s and 1980s played an important role in refreshing the private sector middle class across the entire region. This was partially a result of the increasing differentiation between the economies of the region as the new centre of capital accumulation in the Gulf took off: high wages in professional and managerial roles for migrants could be turned into capital to invest in property and businesses back home. But it also reflected the growing importance of those who could act as brokers between the interests of Gulf capital and their home countries—helping to identify investment opportunities, fixing up trading partnerships, and carrying the social and cultural practices of the Gulf's religiously conservative society to new receptive audiences. As Sameh Naguib points out, there was a layer of the Egyptian Islamist movement's middle class base who were deeply influenced by this social process during the 1980s.[27]

Professionals and proletarians

One of the features of the revolts discussed in this book has been the important role played by 'professionals'. This was perhaps most obvious in the Sudanese Revolution where the Sudanese Professionals Association emerged as a political actor in the uprising. The SPA is a network of independent trade unions and professional associations representing both public sector workers and members of what used to be called 'the liberal professions.' However, in every country discussed here, both collectively and individually groups such as doctors, teachers, journalists, lawyers and engineers played important roles in the uprisings. In some cases, their professional networks became vectors of rebellion, as with the example of the Tunisian Bar Association, which was one of the earliest national organisations supporting the growing revolutionary mobilisation. 'Professional' is a complicated label, however, which can be applied to people in a variety of class positions. A doctor for example could be working for a wage in a public hospital or running their own business selling medical services for a profit (or doing both of these at the same time, as is common for senior doctors in the Egyptian health care system).

While there is not space here for a proper discussion of what constitutes a 'profession' in the contemporary Middle East, understanding some aspects of the role of professionals in the revolutionary crisis is important. Firstly because professional associations (whether formally constituted and regulated by the state or 'alternative' ones) sometimes played extremely important roles as spaces for dissent, as well as taking on practical organisational tasks in generalising protests. In some of the countries discussed here, the state partially or sometimes fully lost control over professional associations representing lawyers, doctors, engineers, journalists, and sometimes even judges, in the decades before the uprisings. This was certainly the case in Egypt, where Muslim Brotherhood supporters were elected to leadership roles in several of the important professional

---

27 Naguib, 2006.

associations during the 1980s and 1990s.[28] To a more limited extent, the professional associations could also serve as a refuge for left and liberal opposition currents. This aspect of the role of professionals in the revolutionary process had strong elements of continuity from previous generations—lawyers and journalists who went through a European-style education were some of the most important carriers of nationalist ideas in the region from the late 19th century onwards.

However, there was a second aspect of this process where the role of professionals can only be understood through the lens of changes in the class structure under neoliberalism. A persistent feature of social changes wrought by the neoliberal turn across the region was the 'downwards' pressure on some of the occupations which historically fell under the term 'professionals', or perhaps more accurately, on some layers within those professions. 'Downwards' here means that their working lives became progressively more like those of workers: their relative pay declined, the advantages conferred by higher levels of education diminished, they lost autonomy in their jobs to managers who imposed tighter discipline and demanded greater productivity through mechanisms such as performance-related pay. This process of proletarianization was uneven, it affected people at the beginning of their careers more intensely, and it did not automatically mean that everyone subject to its pressures automatically drew radical political conclusions. Nevertheless, it was one of the reasons for the combativity of some of the 'professions' which has too often been subsumed under different explanations of 'middle class rebellion'.

One group which was subject to this pressure was junior doctors. During the neoliberal period, they saw the relentless degradation not just of their own pay and conditions, but of the whole public health system. In Egypt, some doctors profited from health privatisation, and made fortunes as medical businessmen. However, increasingly large layers of younger doctors, forced into double-shifts in the public hospitals in the morning followed by more work in private clinics in the afternoon and evening, began to look to other ways to fight back. They started to discuss, and finally to actually mobilise for collective action as wage-workers inside the public health system, taking strike action with the twin aims of forcing the state to improve their own conditions and to

---

28 Wickham, 2015.

invest more in health.[29] Teachers were another group subject to even stronger downward pressures during the neoliberal era than doctors. Reforms to the education system pushed teachers towards supplementing their meagre pay in the public education system with other kinds of work, or by becoming themselves agents of privatisation and commodification. Many were driven into double-shift working offering private lessons (or working for private education providers), thus colluding in increasing the burden of private payments for education falling on working class, poor and even middle class families desperate to secure a decent education for their children.

Egyptian teacher activists often linked the struggle for decent pay to the battle to abolish private lessons as an additional tax on the poor. One striking teacher in September 2011 put it this way:

> First thing to say is that isn't true that we teachers are against Egypt. We want to see a rebirth of education. We are on the side of ordinary people who have to spend up to 50 percent of the money in their pockets on private lessons. We're standing with them, with the Egyptian economy and with the Egyptian people. But we've also got the right to be able to go home at the end of the day and spend time with our kids. This is so that I can have time to sit with my son.[30]

The pressures of proletarianisation were not only reflected in the experience of work for many people who saw themselves as 'professionals', they also translated into new means of collective action and class-based forms of organisation started to emerge in layers of the population which previously had little history of this kind of struggle.

The re-constitution of the working class

We will explore the character and scope of the workers' mobilisations which both paved the way for the uprisings and shaped their trajectories once underway in the next chapter. However, to make sense of that process, we first need to investigate

---

29 Shafiq, 2011.
30 MENA Solidarity Network, 2011.

how neoliberal reforms restructured the economy and society and what difference they made to the nature of work itself.

Across the Middle East as a whole, during the first decades of the 21st century, workers began to mobilise once again in large numbers to defend themselves collectively from the depredations of capital. Despite predictions that waged workers would not fight because they formed a privileged layer inside societies where few enjoyed the luxury of a stable, paid job, millions went on strike. Despite claims that the partial disappearance of 'old' industries would bring an end to traditions of working class militancy, new layers of activists in health, education and the civil service discovered how to build unions and organise collective action. The disruptive capacity of some groups of workers, such as transport and logistics workers was enhanced by the growing reliance of capitalists in different parts of the world on cross-border production chains and international trade.

The scale of the recovery of workers' self-organisation and militancy underscores how capitalism in the neoliberal era, just as in its previous incarnations, still "has no choice about teaching its workers the wonders of organisation and labour solidarity, because without these the system cannot operate".[31] Workers still retain powers of concentration and combination, and the power to disrupt the flow of profit, even in societies where they are not the absolute majority, and under conditions where their bosses have a whole range of ideological tools at their disposal to fragment and disorganise their struggles.

Taking some very broad statistical measures to sketch out the changes in the class composition of the societies discussed in this book, shows some common features which are worth further investigation. Firstly, let's look at the relationship between employees and the other categories of people who are part of the labour force. While there are some employees who are highly paid agents of capital, this category has to be the core of the working class in Marx's definition. One of the long-term trends in the social organisation of labour under neoliberalism has been the promotion of both entrepreneurship and self-employment as alternatives to waged labour. Famously, neoliberal economist Hernando de Soto even claimed Mohamed Bouazizi, whose suicide sparked the uprisings was simply a

---

31 Draper, 1978, p41.

Conditions for popular revolt

frustrated small businessman: "like 50 per cent of all working Arabs, he was an entrepreneur, albeit on the margins of the law, who died trying to gain the right to hold property and do business without being hassled by corrupt authorities.[32]

Yet during the period when neoliberal reforms accelerated in most countries discussed here, the proportion of the total labour force made up by employees as opposed to employers, the self-employed or people working for other members of their own families grew. The exceptions were Iraq and Yemen, where the reduction in waged work was likely an effect of war. In almost all countries discussed in this book, employees formed a substantial majority of the total labour force, except for Sudan and Yemen, where the proportion was 44 percent and 47 percent respectively in 2020. Moreover, in most countries, the category which shrunk the most was what the International Labour Organisation calls "contributing family workers" (in other words people whose boss is a family member, and who have no real say over what happens in the family business) while the proportions for "employers" and "own-account workers" stayed relatively similar.

The trends in data about the proportion of people in the labour force for approximately the same period are complicated by the very large differences between male and female participation, and by the fact that some countries have little data available. Nevertheless, some interesting patterns emerge. Bahrain, which has the most developed economy of the countries discussed here, and almost no agricultural sector to speak of, being largely dependent on oil and services, has by far the highest labour participation rates, including for women. Rates of women's participation in the labour force rose significantly in Bahrain in the two decades between 1991 and 2010, from just under 30 percent to 43 percent.

In Algeria and Tunisia, male labour participation rates dropped noticeably between the 1990s and the present, down from 77.5 percent in 1996 to 66.2 percent in Algeria between 1996 and 2017, while in Tunisia they fell from 75.3 percent in 1989 to 68.3 percent in 2017. However, a rise in female participation partially offset this drop. Egypt's labour participation rates were relatively stable during the same period, hovering around 70 percent for men and 20 percent for women.

---

32 Soto, 2011.

Revolution is the choice of the people

There was a large leap in women's participation in the labour force in Lebanon between 2004 and 2019, up from 20 percent to 29 percent, and a slight rise for men, up from 69 to 70 percent. The small amount of data available for Sudan also showed a big rise in women's participation for the two years available: up from 23 percent in 2009 to 28 percent in 2011, while the male participation rate dropped slightly from 73 to 70 percent. Iraq showed low rates of women working, around 12 percent, while the rate for men was around 72 percent for 2007 and 2012. The largest changes were to be found in Yemen, where women's participation rates collapsed from nearly 22 percent in 1999 to 6 percent in 2014, while the rate for men declined from 69 percent to 65 percent.

In the mid-1990s, Syria's rates of labour force participation were similar to Egypt's and Tunisia's, however after 2000 participation for both men and women declined noticeably, most sharply for women. Unlike Iraq, Algeria and Yemen where the data shows the scars of sanctions and civil war, in the Syrian case this underlines the combined violence of the neoliberal transition and ecological crisis in peacetime conditions before the 2011 uprising.

The general picture which emerges is thus one where either a substantial majority, or a growing proportion of the population are directly dependent on wage labour of some kind, rather than 'being your own boss' or 'becoming a boss', to survive. There are of course other kinds of transformation which have disrupted these patterns, including devastating external military interventions and civil wars, but these trajectories illustrate the continued centrality of waged work under neoliberalism, just as in any other sort of capitalism.

Of course, this does not tell us anything about the kinds of jobs that these wage workers are doing, and to what extent they are likely to confer the powers of combination and disruption we noted above. Workers' ability to resist in an organised way, the history of the workers' movement shows, is affected by factors such as the size of the workplace—with small workplaces, particularly those where people work directly with their bosses in small offices or shops, often being harder to organise than larger workplaces. There is also the separate, but important question of whether workers can take "economically effective action", as Chris Harman put it, in other words whether if they withdraw their labour it hurts their bosses' profits.[33]

So how has the distribution of workers by economic sector changed in recent decades? Although these statistics are very blunt tools for understanding what has happened to the working class, some patterns emerge. Firstly, as we already noted, employment in agriculture declined overall in most countries, except Sudan and Egypt where the number of agricultural workers still dwarfs those employed in other sectors. In Tunisia, by far the largest employment sector in 2020 was manufacturing, followed by construction, agriculture and public administration. In Algeria, the largest sector was construction, followed by public administration, trade and manufacturing. The patterns of change by sector in Algeria show the impact of reconstruction after the 'black decade' of civil war during the 1990s: in the 2000s the steepest increases were in public administration and construction which overtook agriculture as the largest economic sector by numbers employed mid-way through the decade. Manufacturing, education and trade also grew rapidly during the same period. Around 2011, changes in government policy including austerity measures and a hiring freeze in the public sector are visible in the flat-lining of most of these trends except the trade sector.

In Egypt, after agriculture the second biggest employment sector in 1991 was manufacturing. The restructuring of public sector industry in the 1990s led to slow growth in manufacturing employment for the next two decades, and by 2011 construction and trade had overtaken manufacturing. However, after 2011, the growth in manufacturing jobs sharply accelerated again. The numbers employed in public administration in Egypt have been declining since the mid-2000s, as have the numbers employed in education since 2016, although the scale of the education sector in Egypt is extremely large, employing almost as many people as manufacturing in 2011. In Lebanon the largest employment sector since the late 2000s has been trade, followed by public administration, agriculture and manufacturing. Iraq's trade sector is also the second biggest employer: followed by construction, public administration and education.

A lot more detailed investigation would be necessary to provide a better assessment of what changes in the working lives of the people behind these statistics mean for their capacity

---

33 Callinicos & Harman, 1987, p64.

and confidence to resist. However, there are some general points worth making. Firstly, while sectors such as wholesale and retail trade and construction which pose challenges to workers' self-organisation because of either the small size of workplaces and high levels of casualisation and employment of migrant or seasonal workers did grow in many countries, there were either similar numbers or more people employed as state administrators, educators and healthworkers than in these sectors in every country. Although individual government offices or schools may not be especially large workplaces, the fact that they are part of a national infrastructure can be an accelerant to workers' consciousness and self-organisation.

Secondly, although manufacturing in some cases declined or flat-lined, and in others saw a shift from relatively much larger public sector industrial workplaces to small or micro-sized private sector workshops, the picture was highly uneven. Crucially, in several countries discussed here, at the outbreak of the uprisings, privatisation and deindustrialisation had not entirely wiped out the old industrial sectors. For example, in Algeria, despite the closure of many industrial plants during the 1990s, some of the old citadels of labour militancy such as the public sector vehicle manufacture SNVI did survive and played an important role in the strike waves before and during the uprising. A similar point could be made about Egypt's textile sector.

Developments in one other strategically important sector—transport, communications and logistics—are worth mentioning here too. This sector of employment was one of the fastest growing in Egypt since the 1990s and in Sudan since the late 2000s, and remains a major employer in most other countries. What this means for workers' ability to organise is often complex—during the neoliberal period some parts of the transport sector have seen massive growth in 'own-account' working (with the expansion of taxi, microbus and tuk-tuk services for example), and the decline of publicly funded transport infrastructure, for ex=ample.[34]

However, the degradation of transport infrastructure also negatively affects capital accumulation and the past two decades have also seen some investment and modernisation of those parts of the transport systems which are geared towards serving export markets, for example. The struggle of workers

---

34 Alexander & Bassiouny, 2014.

in Port Sudan over the privatisation and containerisation of the port is one example of how such changes can fuel resistance.

Palestinian workers: class formation in exile and under occupation

The experience of Palestine once again conforms to the general patterns of class formation and reconstruction across the region, while the framework of the apartheid political system created by the Israeli ruling class intensifies some aspects and suppresses others. The Nakba was an instance of forced *rural-urban* migration for the majority of Palestinians. One of the outcomes was the partial proletarianisation of Palestinian society, but in a highly uneven fashion and shaped by further experiences of exile and migration. An important section of the Palestinian working class formed during the 1950s and 1960s around the oil industry in the Gulf, for example. Saudi Aramco opened recruitment offices in Beirut in 1949 explicitly aimed at recruiting Palestinians.[35] Other Palestinians were transformed into a new layer of the urban working class in Lebanon and Jordan, although this was often a minority with the majority finding work (when it was available) as rural workers. In Lebanon, for example, Palestinians living in camps such as Nahr al-Bared in the north worked as agricultural day labourers and construction workers, with a minority finding jobs in small manufacturing workshops and services. In the Beirut-based camp of Tel al-Za'atar in the mid-1970s, the majority of the labour force worked in industry, but were concentrated in small workshops, with only 50 out of 1355 in workplaces with more than 50 workers.[36]

Within historic Palestine, the 1967 occupation of the West Bank and Gaza Strip was partially designed by its architect, Israeli commander Moshe Dayan as a mechanism to ensure that Palestinians living there would be available as a disposable labour force and as a captive market for Israeli goods. His policies aimed at achieving "an economic integration and not a political integration. In other words, not an annexation: we should not

35 Thiollet, 2016, p8.
36 Sayigh, 1984.

make them citizens of the state of Israel".[37] Dayan believed it was possible to square the circle and enjoy the benefits of exploiting Palestinian workers and controlling Palestinian agricultural land and water resources, while maintaining the edifice of discrimination which ensured the 'Jewish character' of the Israeli state.[38] During the neoliberal era too, the geopolitical processes which victimised Palestinians continued to deliver social and economic changes aligned with the general trajectories of the capitalist system's development. War and ethnic cleansing once again created outcomes which could be described as neoliberal economic reform and structural adjustment "by other means". Some of these wars did not directly involve Palestinians or even Israelis as direct combatants. Hundreds of thousands of Palestinians living in the Gulf were expelled in the wake of the Iraqi invasion of Kuwait in 1990. This was one of the major milestones in a broader process whereby the Gulf's ruling class disposed of the Arab working class it had imported to build the oil industry and key public services, in order to reorient its migration system towards pulling in workers from South Asia and further East.[39]

Within historic Palestine, the defeat of the First Intifada and the negotiated surrender of the PLO's leadership during the 1990s allowed the Israeli ruling class to also partially reset its labour migration system to exclude tens of thousands of Palestinians and import both Jewish immigrants from the Former Soviet Union and their families alongside non-Jewish migrant workers from a wide range of other countries during the 1990s and 2000s.[40] However, just as elsewhere in the region, the neoliberal era did not only see the destruction of working class jobs, but also the expansion of employment in services, especially in the public sector. Within historic Palestine this took the form of the creation of the Palestinian Authority during the 1990s. The number of Palestinians employed the Palestinian Authority rose from 39,000 at its inception in 1994 to 180,000 by 2013. Although a large proportion of these jobs are in the security services, they also include tens of thousands

---

37 Palumbo,1990, p68.
38 Hirst, 2003, p245.
39 Hanieh, 2011.
40 Alexander, 2022.

of teachers and civil servants.[41] It is politically convenient for the Israeli ruling class and the Western governments with which it is allied to repeat the fiction that Palestinian public sector workers are *not* employed by the Israeli state. Yet the PA is not financially independent and never will be, relying on the transfer of funds by the Israeli government under the terms of the Oslo Accord and donations from the Western powers which guaranteed the peace process to survive.[42] The fact that the Israeli ruling class outsourced the political management of Palestinian public sector workers' discontent to Palestinians does not change that fact.

Youth and revolution

A final point merits some discussion: the question of how the changes wrought by neoliberalism in the economy and society affect people at different ages. For decades officials at the IMF and World Bank have been fretting about the extremely high levels of youth unemployment across the Middle East. The world average was 13 percent in 2018, while the average for the Middle East as a whole peaked at 30 percent in 2017.[43] This is not a new problem, and although the decades since 1991 have seen an acceleration of neoliberal reforms, in general the international financial institutions' prescriptions to solve it have generally focussed on more of the same failed recipes promoting private sector growth, loosening job protection for workers so as to benefit new labour market entrants, changing education and training and attacking pay and conditions in the public sector so as to make poorly-paid, insecure private sector jobs seem more appealing. Part of the issue is connected to demographic growth, most countries in the Middle East have a relatively young population structure. In 2018, 60 percent of the region's population was under 30.

Moreover, there was a surge of rapid population growth in the 1990s and 2000s which has created additional pressures on the labour market since the late 2000s by helping to widen the gap between the number of jobs available and the number of new

---

41 Farraj & Dana, 2021.
42 Farraj & Dana, 2021.
43 Kabbani, 2019.

Figure 8: Youth unemployment, percentage of total

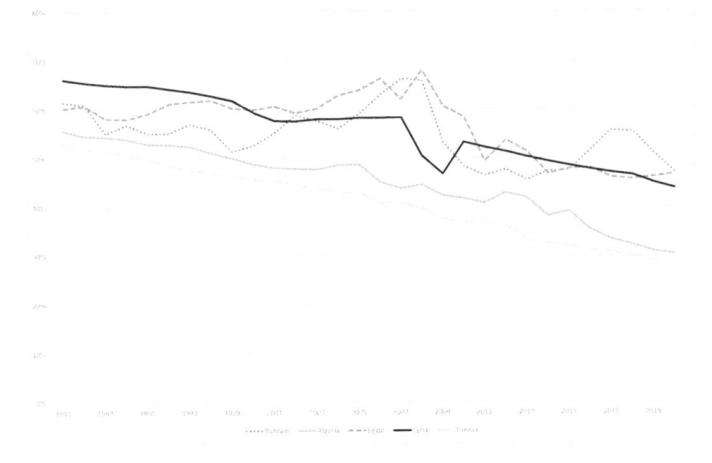

Source: International Labour Organisation

potential jobseekers.[44] The shocks to the economy of the 2008 global financial crisis, the uprisings and revolutions since 2010 and the collapse in oil prices after 2014, and now the Covid-19 pandemic have all affected successive generations of young workers. Another longer-term reason which lies behind the very high rates of youth unemployment in the region is the persistence of a huge gap between men and women's participation in the labour force which is currently triple the rate in 'emerging market' and 'developing' economies.[45] The countries discussed in this book have broadly followed these regional patterns: youth unemployment has been persistently high for decades in all of them.

What is less clear is whether there were *changes* in key aspects of youth unemployment in the run-up to the uprisings which fuelled anger and frustration at specific moments. Young people actually formed a larger proportion of the total numbers of unemployed in 1991 than in the years immediately preceding the uprisings or today. There were noticeable peaks in the share of youth unemployment of the total in Egypt and Bahrain in 2009, but that proportion fell back afterwards (although

---

44 Purfield and et al, 2018.
45 Purfield and et al, 2018, pxiii.

Conditions for popular revolt

it surged again in 2015 and 2016 in Bahrain). Overall, the proportion of young people among the unemployed as a group fell since the 1990s, however.

This does not mean that the young people who were a key constituency in the revolutionary mobilisations lacked real grievances. The reasons for their rebellion were generally more complex than simply the timing of a "demographic bulge" and temporary "tightness" in the labour market. The expansion of higher education is an important part of the picture. In most of the countries discussed here, enrolment rates rose significantly during the 1970s, but growth tailed off as state investment slowed in the 1980s. Growth in student populations surged again in later decades, however. In Egypt, the gross enrolment rate was around 30 percent for much of the 2000s and has risen to around 35 percent in recent years. In Syria, by contrast, the rate was only 12 percent in 2001, but had more than doubled by a decade later, peaking at 42 percent in 2015. In Algeria, gross enrolment was 15 percent in 2001 but had risen to over 50 percent by 2018. Sudan's rate of enrolment started lower—at 6.5 percent in 1999—but still rose considerably, reaching nearly 17 percent by 2015.[46]

The gap between young people's experiences of education and the world of work (and joblessness) they are expected to fit into is certainly one of the factors driving student and graduate resistance. In Tunisia and Iraq, organisations of unemployed graduates played an important role in organising and generalising protests, particularly at early stages of the uprisings. Algerian students have been a relatively well-organised component of the wider popular movement, organising marches on Tuesdays which have complemented the Friday general mobilisations, and creating student assemblies on campus to debate tactics and organise student actions.[47] Student groups were active in opposition networks in Egypt before the 2011 revolution, and student activism expanded massively between 2011 and 2013 with mass mobilisations to defend students' right to organise both inside the public universities and in the private sector.[48]

---

46 World Bank, 2008.
47 Larabi, Smith & Hamouchene, 2020.
48 Alexander & Bassiouny, 2014.

Conclusion

The idea that neoliberalism has not only left a legacy of defeat, but also created objective conditions for popular revolt is counter-intuitive. Yet, the social and economic changes across the region over the last forty years did not only disperse and atomise ordinary people, but also combined them, especially in urban contexts where 'the masses' numbers could be brought to bear. It recreated the conditions for tens of thousands to relearn the arts of insurrection and it created new infrastructures for communication and movement-building. The common threads through the neoliberal remaking of society help to explain why the popular movement looked similar in so many places: the coalition of rebellious lawyers, junior doctors (sometimes software developers, journalists), students and public sector trade unionists, in sometimes uneasy coalitions with the peri-urban unemployed, the marginalised and impoverished.

The crucial thing about neoliberalism was that it was still capitalism, and capitalism needs workers. The missing element in much of the analysis of the revolutions has been failure to take seriously the revival of the workers' movement.

Chapter 9
Revival of the workers' movement

In both 2011 and 2019 strikes and protests in the workplaces played a vital role in the development and trajectory of the revolutionary crisis, although not in every country. This chapter explores how the revival of organised workers' self-organisation and confidence to take independent collective action over the decades before the uprisings in Tunisia, Egypt, Sudan and Algeria played a critical role in creating the conditions for the eruption of revolution. It argues that the intervention of organised workers also made a significant difference to the evolution of the revolutionary crisis itself with high points of workers' struggle often coinciding with the opening of fractures in the state apparatus, such as the wave of strikes which erupted just before the fall of Ben Ali and Mubarak in 2011. Finally, we'll explore the limits of the revival of the workers' movement and the role of reformism both in the form of the trade union bureaucracy and the legacy of Stalinism and Arab nationalism.

Workers' resistance, I will argue here, was firmly rooted in the multi-dimensional social, economic and political crisis which had emerged out of the previous decades of uneven and combined development. It was one of the possible outcomes of the combined crisis of both the neoliberal model of economic development, and the state capitalist model which preceded it, and whose material and ideological legacy continued to shape large parts of the economy. The waves of strikes and protests organised by workers constituted a social movement involving millions of people. Moreover, before the explosion of the uprisings, workers' protests and strikes were by far the most well-organised and often the biggest forms of collective action by the poor. Workers also in many cases pioneered mass public forms of collective action, including street protests and sit-ins which generalised during the uprisings of 2011-2013 and 2018-2020.

An upturn in workers' collective action

Despite the lack of reliable statistics and all the challenges mentioned above, there is overwhelming evidence of huge upsurge in strike activity across the region from the mid-2000s onward. For Tunisia, where the official data probably bears some relationship to actual patterns of strike activity, the graph below shows three major peaks of legal strike activity since 1970—in 1977, 1985 and 2011, with the 2011 peak being significantly higher than the 1977 peak. Bearing in mind that the graph only shows legal strikes, and thus illegal strikes are not represented in the data at all, in terms of numbers of strike days 'lost', 2011 represented a huge leap compared to previous years.

Unusually for the region, Tunisian workers have been able to exercise the right to strike legally. Since the 1970s the Tunisian state has also recognised the UGTT trade union federation's right to negotiate collective bargaining agreements with employers.[49] These two mechanisms have allowed the union bureaucracy to use strikes and threats of strikes as a tactic to pressurise employers into making concessions, while also often acting as a kind of "safety valve" for the frustrations of rank-and-file workers.[50]

In Egypt, there was no mechanism for workers' resistance to find an outlet in legal strike action, and before the growth of independent media in the 2000s, there was precious little reporting of strikes to serve as an alternative source of data. However, both Egyptian activists and academics with long experience of research on the Egyptian workers' movement broadly agree that there was a dramatic qualitative shift in

49 Beinin, 2016, p32
50 Del Panta, 2019

Revival of the workers' movement

Figure 9: Legal strike days lost per 1000 population, Tunisia

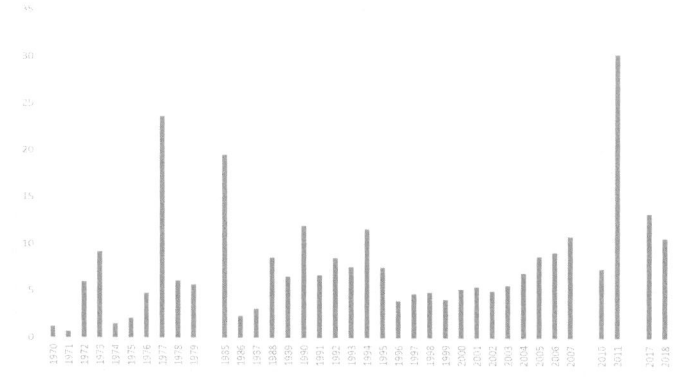

Source: International Labour Organisation

the numbers of strikes from the mid-2000s onward. This accelerated after December 2006, when textile workers at Misr Spinning in al-Mahalla al-Kubra won a historic victory in a major strike which mobilised thousands of workers against their bosses and the state.

The timing of Algeria's uprising and the workers' revolt which preceded it differed from those in Tunisia and Egypt, although the overall pattern was very similar. The economic crisis of the late 1970s, which propelled the Algerian ruling class towards neoliberal restructuring triggered major waves of strikes. Despite a crackdown on the left in the UGTA trade union federation, the strike wave continued to build in strength during 1983-6, with 3528 strikes in the public sector and 2298 in the private sector across the country during this period.[51] The strike wave paved the way for the explosion of riots and protests across Algeria in October 1988, ushering in an intense period of crisis in the state, which was only resolved by the intervention of the army in 1992. The catastrophe of the 'Black Decade' of military repression and the civil war which followed it was a major factor inhibiting Algerians' willingness to risk collective action for the ten years afterwards, helping to explain why Algeria joined the 'second wave' of uprisings in 2019-20 and not the 'first wave' in 2011. However, the ten years before the mass popular mobilisation of 2019 saw major strikes in education, health, transport and industry, many of which

---

51 Larabi, Smith, & Hamouchene, 2020

involved thousands of workers at a time, and some of which mobilised tens of thousands (such as the teachers' strikes).

Sudan's experience of strike action in the decades before the uprising began in late 2018 had something in common with Algeria, in that the crisis of the 1970s had come to a head in a popular uprising in 1985 resulting in a political revolution which removed Jaafar Nimeiri from power and installed a democratic government under Sadiq al-Mahdi, which was itself overthrown in a coup led by Umar al-Bashir working in alliance with Hassan al-Turabi's Islamist movement in 1989. Strikes by doctors and lawyers and judges in 1983 and 1984 had paved the way for the 1985 uprising, while during the revolution they joined railway workers, textile workers, bank workers together with engineers, academics and nurses in a general strike.[52] A combination of worsening economic crisis and an intensification of struggle over South Sudan created conditions for Al Bashir's coup in 1989, which was accompanied by fierce repression of independent trade unions and professional associations. The revival of strike activity pre-figured the uprising of 2019. There were doctors' strikes in 2010 and 2011, following strikes by teachers, railway workers and water carriers in 2009.[53] Despite difficult conditions, some of the strikes became much more than localised battles. For example, a strike by doctors in 2016 demanding protection for healthworkers from assault in the workplace spread to 65 hospitals nationwide.[54] Strikes were not restricted to public services: strikes against privatisation by stevedores in the cargo port in Port Sudan mobilised 20,000 workers in May 2018.[55]

The public services in revolt

The character of the strike waves demonstrates their roots in the twin crises of industry and public services under neoliberalism. In public services, strikes were a response from below to the neoliberal assault on education, health and public administration, which encompassed the relative degradation of

---

52 Abbass, 2010
53 Freedom House, 2010; Berridge, 2014
54 Radio Dabanga, 2016
55 Radio Dabanga, 2018

pay and working conditions, increasing use of sub-contracting and various models of precarious labour, and the intensification of managerialism and factory-like discipline. Striking workers in the public services, especially those in education and health also sometimes explicitly positioned themselves as fighting for broader social goals, defending the rights of the poor to healthcare and education and challenging the logic of the market and competition.

Almost every country discussed here shared a common experience of mass strikes in public services in the years preceding the popular uprisings. One exception is Syria, which we will discuss in more detail below. Teachers, health workers and low paid clerical workers in public administration (*muwazzafin* in Arabic) were the main groups whose collective action powered repeated strikes which were not only often some of the largest in terms of numbers of participants but also among the most significant in terms of mobilisation on a national scale and engaging the state in direct confrontation. These public service strikes were often highly participatory, mobilising thousands of people in creative and democratic forms of organising and left a rich organisational legacy both inside existing trade unions and professional associations, and outside them in the form of new independent union networks and trade unions. The other significant feature of public services was that the institutions of the state could act as a kind of scaffolding for collective action, providing a platform for workers to aggregate their grievances and frustrations and gather in sufficient numbers to begin to have an impact on national politics and state policies in relation to both their own terms and conditions of employment, but also crucially by positioning strikers as fighting on behalf of wider layers of the population to demand greater investment in health, education and local government services.

Mass strikes by teachers in primary and secondary schools were a ubiquitous feature of the public services revolt in almost every country discussed here. Tunisian primary and secondary school teachers staged several national strikes in the years before the popular uprising began in 2010, including a national strike over working conditions and pay in late October that year. The teachers' strike movement grew further in size and scope during and after the 2011 uprising. There were national primary and secondary school strikes almost every year between 2012 and 2019. Demands over pay and conditions continued to be important but the movement also set its sights on curriculum reform, calling for the revision of materials from the Ben Ali era.

Teachers in secondary and primary schools have also been central to the public service strikes in Algeria during the last two decades. Some of the most militant struggles have been led by casualised teachers, who organised a "March of Dignity" in March-April 2016. Following the government's refusal to provide permanent jobs for nearly 30,000 teachers on temporary contracts, activists organised a march from Béjaïa to Algiers which captured the imagination of local people in the towns *en route* who came out to offer solidarity and support. The March of Dignity followed a seven-week long strike by teachers in the southern regions in 2013, and a month-long stay-away in March 2014.[56]

In Egypt the initial spur for collective action among teachers was the implementation of a new pay and grading structure by the Ministry of Education in 2017 which imposed new professional standards and performance-related pay.[57] The new 'Cadre' sparked a ferment of grassroots organising and protests, which laid the basis for the emergence of a new independent union for teachers in July 2010. Just over a year later, in September 2011, the new union was leading hundreds of thousands of teachers in national strike action with far-reaching demands encompassing pay, conditions, and the resignation of the Minister of Education.[58] Teachers' strikes have also been major vectors of resistance in Lebanon, Sudan and in other countries such as Morocco and Jordan.

Strikes by health workers, particularly junior doctors, are also an extremely common feature of the public service strike waves of the past decade across most of the region. There were mass strikes in the health sector in Algeria 2010, 2011 and 2013 leading to a major open-ended strike in November 2014. Junior doctors were an active component of the healthworkers' strike movement: from late 2017 until the summer of 2018, they were on strike against poor pay, job insecurity and appalling working conditions. Other health workers joined them for a three-day national general strike in hospitals in

---

56 Del Panta, 2020.
57 Ministry of Education, 2007, p32.
58 Raslan, 2011; MENA Solidarity Network, 2011.

Revival of the workers' movement

January 2018.[59] Strikes by doctors and health professionals has played a key role in developing combative forms of union and strike organisation in the health service in Sudan. A major strike by doctors in 2016 demanding protection from assault for frontline health staff spread to 65 hospitals across the country by 9 October.[60] The road from 'economic' to 'political' demands was short. In the same month as the Doctors' strike, one of the key coordinating bodies, the Sudan Doctors' Central Committee (SDCC) joined with the Sudanese Journalists' Network and the Alliance of Democratic Lawyers to form the Sudanese Professionals' Association.[61]

Teachers and healthworkers were not the only public service workers whose frustrations boiled over into strikes and protests. In Egypt, low-paid civil servants in the Property Tax Agency organised a historic national strike in 2007, which laid the foundations for the first independent union for more than fifty year. The strike was notable not only for its scale—mobilising tens of thousands of property tax collectors across the country—but also for the strikers' creative tactics. The journey towards the strike started in September 2007, at a rally called by activists in the Property Tax Agency's Giza office to demand parity between their pay, and that of colleagues doing similar work for the Ministry of Finance. Sit-ins and protests spread to other offices around the country, and local mobilising committees began to come together on a regional basis. Mahmud 'Uwayda and activists from al-Mansoura travelled in a 22-bus convoy with activists from other offices in Daqahiliyya province, reaching the centre of Cairo after a 25-km march from the Ministry of Finance. They found thousands of their colleagues already waiting for them:

> "We were greeted with open arms and cheers, by smiling, laughing, cheerful faces as if we had known them for years. The place itself was no stranger to us either, as we had walked there the 25km from the Ministry of Finance... The drums, tambourines and megaphones, the joy and the shouting: some people cannot believe that the numbers on that day were

---

59 Del Panta, 2020.
60 Radio Dabanga, 2016.
61 Sudanese Professionals Association nd; El Gizouli 2019.

more than ten thousand. And everywhere you heard the beautiful chant: 'a decision, a decision ... we're not going home without a decision'".[62]

Holding their nerve for 9 days of constant protest, which ended with marathon negotiations between the Higher Strike Committee and the Minister of Finance, Boutros Ghali, the tax collectors won a significant victory, equivalent to a 300 percent pay rise. As we will discuss later, this victorious strike was also the first step towards the founding of the first independent union in Egypt for fifty years. Workers in public utilities, such as water and electricity have also played an important role in the strike waves. Workers employed by the Lebanese state electricity company, EDL fought major battles in an effort to reverse the trend towards casualisation.

Patterns of industrial resistance

The crisis in industry was of a dual nature, comprising the unresolved problems of the 'old' industries of the state capitalist era, combined with the cyclical crises of 'new' industries which had either transitioned to private ownership or were built up during the neoliberal era and oriented on the export market. Despite the best efforts of the state, employers and compliant national trade union leaderships to prevent it, neither privatised industries nor the new manufacturers proved able to completely stop the re-emergence of strikes and the rebuilding of workers' self-organisation in the workplaces. Meanwhile, sectors of the economy which retained their importance from the state capitalist era, including some sections of heavy industry such as steel and cement; transport, communications and logistics, also saw major strikes in most countries discussed here.

Regional UGTT offices in Tunisia built up their industrial muscle and resources through coordinated strike action in the major industrial zones in Ksar Hellal, Monastir, Sfax and Bizerte, winning wage rises but also rights to hold union meetings on company premises and paid facility time for union activists.[63] Throughout the 1990s, strikes in manufacturing made up a large

62 Uwaydah, 2008, p53–54.
63 Beinin, 2016, p55.

Figure 10: Legal strike days, manufacturing: Tunisia

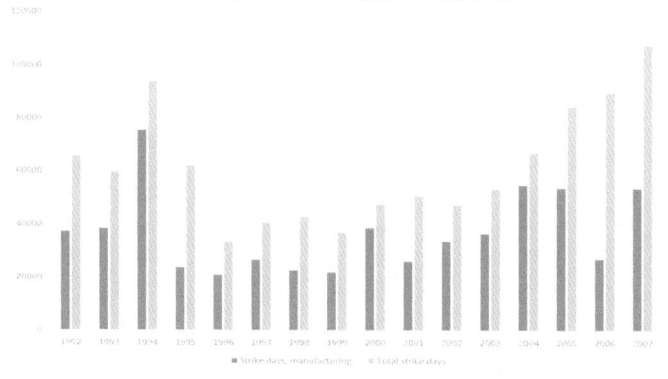

Source: International Labour Organisation

percentage of all official strikes, peaking in 1994. By 2005-2007, however, the overall number of strike days was rising sharply, as other sectors took the lead. In Algeria, the 2016 strike at the SNVI (SNVI - Entreprise National des Véhicules Industriels), a major vehicle manufacturing plant in Rouïba played a role in preparing the way for the popular uprising in 2019. Although the industrial area where SNVI is located employed much smaller numbers than in the late 1970s, it still represented a significant concentration of around 32,000 workers in 100 productive units, the largest and most important of which was SNVI itself, with a workforce of 7000.[64] Following two violent clashes between workers and riot police in January 2010 and December 2015 an 8-day strike erupted in November 2016 over the impact of the government's national pension reform and the mismanagement of the factory. The strike was organised through the local UGTA branch, which called the action under pressure from rank-and-file and mid-ranking activists, despite the closeness of the UGTA national leadership to the regime. Pressure from the UGTA centre did bring the strike to a close in return for a management promise to consider workers' demands, but without closing down all avenues for further resistance.[65] Rouïba would emerge as one of the centres of the revolt against the UGTA leadership during the uprising in 2019. Relatively profitable industries, such as steel and the crucial

---

64 Del Panta, 2020.
65 Del Panta, 2020.

Revolution is the choice of the people

hydrocarbon sector were not immune from strikes either. At the El Hadjar steel complex there were several major confrontations between management and the workforce between 2010 and 2013, leading to a rupture with the UGTA and the foundation of an independent union by 5,000 of El Hadjar's workers.[66] Falling hydrocarbon prices on the international market and the decline in proven energy reserves led to the government implementing austerity measures targeting workers' pay and living conditions, leading to a long series of protests in the state oil and gas company SONATRACH including hunger strikes by workers in 2013, 2016 and 2018. The state-owned gas and electricity company SONELGAZ also saw the growth of an independent union and workers' protests which triggered a wave of arrests of union leaders and the jailing of Raouf Mellal, the union president in 2017.[67]

In Egypt, large scale strikes in industry preceded the public services revolt. A major breakthrough came in December 2006 with the strike at Misr Spinning in al-Mahalla al-Kubra. The giant Misr Spinning plant, employing tens of thousands of workers and dominating the neighbouring town, was one of the iconic centres of the public sector textile industry (although its foundation by industrialist Talaat Harb in the 1930s actually long preceded the state capitalist turn in national economic policy). The factory had also a long tradition of militancy, having been the site of major strikes going back to the 1940s. The strike was triggered by a dispute over the payment of bonuses, and resulted in a complete victory for the workers, not only over their own management but also symbolically over the state, as the Minister of Labour Ai'sha Abd-al-Hadi was forced concede that the strikers' demands would all be met and even that the strike days would count as paid holiday.[68] The stunning success of the Misr Spinning strike soon triggered a wave of strikes over similar demands in other major textile factories across Egypt, with walkouts in Shibin al-Kom, Kafr al-Dawwar, Zifta, 10th Ramadan City, Al-Salihiyya and Burg al-Arab. By April the strike wave had spread from public sector textile plants (or those which had recently been privatised) to private sector textile firms including Makarem Group in Sadat City and Arab Polvara

66 Del Panta, 2020.
67 Del Panta, 2020.
68 Alexander & Bassiouny, 2014.

in Alexandria.

The Egyptian strike wave was notable for the way in which workers' collective action rapidly generalised across the divide between the public and private sector industries. One of the first signs of the recovery of workers' confidence and willingness to fight back was not in the 'old' public sector industries, but in new industrial centres which had often been deliberately located in entirely new areas far away from the traditional centres of working class organisation.

Transport, communications and logistics workers also flexed their muscles during the strike waves. Major transport strikes in Algeria included action by staff at the state airline, Air Algerie in 2013, 2015 and 2018; railway workers who staged protests in 2014 and organised a 9-day strike in May 2016 demanding a 100 percent salary increase, and 3,000 public transport workers in Algiers who walked out on open-ended strike in December 2015.[69] Transport workers in UGTA-affiliated unions generally organised strikes in defiance of the national union leadership's efforts to maintain "social peace" with the government, in particular after the signing of a formal economic and social pact committing the unions to a four-year truce in 2006.[70] The cargo workers and stevedores in Port Sudan have been one of the major groups of workers involved in strikes and protests to defend their jobs against plans to privatise the port. Attempts by the state-run port company to bring in new private investors on long-term concessionary contracts has met with determined resistance, including mass strikes involving 20,000 workers in May 2018.[71]

The revival of rank-and-file organisation and the contradictions of the trade union bureaucracy

One conclusion which can be drawn from the mass strikes of the last decade in the Middle East is that workers' capacity for self-organised collective action was embedded deeply in the labour process under capitalism, and not conditional on either pre-existing trade union organisation willing to organise

---

69 Del Panta, 2020.
70 Larabi, Smith, & Hamouchene, 2020.
71 Radio Dabanga, 2018.

collective action or legal frameworks permitting strikes. It is hard otherwise to explain why although these last two conditions were only met in Tunisia, the strikes were equally strong in Egypt, where legal strikes were almost impossible, and union structures were not merely passive but deeply hostile to workers' interests and self-organisation, functioning as another arm of the ruling party and the state bureaucracy.

The strikes were driven by activity from below, through the painstaking recreation of cultures of solidarity and self-organisation at the level of individual workplaces. Workers' collective action was the 'prime mover' for building workplace organisation, not the other way around. What is important about the mass strikes in the Middle East, however, it is that these waves of collective action provide confirmation that *neither* neoliberalism's entrenching of competition between workers and the poor *nor* the legacy of the state capitalist ruling parties' attempts to mobilise them behind the 'national' goals of the ruling class was able to prevent the resurgence of workers' resistance.

As anyone who has ever organised one will tell you, strikes both *require* and *create* organisation. Moreover, where they emerge 'from below' they have a tendency to create highly democratic and participatory forms of organisation, in contrast to strikes organised in top-down manner by trade union bureaucracies.[72] The 'sit-in' strike, for example, creates a large, permanent assembly of strikers, which can act as a forum to decide tactics and strategy in open debate. Crucially these mass meetings can also provide a mechanism for holding elected delegates to account.

Whether they have been tasked with negotiating on the details of the salary scale or putting the case for the strike on the local television station, strikers' representatives have to return and justify themselves before their colleagues. Certainly, hundreds of thousands - and possibly millions - of working class women and men across the region gained experience of strike organisation with a heady dose of direct democracy in the last decade and a half. This is a significant achievement in societies where even the most threadbare kinds of democracy are absent from the political sphere.

Yet localised, small-scale battles were reflections of a

---

72   Cliff, 1985.

systemic crisis, the problems they exposed—such as the coordinated assault on jobs and conditions in manufacturing in order to boost international competitiveness, or the decline in state funding and resources for public health and education—could not be resolved within individual factories, hospitals or schools. They demanded mobilisation and contestation at the level of the national state and beyond. In Tunisia, the structure of the UGTT meant that the union federation's regional offices tended to be much more susceptible to rank-and-file pressure than the national Executive Board. Thus regional strikes and sometimes inter-regional coordinated action could provide a mechanism for generating nation-wide strikes.

Activists in other countries also repeatedly proved that it was possible to create forms of coordination which enabled national strikes to take place despite the lack of usable national trade union structures. The formation of the independent union representing Property Tax Collectors in Egypt (RETAU) flowed out of just such a process of scaling up local and regional initiative into nationally coordinated action which successfully forced major concessions from the government. Hala Talaat, a teacher from Giza and one of the founding activists in the Egyptian Teachers' Federation after 2011, recalled how it was the imposition of the new pay and grading structure, the Teachers' Cadre in 2007 which provided impetus to transform local groups of teachers, organised in Teachers Leagues, into nodes in a national network of activists:

> A league [rabita] was a group of teachers in a governorate or a locality, who got active to demand teachers' rights. But there was no co-ordination between us and other governorates. Co-ordination began to develop over issues like the Teachers' Cadre which led to a crisis between the teachers and the Ministry.[73]

In Algeria, too, the strike wave paved the way for the emergence of autonomous unions, some of which were powered by the energy of rank-and-file mobilisations by public service workers, particularly school teachers and other education workers. The blockages and obstacles they faced to mobilising within the UGTA were one of the factors which drove the

---

73 Talaat, 2012.

formation of networks such as the Conseil des Lycees Algeriens (CLA) which led major school teachers' strikes in the early 2000s. The legislation which partially ended the UGTA's monopoly over trade union organisation came into force in 1990 in the wake of the mass strikes of the 1980s and the 1988 nation-wide uprising triggered by subsidy cuts. The government's sudden conversion to union pluralism was designed to weaken the workers' movement by introducing competing union centres to the UGTA. One of the first beneficiaries was the Islamist movement, the Front Islamique du Salut, which launched its own union federation in June 1990. The FIS-affiliated union failed to make much headway against the UGTA, nor did it prove a successful launchpad for resistance to the government. [74] Moreover, instead of siphoning off the UGTA's militant industrial rank-and-file, the autonomous unions which grew outside the historic union federation have almost all been concentrated in public services:[75]

> They have challenged the finance laws, rejected the undermining of Algerian workers' achievements in terms of retirement, and denounced the preliminary draft of the Labour Code. They have moved on from just bonus claims for this or that sector.[76]

A new federation of autonomous unions, the CSA, was created in 2018, bringing together 13 unions from different sectors, dominated by the education unions which led the teachers' strikes in the early 2000s, in addition to unions representing public health practitioners, vets, higher education teachers, aircraft maintenance technicians, imams and postal workers.

There are in fact more similarities between the struggles to create independent unions and the battles within existing organisations, such as the UGTT in Tunisia, that might appear at first glance. The UGTT was formed through the struggle against French colonialism and served essentially as a powerful wing of a nationalist, rather than a social democratic movement.[77] More than this, the UGTT emerged as a uniquely well-organised force

---

74 Alexander, 2000, p481–82.
75 Larabi, Smith & Hamouchene, 2020.
76 Larabi, Smith & Hamouchene, 2020.
77 Yousfi, 2018.

compared to other trade union movements in the region during the 1950s and early 1960s. Its leadership could lay credible claim to the title of co-founders of the independent Tunisian state, and although the 'socialist experiment' in state capitalist economic policies under Ben Salah during the 1960s did not last out the decade, the UGTT was able to consolidate its role as bargaining partner to the employers and the state in the 1970s. Although the confrontation between the workers' movement and the regime in the late 1970s ended in fierce repression and strenuous efforts by the regime to co-opt the upper leadership of the UGTT, the middle and lower levels of the federation remained a refuge for several generations of trade union militants influenced by leftist and Arab nationalist ideas.[78]

None of this should be taken to suggest that it is easy to keep any of the regimes which have ruled Tunisia since independence from capturing the UGTT and turning it into essentially an arm of the state. The UGTT's national leadership has more often worked with, rather than against, the ruling party. Even Habib Achour, the UGTT general secretary at the height of the massive wave of strikes and workers' protests in the late 1970s who was jailed for several years, was pushed into confrontation with the regime by pressure from rank-and-file organisation.[79] And just as in other countries, the revival of collective action in the workplaces was driven from below. In 2009 activists in the secondary school teachers' union, SGES began to document local strikes and protests. These reports show how the national battles from 2010 onwards followed years of school-level protests and strikes, and also illustrate how teacher activists were connected with (and contributed to) wider networks of solidarity. In October 2009 alone the blog reported on strikes or planned strikes in El Kaf, Sidi Hussein, Mednin, Ben Arous, Bou Salem, Bizerte and Bargou. Violence in the workplace was a cause of several of the strikes or strike threats: teachers in Ben Arous staged a one-hour 'lightning' strike in protest at the security forces storming the school, while the strike in Sidi Hussein was in response to deteriorating conditions inside the schools, including attacks on a schoolgirl.

The victimisation of teacher activists sparked protests

---

78 Yousfi, 2018; Beinin, 2016.
79 Bellin, 2002; Yousfi, 2018.

and solidarity meetings involving other trade unionists in Sfax and a rally by hundreds of teachers on 17 October. In the meantime, teachers were also active in mobilising solidarity for others, such as the Redeyf coal miners and their families. Strong traditions of building solidarity were deeply embedded in the Tunisian teaching unions. Activists from the secondary school teachers' union SGES were central to mobilising support for the uprising in the phosphate mining area Gafsa following the revolt there in 2008, and several members of the union, including Adnan Haji, were sentenced to long terms in prison in 2009 prompting a protest strike. The Gafsa uprising in fact was emblematic of the contradictions inside the UGTT, as it pitted a coalition of local unemployed youth and UGTT activists in the public sector unions, such as Haji against the UGTT branch in the Gafsa Phosphate Company, which was famed for its clientelism and collusion with management.[80]

Nevertheless, the fact that both in the 1970s and in the run-up to the 2011 revolution, the combined pressure of revived rank-and-file militancy and burgeoning street mobilisations forced the top of the bureaucracy to break with the regime was highly significant. This, in itself, reveals something important about the UGTT bureaucracy, that for all its accommodation and collaboration with the Ben Ali regime, it remained a trade union bureaucracy, rather than having simply the character of regime apparatchiks. The Algerian UGTA by contrast, lost more of its independence in the bruising battles with the state during the 1980s. Then the combination of a devastating civil war with brutal neoliberal structural adjustment and the asset-stripping of the public sector in the 1990s battered workplace organisation further. However, when workers' confidence and combativity began to revive in the first two decades of the 21st century, this did find limited expression *within* the UGTA and not just *outside* it. In some public sector industries UGTA branches were able to mobilise for strike action in defiance of the upper levels of the bureaucracy, such as the SNVI plant in Rouïba in 2016.

Moreover, both the creation of new trade unions, and the renewal of old ones through the ousting of compromised and collaborationist leaderships, quickly posed a new challenge: how to maintain the democratic gains in organisation at the same time as keeping up pressure on employers and the state

80 Gobe, 2010.

not to backslide once the intensity of mobilisation slackened. In particular, the pressures of bureaucratisation on those in leadership roles who assumed longer-term positions as mediators between the mass of members on the one hand and employers and the state on the other intensified. This was not fundamentally to do with any personal failings or character defects on the part of the activists concerned but reflects the intrinsic problem of bureaucracy within trade unions.

The roots of this process of bureaucratisation lie in the unique class position of trade union officials: they are neither employers or workers, but exist as a mediating layer between them, susceptible to pressures from both sides. This 'Janus-faced' character is vital to distinguishing a genuine trade union bureaucracy from officials who form part of the state or ruling party bureaucracy.[81] It is not accidental, as Tony Cliff and Donny Gluckstein have argued. Two key points stand out in their approach to this question. Firstly, that full-time trade union officials occupy a distinctive and unique position in capitalist societies—they are neither workers nor employers, but are located between the two sides in a role which is structurally designed to mediate between them. This role is carved out for trade union officials by the pressures from both sides—their salaries (if they have them) and their leadership roles are conditional on workers' organisation remaining strong enough to force concessions from employers and the state. However, their status as mediators and negotiators would also be threatened by revolutionary change which might destroy the bargaining machinery that gives them their special function. Thus, there is an inevitable tendency towards conciliation with employers and the state.[82]

The second essential point which Cliff and Gluckstein make is that a conflict of interests exists between the trade union bureaucracy and the mass of union members—or more accurately the mass of ordinary workers in the workplaces—is a permanent feature of trade unionism.[83] The corollary of this argument is that the tendency of trade union officials to conciliate and compromise with the capitalist ruling class and

---

81 Hyman, 1975; Cliff and Gluckstein, 1986; Darlington & Upchurch, 2012.
82 Cliff and Gluckstein, 1986.
83 Darlington and Upchurch, 2012, p91.

its state is not something which is simply a reflection of personal venality or cowardice (although trade union leaders with these traits certainly exist). Nor is it just a reflection of the political allegiances of trade union bureaucrats: electing leaders who are clear about their opposition to the existing regime is not in itself enough to guard against their eventual co-option by the ruling class at moments of crisis.

Strikes and the road to revolution

While workers' revolts preceded the uprisings in several cases discussed here, there was no inevitable progression from strikes to revolution. Morocco, for example, provides examples of mass strike waves which shared many similar features to those discussed in detail here, including the leading role played by young teachers and junior doctors, and the creation of highly democratic coordinating committees to mobilise action alongside the existing union structures.[84] There have been both national battles over issues such as public sector pension reform and local and sectoral struggles over pay, conditions and union rights. However, the rising tide of popular mobilisation in February 2011 did not succeed in rupturing the state as it had done in neighbouring Tunisia, or in Egypt. The trade union bureaucracy actually played a significant role in dampening the movement from below by accepting the King's invitation to join a social dialogue about meeting unions' economic demands, and calling off strike action, thus separating the mobilisation over social grievances from the mass movement for political change.[85] In the case of Libya and Syria, there was no mass strike wave in the years preceding the uprising, which meant that there was no flowering of independent unions or rank-and-file coordinating committees. The very high levels of repression, combined with the embryonic state of the working class before the oil era and the peculiarities of al-Qadhafi's "Jamahiriya", which purported to embody popular control of society, while concentrating power in personal and family networks around al-Qadhafi himself, probably explain why it proved very difficult for workers' organisation to emerge in Libya. The situation in Syria was

84 Rafiq, 2019.
85 Feltrin, 2019, p55.

different, however. There were historic traditions of workers' organisation going back to the 1940s, and the late 1970s and early 1980s had seen important episodes of strikes and a revival of rank-and-file activity, challenging the suffocating grip of the regime-affiliated trade unions. There was fierce repression in the years which followed, aided and abetted by the regime's trade union arm, the General Federation of Workers' Unions. [86] Does the intensity of that repression explain the failure of workers' struggle to revive in later decades? Clearly it was an important factor, although the workers' movements in Algeria and Sudan also went through searing experiences of civil war and intense repression during the same period and this did not prevent the eventual recovery of workers' agency.

Does an explanation lie in the restructuring of the class structure of Syria during the neoliberal period, and the restructuring of the working class in particular? The most intense shifts in class structure occurred in rural areas, where the neoliberal crisis in agriculture prompted migration from the countryside to the impoverished suburbs. There was a significant change in the relative weight of the public and private sector in industry, and by 2009 manufacturing accounted for 6.9 percent of GDP and 15 percent of the labour force. Public sector manufacturing enterprises tended to be larger and employed 96,000 people, a reduction from 105,000 in 2005.[87] By contrast 450,000 were employed in the much smaller (sometimes micro) firms in the private sector. The percentage of the labour force employed in manufacturing in Syria in 2010 was 16.5 percent, compared to 12.1 percent in Egypt and 18.2 percent in Tunisia, and 7.7 percent in Sudan.[88] . Moreover, this does not explain the absence of revolt from below in either the public services or the strategically important transport and logistics sectors, both of which featured strongly in the revival of the Sudanese workers' movement and were a nearly ubiquitous feature of the mass strikes across the entire region. The regime had criminalised strikes by employees in public services in the 1980s, it is true, however this was not unique to Syria, as similar provisions operated in Lebanon, where there were significant strikes by teachers and electricity sector workers in the 2000s.

86 Daher, 2020, p9.
87 Lawson, 2018, p85.
88 ILOSTAT, 2022.

Revolution is the choice of the people

A possible explanation lies in the relationship between the "mass organisations" of the Syrian ruling party and the layers of the working class whose capacity to inflict disruption on the state was greatest. As with ETUF in Egypt, the GFWU had lost much of its political influence within the regime as neoliberal reform intensified, which simultaneously degraded its capacity to act as conduit for the delivery of services to its members.[89] However, as Joseph Daher notes, the GFWU and its sister organisation in the countryside, the General Federation of Peasants, "continued to play notable social roles for their members and other segments of the population who benefited from certain services they provide, which are usually free or relatively affordable in comparison to institutional alternatives. The GFWU, in particular, was very effective in the field of public health".[90] The regime also mitigated the impact of neoliberal restructuring on state employees and public sector workers to a degree, through bonuses and grants and maintenance of their salaries in the years immediately prior to the uprising.[91]

A further element to consider here is the political consequences of the interaction between the assault on job security in the public sector, labour law reform and workers' collective action. In Egypt, the 1990s saw a huge restructuring of employment with hundreds of thousands of jobs lost in public sector industry or transferred to the private sector. In 2004, the regime felt confident enough to seal this process with a new labour law which theoretically granted workers the "right to strike" while employers were simultaneously given greater legal rights to terminate jobs.[92] Although the number of legal strikes was tiny, illegal strikes significantly increased after the law was passed. A similar law was also enacted in Syria in 2010, which also gave employers the right to dismiss employees without justification and with limited compensation.[93]

Part of the answer to the puzzle as to why there was no mass strike wave in Syria before the uprising in 2011 may lie in differences in timing by the actions of the regime, compared to its counterparts elsewhere. In the Egyptian case, the 2004

89 Lawson, 2018, p83.
90 Daher, 2020, p10.
91 Lawson, 2018, p85.
92 Bassiouny & Said, 2007.
93 Daher, 2020, p7.

labour law was one of the outward signs of a deeper political and social process: the rupture from above and below of what is sometimes called "the authoritarian bargain" or the "Nasserist social contract". It was one of the markers of the shift by the ruling class away from the mechanisms by which it engineered workers' consent to their political subjection in the state capitalist era. The strike waves could be read as signal that large sections of the working class too were withdrawing from their side of this bargain and would henceforth deploy their collective strength in the workplaces, not in order to try and make the state revert back to its old role as an organiser of production and national development, but in order to disrupt the flow of profits through the circuitry of capital accumulation. As Mostafa Bassiouny points out, in Egypt, there was a highly significant change in the prevalence of *strikes* as opposed to other forms of collective action by workers from the mid-2000s onwards, in contrast to some of the major battles in the 1990s and 1980s when workers occupied public sector industrial enterprises but continued to work in defiance of the state.[94]

Of course, it would be naïve to pretend that this shift in workers' consciousness was anything but messy and confused. There were plenty of striking workers in the public sector in Egypt who still did want the state to return to its former leading role in the economy. The ideological legacy of nostalgia for the state capitalist era turned out to create points of confluence between some of the Nasserist elements in the trade union bureaucracy and counter-revolutionary forces. Nevertheless, it is clear that this process of rupturing the old social contract of the state capitalist period between the urban working class across services and industry worked out differently in Syria. The consequences of those differences to the trajectory of the uprising would be profound and tragic.

The working class and the Palestinian struggle

What about the role of organised workers in the Palestinian national movement? Does this represent an exception to the general patterns outlined above? Far from it: the First Intifada which erupted in 1987, followed nearly two decades of growing

---

94 Bassiouny & Said, 2007.

Revolution is the choice of the people

trade union organisation shaped by the dramatic shifts in the structure of the Palestinian working class as a result of the Israeli economic strategy of using the Occupied Territories as dormitories for "migrant" Palestinian labour in the wake of 1967.[95]

By 1987 there were 130 unions in the West Bank, mostly relatively small with less than 250 members, although some such as the Construction and General Institutions Workers' Union in Ramallah and the Hotel, Restaurant and Café Workers Union in Jerusalem, averaged a 1000 dues paying members.[96] Unions did not focus solely on workplace issues in a narrow sense, but developed a dense mesh of organisations supporting their members in a wide range of areas, with committees to run their financial affairs, medical and health services, insurance and savings, social and cultural activities, voluntary work and even sports activities. Most of these structures were elected and in theory at least, there were democratic mechanisms which allowed activists at the base of the union movement to shape the decisions of the leadership through electing delegates from local to national leadership positions.[97]

Unions which represented Palestinians working in Israel were (and still are) prevented from direct engagement or negotiation with Israeli employers by the legal structures of the occupation itself, which banned Palestinians from organising their own unions "inside" Israel. There was also pressure on Palestinian unions organising workers employed by Palestinian businesses to suspend, or at least moderate, the class struggle in order to maximise national unity. Competition between the Communist Party and the major nationalist currents (particularly Fateh, the PFLP and DFLP) over this reviving workers' movement intensified during the late 1970s. In the early 1980s this competition led to splits in the trade union on factional lines, and in some cases the proliferation of duplicate, factionally-aligned unions representing the same groups of workers.[98]

The period of the Oslo Accords during the 1990s and the creation of the Palestinian Authority saw the retreat of both grassroots union organizing and neighbourhood-based

---

95 Hiltermann, 1993, p64.
96 Hiltermann, 1993, p69.
97 Hiltermann, 1993, p70.
98 Hiltermann, 1993, p69.

mobilizational networks. The energy of a layer of activists in the mainstream nationalist organizations, particularly Fatah, was absorbed by building the structures of the Palestinian Authority, which many of them hoped would be a step towards an independent Palestinian state. In reality, the Oslo Accords were a trap: the Israeli settlements expanded, Israel's "Matrix of Control" tightened over Palestinian land, water resources and population centres.[99]

The major nationalist factions have traditionally called on workers to refrain from fighting from their rights against Palestinian-owned businesses, or challenging the Palestinian Authority, arguing that the struggle for national liberation was paramount. There are signs that this "freezing" of the class struggle has begun to thaw with strikes by taxi drivers in 2012 and teachers in 2016 and 2020.[100] The 2016 action involved nearly 35,000 teachers, who organised the largest teachers' strike in Palestinian history despite their union acting "more as mediator for the PA than advocate for union members".[101]

Yet the way in which the Israeli apartheid system functions creates structural obstacles to the realization of Palestinian workers' class power in the areas dominated by Israel. The Palestinian public sector is reliant on a combination of international aid and funding from Israel, while Israeli road closures, and the seizure of land and water resources by settlers have destroyed or badly damaged much of Palestinian agriculture and industry. This process of "de-development"[102] has weakened the strategic power of the Palestinian working class.

The same apartheid structures have politically neutralized the economic struggles of Jewish Israeli workers. Strikes and even large-scale social protest movements, such as the wave of huge "social justice" demonstrations in 2011 have not been able to break through the confines of Zionist ideology to show solidarity with Palestinians. In fact, Israel's historic trade unions have been part of the settler-colonial enterprise for longer that the Israeli state: the Histadrut was a pioneer of the racist "Jewish labour" policy of excluding Palestinian workers under the British Mandate having previously founded the Haganah,

---

99 Halper, nd.
100 Beinin, 2021.
101 Abu Moghli & Qato, 2018.
102 Roy, 1987.

Revolution is the choice of the people

one of the major Zionist militias which would play a pivotal role in the ethnic cleansing of Palestinians during the Nakba.[103] For decades this "union federation" was a major employer and state institution. It collected millions of pounds in compulsory wage deductions for health insurance and social protection from Palestinian workers it refused to represent and refused to even transfer these to Palestinian unions in the West Bank as had been agreed under Oslo Accords.[104]

Although the Histadrut's membership collapsed in the mid-1990s following changes to the Israeli healthcare system which broke the link between union membership and access to health insurance, it has not been replaced by more progressive alternatives. After the shrunken Histadrut, which now represents around 700,000 members, the second largest union federation is the Likud-affiliated Histadrut Leumi with 100,000 members, followed by the more left-wing Koach LaOvdim,[105] which only counted 13,000 members as of 2018 (although it claims to represent around 35,000 workers through collective bargaining agreements).[106] Koach LaOvdim and the 2300-member WAC-MAAN union do recruit Palestinians but as Sumaya Awad and Daphna Thier point out, neither have made any progress in shifting their Jewish members away from acceptance of Zionism. The enmeshing of trade unionism with settler colonialism means that:

> unions in Israel are pulled rightward by their Jewish members. In order to recruit, they must set aside the question of the occupation. Otherwise, they doom themselves to marginality. This is the nature of labor in an apartheid economy. Almost complete separation means that, by design, Jews and Palestinians rarely work alongside one another as co-workers. Instead, they are segregated in ways that entrench racism and ensure that national loyalty trumps class consciousness.[107]

---

103 Pappe, 2015.
104 This process was only halted after a court victory by the Israeli trade union, WAC-MAAN in December 2020.
WAC-MAAN, 2020.
105 Bsoul, 2017.
106 Koach La Ovdim, nd.
107 Awad & Thier, 2021.

Conclusion: workers' collective action in the uprisings

There were three major ways in which organised workers specifically contributed to the uprisings. Firstly, as we have already noted, the mass strikes of the pre-revolutionary period functioned precisely as the "schools of war" for working class activists that Frederick Engels named them back in 1845.[108] Through involvement in the mass strikes, millions of people, the vast majority of whom were not otherwise engaged in political activity at all, and certainly not members or supporters of opposition groups, learned for themselves how to organise protests, make placards, write leaflets, provide provisions for strikers, secure their sit-ins and ensure that strikers acted in a disciplined manner, communicate securely under the noses of the security forces, talk to the media, mobilise solidarity from their communities and other groups of workers. In addition, they gained experience in debating and deciding on strategy and tactics collectively and often with a high degree of democratic accountability. Before the uprisings erupted, there was no other political or social movement on the same scale which provided space for ordinary people to try out these things for themselves: even in countries where mass opposition movements did exist these tended to be Islamist in character and considerably less open to working class people taking on leading roles.

A second way in which the mass strikes contributed both to creating the conditions in which popular uprisings could take place, and in many cases accelerated the crisis of the state once an uprising was underway was by transmitting the energy of the revolutionary process from the domain of politics into economic struggles and back again. In the case of Egypt, this dynamic was visible both before 2011 and during the initial phase of the revolution, in the 18-day long uprising which began on January 25. It continued for much of the first year after Mubarak's fall.

The final years of the old regime were characterised by interlacing waves of political protests and mass strikes. The regime was at times successful in forcing political protesters to retreat from the streets through repression, which even extended to protesting members of the judiciary who were beaten and abused by security forces in 2006. Yet just as the street mobilisations

---

108 Engels, 1845, Ch10.

declined, mass strikes took off, and workers "took by storm" as Rosa Luxemburg would have put it, the same rights to protest and organise that the regime's crackdown denied to opposition activists campaigning for political reform, opening the door to a new phase in the struggle.[109] A very similar dynamic was in operation during the 18-day uprising itself. In particular, the wave of strikes which began to gather pace from the weekend of 5-6 February onwards in Suez, and then across other towns and cities including the capital over the following days, played a significant practical and political role in tying down the regime's resources and energies and puncturing its claims that the protesters in Tahrir Square and other sit-ins in the city squares were isolated groups, organised by sinister "foreign hands".[110]

A third aspect of the mass strikes' contribution to the dynamics of the uprisings and the regime's efforts at counter-mobilisation was in the way that they rendered the "zombie parties'" mass organisations unusable just at the moment that the regime needed them. Again the contrast in this respect between Tunisia and Egypt on the one hand, and Syria on the other is stark. In Tunisia, trade unionists opposed to the regime were able to maintain organisation in the lower levels of the UGTT union federation even when the top layers of the bureaucracy were thoroughly compromised. ETUF in Egypt proved impervious to rank-and-file pressure, but by 2011 the emergence nascent independent unions and the much wider experience of strike organising meant that the ETUF leadership was unable to mobilise anyone at all for pro-regime counter-protests in the early days of the uprising. One reason why the sit-in at Tahrir Square found itself under attack from a motley collection of thugs riding horses and a camel on 2 February 2011, was that pro-regime trade unionists simply didn't show up, despite increasingly desperate attempts by the ETUF leadership to encourage them to take to the streets and defend the dictatorship.

By contrast, the Syrian regime continued to successfully mobilise counter-protests opposing the revolution through its mass organisations, including the General Federation of Workers' Unions, throughout 2011. Combined with fierce repression, these pro-regime mobilisations played a significant role in denying the streets of the capital and other major cities to

---

109 Luxemburg, 1906.
110 Alexander & Bassiouny, 2014.

Revival of the workers' movement

revolutionary activists. On 25 March, as tens of thousands tore down a statue of Hafez al-Assad in Dera'a on the second "Friday of Dignity" and thousands gathered in Homs, Hamas, Lattakia, Deir-ez-Zor in solidarity with the besieged town, the regime also mobilised thousands of supporters in central Damascus.

> Many participants, wearing Bashaar T-shirts and kissing his image, seemed to be genuinely passionate in their love for the leadership; many others—schoolchildren and civil servants—were bussed in for the occasion.[111]

In Syria, therefore, the regime did not face the paralysing effect of workers' withdrawal of labour in key public services, government offices, transport networks, manufacturing enterprises and media organisations in the capital and provincial towns in the early stages of the uprising. In Egypt, even though the strike wave during the uprising was not coordinated or as well-organised as in Tunisia were, nevertheless, in the days immediately before Mubarak fell, strikes shut down key industrial enterprises in steel, cement and textiles, municipal cleaners blocked the road in Giza, telecoms workers protested outside telephone exchanges, the staff of major hospitals and universities walked out, bus workers in Cairo shut down several garages in the Public Transport Authority and railway workers joined the strikes. By 11 February, nine military production factories in Helwan, where workers faced courts-martial for insubordination, were on strike.[112] Journalists in the state-run media were in revolt against their editors, in some cases literally throwing them out of the building while they took control of the newsroom and set about reporting the unfolding revolution.

These kinds of strike waves which carried the revolution simultaneously through the streets and the workplaces took place in several of the countries discussed here. In many cases the timing correlated with turning points in the revolutionary process and major setbacks for the regime. In Tunisia, the national general strike on 14 January 2011 prompted Ben Ali's flight into exile. In Egypt, the strike wave was the major innovation in the dynamics of the popular uprising in the days before Mubarak fell on February 11. A general strike on

---

111 Yassin-Kassab and Al-Shami, 2018, p39.
112 Alexander & Bassiouny, 2014.

10 March 2019 is widely seen by Algerian activists as pushing the Algerian ruling class to finally abandon Bouteflika. Sudan's 2019 uprising saw several mass strikes, most importantly on 28-29 May and 9-11 June at the height of the struggle against the Transitional Military Council.

Chapter 10

Partners in revolution? Women and the uprisings

In April 2019, as the first phase of Sudan's revolution was nearing a climax, graffiti artists in the Syrian town of Idlib captured one image from the sit-in outside the Army General Command in Khartoum in a new mural. Draped in the folds of a traditional white robe, raising her hand to lead the crowds in chanting, Alaa Saleh appeared on the wall just as she did in countless images on Twitter and Instagram.[113] It is often tempting to consider the images of the women who like Alaa Saleh, came to represent turning points in the revolutions as mere symbols. Yet, women's participation in the revolutions was anything but symbolic. The uprisings were driven by the desire for millions of women for social and political change and their growing frustration with the existing system. Both regimes which had posed as "secular" and "progressive" guarantors of women's rights and those which used the language of Islamism continued to impose sexist laws and carry out gendered forms of repression. Meanwhile, the growing burdens of care and family responsibilities in a world shaped by neoliberal reforms which degraded public services and destroyed jobs, gave the lie to claims by officials of the international financial institutions such as the World Bank and IMF, that the market would break the chains of women's degradation.

Women participated in the uprisings in large numbers,

113   Enab Baladi, 2019.

however, the revolutions in many cases appeared to result in a "gender paradox" where this was not matched by equality of representation in key bodies negotiating or implementing the political reforms required for a "transition to democracy".[114] The growing influence of Islamist groups in countries where they dominated opposition to the old regimes raised fears that the expansion of democratic rights would inevitably lead to a degradation of women's rights and status. However even in contexts where the uprisings were directed at regimes of an Islamist character, or allied with Islamist currents, such as Sudan, similar problems were visible.

Moreover, as events moved from revolution to counter-revolution, a common pattern emerged of the state reasserting ideological and sometimes physical domination over women's bodies in explicit attempts to break the revolutionary movements through sexist violence.

This chapter examines the roots of women's participation in the revolutionary uprisings, arguing that there were deep-rooted social and political causes of their role as "partners in revolution".[115] The "gender paradox" of the revolutionary decade points not towards the determining role of religious ideology and patriarchal culture, but instead shines a spotlight on the nature of the capitalist state and its structural role in recreating and sustaining women's oppression despite capitalism's promise that equality of persons should be the inevitable outcome of the operations of an abstract labour market where purchasers of labour power are intrinsically uninterested in whether the bodies containing it are male, female or even transcend this binary altogether.

The dilemmas of generational reproduction

The question of how to reproduce labour power in capitalist societies is fundamental to the issue of women's oppression. For profits to continue to flow to the ruling class, there must be a continuous supply of new workers entering the labour market. Moreover, as capitalism develops, the issue of generational reproduction becomes more challenging, as more is expected

---

114 Khalil, 2014b.
115 Khalil, 2014a.

of workers in terms of their level of education and ability to use technology. Literacy and numeracy become a baseline for many kinds of work, not simply a specialised set of skills for a small range of professions serving the elite. The interaction between these different sets of pressures helps to explain why capitalist ruling classes have to pay close attention to perfecting "home-grown" methods of bringing up the next generation of workers. This means contending not just with the practicalities of ensuring that working class children live through to adulthood and acquire the skills to play a productive role in the workplace, but also that they are socialised to accept their subordinate position in society.

At the same time, there are pressures on capitalists to increase the overall potential pool of labour power available for exploitation, creating a trend towards the socialisation of some of the tasks which used to be carried out in the household. The basic trade-off from the capitalist's point of view is fairly simple: he or she is not that interested in whether the body which comes with the labour power is male, female or non-binary, what matters in the long run is how much of their surplus labour can be seized to make a profit. In other words, how long is the part of the working day when a worker is no longer simply working to meet her own needs for subsistence but is purely working to profit her boss. This, as Lise Vogel points out, is the feature of capitalist societies which underpins bourgeois rhetoric about the essential equality of persons.[116] So long as capitalists as a class gain more by exploiting women in the workplace than they save by having them work unpaid, but nevertheless requiring food, shelter and healthcare in order to fulfil their necessary role in child-bearing, strong pressures towards enabling women to join the workforce will exist.

Besides these basic trends, however, there are other pressures which affect the timing and degree to which capitalists mobilise women's labour power in the workplace, and what demands they also make of women in relation to social reproduction outside the workplace. One of these is the way in which competition between workers can be used to drive down wages or weaken their collective resistance to efforts to extend the working day. Historically, women's labour has often been mobilised by capitalists to compete with men, often linked

---

116 Vogel, 1987.

with technological changes which have allowed capitalists to benefit initially from employing relatively less skilled and less experienced workers who they can get away with paying less.

There is also an aspect of this which is related to competition between younger and older workers, and its specifically gendered form is deeply connected to previous patterns of women's oppression. Thus, the feminisation of sections of the industrial workforce in Britain in the late 19th century, would not have pitted young women workers who gained jobs, apparently against the interests of older men who lost them or were forced in to less skilled and less secure work, without the reconstruction of the working-class family in the previous generation.

This brings us to the question of the relationship between women's oppression, the role of the family in social reproduction, and the multidimensional crisis (or crises) of capitalism. The early phase of capitalist industrialisation in Europe in the 19th century drew men and women and children into work in factories, mines, construction and transport. It was intimately bound up with processes of rural-urban migration which created huge cities so that capitalists could have a ready supply of labour to dispose of as they wished.

Some of the pressure from within the capitalist ruling class toward reconstituting working families as spaces where some of the essential tasks of reproducing labour power could take place, where workers could recuperate and replenish their energy, find solace and refuge from the pressures of the market, and healthy children could be born and raised, came from the realisation that these industrial cities were catastrophic for human health and reproduction, with mortality rates so high that their population would have remained below replacement levels without the constant influx of new migrants and the disastrous spread of epidemic diseases (which turned out not to entirely respect distinctions of social class, infecting the rich as well as the poor). In addition, and equally importantly, the mid-19th century also saw the birth of the first mass workers' movements, and the intensifying battle by workers to win shorter working days, higher wages and better conditions. The compromise which held for a good part of the mid-19th century in Britain was to raise wages for a layer of male workers to a point where they could sustain a family, leaving women under less pressure to work outside the home. As Sheila McGregor points out, the fact this process left women back at home and men going out to work was not inevitable, but:

> the failure to fight for an alternative based on state provision of nurseries, cleaning, laundry, cheap restaurants and the like meant that the exigencies of biological reproduction made it highly likely that the outcome would be a family based on a division of labour.[117]

The other kinds of crisis which have historically played a crucial role in regulating the balance between capitalists' demands on women in relation to production and social reproduction are economic crises. It is enormously convenient to the ruling class to force individual families to absorb the social shocks which result from economic crisis, ranging from supporting "surplus" labour laid off as production shrinks, to filling in the gaps in service provision as a result of reductions in state spending. In the case of women, the ideology of the sexual division of labour can usefully justify this process by promoting the idea that women's "natural" place is at home.

A final point needs to be made here about the role played by migration in providing a temporary relief for the capitalist ruling class from the dilemmas posed by generational reproduction. Mobilising migrant labour can provide a mechanism for reducing the costs to capital of social reproduction. If adult workers migrate, they arrive at their new workplaces without their bosses having had to contribute anything to their education and healthcare while growing up. Moreover, racism and the denial of citizenship rights can render them less resilient in the face of repression and impede their ability to fight back collectively. If they become ill, get injured or simply become too old to work efficiently, they can be shipped back to their countries of origin, again without their bosses having to contribute anything to their upkeep in old age. Just as women face being thrown out of work back into what Marx called "the reserve army of labour" at moments of economic crisis, so too migrant workers are often the first to lose their jobs when the slump hits.

Nevertheless, the long-term trajectory in capitalist societies is towards the exploitation of the majority of women in the workplace. This has taken place alongside the maintenance

---

117 McGregor, 2018.

of the family as a flexible 'private sphere' where some of the essential tasks of reproducing labour power take place, but the capitalist ruling class cannot escape the need to intervene actively in social reproduction. These processes have fed into another societal change: the overall long-term decline in fertility rates.[118] The 'fertility transition' has happened unevenly, but the general historical trend throughout capitalism's existence is for women to give birth to fewer children. The impact of changes in fertility has increasingly been concentrated in much shorter time scales, as the capitalism system has matured. In 1815, women in Britain on average gave birth 6 times. It took 95 years for that number to fall to 3 births per woman. By contrast, in Iran, the same drop in the average number of births took only 10 years between 1986 and 1996.[119]

The gap between women's access to formal education compared to men's has also dramatically narrowed over the history of capitalism, although in a highly uneven manner. Although there are persistent gaps in girls' and women's access to education and their attainment in school, the general pattern has been for these gaps to narrow over time. All of these elements are broadly consistent with the argument that in capitalist societies, establishing the conditions for the efficient exploitation of women's labour power, has historically been more important to capitalist ruling classes in the long run than their capacity to give birth.

Women's changing social role in the Middle East

The Middle East in general, and the countries discussed in this book in particular, are not exceptions to these general trends. Women's participation in the labour force has grown overall, even if at uneven rates. Fertility has declined dramatically, while inequality in access to education has also shrunk considerably. As the charts above show, the Middle East overtook Asia and the Pacific and Sub-Saharan Africa in this respect in recent decades.

Yet there are also significant differences between the Middle East and other regions of the world in terms of women's participation in work outside the home. Compared to other

---

118 Roser, 2014.
119 Roser, 2014.

Partners in revolution? Women and the uprisings

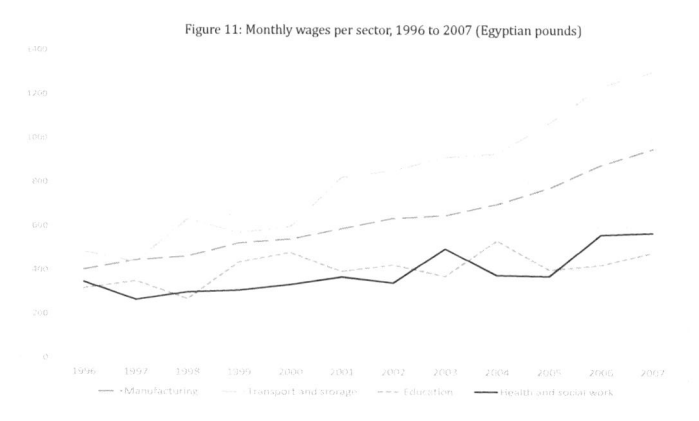

Figure 11: Monthly wages per sector, 1996 to 2007 (Egyptian pounds)

regions women form on average a smaller proportion of the labour force in most countries in the Middle East.

For both the women who took part in the revolutions and uprisings discussed in this book, and those who did not, these societal changes form the backdrop to their decisions to revolt or conform. Within a single generation, and in some countries even shorter time scales, they had experienced huge declines in fertility rates and rapid increase in access to education. By contrast, the world of work had only partially opened up, and in some cases working women entered the labour force while working class men were shut out of it through the restructuring or closure of public sector industries. Job security, pay and conditions at work remained under pressure throughout the neoliberal period.

The experience of cleaning and security jobs in the Tunisian public sector led to large pay cuts, cash-in-hand payments and the loss of health insurance and pension rights, for example. This process specifically disadvantaged women, whose working hours became very difficult to manage with early-morning and late evening shifts broken up by long periods without pay in the middle of the day.

The revolts in public services we discussed in previous chapters convulsed sectors of the economy where women form large proportions of the workforce. In 2007, 75 percent of women employees in Egypt worked in education, public administration and social care. Meanwhile, during the decades before the revolution of 2011, the pay differential between sectors where women workers were concentrated and other sectors widened considerably as the graph above illustrates.

Beyond the workplace, the impact of neoliberal economic reforms had the effect of making women's lives harder in several dimensions. Women already performed a much larger share of unpaid care work than men, but the declining quality of public health and education services increased pressure on them to earn more to pay for private services, or to fill in the gaps as best they could.

Cuts to subsidies on fuel and consumer goods also hit women hard, eating into household budgets which were generally their responsibility to manage, forcing them to spend even longer times queuing or searching for cheaper alternatives or making their own. Meanwhile rising costs of public transport affected not only women's ability to travel to work and study, but also their safety, with cheaper modes of transport tending to be more overcrowded and sometimes exposing them to greater risk of sexual harassment and assault. The deterioration of public health systems, like education affected women twice—firstly as workers in an increasingly badly-paid, deskilled and violent environment, and secondly as patients or patients' relatives.

Political bodies and the body politic

In addition to these societal changes affecting women's lives, the decades before the uprisings also saw intense political struggles around women's public presence (often symbolised by questions of their dress and behaviour), and over the balance between women's rights and duties in relation to the family and marriage, which usually crystallised around questions related to divorce, inheritance and child custody laws and issues of women's autonomy from husbands and male relatives. How these struggles played out in specific countries was affected by the political character of the social movements which took up these questions, by the ideology of the regimes in power and also by how women individually and collectively intervened around the issues. Yet there was also a degree of convergence between different countries, as the demands of capitalist accumulation shaped law and politics across the region. Both Islamist regimes

Figure 12: Total fertility rate 1950 to 2017

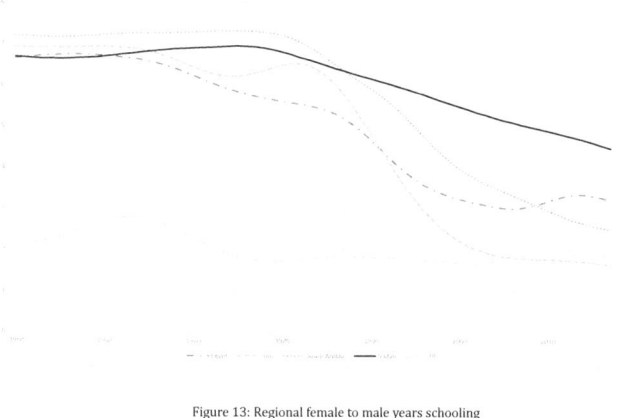

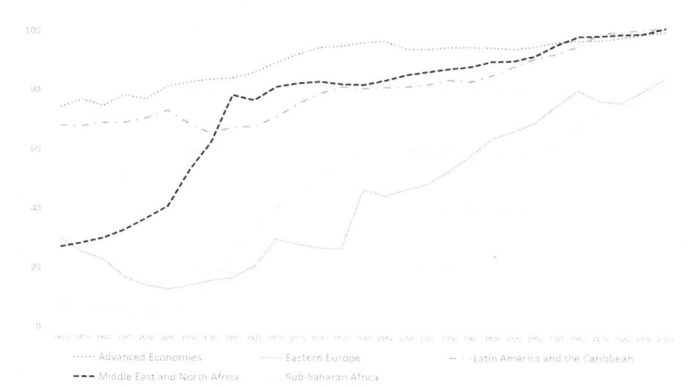

Figure 13: Regional female to male years schooling

Source: Our World in Data

and the former state capitalist ruling parties sought to police what women could wear and what they could do in public spaces. Support for oppressive laws restricting women's rights to divorce, custody of their children and autonomy from their husbands crossed ideological boundaries as well.

Regardless of the politics of the people running them, states across the region remained committed facilitating women's "reconciliation between her work in society and her duties in the family".[120] This phrase, which has been enshrined in the Egyptian constitution since 1956 in various guises, sums up neatly the way in which the ruling class in capitalist societies imposes a double burden explicitly on women, who are mobilised for exploitation outside the home at the same time as retaining "duties" (which are not imposed on men) towards privatised social reproduction in the family. It was no accident that this specific framing survived from the state capitalist era, into Sadat's 1971 Constitution which paved the way for the neoliberal turn in state policy, reappeared in the 2012 constitution which was proposed by an Islamist-dominated commission in the wake of the revolution. In a slightly modified form, it was incorporated into the 2014 constitution promulgated by al-Sisi after smashing the Islamist movement in 2013.

Two other points about how societal changes shaped women's experiences across the region are worth noting. Firstly, during the decades before the revolutions, women were more likely than ever before to have to negotiate entry into urban public spaces on a daily basis for study and work. As Assef Bayat notes, the 'outside-in' nature of the urban spaces in the neoliberal era, and the growth of 'informal' work made being 'in public' an inescapable way of life for many poor women as well as men.[121] Another significant shift in women's experience of public visibility (as well as highly gendered efforts to control and manage this visibility) was starting to take place in the realm of communications with the rise of social media. Although access to social media is unsurprisingly concentrated among wealthier sections of the population, and is highly uneven across the region, nevertheless, platforms such as Facebook did start to develop mass user bases, including large numbers of women over the last decade.

Women's use of social media platforms also marked a kind of being in public, and the similarities of the ways in which this was 'policed' in a direct way by the state, but also in more indirect ways through online sexist abuse by men individually or collectively, bore striking resemblances to the ways in which women's bodies into physical public spaces were policed. Women activists who used social media in Bahrain and Egypt—like many women social media users elsewhere in the world—have often faced harassment and abuse on social media platforms,

---

120 Arab Republic of Egypt, 1956.
121 Bayat, 2017, p109.

threatening them with rape, assault and violence, commenting on their bodies and sometimes exposing details of their private lives to intimidate and silence them. Since 2013 the Egyptian authorities have used 'indecency' laws to prosecute women who published images or videos of themselves enjoying themselves in public (or even semi-private) spaces, documented their experiences of sexual harassment on social media, or became prominent social media influencers even where the content revolved around topics such as fashion and make-up advice.[122]

One of the most visible ways in which struggles over women's public presence (and by women to assert their autonomy) played out was around the question of "Islamic dress". In Egypt, for example, this took the form of a visible trend during the 1970s and 1980s onwards of women wearing headscarves, long-sleeved shirts and skirts or trousers in ways which differed both from "traditional" urban or rural women's dress, and from trends of "Western" style dress which had been popular among middle class women during the previous generation. Although some women adopted it out of political conviction it was a much bigger societal trend than levels of support for opposition Islamist currents.[123]

This phenomenon was also visible in Tunisia during the same period, where women who wore headscarves faced discrimination and repression by the authorities for their choice, as Andrea Khalil notes:

> Islamist and Muslim-identified people were oppressed because of their religious practice, and women suffered especially under Ben Ali's secularist policies because of the female Islamic identity made visible by the veil. Under the dictatorship, men and women could only get promoted if they had some direct relation to Ben Ali's Constitutional Democratic Rally (RCD), and because the veil is a visible sign of religiosity, professional women were particularly vulnerable to this form of socio-economic discrimination. Many veiled women recounted having their head scarves pulled off in public by Ben Ali's security forces.[124]

---

122 AFP, 2020.
123 Macleod, 1993.
124 Khalil, 2014a.

The regime justified its targeting of Islamist women for their choice to display their beliefs through their dress by presenting itself as a bulwark against Islamist attempts to roll back Tunisian women's legal rights, including the country's relatively progressive personal status laws, adopted in the wake of the struggle for liberation from French colonial rule.

In the minority of countries where Islamist movements attained power, important battles over women's dress and presence in public spaces were also fought out over the past few decades. There is not space here to properly do justice to the experience of women in Iran, but as the only revolution which brought about a lasting change in political regime, the Iranian example was important for the rest of the region. The laws imposing an Islamic "uniform" on women in public spaces were imposed in a context where the faction around Ruhollah Khomeini was striving to assert control over the streets and workplaces. Women mobilised both for and against this policy, and one of the new regime's arguments which found support across a wider political spectrum was the way in which it linked its ideal of women's dress with an ideal of "anti-imperialist" resistance. Thus a reactionary and disciplinarian move, which women activists were right to oppose, became entangled with a set of wider questions in the context of the escalating conflict between the Islamic Republic and the United States.[125] The alliance between Umar al-Bashir's military regime in Sudan and the Islamist movement led by Hassan al-Turabi after the 1989 coup which brought el-Bashir to power also led to the imposition of reactionary laws regulating women's dress and behaviour in public. The Criminal Penal Code of 1991 allowed police to subject anyone considered to have committed "indecent act or an act contrary to public morals or wears an obscene outfit or contrary to public morals or causing an annoyance to public feelings," to flogging. Women were disproportionately affected by this law, with an estimated 40-50,000 detained each year and punished under the public order regime in Khartoum alone by 2015.[126]

The Egyptian regime also developed its own brand of "state feminism". The regime was driven by two primary motivations, firstly accessing international aid and loans was conditional on demonstrating progress in improving women's legal rights.

---

125 Harman, 1994; Poya, 2010.
126 Habani, 2015.

Egypt initiated reforms of the personal status laws championed by Jehan Sadat, the wife of President Anwar al-Sadat, signing the international Convention on the Elimination of all Forms of Discrimination Against Women (CEDAW), in 1980.[127] The second driver behind the regime's backing for legal reforms was political: as in Algeria and Tunisia, it offered a kind of "trade-off" between support for women's legal rights and widescale repression in the name of preventing the growth of Islamism. Further reforms followed in the 2000s including the *khul* law, which allowed women to seek a divorce without their husband's consent, the extension of women's rights to custody over their children in the event of divorce, and the abolition of a husband's right to forbid his wife to travel abroad.[128] These reforms which were popularly associated with Suzanne Mubarak, the president's wife, and triggered opposition from across a wide political spectrum, including within the Islamist movement (both within the Muslim Brotherhood and the Salafist movement), but also among liberals including prominent figures in the Wafd party.[129]

Women as leaders in workplace organising: The case of Egypt

While women could be found engaged in a wide range of political and social activism before the uprisings, by far the largest mobilisation in terms of numbers was women's participation in the mass strikes detailed in Chapter 10. The strikes and protests also gave working class women the chance to develop themselves as leaders and organisers. In 2008, Farah Koubaissy interviewed Aisha Abd-al-Aziz Abu-Samada, better known as Hagga Aisha, the organiser and spokeswoman for workers at the Hennawi Tobacco factory in Damanhour. Following years of relentless speed-ups in the pace of work and cuts to basic safety equipment, the final straw came when the tame union committee signed up to a deal with management agreeing to slash workers' bonuses and social allowances.

---

127 Sonneveld, 2018, p334.
128 Sonneveld & Lindbekk, 2015.
129 Sonneveld & Lindbekk, 2015.

Revolution is the choice of the people

On 4 August 2008 Hagga Aisha and a group of colleagues informed management and the union committee that unless their bonuses and allowances were paid a strike would begin the next day. The following morning around 100 workers occupied the factory, while another 100 piled into a flotilla of buses and headed off to Cairo for protests outside the Ministry of Labour and the General Federation of Trade Unions. Hagga Aisha took on the role of spokesperson as well as organising the strike. She liaised with the media and made sure that journalists were there to hear the strikers' stories on 5 August. She arranged the transport from Damanhur to the ministry headquarters in the Cairo suburb of Madinat Nasr and led a delegation of workers to the General Federation of Trade Unions.[130]

Women garment workers at Misr Spinning in al-Mahalla al-Kubra began the historic strike in December 2006 which triggered a major escalation in the strike wave.

Prime minister Ahmad Nazif, a staunch neoliberal and enthusiast for privatisation, had promised all public sector workers an annual bonus equivalent to two months' pay. Disappointment quickly turned to fury as workers discovered that they had received only the standard bonus. Some 3,000 women garment workers stormed into the main spinning and weaving sheds and demanded that their male colleagues stop work. "Where are the men? Here are the women!" they chanted. Then 10,000 workers gathered in the factory courtyard and once again women were at the forefront. Strike leader Muhammad Attar later recalled, "The women almost tore apart every representative from management who came to negotiate".[131]

At the Mansoura-Espana garment factory, women workers organised an occupation for two months, sleeping on the shopfloor along with male colleagues in a bid to stop the owner selling up and closing down the company. The public services

---

130 Alexander & Koubaissy, 2008.
131 Alexander & Koubaissy, 2008.

Partners in revolution? Women and the uprisings

also saw women activists gain experience of strike organising and building independent unions. Women activists were among the organisers of the Property Tax Collectors' strike in 2007 and the first independent union which was founded in 2008 following the strike's success.

In 2011-13, I interviewed women working in a wide range of sectors who were active in organising strikes and building independent unions, including junior doctors, hospital admin workers, local government workers and property tax collectors, aviation workers and teachers. Some were leaders in their own workplaces but others had also taken on national roles in strike organising such as Dr Shima'a Mosallam, founding member of the independent union at Abbassiya General Psychiatric Hospital in Cairo and a member of the Higher Strike Committee of the Doctors' Union which organised two nation-wide strikes in May 2011. As Dr Mosallam explained, her role at national level built her activism within the hospital where she was one of a group of health workers who organised a successful campaign in November 2010 to stop the Ministry of Health transferring the hospital to new premises outside Cairo in order sell the land to property developers. The petition campaign against the land sale created new networks of activists across the hospital and raised their confidence. Following the uprising in January 2011 they began to organise an independent union representing all grades of staff, following the model developed in another Cairo hospital, Manshiyet al-Bakri.

Dr Mosallam was not the only woman activist playing a prominent leadership role at a national level in the Doctors' Union during this period. Dr Mona Mina was elected to the union's national executive and then to the role of General Secretary during the same period, reflecting the success of the left in winning support of a wide layer of members, and the growth of a layer of activists inside the union who began to look toward more militant tactics to defend both their rights at work and the rights of Egyptian citizens to public health care. Dr Mina's electoral victory installed a Coptic woman as the national leader of a major health workers union after more than twenty years when the dominant political current in the Doctors' Union had been the Muslim Brotherhood.

The ferment of activism in the public hospitals did not only extend to better-paid and highly educated doctors, but also to some of the most low-paid and precarious workers, such as Fatma Zahraa, an administrator at Manshiyet al-Bakri hospital. Before the revolution she earned seven Egyptian pounds a day working as a secretary on a rolling contract which was renewed every 55 days. Without rights to paid holidays or health insurance she and other temporary workers also had to deal with bullying and aggressive managers. The independent union not only gave her and colleagues a collective route to improve their conditions, it also empowered them in relation to other grades of staff, starting to break down some of the deeply-ingrained hierarchies between doctors, nurses, admin staff and manual workers.

> After the revolution, we found that the issue of democracy and the legitimacy of the majority opinion became an 'open area' for everyone. I wanted to have a role in this because I hadn't been able to do this before because of personal restrictions. Now we're spreading the idea of the union among all sections of the hospital and we're trying to win new members. If there are more than 70 members in a particular section, they elected five reps, and from among those reps, one is elected to represent the section on the union council. There are actually unions for all the different grades, there is a Doctors' Union, a union for the nurses, and a union for the admin staff. But the independent union knits everyone together. In the meetings of the union council, for example, the manual worker rep sits next to the doctors. There is equality. It's a great gain for democracy. One hundred per cent.[132]

It was not only in public services that women emerged as leading union organisers. In 2013 I spoke to Abeer Ashour, the president of the Union of Bread Sellers in Suez about how she and colleagues were starting to organise the workers who distributed the flat, round government-subsidised loaves from street kiosks:

> There is a lot of corruption, and the whole system of bread production is failing. Of course, it is us the bakery

---

132 MENA Solidarity Network, 2013.

workers and bread sellers who face the anger of our customers when the system goes wrong. They shout at us and a colleague was attacked with hammer. I have a degree in Commerce, but as a divorced woman I've had no choice but to take this job, even though it doesn't pay enough to feed my two kids. Our working conditions are really unsafe, particularly for women. We work in wooden kiosks in the street to distribute the bread from the public bakeries. I end up taking money from my own pocket to repair the kiosk where I work.

We are trying to build an independent union and have around 60 members now. Our wages are very low, we get around 265 LE a month. The old unions have done nothing for us, they worked hand-in-hand with the old regime and don't really represent workers' interests".[133]

The growing space for women to organise at work did not mean that sexism and discrimination disappeared overnight. While women participated in the overnight sit-ins and workplace occupations alongside men, they were more likely to end up organising the provisions than their male colleagues, some women activists told me. Women's representation at the highest levels of the new unions was unequal too, even in sectors where they formed a majority or near-majority of the workforce.

In 2012 I was sitting with activists from the Women's Committee of the Egyptian Federation of Independent Trade Unions discussing how the revolution had opened up new prospects for women to organise at work, when Kamal Abu Aita, the EFITU president walked into the room. Several of the women I was talking to rounded on him immediately: "Mr Kamal, why is it that us women never get picked for foreign trips or to talk to the media? It isn't fair that men get all these opportunities".

Women as protest leaders and organisers

One of the important roles played by the mass strikes in the pre-revolutionary period was that the spaces they created for women to emerge as organisers and leaders pre-figured

---

133   MENA Solidarity Network, 2013.

the partial opening of such spaces in the streets and on the barricades in confrontations with the security forces. Women's roles in revolutionary organising on the streets reflected both the constraints of the sexism and oppression they faced and how the uprisings began to challenge and break down the ideas and structures perpetuating them, both among women themselves and men.

Women in Tahrir Square were visible in a range of critical roles during the 18-day uprising, including running security cordons at the entrances so that women entering would have their ID checked and their bags could be searched by other women. In the early days of the uprising this organisational role was often taken by young Islamist women. Inside the square, women also led chants and spoke from the platforms, and Coptic Christian women were visible leading joint prayers for Christians and Muslims on 'Revolution Sunday'.[134]

Women doctors and pharmacists helped to run the Square's 'field hospitals', a role which they continued in later sit-ins as confrontations with the security forces escalated again in November 2011. Dr Rania Fouad, a recently-qualified doctor, died after inhaling tear gas after the police attacked the field hospital where she was working, according to other activists.[135]

Women played a visible role as protest leaders and organisers in other revolutions and uprisings. In Sudan, for example, women activists helped mobilise in the neighbourhoods where regular street protests kept up the pressure on the regime through the months after the uprising began in December 2018. Fatima Joda spoke to *Middle East Solidarity* magazine about her experience of protest in Khartoum's Burri neighbourhood in January 2019:

> On 17 January I was in the crowd, out on the streets of Burri, one of the most politically active neighbourhoods of Khartoum. As we were moving peacefully along, women and children from the area joined the protest and started chanting with us. Security Forces started breaking up the crowd by throwing teargas at us. Everyone began running and hiding inside the houses, which the neighbourhood families opened up in order to hide the protesters. After a couple of minutes, we

---

134 Alexander, 2011.
135 MENA Solidarity Network, 2012.

began to gather again as security forces and police drove to a nearby street to separate other protesters.

We are no longer scared of death, and you can tell this from the increasing numbers of people joining the protests every day. Everyone is out on the streets now. It's not easy to overthrow a dictatorship that has been in power for 30 years. It will take months and maybe years till we get our freedom. The only thing I am sure about now is that we are not going to be silent anymore.[136]

Some young women emerged as icons for the whole revolutionary movement based on their roles in the street protests and sit-ins. While Alaa Saleh whose image became a global symbol of the Sudanese Revolution was the most famous, there plenty of others, such the young woman who was nicknamed 'Tear-gas girl' (Bint al-bomban) as a video clip of her picking up smoking tear gas canisters and hurling them back at the police went viral on WhatsApp chats and social media pages.

Dr Sara Abdelgalil argues that from the beginning of the revolution, women and girls were in the frontline. The spaces they used to organise included the newly-formed independent unions and professional associations, but also apparently 'apolitical' forums where women had previously focussed on topics considered traditionally "feminine". This extended to using women's networks to call out and shame police officers who were involved in attacks on protests.

For me as a Sudanese woman, it is interesting to see how wide the support for this movement goes among Sudanese women. We have seen Facebook groups which were previously just for discussions about beauty and cooking showing their support for the protests. They have even been using the Facebook groups to identify police officers involved in beating protesters and warning people to stay away from them. Young women from these groups put out a statement on 31 January. This shows that all sections of the community are standing together.[137]

---

136 Joda, 2019.
137 MENA Solidarity Network, 2019.

Revolution is the choice of the people

The Sudanese sit-ins created spaces for women to be active in a variety of organisational roles, as in the Egyptian workers' sit-ins, some of this replicated existing the existing gendered division of labour in social reproduction by organising provisions and food for the thousands of people in the protest camps.

However, these revolutionary spaces also opened up opportunities for political discussion and debate on an unprecedented scale, as well as political education. The major sit-in outside the Army General Command in Khartoum which was established on 6 April was organised on a day-to-day basis by a structure of revolutionary committees. Some of these were focussed on practical issues of security, provisions, cleaning and logistics, but they also included political education among their priorities, including specifically organising discussions to raise awareness of sexism and racism.

> Since the first day in the sit-in we have been holding discussion circles. They are to raise awareness, both of the committee members and all the protesters at the General Command sit-in. We talk about the importance of peace, the acceptance of the other and the rejection of racism in all its forms, whether ethnic or religious, and discrimination against women. These have really raised the political awareness of the protesters.[138]

Uprisings in the other countries discussed in this book include similar examples of women taking on crucial roles in street protests and sit-ins. In videos of the massive street protests which shook Iraq during 2019 and 2020 young women could be seen leading the chants on megaphones. Unemployed women graduates played an important role in sparking the popular movement in Iraq, through sit-ins and road blockades demanding access to jobs in the months before the establishment of the major sit-ins in Baghdad and other cities.

As Selma Oumari explains, the explosion of the mass movement in Algeria in 2019 also created spaces for women to organise in public despite deeply-engrained sexism.

> Women are marginalised in public spaces, and only

138 Alexander, 2019

> 18 percent are able to get a job. They are second class citizens as they don't have the same rights as men. That is why they are very concerned and active in the process of social change. They are visible in the movement and are shaping the political debate around their own issues. Feminist blocs are very lively on the Friday demonstrations, raising debates within the movement about women's rights. They are pushing for the abolition of the Family Code, which enshrines women's legal status as inferior to men. As organisers, they are active in the student movement, and in the trade unions.[139]

The character of the street protests did shape whether women were likely to participate *en masse* and what roles they were likely to play, however. Although young women were to be found on the frontlines of protests in all the revolutions, including facing down attacks from the police and security forces, the participation of women across a wider range of ages and women with children unsurprisingly tended to increase where there was less likelihood of violence. In Egypt, when clashes with the security forces escalated into pitched battles around the perimeter of Tahrir Square and along Mohamed Mahmoud Street, a gendered division of labour on the protesters' side reasserted itself, with women more likely to be cast in "supporting" roles in the field hospitals or behind the frontlines dominated by young men. This was captured in graffiti stencils along Mohamed Mahmoud Street showing a young woman activist telling a young man "I've got your back".

In all the revolutions and uprisings, women faced specifically gendered forms of repression for their public defiance of the old order, sometimes also sexism and assaults from male protesters and activists, and in countries where new constitutions or amendments to existing ones were promulgated as a result of the political crisis, the question of women's rights in the post-revolutionary period was also hotly contested, often along the political fault-line dividing secular and Islamist currents. In Egypt, as we will discuss in more detail below, the revolution also saw activists increasingly focussing on the question of sexual harassment and assault, both in response to the growing frequency of violent attacks on women during protests.

---

139 MENA Solidarity Network, 2019.

Perpetrator or protector? The role of the state in violence against women

The challenge which women's highly visible role in the uprisings posed to the state is summed up by the experience of women activists in Egypt who were subjected to the violence of so-called "virginity tests" by the military police after being arrested from the Tahrir Square sit-in. Young women detainees such as Samira Ibrahim, who took her abusers to court and gave public testimony which spurred a broad debate about violence against women, were stripped while military doctors penetrated them with their fingers or other instruments supposedly in order to ascertain whether their hymens were intact. Samira and other young women arrested at the same time were also beaten, subjected to electric shocks and deprived of sleep and food. When challenged in public about the "virginity tests", military officials at first denied the story, but then admitted the abuses, justifying their actions by arguing that this was necessary to "protect" the reputation of the army from claims of sexual assault and rape. As one of the generals later explained to a male reporter on CNN, "these women were not like your daughter or mine", for they "had camped out in tents with male protestors". The army had to protect itself: "[w]e didn't want them to say we had sexually assaulted or raped them, so we wanted to prove that they weren't virgins in the first place".[140] By violating Samira Ibrahim's body, in order to "prove" she had already forfeited her right to protection as a dutiful girl who knew her place in a gender-divided society, the army staked a larger claim about the role of the state, as "protector" of women's dignity.

In parallel with the use of "virginity tests" and the debate that Samira's courageous legal challenge to her abusers provoked, another disturbing phenomenon spread: gangs of men assaulted and raped women in public spaces during major protests. As Nadje al-Ali notes, these attacks often followed a distinctive pattern.

> On 25 January 2013, the second anniversary of Egypt's revolution, at least nineteen women were sexually assaulted by gangs of men. These attacks were similar to previous assaults during protests: large numbers of men move jointly through crowds, working in a systematic

140 Sekaily, 2013.

Partners in revolution? Women and the uprisings

and orchestrated way, surrounding individual women, first in a U shape, then fully encircling a woman in several lines of men. Victims report feeling confused by some men speaking about protection while closing in on them and attacking them in a most brutal manner, including stripping off their clothes and raping them with objects and fingers.[141]

One of the first cases of this kind to come to international attention was the attack on American journalist Lara Logan in Tahrir Square on 12 February 2011, as huge crowds celebrated the fall of Mubarak.[142] However, over the following two years, many other women, mostly Egyptian, would recount similarly brutal experiences while attending major protests. Revolutionary activists began to organise over the issue of women's rights to participate in protests without facing such attacks, in some cases organising practically to try and reclaim the streets and squares as spaces for women through physically protecting women demonstrators from attack or using volunteers to creating women-only areas in the protests.[143]

Other tactics included mapping and documenting attacks on women, campaigning to challenge the "everyday" and pervasive nature of violence against Egyptian women (which largely occurs in private spaces rather than public ones), and mobilising a major protest march on 20 December 2011, which brought around ten thousand women onto the streets of Cairo. The spur for the protest was once again the violence of the military against women protesters, in particular the image of a young woman being dragged across the floor and stamped on by military police, as they tore off her black robe and exposed her. As Nadine El-Enany noted, many of the women involved in the protest presented revolutionary solidarity between women and men as the answer to the urgent question of the state's violence against women.

> The women were urgent, angry and determined to make their voices heard, and themselves and their role in this revolution, visible. They were of all ages.

---

141 Al-Ali, 2014.
142 Stelter, 2011.
143 Al-Ali, 2104.

Revolution is the choice of the people

They chanted, "Egyptian women and Egyptian men are one hand". Women showed passers-by the image of the woman being attacked by soldiers, thrusting it in people's faces, forcing them to witness the crimes of SCAF. Many had not seen the image and didn't believe it, accusing the protesters of fabricating it, but the women marched on, all 10,000 of them, their voices one voice, propelling the Egyptian revolution along.[144]

The question of whether the state's main role was as a channel amplifying sexism and misogyny in wider society, or whether it had an organising and directing role in women's oppression became both more contested and more urgent to answer as time passed from the initial uprising in 2011. Between 2012 and 2013 debates over this issue also became wrapped up in the growing polarisation between secular and Islamist political currents, with some feminist activists arguing that it was the presence of Islamists in elected office in Egypt and Tunisia, and the emergence of conservative Salafist groups as players in "street politics", the electoral arena, and acting as armed organisations, which underlay the upsurge in violence against women.[145]

However, the attacks did not end with the fall of Mohamed Morsi in July 2013. Nearly a year later after public celebrations marking the inauguration of Abdelfattah al-Sisi as president in June 2014, a graphic video showing a naked, injured woman being dragged through Tahrir Square went viral online. In the outcry which followed, other women testified that they had also been attacked by groups of men in the square that night. Al-Sisi made a statement condemning sexual harassment and prosecutors began to apply a new law which punishing sexual harassment with at least six months in jail or fines of 3000 Egyptian pounds.[146]

As head of Military Intelligence at the time its officers were raping women detainees in order to protect the army's good name, al-Sisi's credentials as a defender of women's rights are more than a little thin. The continuing attacks on women in public spaces can be read in more than one way. On the one

---

144 MENA Solidarity Network, 2012.
145 Tadros, 2006.
146 Saleh, 2014.

hand, they reminded everyone of the on-going need for women to be protected from men, with the state posing as defender of their rights.

On the other, they emphasised that women's presence in public spaces was not theirs by right, but conditional, even in cases where women were expressing their support for the regime in power, rather than their dissent. Meanwhile women were enlisted to help promote "Sisi-mania" which projected the slightly paunchy, balding, middle-aged general as a sex symbol. Sisi's face adorned cheap chocolates in shop windows, while columnists in the official media gushed over his "virility":

> He was called upon at a supreme moment in history; a kind of mysterious rendez-vous with destiny. He was a hero like no other! He aroused attention without exhausting it. Nothing that touched the common run of mortals made any impression on him. All in all, he is but a common man, with an almost aristocratic aura of a nobleman. Composed and cool, El-Sisi is everyman's man, with a sort of serene majesty on his brow... He will lead us to victory and never renounce the struggle, and we will be right there at his side.[147]

Another facet of the military regime's counter-revolution was the unleashing of a vicious homophobic crackdown. This included whipping up a moral panic about LGBT+ people through sensationalist reporting, including journalists accompanying police in "raids" on men's bathhouses, filming and publishing information about the men detained in the process who were later put on trial for "sexual deviance" and "debauchery". Despite the long history of state-sponsored homophobia, many LGBT Egyptians considered the intensity of the crackdown under al-Sisi's rule unique. As Ramy Youssef put it in a 2015 interview:

> I think the crackdown under al-Sisi is definitely the most violent of all time. His government controls all the state's institutions, including the supposedly-free ones. Journalists and the media work according to the directions of the government. Police are more violent than ever: they are using tracking techniques which they

---

147 Marfleet, 2014

have used previously in 2003 but on a larger scale.[148]

Not only gay men but a wide spectrum of LGBT+ people faced systematic repression. One of the most high-profile examples was the arrest and torture of Sara Hegazy, who was seized by police and charged with raising the rainbow Pride flag at a 2017 concert by Lebanese band Mashrou' Leila. However, human rights groups and activists documented dozens of examples of arrests, public outings, prosecutions and torture, while pro-Sisi politicians such as MP Riad Abdel Sattar pushed for even more draconian laws aimed at "punishing, jailing, extirpating anything even remotely connected to homosexuality".[149]

Women's rights and the law in the revolutionary period

The fall of Ben Ali and Mubarak opened up possibilities for legal and constitutional reform on a scale not seen for decades in Tunisia and Egypt—ushering in competitive elections, the writing of new constitutions, and created space for political organisation from below, with new parties, movements and campaigns flourishing. However, as we will discuss in the next chapter, questions of reform were addressed within a political framework which ruled out revolutionary challenges to the structures of the existing state, and thus the consensus among the major currents in the opposition was strongly in favour of negotiating their access to the corridors of power with the still-functioning core institutions of the old regime. In both cases, the largest and best organised opposition *parties* were Islamist—Ennadha in Tunisia and the Muslim Brotherhood in Egypt. In Tunisia, the main trade union federation, the UGTT was in fact the largest reformist organisation in the country.

In both countries, the issue of women's legal rights and political representation in the wake of the dictators' fall was a site of intense struggle reflecting competing political and social pressures. At a political level, the growing polarisation in Egypt between Islamists and 'secular' forces, which opened the door to the political rehabilitation of elements of the old ruling

148 Finden, 2015.
149 Long, 2017.

Partners in revolution? Women and the uprisings

party through the "National Salvation Front" which launched in the autumn of 2012. For some of the women politicians who had worked closely with the old regime, this provided the opportunity to rebuild a platform for a renewal of the "state feminism" of the previous era.

Former Mubarak-era cabinet minister and diplomat Mervat el-Tallawy who was appointed by the Supreme Council of the Armed Forces as chair of the National Council for Women, told the *Mail on Sunday* that women had everything to gain from the ousting of Mohamed Morsi by al-Sisi in July 2013:

> In February 2012, members of the Shura Council, Egypt's legislative body, blamed women for the increase in sexual assaults "because they put themselves in such circumstances". In doing so, they sent the signal that it is OK for a man to touch any woman in the street. Morsi's government moved to deny women the right to right to seek a divorce under Islam, supported female circumcision, sacked women in top government jobs and tried to lower the age of consent for girls to marry from 18 to nine. They want to treat us like slaves whose role is to bear babies and serve the sexual needs of men. They have tried to take us from a modern, civilised and religiously tolerant country back into the dark ages.[150]

El-Tallawy's support for women appeared stretched thin when it came to the rights to peaceful protest and assembly, however. In 2015 she said of young women political prisoners "they live better than they were living on the outside". Among those women whose plight she dismissed included young activists condemned to up to 15 years in jail for assembling in the streets of Alexandria on the way to school.[151]

But what about El-Tallawy's accusations that the Muslim Brotherhood while in power launched an all-out assault on women's legal rights? In reality, the picture was more complex than simple binaries between 'Islamist' and 'feminist' constituencies mobilising around these issues. As researchers Nadia Sonneveld and Monika Lindbekk point out, divorced fathers' groups which began to mobilise demanding changes

---

150 Johnson, 2013.
151 Ibrahim, 2015

to the divorce and child custody laws did seek the support of Salafist and Muslim Brotherhood deputies in parliament but did not always simply call for a restoration of the previous legal position for men. Some instead argued for childcare as a shared responsibility between parents, in effect weakening the idea that men's primary role was as a breadwinner and women's role as carers, which paradoxically was the consensus among most Islamists.[152] Feminist groups, such as the Coalition of Egyptian Feminist Organisations (CEFO), opposed amendment of the personal status laws, although rather than relying on arguments from Islamic shari'a like the divorced mothers' groups, they focussed on Egypt's obligations under international law.

When it came to the writing of a new constitution, the Muslim Brotherhood and the Salafist movement dominated the body which prepared the draft. As feminist activist Hala Kamal was right to argue, this committee was "a product of a process in which a vast majority of Egyptians were excluded and their demands ignored," including women who were hardly mentioned explicitly at all in the document. Yet the idea that the text which emerged represented a completely reactionary perspective on women's rights is challenged by Ellen McLarney, who notes that the 2012 constitution establishes a constitutional right to "equality and equal opportunities for all citizens, men and women (muwatinin wa-muwatinat), without distinction, favouritism, or partiality, in rights or duties". As McLarney points out, this puts the constitution proposed by the Islamist-dominated Constituent Assembly on more progressive legal terrain than the US, where an Equal Rights Amendment has yet to be passed.[153]

It is true that the 2012 Constitution also contained phraseology which was a clear concession to the most reactionary elements of the Islamist movement in terms of opening up scope for interpretations of Islamic law which could radically restrict women's rights and that some sections of the Islamist movement actively campaigned on a reactionary platform which did indeed call for women to return to an exclusive role as homemakers and mothers. However, the leadership of the Muslim Brotherhood faced competing pressures opposing these perspectives.

152 Sonneveld & Lindbekk, 2015
153 McLarney, 2013

Partners in revolution? Women and the uprisings

Firstly, the Brotherhood itself, with its contradictory class base drawn from sections of the working class, the middle class and a small layer of wealthy businessmen, was also affected by the social changes we have discussed earlier in this chapter. It included among its ranks quite large numbers of women activists, particularly from the middle classes who had engaged in politics for decades, and whose public role was seen by the generation of reformists which emerged to challenge the party's "old guard" during the 1980s and 1990s as essential to winning women's votes in elections.[154] Secondly, Egyptian capitalism requires women's labour in the workplace: it cannot afford to raise wages for the majority to a level where women do not need to go out to work, and the Muslim Brotherhood's leadership was well aware of this: its' economic policies certainly praised women's labour in the household economy, but also in "private enterprise".[155]

In Tunisia, also the issue of women's rights was highlighted during the constitutional drafting process, with Islamist and secular activists apparently lining up on different sides of the debate about the phrasing of a clause which feminists argued relegated women to a position which was "complementary" rather than "equal" to men in the family. As Mounira Charrad and Amina Zarrugh note, the meaning of the phrase *'yetekamel durhuma'* in the original Arabic is open to other possible interpretations:

> We see an alternative translation of the term as 'integrate with one another'. This translation points to a sense of fulfilment and unity between men and women that suggests the essential significance of the roles of both men and women to the nation and the family.[156]

Nevertheless, a lively campaign of petitions and protests resulted in the wording being dropped from the version of the constitution which was adopted in 2014, as members of Ennadha's leadership publicly emphasised their support for protecting Tunisian women's legal and constitutional rights.[157]

---

154 El-Ghobashy, 2015.
155 McLarney, 2013
156 Charrad & Zarrugh, 2014.
157 Charrad & Zarrugh, 2014.

Conclusion

The intensity with which women's public presence, their dress and their bodies were politically contested during the revolutions did not appear in a vacuum, but reflected the contradictory ways in which capitalist development on the one hand perpetuated women's oppression—objectifying and commodifying their bodies, demanding unequal burdens of unpaid work from them in the process of social reproduction—but also drew them into urban public spaces, workplaces, schools and universities in greater numbers than ever before bringing with it greater opportunities to organise collectively for their own liberation. However, this was not a linear, straightforward process, as it took place in the context of long histories of colonialism and imperialism which accelerated some aspects of economic development while holding back others. Contrary to simplistic and often racist assumptions in Western media commentary the positions taken by individual women and men on these questions, and the influence of specific sexist ideas and practices in any of the societies discussed in this book could not be reduced to a simple binary of either an index of 'modernity' versus 'backwardness' or the influence of 'secular' versus 'Islamist' political currents in the state and wider society.

Women's participation in and leadership of the mass strikes before and during the revolutions very clearly signalled their resistance to the conditions under which exploitation was taking place, and their growing confidence to change those conditions for themselves alongside working class men. However, women's mass participation in street protests and sit-ins was also a huge challenge to a political order which at times claimed explicitly to be speaking on their behalf and defending their interests. The reaction at the core of the state to this challenge demonstrated quite clearly just how important sexism was to the counter-revolutionary project.

Revolution is the choice of the people

Section four

The crisis of the state and permanent revolution

Revolution is the choice of the people

Chapter 11
Faust's bargain: the failure of reformist strategies

This book began with an overview of the mass popular mobilisations which have shaken country after country across the Middle East over the last ten years. The following two sections explored the long-term roots of the multi-faceted crises and outlined some of the principal collective actors among the people whose intervention would shape the dynamics and outcomes of the revolutionary contests with the regimes. In the final chapters we will look beyond the revolutions as movements to address the question of "revolution as change", as Assef Bayat puts it.[1] This also means addressing the paradox which Bayat has identified: how could popular uprisings on this scale have altered the state so little? Does the problem lie in a lack of genuinely revolutionary ambition on the part of those who led them? Or the tactics they adopted to achieve their goals?

In this chapter we will investigate two theorisations of *how* political change was meant to happen as a result of the popular uprisings and explore why the actual outcomes of the revolutions failed to follow either of these scripts. The first theorisation of the process of change concentrates on the mass mobilisations themselves, proposing an overarching framework of these as "nonviolent resistance" or "civil resistance". Popularised by US-based academics such as Gene Sharp and Erica Chenoweth, this approach to understanding the path "from dictatorship to

---
1 Bayat, 2017, p17

democracy"[2] regards mass collective action as a prerequisite for achieving change, including mass strikes and civil disobedience. While not necessarily labelling this as a "revolutionary" strategy, theorists of "civil resistance" such as Erica Chenoweth are clear that political regime change through extra-parliamentary, nonviolent means will be a likely goal of such mobilisations.[3]

The second theorisation of political change is the model of "democratic transitions" promoted by Western governments and accepted in some form or other by major reformist opposition movements across the political spectrum from Islamists to liberals, nationalists and the left, in most of the countries discussed in this book. In contrast to the "civil resistance" paradigm which explicitly excludes parliamentary routes to achieving the reforms demanded by the mass movements involved, the concept of a "democratic transition" lays out an electoral "road map" for the processes of moving from authoritarian to democratic forms of government. This model is of course also explicitly aimed at avoiding radical changes to the state which might harm the interests of the broader capitalist ruling class within the country and the Western powers outside it.

The end goal of the "transition" is presumed to be the consolidation of a Western-style democracy with regular parliamentary elections, a free press, well-behaved policemen who don't randomly torture citizens and militaries who know their proper place and don't interfere in politics. Democratic transitions have been inevitably paired with measures to enforce economic liberalisation alongside political liberalisation creating an explosive paradox for the local reformist partners in such processes who have been left to deal with the collapse of popular support for the project in the context of deepening economic and social crisis and plummeting living standards for the poor.

These two strategies are not precisely counterposed as alternatives to each other. In almost every case discussed here the eruption of mass popular movements calling for systemic political change took established opposition parties, including those formally committed to achieving democratic reforms,

---

2 Sharp, 2008.
3 Chenoweth, 2021.

Faust's bargain: the failure of reformist strategies

by surprise.[4] The popular mobilisations bypassed opposition party leaderships and hierarchical decision-making structures, although frequently they were supported by large sections of these movements' base and sometimes by prominent individual members. However, a democratic transition was often proposed as a completion of the political task begun by the popular mobilisations, usually as an explicit substitute for further collective action and as part of the process of achieving the subordination of political struggles in the streets, neighbourhoods and workplaces to the leadership of parliamentary parties.

This chapter will argue that despite their apparent differences, what links these two theories of change is their acceptance of a Faustian bargain with the capitalist ruling class. Their commitment to the continuity of the existing form of the state and expectation that a change of heart in the leadership at the top will be enough to effect a lasting shift from authoritarianism to democracy has often led them to disarm and demobilise the mass movements which are the only protection against the revenge of old order. Or in some cases, the political and social forces leading the counter-revolution have proved capable of seizing the streets, organising protests and simulating civil disobedience (backed up by threats or actual violence rather than promises of "nonviolence").

Rethinking reformism

The term "reformist" in this book is not simply a shorthand for those who promote "reforms". This commonly-used definition can be found regularly in use by media commentators and academics, including in risible contexts such as descriptions of various kinds of despots as "reformers". Rather, it is used here as a label for a family of ideologies, organisations and political practices which combine two key characteristics: an insistence that the capitalist system must be reformed rather

---

4 Sudan, it could be argued, constituted a partial exception to this, in that the Forces of Freedom and Change included long-established political forces such as the Umma Party. However, the most dynamic components of the FFC during the uprising were not established parties, but new movements such as the Sudanese Professionals Association.

than overthrown and that the self-organisation and activity of ordinary people can play a role in this process. The two parts of this definition are equally important and distinguish reform*ism* from *reforms* (which can be initiated by other players in the political game, including members of the elite looking to contain or diffuse anger from below). Revolutionaries are very likely to be involved centrally in agitation for reforms with the opposite intention. As using such partial victories can build the self-confidence of ordinary people that their actions can change things for the better and act as a stepping stone towards them concluding that the system itself has to go.

These twin characteristics give reformist movements and currents a special role in revolutionary crises, as they provide an essential 'safety valve' for the capitalist system. They work systematically to channel the pent-up energy of the revolutionary pressure from below into parliamentary institutions or into into the "maze of trenches impeding access to a now defensive citadel," of the core of the state.[5]

This definition of reformism expands one which is commonly used on the revolutionary left and has a long history in the Marxist tradition, where the label "reformist" has been applied to Social Democratic parties and the trade unions.[6] However, refusing to extend the label to other political traditions, such as liberal, nationalist and Islamist movements can lead to immense confusion and political misjudgements. This is particularly a problem outside Europe where the historical experience of creating Social Democratic-type parties with a mass base among workers or other sections of the poor is relatively restricted. Various types of secular nationalist parties, Stalinist and Maoist Communist groups and some

---

5 Thomas, 2009, 148. Thomas's work on Antonio Gramsci's theory of the "integral state" is especially useful in this context, see Thomas, 2009 pp137-148.

6 See for example, debates within the German Social Democratic Party (SPD) between Rosa Luxemburg and Edward Bernstein at the turn of the 20th century (Luxemburg, 1900). Luxemburg popularised the term "reformism" in her polemics against Bernstein, who argued that socialism would come about not through the revolutionary seizure of power, but gradually through social reforms enacted as result of SPD electoral victories and trade union activity. See Luxemburg, 1900, Chapter 5, for example

Faust's bargain: the failure of reformist strategies

Islamist organisations frequently occupy the political space which in the European context has often been filled by Social Democratic organisations.[7] Failing to understand the variety of political currents which can play a reformist role, especially in the context of a revolutionary crisis can also lead to pessimistic or abstentionist conclusions by the revolutionary left.[8] This was the case with sections of the Egyptian revolutionary movement in 2012 which refused to support Islamist candidate Mohamed Morsi in the last round of the presidential elections against his rival, the open counter-revolutionary candidate Ahmed Shafiq.

Reformist movements don't only internalise ruling class ideas, but they are almost always cross-class bodies, usually led by members of the middle class. They are however, distinct from ruling class parties which advocate reforms and seek to win support of workers or the poor on that basis. —In its expanded meaning, reformism combines the acceptance of ruling class ideas by people outside the ruling class with the mobilisation of people from classes beyond the ruling class in organisational forms which are not simply led by warring factions of the elite. Nor is reformism the same as the *deflection* of anger at the system onto other targets by right wing or fascist movements. Such movements take real grievances and frustrations and ultimately divert them away from the ruling class, towards religious or ethnic minorities for example.[9]

A final note is necessary here. Reformism operates at very deep levels in capitalist society and is not only carried by formally organised parties or movements. Participation in mass popular mobilisations which dislodged the dictators and opened the floodgates of revolution did not automatically lead to the conclusion that deeper and more radical change was required. In fact it was more common of such explosions of revolutionary energy to propel reformists into the limelight, even if they had not called for or necessarily even supported the popular uprising.

It is at precisely such moments, that reformism plays a crucial role in protecting the state and perpetuating the rule

---

7 Harman, 1994 provides an important example of an extension of the label reformist to non-Social Democratic-type movements and ideologies in his analysis of Islamism.
8 Alexander & Bassiouny, 2014 p167
9 See Harman, 1994 on this point.

of the capitalist class. In this drama, someone always has to play the role of Faust, bargaining with the Devil for a share in his power. Those who cannot plausibly present themselves as having shared in the struggles which have broken down the doors to the corridors of power are unlikely to be able to take on Faust's mantle in such contexts. This is the hour of the former political prisoners, of the exiles, of those who have sacrificed years of their lives in opposition to the rulers. People of this calibre are the ones who must sell their soul in order to save the system, because revolution has temporarily altered the balance of power between rulers and ruled and those who are accustomed to command have to learn new languages of persuasion if they are to survive.

Reformist ideas often spread extremely fast in such contexts. They thrive in the gap between ordinary people's revolutionary *actions* and the political *conclusions* they draw from the results of those actions. The absence of mass reformist parties in the pre-revolutionary period does not mean for example that these kind of organisations will not appear during the revolutionary crisis itself. The emergence of the Socialist Party in Portugal after the uprising against the fascist regime in 1974 despite the relative weakness of social-democratic and parliamentarian political traditions and very high levels of workers' struggles, provides a classic example.[10]

Unarmed movements take on the authoritarian state

Confronted with the regimes' enormous apparatuses of violence it seems extraordinary that mass protest movements could have arisen in the first place. Yet in country after country, similar methods of unarmed mass mobilisation opened revolutionary processes on a gigantic scale which led to the panicked flight of dictators, forced political reforms and opened the floodgates for explosion of popular organising, political activity and artistic creativity. The rapid fall of authoritarian regimes in 2011 confounded academics who considered them 'resilient' and 'adaptable.[11]' The resurgence of mass popular movements in 2019 in several more countries in the region surprised those

---

10 Birchall, 1979.
11 Hinnebusch, 2006 has an overview of some of these debates,

who had assumed that the violence of the counter-revolutions and civil wars would have deterred a repeat of the same tactics for confronting the armed power of the state. What was the secret behind the uprisings' initial success? However, in every case discussed here, military forces emerged from the revolutionary crisis with an expanded role in the state and society, usually leaving trails of destruction and violence in their wake. Moreover, there was no 'electoral exit', or a 'negotiated transition' similar to the reformist compromises which ended the Eastern European uprisings of 1989 and after or smoothed the path from resistance to dictatorship to capitalist democracy in Latin America, South Korea or South Africa.

In some cases, military coups installed a revived authoritarian regime and removed civilian politicians who had attained government office as a result of the popular uprising. Egypt in 2013 and Sudan in 2021 fall into this category, although at the time of writing the final outcome of the Sudanese Revolution still hung in the balance. In other cases, armed forces loyal to the old regime attempted to abort popular mass movements through declaring war on sections of the civilian population (Syria, Libya and Yemen fall into this group). Although the outcomes varied as to whether the armed forces of the old regime would claim military and political victory in the end (Syria) or their military competitors (Libya and Yemen), the unarmed civilian movements were the clear losers. In Bahrain, the beleaguered monarchy was rescued by Saudi forces who invaded and crushed the uprising at an early stage.

In Algeria, there was no bloody counter-revolution in the style of Egypt in 2013, and the security forces, as opposed to the military played the leading role in repression. However, the demands of protesters for the military to retreat from politics for good, ending a regime which they characterised as analogous to the French colonial occupation, were clearly not met. In Lebanon and Iraq, the mass movements of 2019 tended to counterpose the idea of a revived and expanded "national" army to the paramilitary formations attached to the ruling sectarian parties. In both cases the unarmed protest movement was unsuccessful in forcing more than superficial changes in government, aided both the onset of the pandemic and by vigorous repression. Tunisia, which appeared a partial exception with its longer democratic interlude, has recently succumbed to a new authoritarian regime, underpinned by the dramatic expansion of the army's influence within the state.[12] Why did the revolutionary mobilisations ultimately fail to end authoritarian rule?

Mainstream academic approaches to analysing these questions have often tended to either focus exclusively on the state and institutions, including the armed forces and security services themselves, or focussed on a critique of the strategy and tactics adopted by the movements opposing them. The latter approach has been taken by Erica Chenoweth, whose analysis of "nonviolent" or "civil resistance" movements has been influential not just within academic circles, but among recent movements such as Extinction Rebellion (XR).[13]. Chenoweth's theorisation of "civil resistance" movements coincided with the aftermath of the 2011 wave of uprisings but draws heavily on the work of Gene Sharp, an American political scientist whose writings have been widely translated and distributed by democracy activists. Sharp's major work, *The Politics of Nonviolent Action*, which appeared first in 1973, addressed theories of power and the "methods and dynamics of nonviolent action".[14]

Chenoweth and Sharp recognise some of the contradictions within military institutions and other "power structures", and propose strategies and tactics for activists who want to constrain these bodies' capacity for violent repression.[15] Persuading the people inside these "power structures" to switch sides thus emerges as the end goal of "civil resistance" movements". What is it that persuades the men with guns to change their minds about using them against protesters? According to Chenoweth and other theorists of nonviolence, there are two key factors at play. The first is the capacity of the movement opposing them to mobilise massive numbers through various forms of collective action—including protests, strikes, tax strikes, boycotts. She goes as far as claiming that no revolution has ever been defeated once 3.5 percent of the population has participated in a "peak event".[16] The second is the movement's capacity to maintain "discipline" by refusing to carry out acts of violence, whether armed or unarmed. major weaknesses in theories of nonviolent resistance

---

12 Fassihian, 2018; Nassif 2022.
13 Empson, 2020.
14 Sharp, 1973.
15 Chenoweth, 2021, p100.
16 Chenoweth, 2021, p114.

is that without a clear understanding of where the violence of the military and security forces comes from, it is impossible to pinpoint what factors enable or constrain it. We will return to this point in the next chapter. This can lead to a collapse into moralistic lecturing, as Chenoweth does to the Palestinians, whose failure to attain self-determination she ascribes to their lack of nonviolent discipline in the wake of the First Intifada.[17]

The everyday ideology of the popular *hirak*

Nevertheless, at first sight, the model mapped out by the "civil resistance" theorists does appear to describe the beliefs and practices of large numbers of people involved in the popular mobilisations discussed here. Support for tactics of peaceful (*silmiyy*) protest, demands asserting the civil (*madaniyy*) character of the state and positive belief in a broad and apparently inclusive national (*wataniyy*) identity counterposed to the narrow interests of existing elites, were influential and much debated during most of the popular uprisings. The desire for "peaceful" change had a particular powerful resonance in contexts scarred by civil war, such as Sudan and Algeria, where some dubbed the 2019 popular uprising "the revolution of smiles". "Violence, we think, does not lead to democracy," Algerian lawyer and human rights activist Moustapha Bouchachi told *The National* in December 2019".If you use violence, you legitimise their violence".[18]

In Arabic, the word *madaniyy* and the concept *madaniyya* has a complex set of associations. The term could be counterposed to military (*'askary*) or Islamist/ Islamic (*islamiyy*). In Egypt during 2011 struggles in some workplaces to force out the unelected generals embedded across the state used the term *madaniyy* to demand the extension of civilian as opposed to military control. However, the opposition between *'askary* and *madaniyy* was reframed by the growing polarisation between secular nationalist and Islamist political currents during 2012, which allowed the elision of the "civil" character of the state with an anti-Islamist, but pro-military agenda.[19] In the case of Sudan, where the

---

17 Chenoweth, 2021, p165.
18 Cookman 2019.
19 Alexander& Bassiouny, 2014, p317.

Islamist movement had been part of the regime was deeply, the *'askary / madaniyy* dichotomy was much clearer in relation to the state. *Madaniyya* took on a much broader set of meanings encompassing ideas of "civicness" and became a key slogan of the mass movement.[20] The assumption that the only possible vehicle for change was the existing national state, and therefore required a revitalised and reformed national consciousness (*wataniyya*), was rarely challenged as could be seen by the ubiquitous adoption of the national flags by protesters.

The prevalence of such ideas does not mean that somehow the popular uprisings were pro-US conspiracies of activists trained in the dark arts of "democracy promotion" by the State Department. US-government funded groups certainly did provide "training" to small numbers of activists in several of the countries discussed in this book, sometimes to the great irritation of their long-standing allies in the regimes which the uprisings confronted.[21] Erica Chenoweth's collaborator and co-author, Maria Stephan has worked at the US State Department.[22]

Moreover, one of the core assumptions of important strands of the movements which have adopted the language and practice of nonviolence and parallel ideas about the universality of human rights, is that there is an "international community" to which they can appeal. As detailed in previous chapters, the US and other Western powers have long sustained various kinds of authoritarian regimes both the region and beyond it, and rather than being driven by a principled desire to turn liberal rhetoric into reality, Western interventions supporting protesters against violations of their rights are not determined by whether the protesters use violence but by calculations of imperial self-interest.

A way of understanding the apparent alignment between arguments promoted by "civil resistance" theorists and practices adopted in the mass popular mobilisations, is to see this an instance of how reformism often works in the context of revolutionary crises. Theories of nonviolent action developed by academics and activists (especially those working in more professionalised roles for NGOs) have taken some of the ideas and practices that participants in revolutionary mobilisations

---

20 Berridge, De Waal & Lynch, 2022, p2.
21 Nixon, 2011.
22 See Caldwell, 2019 for more detail on this point.

Faust's bargain: the failure of reformist strategies

learn through a "method of successive approximations" (as Trotsky put it)[23] and synthesize these into what appears to be a coherent theory of political change. But the horizon of that change is limited to what can be achieved within current norms of what the state should look like, even if this may be dressed up as an idealised version of its liberal democratic manifestation rather than necessarily any actually-existing state. Such ideas have become resonant with much wider layers of people in many contemporary revolutionary crises because they combine things that ordinary people have learnt from their own practice (for example that demonstrations can bring about change) with pre-existing ideologies about how liberal democracy is meant to work or why it is better to negotiate with power-holders to persuade them to modify their behaviour rather than overthrow them.

It is not only at the level of ideas that the approach mapped out by civil resistance theorists and democracy activists can be considered reformist. The obsession among "civil resistance" theorists with "training", "discipline" and "professionalism" for movement leaders and participants is analogous to some of the processes which feed into the emergence of the trade union bureaucracy as a distinctive social layer within the workers' movement. If organising is a function exercised by specialists (whether they have been trained in a craft or professional sense) this can lead to the conclusion that training the right kind of organisers is more important to movement success or failure than whether leadership roles are democratically exercised, widely distributed and constantly refreshed from below. The role of "specialists" in civil resistance movements is not the only (or necessarily even the main) critique of such theories of political change, but it is important because it demonstrates how the instrumentalization of ordinary people's self-activity to change the world is embedded in reformism.

The tendency to frame collective action by workers and the poor as a weapon which can be *used* in a struggle to exact concessions from the state, employers or the ruling class more broadly, begs the question of *who* is going to attempt to wield it. The answer in the immediate wake of uprisings which dislodge autocrats from power has often tended to be other reformist movements or opposition politicians looking

---

23 Trotsky, 1930.

to bring about change through parliament, rather than the streets, or sometimes other political forces including parties and movements led by segments of the existing ruling class but excluded from the current governing coalition.

Violence and nonviolence in the uprisings

One pattern of confrontation between popular revolutionary movements and the state can be seen in Tunisia, Egypt and Sudan. A version of the same process played out in Algeria between 2019 and 2020 but with a much smaller degree of rupture at the top of the regime, where the damage was limited to the president and his immediate circle than in the other cases. In these cases, the eruption of mass mobilisations by unarmed protesters demanding the fall of the regime created a crisis for the security forces who lost their ability to control the streets. These were *not* nonviolent mobilisations, and all involved unarmed protesters responding to police attacks with self-defensive violence. Often protesters also engaged in pre-emptive, strategic violence aimed at destroying police buildings and forcing police officers and troops to retreat from the streets. Such actions were often highly effective in creating conditions for much wider layers of people to join the mass protests. To put it bluntly, the defeat of the police through the physical resistance and unarmed violence of the protesters was a necessary step for the majority of Egyptians to feel safe enough to join them. In all of these examples, the efforts of the regime to halt the mass mobilisations through "deterrent" or "exemplary" forms of violence failed. In fact, such deliberate interventions by the security forces are widely attested to have accelerated and generalised the uprisings, rather than slowed their progress.[24]

Although the exact sequence of events differed, the outcome of the retreat of the regimes' security forces, was the deployment of the state's *other* armed forces—usually the national military—in the streets as an "alternative" to the discredited and hated police. More importantly, this moment also marked the entry of the armed forces' leadership into the political field of battle as they sought to secure an end to the

---

24 Alexander & Bassiouny, 2014.

crisis which would limit damage to the state (even if that meant accepting some casualties at the top of the regime). Crucially, the scale of the mass mobilisation meant that such damage limitation required persuasion and negotiation rather than mere force to clear the streets, and the identification of suitable interlocutors who would be trusted by "the people".

That leaders of the armed forces had become the pivot around which the efforts of what remained of the old regime and wider layers of the ruling class to regroup their forces is clear from a quick succession of thumbnail sketches. These include the Tunisian Chief of Staff, Rachid Ammar (a careerist who owed his position entirely to the old dictator, Ben Ali), reinventing himself as a "protector of the revolution" and becoming a reference point for all and sundry in the new government after Ben Ali's fall.[25] Or the dismissal of Hosni Mubarak in Egypt and assumption of power by the Supreme Council of the Armed Forces (SCAF). Gaid Saleh, the Algerian Chief of Staff was the one called on to administer a "mercy killing" to Bouteflika's presidency in April 2019, in the form of a "medical coup" declaring him unfit to rule. At almost exactly the same time in Sudan, the mass movement was directly pulling the armed forces into the revolutionary crisis by choosing the Army General Command as the site for the wave of major sit-ins which led to the army's removal of el-Bashir on 11 April. Under the pressure of these mass mobilisations, leaders of two key components of the regime's repressive apparatus, the Sudanese Armed Forces (led by Al-Burhan) and the Rapid Support Forces militia (led by Hemedti), removed el-Bashir from power and set up a Transitional Military Council to run the country instead.

Here is important to note that events in Sudan and Algeria diverged from Tunisia and Egypt, in that rather than accepting military custodianship over the state, opposition movements and protesters in the streets continued to mobilise in explicit rejection of military rule. In Tunisia, where the armed forces were to begin with institutionally and materially much less powerful than its counterparts elsewhere in the region, the military's role remained primarily behind-the-scenes. Far from being held to account for the crimes of Ben Ali's regime, the army's reputation as a victim of the former dictator was

25 Grewal, 2016.

promoted through the rehabilitation of former officers who had been arrested, tortured and dismissed from service on suspicion of organising a coup in 1991.[26] The slogan of "the army and the people are one hand" initially reverberated in Egypt as SCAF's assumption of state power for a transitional period until the completion of constitutional reforms, parliamentary and presidential elections was accepted across the spectrum of the mainstream opposition and only publicly challenged by a handful of small revolutionary groups.

By contrast, in Algeria mass protests continued to reject any accommodation with the military over the summer and autumn of 2019, insisting "get rid of them all". And in Sudan, the opposition parties and independent trade unions grouped under the umbrella of the Forces of Freedom and Change (FFC) demanded an immediate entry to the corridors of power rather than waiting on elections to open the door to the state. As we will discuss below, the end result of this attempt at forging a workable "partnership" with the military bore striking similarities to the Egyptian case, at least in so far as the behaviour of generals was concerned.

While the response of the popular movement to the Sudanese military coup of October 2021 differed dramatically from the Egyptian case, the general's unceremonious ejection of their civilian "partners" from office proved once again that the military themselves turned out not be the guarantors of a new liberal democratic order, but rather its gravediggers.

The events which led up to the military-led counter-revolutionary restorations of authoritarian rule underscore a major weakness in the "civil resistance" model outlined by Chenoweth and others. Slogans such as *"irhal!*—leave!" or *"tasgut bas!*—just fall!" were a powerful unifying cry, once the dictator had gone, the question of what to do about the rest of his regime remained unsolved. Changing a regime (let alone altering the basic institutions of the state) through collective action from below turns out not be easily reducible to a campaign with limited goals, but a far more complex affair.[27]

---

26 Grewal, 2016.
27 Empson, 2020.

The disasters of war

Several other revolutionary crises discussed in this book ended in even more disastrous outcomes for ordinary people: civil wars which became regional and global conflicts leaving hundreds of thousands dead and millions as refugees.

Why did mass movements which began by adopting many of the tactics recommended by "civil resistance" theorists end up following such different trajectories? One strain of analysis seeks an answer in the recruitment strategies of the security forces and military themselves, in particular whether this follows a "communal" pattern (building military or security bodies around a specific sectarian, tribal or regional identity). According to this perspective Syrian regime's mobilisation of largely Alawite sections of the military and the Bahraini regime's reliance on Sunni recruits (including large numbers from outside Bahrain) created higher barriers to the defection of sections of the military from the regimes.".[28]

Reliance on communal or regional identities to ensure the loyalty of military and security forces did not always work for dictators under pressure from mass movements in the streets and workplaces. The Rapid Support Forces, which has a strong regional and ethnic identity as it was created from the Janjaweed militias in Darfur, did not stand by Umar al-Bashir in his hour of crisis, but like the Sudanese Armed Forces dumped the dictator to set up a new ruling military body. Sudan's long experience of armed conflicts, the highly fragmented nature of the armed bodies of men associated with the state and the importance of ethnic, religious and regional identities in those conflicts might have been expected to place the revolution there closer to the experience of Iraq, Lebanon or Libya than Egypt. Yet a mass, unarmed movement from below, using a repertoire of protest marches, sit-ins and strikes, proved capable of extending the revolutionary process beyond the first wave of mass mobilisations without turning into an armed struggle and civil war.

There was however, one factor which the Sudanese revolution shares in common with the revolutions in Tunisia and Egypt and the uprising in Algeria (and which was missing in Syria, Libya, Lebanon and Iraq). That was the intervention of organised workers directly in the revolutionary process

---

28 Makara, 2013, p341.

through strike action. The Sudanese general strikes of May and June 2019 moreover built on a long-standing tradition which embedded workers' collective action into the repertoire of revolutionary tactics.[29] In Tunisia, Egypt and Algeria, general strikes also took place in close proximity to the fall of the dictator, palpably contributing to the crisis of the regime and often demonstrably helping to seal his fate. The only real exception to the correlation between mass strikes and a prolonged period of largely unarmed contention between the popular movement and the state was Bahrain, where a general strike was not able to counter-balance the external military intervention led by Saudi forces.

The failure of the "democratic transitions"

In Tunisia, Egypt, Algeria and Sudan therefore a pattern emerged of mass, unarmed (though not nonviolent) collective action (including significant interventions by organised workers through strike action) which opened up a period characterised by the interplay of several contradictory conditions. The first of these was that millions of ordinary people were able exercise various democratic rights and freedoms in ways which had often been impossible or unthinkable just a few weeks before. These included the rights to assemble, protest and march, rights to free expression, to found and organise political parties and trade unions. The seizure of these political rights through the conquest of the streets was paralleled by increasingly confident demands for political and social rights in the workplaces and neighbourhoods.

The second condition was that the security forces and military were clearly acting under some constraints on their capacity to use violence. Many old repressive laws forbidding assembly or organising could no longer be enforced, and hastily written new ones were often contested, sometimes politically in the newly argumentative press and social media platforms or physically through protests and other forms of collective action. One of SCAF's first acts in Egypt for example, was to issue a decree banning strikes in March 2011. While clearly highly repressive in intent, it had very little immediate effect as the

---

29 Berridge, De Waal & Lynch, 2022, p45.

country was gripped by the largest strike wave for generations. Figureheads from the old regime were put on trial and the heads of security services sacked from their jobs. Of course, it was usually a symbolic handful of small fry among the old regime's torturers and thugs who were dragged before courts for their share of "transitional justice," but the days when the secret police owned the state and could do what they liked in society seemed to have gone for good.

The framework which was meant to govern the emergence of reformed state institutions and the transition to a democratic political system systematically marginalised street protests and strikes, however. The various milestones on the road to political reform in Egypt signposted that it was as voters, not protesters, that citizens should now raise their voices and exercise their influence over political life. These included the referendum on amendments to the Egyptian constitution in March 2011, which was backed by both the new military rulers and the Muslim Brotherhood, delivering a resounding 'yes' vote for the changes. This was followed by parliamentary elections between November 2011 and January 2012, presidential elections in June 2012 and a December 2012 referendum on the new constitution which had been developed by a Constituent Assembly negotiated between the newly elected parliament and a range of political parties (albeit following fractious battles in the courts over the number of Islamist members). While at a surface level, these processes appeared to point towards the expansion of democracy, the military tightened its grip on the state, and secular opposition parties appealed to the generals to rein back the influence of elected Islamist politicians. Over the same period, the army stepped in to fill the space left by the retreat of the Interior Ministry's forces by taking on the day-to-day work of repression. By September 2011, nearly 12,000 Egyptians had faced military judges after being arrested, more than the total number of civilians tried in military tribunals during the entirety of Mubarak's rule.[30]

Military figures often consolidated their position within the civilian apparatus of the state. In Tunisia for example, one only military officer was appointed to a provincial governorship during Ben Ali's reign, but between 2011 and 2016 eleven

---

30 Human Rights Watch, 2011.

assumed these important administrative roles.[31] Nearly half of Egypt's provincial governors (14 out of 29) were already from a military background on the eve of the revolution in 2011, while a further six were police generals. Between 2011 and 2013 the armed forces officers continued to be appointed to governorship roles even if police generals were temporarily excluded by vociferous protests.[32]

In Sudan, the Forces of Freedom and Change negotiated a 39 month period of power-sharing with the Transitional Military Council *before* holding elections. This arrangement aimed to give time for reforms and new appointments to reduce the influence of supporters of the old regime, particularly members of the Islamist parties allied with Umar al-Bashir who had been rewarded with powerful positions throughout the state during his rule.[33] The FFC parties also hoped to reduce the risks of an electoral comeback by the Islamist parties by giving their opponents time to prepare.

The tide of change at first appeared to be flowing the civilian parties' way. Civilian provincial governors replaced all military appointees in July 2020.[34] Committees tasked with uncovering the old regime's corrupt networks which warrened the state got to work. Yet with the presidency of the Sovereign Council held by General al-Burhan of the Sudanese Armed Forces and the vice-presidency in the hands of the RSF militia's Hemedti, there were many ways these two armed bodies could exercise their influence over the state.

Some of these were financial, rather than political: Hemedti was fond of boasting that he had bailed out the cash-strapped central bank for example.[35] Meanwhile, the RSF continued to arrest and torture activists, while none of its members or commanders (or those of other participating forces) were held to account for their role in the massacre of protesters during the attack on the Khartoum sit-in on 3 June 2019. Unlike El-Bashir's civilian allies among the Islamist movement, the military and militia institutions which had underpinned his regime were shielded from scrutiny and accountability by being parties to the

---

31 Grewal, 2016.
32 Alexander & Bassiouny 2014.
33 Berridge, De Waal & Lynch, 2022, p48.
34 Middle East Eye, 2020b.
35 Alexander, 2020.

Faust's bargain: the failure of reformist strategies

agreements which underpinned the Transitional Government.

In both Egypt and Sudan the accommodation between civilian politicians who had been catapulted into office by the popular revolution and the military would break down in the military coups of 2013 and 2021. Or rather the military would in both cases seize back political control of the state, forcibly eject their erstwhile civilian partners and attempt to assert their domination of the streets. In Egypt, the armed forces under the leadership of al-Sisi were successful in doing both. In a short space of time they led huge massacres of their civilian opponents (to massive acclaim in the streets), politically rehabilitated the police and Interior Ministry forces, outlawed strikes and street protests. Although fully demobilising the mass movements of the previous two years took time, it was clear by August 2013 that a military-led counter-revolution was well underway.[36]

In Sudan, during the period of the Transitional Government, Al-Burhan and Hemedti expanded their political alliances with armed groups from Sudan's peripheries through the Juba Peace Accord and gave them a place in government, eventually working with them to remove the civilian members of the FFC from office and institute a new period of military rule. This included the restoration of many supporters of the old regime into the government departments they had previously managed before being removed by the civilian-led Transitional Government.[37] They were met with determined resistance from a revived mass movement, with civil disobedience and continued street protests. Steadily increasing levels of violence in the capital and other major cities against protesters was coupled with intensifying police repression.

But in contrast to Egypt, the military and its partners in crime had been unable to carry massacres in the capital and other major cities on the scale of those perpetrated by the Egyptian military in the wake of its coup in 2013. Unlike Egypt the revolutionary movement opposing the military developed politically and organisationally, with the neighbourhood-based Resistance Committees leading the mass mobilisations against the generals' regime, and sidelining the civilian opposition parties. The picture was different in the provinces. In areas such as West Darfur, hundreds were killed in

---

36 Marfleet, 2017
37 MENA Solidarity, 2021.

"tribal" conflicts in early 2022. Activists from the Resistance Committees in the West Darfur provincial capital, El Geneina said that the military authorities were responsible for the escalating violence, driven by conflicts over resources stoked by the government itself.[38] A horrific massacre of over 200 people in El Geneina, in the last week of April 2022 was widely attributed to the Rapid Support Forces militia.[39] While the ultimate outcome of the Sudanese Revolution was still in the balance at the time of writing, it was clear that as in Egypt, the strategy adopted by the Forces of Freedom and Change, including the leadership of the Sudanese Professionals Association, of securing a "transition to democracy" through a negotiated partnership with the military and militia leaders of the Transitional Military Council had failed.

In both Egypt and Sudan, the military-led counter-revolutions underlined that the premise of the "transition" was essentially a Faustian bargain between civilian opposition leaders and the military. Despite the difference in their political ideologies, Islamists in Egypt and the heterogenous mixture of "technocrats", representatives of "traditional" Islamic parties and reformist movements making up the civilian FFC component of the Sudanese Transitional Government found themselves facing versions of the same problem. The generals had no intention of relinquishing their dominant role in the state.

A further important parallel between Egypt and Sudan can be drawn between the role of the "international community" and powerful regional states in abetting and enabling the military coups. Western governments had lauded the beginning of Egypt and Sudan's "transition to democracy" but did very little concrete to stop the military takeovers in either case. In the case of Egypt, the massive flows of arms from the US and Britain were interrupted in the wake of the 2013 coup but reinstated a few years later.

The US government suspended aid to Sudan following the October 2021, but rather than actually punish the coup leaders, Western governments worked hard behind the scenes to try and restore a civilian cover for the new military regime. Meanwhile, regional states allied with the West, especially Saudi Arabia and UAE, worked hand in glove with

38 Radio Dabanga, 2022a; 2022b.
39 Radio Dabanga, 2022c.

the military in both cases providing financial, diplomatic and military support. In the Sudanese case, two further members of a regional counter-revolutionary quartet—Egypt and Israel—also played significant roles in bolstering the generals' confidence that ridding themselves of their troublesome civilian "partners" would not result in any serious repercussions from the US or its allies.

Armed alternatives? Military insurgencies and political change

The preponderance of strategies for political change which combined unarmed mass collective action with constitutional and parliamentary processes marked an important shift from the dominant model of revolution during the period after World War Two. As discussed previously although the revolutionary struggles which led to the establishment of the independent states of the post-colonial era did often involve mass mobilisations on a similar, or sometimes greater scale than those discussed in this book, the idea that a military vanguard was a necessary element for success was widely accepted. In some cases such as Algeria, armed struggle for liberation was led by a guerrilla movement, while in Egypt, Iraq and Libya, military action to establish a new political order took the form of mutinies and military coups led by nationalist junior officers.

The anti-colonial or national revolutions are deserving of the label "revolutions" because even though they were usually consummated by armed minorities who then set about consolidating their position at the core of a new ruling class and demobilising or repressing street protests and strikes, mass collective action by the urban and rural poor and in some cases the urban working class was essential to break down the old political order. Moreover, while these were clearly political revolutions, they also form part of the great historical wave of *social* revolutions through which the bourgeoisie established capitalism on a planetary scale by creating the conditions for the rise of independent centres of capital accumulation outside the historic core of the capitalist system. This is one of the reasons why the model of armed national liberation struggles has declined in importance as the years have passed. It does not mean that armed political movements have vanished from the world, of course, but these are more likely to take the form of vanguardist movements who resort to armed "propaganda of the deed" as a mechanism to extract concessions from a repressive regime (often after the regime has blocked nonviolent mobilisations). Many of the armed Islamist movements of the last four decades fall into this category. By and large, this is different from integrating armed struggle into a revolutionary strategy to build a new state.

There are certainly important examples of reactionary and counter-revolutionary movements, principally the Islamic State and its emulators, which did seize power by military means, overthrow the existing political system and build different state institutions in its place. However, these notably only arose in contexts of civil war and widespread societal destruction and did not establish stable new states, even in areas where there was arguably a viable social and economic base to do so, such as Mosul and its hinterland in northern Iraq. The failure of the IS project to rip apart the borders established by the imperial carve-up of the Levant at the end of World War I underscores the continued disciplining effect of the existing national state system on would-be state builders.

This has implications for the two major instances of "unfinished business" from the era of national liberation struggles: the Palestinian and Kurdish national movements. Unlike IS which turned armed resistance to the US occupation of Iraq into sectarian civil war, and took root in Syria, Libya and Yemen as a reactionary reflex of despair at the conditions created by counter-revolution, armed movements in Palestine and the Kurdish on the Syrian-Turkish border could justifiably still claim an organic relationship with movements resisting national oppression and pointing towards broader goals of social and political transformation. Only the Kurdish movement was actually able to establish territorial control in new areas and build new state institutions. However, as Chapter 13 will discuss in more detail, the experiment in Kurdish self-rule trapped in an irresolvable paradox. The strongest Kurdish movement in Northern Syria, the PYD, was well-organised enough to create new state structures following the partial collapse of the Ba'athist state's authority in the area, and to defend these for a while through force of arms. However, this was only possible because the Syrian government accepted the separation of the northern provinces for tactical reasons in order to concentrate on destroying the revolutionary movement and armed rebellion in the rest of Syria.[40] It was also conditional on military support from the US and its allies who mobilised Kurdish forces against the IS statelet in Raqqa.

The gravediggers of revolution

The role of the military and security bodies of the existing nation states of the Middle East in turning the cycle of revolt from revolution to counter-revolution is a persistent feature of the uprisings discussed in this book. Across both the first and second waves of revolutions and crises analysed here, the most common fate for the popular revolutionary movements was defeat at the hands of the national armed forces, both in the political arena and on the streets. Even in Tunisia, often lauded as the one democratic success story to emerge from the region's revolt, President Kais Saied's coup of 25 July 2021 was implemented by army officers, who flanked him as he announced the closure of parliament and the Prime Minister's office. Underlining the fact that the army's role was anything but symbolic, tanks stood outside the parliament building while soldiers blocked the entrance to MPs.[41] Saied's framing of his action was to speak of acting in the people's name against the parliamentary institutions which had been revived in the wake of the 2011 revolution after years of dictatorship, accusing them of corruption and incompetence in the face of the deepening economic crisis. Saied's coup followed months of protests demanding social justice in the impoverished towns of the interior such as Sidi Bouzid and Kasserine which were the cradle of the 2011 revolution. The government's response had been to unleash repression. Security forces killed a demonstrator and arrested hundreds for Facebook posts 'insulting the police'. Hichem Mechichi, the Prime Minister who would find his office blocked by tanks on 25 July, said at the time that the police acted "professionally".[42]

Tunisia's backsliding towards authoritarianism, underscores

---

40 Burchfield, 2017.
41 Masmoudi, 2021.
42 Human Rights Watch, 2021.

that the problem facing those wanting to expand democracy and extend civilian control over the state does not disappear even in contexts where the army is a relatively small, "professional" body which has a much less overtly political role than most of its counterparts. It also shows that strengthening *national* armies in order that they can assert their dominance over unruly paramilitary bodies and militias provides no solution to the dilemma facing would-be reformers. In order to understand why these bodies of armed men inevitably seek to play a counter-revolutionary role when threatened by an uprising from below, we need to approach the question of the state and revolution from a different angle.

Chapter 12

'You became a whip in the hands of the powerful'

Hey soldier standing in line
Fearful, not understanding the banner in my hand
or my chants
Your imagination fails—is this just a dream?
Don't forget that blood's all one colour
What did you get out of the rule of those greedy
bastards?
Just degradation for you and all those who serve.
A farmer like your father before you,
Your only legacy is struggle
Why do the pashas rule you?
It's not their country
Take a look at the street, there are millions like you
There's no shame in your galabiyya and your roots
It's only shameful you became a whip in the hands
of the powerful.

Ramy Essam[43]

---

43 Author's translation of Egyptian singer Ramy Essam's Ya Askary (Hey soldier!). Watch the video here: youtu.be/pXuv5UjGo5E

Revolution is the choice of the people

The central role played by armed forces in turning the cycle of revolt from revolution to counter-revolution is not a problem restricted to the Middle East, of course. In an analysis of the defeats of left governments in Latin America, Juan Carlos Monedero points out that parties entering government with redistributive agendas are immediately confronted with obstacles.

> They do not enter into full possession of the state, as if it were a new home: the rooms may be booby-trapped, the stairs barricaded; there may be snipers in the kitchen—shooters who are unseen because they are taken for granted, and all the more effective because unseen.[44]

As Magdi el-Gizouli noted, the question of what to do about the "snipers in the kitchen" also confronted the reformist politicians in Sudan who entered a power-sharing agreement with the military to jointly oversee the "transitional period".[45]

Reformists of all shapes and colours certainly recognise this problem - liberals, Islamists, left nationalists, socialists. Many of them have personally experienced it—through detention, torture and exile. Yet the question remains: can the 'benevolent' and 'civil' aspects of the state's public power actually control the violent and coercive parts? In public, liberal reformists may point to ideals of checks and balances, of the constitution and the rule of law. Ask them privately and they are often more sanguine—the armed men cannot be destroyed, they must be appeased and pacified, persuaded that there remains a place for them in the state, their interests will be protected and their privileges respected. Then they can slink off back to their barracks to await the next crisis. The snipers need to be persuaded to leave the kitchen, but they are indispensable to the maintenance of an order which has no viable alternative and thus cannot be told to lay down their arms or relinquish their special role for good.

This chapter examines the role of the state's armed men in the process of rolling back the revolutionary tide from a different perspective. Taking as its theoretical framework the analysis of the state developed by Marx and Lenin in their discussions of the Paris Commune, it argues that the failure to

---

44 Monedero, 2019.
45 El-Gizouli, 2020b.

confront and break the military-bureaucratic machine at the heart of the state lies at the root of the success of the counter-revolutionary offensive against the first wave of uprisings, and offers vital strategic lessons for future revolutions.

The way that military, security and paramilitary forces behave in revolutions goes back to one root: the capitalist state's need for what Lenin called "special bodies of armed men" to maintain the rule of the capitalist class.[46] This is why revolutionary movements which confront the state's repressive apparatuses are not just dealing with institutions composed of men with guns, but key elements in the ideological machinery which justifies the continuation of exploitation and oppression. Rather than expecting these violent institutions to simply "defect" through their officers or commanders switching sides and accepting a future subordinate to civilian control, a Marxist analysis of the state and revolution maps out the route to an alternative strategy. This seeks to create the conditions for the brutalised rank-and-file, the men who have been made into whips for the ruling class and its state, to recover their humanity and revolutionary agency.

Officers, warlords, secret policemen

One key assumption of the critique of the behaviour of the military sketched out above is that the problem with 'the snipers' is that they are the wrong place—in the kitchen rather than where they belong, in their barracks (or possibly guarding the front door). Indeed, the demand for the army to "return to the barracks" and leave the realm of politics (let alone invading ordinary people's homes and workplaces) has been raised in many of the revolutions and uprisings discussed in this book. According to this logic, a fundamental task of the popular revolutions is to reassert that there *is* a 'right place' for military bodies, a proper sphere where they can exercise their role safely. On occasions the most badly-behaved 'snipers' are affiliated with paramilitary organisations, rather than the national military. In these cases, often the argument emerges that their behaviour is a reflection of the weakness of *public* armed power and its inability to exercise authority over *private* interests? This has

---

46 Lenin, 1917a.

sometimes been framed explicitly as a call for the strengthening of national armed forces against party, regional or sectarian militias, this problem has particular resonance in countries such as Lebanon, Iraq and Sudan, where militia leaders and warlords play significant (and sometimes dominant) in government.

A further variation on this theme is the widely-used concept of the "deep state," initially coined to explain the ways in which the Turkish military and security agencies worked with organised criminals and paramilitary groups to thwart and subvert democratic institutions.[47] In this case, the way that military and security bodies operate to counter the actions of elected politicians or the rise of protest movements and strikes is explained as a reaction to threats to the narrow interests of their members. This seems on the face of it to offer a potentially compelling paradigm to explain the counter-revolutionary role of the military and security services. Certainly, the relationship between military, security and criminal networks has been a direct cause of popular anger with the regimes in Syria, Algeria and Sudan. The Assad regime's use of *shabiha* criminal networks to carry out sectarian kidnappings and murders is notorious, but not exceptional.[48] It finds parallels in the role of Algerian military and security networks in drug smuggling and other forms of organised crime.[49] Meanwhile in Sudan, the role of the Janjaweed militias in various forms of criminal activity including smuggling and people-trafficking, long after their evolution into the Rapid Support Forces under Hemedti's leadership has been well-documented.[50]

When considering the role of the military in the states which were challenged by the revolutions and uprisings discussed in this book it quickly becomes clear that the problem of their overreach is a systemic one across the Middle East as a region. A whole range of indicators show that the region is one of the most heavily militarised in the world. This does not mean that these military and security forces have necessarily the largest military budgets in absolute terms, nor are they the most effective in the world at winning wars. Only one state in the Middle East, Saudi Arabia, made the top ten military spenders of 2021 ranked in absolute terms.

47   Wills, 2017.
48   Kellier, 2012.
49   BBC News 2018b; 2018c.
50   Sudan in the News 2019.

'You became a whip in the hands of the powerful'

Country	Military spending 2021 ($bn)
United States	778
China	252
India	72.9
Russia	61.7
United Kingdom	59.2
Saudi Arabia	57.5
Germany	52.8
France	52.7
Japan	49.1
South Korea	45.7

Source: SIPRI Military Expenditure Database, 2021

Country	Military spending 2021 as % GDP
Oman	7.3
Kuwait	6.7
Saudi Arabia	6.6
Algeria	5.6
Azerbaijan	5.3
Israel	5.2
Jordan	5.0
Qatar	4.8
Armenia	4.4
Pakistan	4.0

Source: SIPRI Military Expenditure Database, 2021

Revolution is the choice of the people

Region	Avg. mil budget 2021 % of GDP
Americas	1.5
Africa	1.8
Asia and Oceania	1.8
Europe	1.8
Middle East	4.9

Source: SIPRI Military Expenditure Database, 2021

Country	Total military personnel (estimate)	Military personnel as % of total population.
China	3134000	0.2
USA	1832000	0.5
Russia	1350000	0.9
Egypt	1230000	1.2
Iran	1015000	1.2
Turkey	775000	0.9
Israel	646000	7.4
Algeria	465000	1.1
Yemen	420000	1.4
Saudi Arabia	350000	1.0
Iraq	330000	0.8
UK	231000	0.3
Sudan	205000	0.4
Syria	150000	0.7
Lebanon	100000	1.9
UAE	770000	0.8
Bahrain	13000	0.9

Source: Total Globalfirepower, 2022, Total military personnel includes active forces, reserves and paramilitary forces

However, when considered from a perspective of military expenditure as percentage of GDP, the picture changes dramatically. Overall, the average military budget across the Middle East was 4.9 percent in 2020, a dramatically higher average than any other region of the world.

The numbers of active military personnel are also extremely high, representing an average 2.4 percent of the total labour force across the MENA region in 2019.[51] In numerical terms this means there are very large numbers of men (and occasionally women) bearing arms or trained to do so. The figures for 'military personnel' also considerably underestimate the real size of the armed bodies of men associated with these states, as they do not include the armed security forces and police. The military functions of the police and security services in Egypt, for example, would add around 400,000 armed men to the totals above, as part of a much larger police and security complex run by the Ministry of the Interior. As Omar Ashour noted in 2012,

> The ministry comprises a massive bureaucracy employing more than 1.5 million people: officers, petty-officers, soldiers, conscripts, and civilian administrators. This labor force includes more than 831,000 full-time jobs and a complex network of more than 300,000 paid informants and ex-convicts.[52]

Umar al-Bashir in Sudan, cultivated the Rapid Support Forces paramilitary forces out of the Janjaweed militias in Darfur but integrated them into the armed bodies of men under the state's direct command through the National Intelligence and Security Services (NISS) which reports to the Sudanese Presidency.[53] After the revolution of 2019, the commander-in-chief of the Sudanese Armed Forces, Abdelfattah al-Burhan insisted that the RSF were an "integral part of the Sudanese Army".[54] The question of whether paramilitary forces owe allegiance to the state, or some other entity, is also often difficult to answer, and it is not clear in the data above which paramilitary forces have been included in the totals.

51 World Bank, 2021.
52 Ashour 2012, p22.
53 Human Rights Watch, 2015.
54 Radio Dabanga, 2019f.

Revolution is the choice of the people

Calculated in terms of the number of people who make their living on a daily basis from the business of war and security, most of countries discussed in this book count as highly militarised (regardless of whether these militaries are necessarily effective at fighting wars against external or internal challengers).

However, the reach of the military and security forces into the civilian apparatus of the state and the economy goes much farther than that. One of the problems with the "deep state" model is that it cannot deal analytically or empirically with the degree to which the military and security forces permeate the "shallow state" as well in countries such as Egypt, where the management of large parts of the "civilian" administration, publicly owned industries and key transport services is considered the prerogative of the officer class. Yazid Sayigh has documented the functioning of Egypt's "Officers' Republic" in meticulous detail. In a 2012 report he outlined how

> Senior officers were incorporated into Mubarak's crony system through the promise of "a loyalty allowance" they would receive upon retirement in return for abstention from political engagement—and acceptance of relatively poor wages—during their years of service in the EAF [Egyptian Armed Forces]. For the vast majority that consists of the opportunity to resume a career in the state sector, which means they receive a second salary in addition to military pensions. Each of those positions comes with its own associated bonuses and allowances.[55]

As we saw previously, the role of the military in the civilian economy did not recede with the shift from state capitalist to neoliberal policies, but was instead reconfigured. In fact in many cases, military entrepreneurs and managers ushered in the transition, enriching themselves and their families in the process).[56]

A similar problem emerges in relation to paramilitary bodies. The leader of the Sudanese Rapid Support Forces, Hemedti, is the lynchpin of what NGO Global Witness describes

---

55 Sayigh, 2012.
56 Alexander & Bassiouny, 2014, p55-6.

a "paramilitary-industrial complex",[57] a network of companies headed up by members of his family with interests in transport, tourism, infrastructure, iron and steel in addition to gold mining, and illicit activities such as drug smuggling and human trafficking.[58]

Imperialism, militarisation and the state

The underlying condition which drives the militarisation of the regional economy is the intense imperialist competition between the Great Powers in the area, rather than simply the appetite for power of local military elites. This in turn reflects the region's historic importance in geostrategic terms and the centrality of oil and gas to the global economy for much of the last century. One expression of this competition has been the development of a large military 'footprint' throughout the region in the form of bases, military exercises and the provision of training and advisors to their junior partners by the Great Powers (the US and its allies on the one side and the Soviet Union on the other). Another is the strong mutual interest of the global imperialist powers and the military sections of the local ruling classes of the region in the purchase and consumption of arms and other military technologies.

How does the system of unequal partnerships between the US and its local allies actually work? The relationship between the US, Israel and the other ruling classes of the region has been internalised by state institutions across multiple countries. It is felt through the presence or absence of experts, the circulation of their policy manuals and directives, the flows of aid and diplomatic exchanges. Most importantly it is woven into the fabric of the military and security apparatuses of these states. The type and quality of equipment soldiers carry, the training and career histories of important layers of officers, relations between military institutions, rest of the state, and their role in wider society are all to some extent or other its correlates.

Foreign Military Training (FMT) programmes operated by the United States play a major role in structuring both long-term and short-term relationships between key members of the

---

57 Global Witness, 2019.
58 Sudan in the News, 2019.

militaries of most of the countries in the Middle East discussed in this book and the US military. These training courses form only one part of a global programme which in 2018 involved approximately 62,700 students from 155 countries who participated in training, the total cost of which was approximately $776.3 million.[59] The total number of students can fluctuate considerably from year to year: in 2016 it was 122,000 students and cost around $900 million.[60] The stated "operational benefits" of the programme explicitly include "influencing the development of foreign military institutions and their roles in democratic societies".[61] As numerous critics have noted, these and their predecessor programmes have in fact trained generations of military leaders who have gone on to inflict huge damage on their own societies, whether through brutal "counter-insurgency" campaigns, military-led repression of civilian protest movements or through seizing power themselves. Researchers Jesse Dillon Savage and Jonathan Caverley even concluded in 2017 that the presence of trainees from just one FMT programme, International Military Education Training (IMET) doubled the likelihood of an attempted coup d'etat occurring between 1970 and 2009, and that militaries which had received IMET training accounted for two thirds of the successful coups.[62]

The relevance of this question for the discussion in this chapter of the challenges posed to revolutionary movements by the military institutions is underlined by the fact that both Abdelfattah al-Sisi and Sedki Sobhy, his second-in-command during the 2013 coup undertook graduate studies at the United States Army War College.[63] Sisi spent an academic year at the War College in 2006, writing a thesis which ruminated on the challenges of "Democracy in the Middle East".[64] The FMT programme involves thousands of students every year from across the Middle East, most of them serving members of the military. Between 2007 and 2018, the total number of students

---

59 US Department of Defense, 2019a, ES-2. Totals are for the US government's fiscal year, which runs from 1 October to 30 September.
60 US Department of Defense, 2019b, ES-2.
61 US Department of Defense, 2019a, pI-1.
62 Savage & Caverley, 2017.
63 Savage & Caverley, 2017.
64 Stewart, 2013.

'You became a whip in the hands of the powerful'

enrolled on the various programmes was over 106,000 in total from across the countries counted as the 'Near East' (Algeria, Bahrain, Egypt, Iran, Iraq, Israel, Jordan, Kuwait, Lebanon, Libya, Morocco, Oman, the Palestinian Authority, Qatar, Saudi Arabia, Syria, Tunisia, UAE and Yemen) with numbers ranging between 5000 and 12000 per year.[65] The total cost of the training attended by students during this period was just over $3,000,000,000.

Patterns of spending shifted according to changing circumstances. There was a dramatic increase in the overall number of students on the Near East programmes after the uprisings of 2011: the average for the years 2012-18 was 145 percent of the average for the previous period. This increase was not evenly distributed either in terms of student numbers or in terms of investment in more expensive forms of training. Not only were there twice as many Saudi students on average during the period 2012-2018 as there had been during 2007-2011, their training costs were 134 percent more during 2012-2018. The surge in spending on high-value training after 2011 underscores the importance of the Gulf militaries led by Saudi Arabia and UAE to the changing regional architecture of imperialism which we discussed in previous chapters. It also provides a confirmation of the subordinate place occupied by the Egyptian military in the regional hierarchy. The "largest army in the Middle East" is centrally integrated into the US-led military system, but its main military functions have long been as expensive border guard on the desperate population of the Gaza Strip and as internal gendarme propping up decades of authoritarian rule. Sisi's recent arms purchases and apparent efforts to modernise Egypt's military institutions indicate a desire to enter the regional competition for military supremacy, but there is a long way to go before that becomes a reality.[66]

Arms, equipment and training also flow to security and paramilitary bodies from the Western powers to their regional allies. In the case of the EU states, this has taken the form of directly "externalising" Europe's borders, recruiting paramilitary formations in Libya and Sudan's notorious RSF to hunt down would-be migrants and prevent them from reaching Europe. The rise of the RSF within the Sudanese state,

---

65 US Department of State, nd.
66 Springborg & Williams, 2019.

despite its role in genocide in Darfur was aided and abetted by the European Union's "Khartoum Process".[67] This agreement channelled security equipment and training to the Sudanese state as one of the regional partners of the EU in efforts to intercept migrants attempting to reach Libya as the first stage in their perilous journey to Europe. Although the EU denied that the RSF was either the direct or indirect beneficiary of its "Better Migration Management" project, this was contradicted by researchers who described how the RSF's rising status in the state allowed it to alternate between trafficking migrants, taxing them and arresting them.[68]

The RSF's other major role was to act as mercenaries for El-Bashir's allies, Saudi Arabia and UAE, in the devastating war in Yemen. Other regional powers also adopted similar strategies: Turkey mobilised Syrian fighters in order to intervene in the conflict in Libya.[69] Sometimes the primary drivers were ideological, rather than financial as in the case of the RSF's role in Yemen. Hezbollah and militias affiliated with the Iraqi Islamist parties played key roles in the Syrian regime's counter-revolutionary war, often using sectarian slogans to mobilise volunteers.[70] Such trends in the paramilitarisation of warfare are not just the result of instability on the margins of the global system, they are driven from the centre. The presence of thousands of 'private military contractors' (PMCs) working for US-based firms such as Blackwater in Iraq during the US occupation highlighted how military operations work "in the era of outsourcing".[71]

It is sometimes tempting to look at the archipelago of US bases across the region, and track the career paths of the senior officers serving in the armies of US allies through US military academies and conclude that little has changed since the period of direct colonial rule. This would be a mistake, however. There are other factors at play in the long-term militarisation of the region. One of these is the general weakness of the indigenous bourgeoisie (largely a result of the stunting and distortion of

---

67 Jalal, 2019b.
68 Lumley-Sapanski, Schwarz, & Valverde-Cam, 2021.
69 McKernan & Akoush, 2020.
70 Karouny, 2013.
71 Singer, 2004.

its development by colonialism).[72] Junior officers drawn from middle class and even relatively poor backgrounds (sometimes from religious minorities as was the case in Syria) often formed one of the most energetic and cohesive components of the modern middle class which substituted itself for the missing or weak indigenous bourgeoisie by seizing state power and ousting the political regimes allied with the colonial powers.[73]

In the wake of the anti-colonial revolutions, military institutions have also for most that period acted as *direct agents* of capital accumulation across large parts of the region, with military officers playing various roles as managers, owners and investors in capitalist enterprises. This is distinct from, but evidently complements, the classic role played by military institutions in capitalist states as *indirect agents* of capital accumulation, as mapped out by Frederick Engels, Vladimir Lenin and Karl Liebknecht during the late 19th and early 20th centuries.[74] In this model of the role played by military institutions under capitalism, the leadership of the armed forces are part of the wider ruling class and form the coercive core of the capitalist state. Their primary role is as guarantors of the conditions for capital accumulation to take place. 'Indirect' here should not be taken as meaning subordinate or peripheral, in fact as Lenin articulated clearly in his classic work.[75] This role has two complementary faces: that of the *internal gendarme* who enforces the rule of the capitalist class over all other classes, and that of *external predator* against the other rival capitalist classes.

Confronting the 'military-bureaucratic machine'-

Chapter 10 discussed the abuse of Samira Ibrahim and other young women protesters by Egyptian Military Intelligence. What does this case reveal? Firstly, it tells us about the military's ideological compulsion to present itself as a power standing above society and acting for society's 'own good,' in the name of the state. In this case, that meant acting to preserve misogynist

---

72 Trotsky, 1930.
73 Cliff, 1963.
74 Engels, 1884; Liebknecht, 1907; Lenin, 1917c.
75 Lenin, 1917b.

codes of 'morality' which prescribe the circumstances in which men and women can mix and what they can do together. Secondly it demonstrates that ideology on its own is not sufficient for the state to carry out its functions: for that purpose violence is necessary. It was not enough for state officials, whether army officers or civilians, to denounce young women in the media for transgressing sexist norms by staying out overnight in the streets to protest and hope that some men would take the hint and punish them on the state's behalf (although this certainly also happened). In Samira Ibrahim's case, the "special bodies of armed men", were acting in their official, public function to violate her body. This is what the process of acting out these rapes as "virginity tests", giving them the fictitious cover of a medical procedure, tells us. This violence was not solely deployed for the personal satisfaction of the men who carried it out, rather it served a wider strategic purpose: that of enforcing the domination of the existing ruling class.

It underlines the point that the 'separateness' of state institutions from society is an illusion—an ideological veil which conceals that it represents not the interests of the whole of society, but of the ruling part. And there were many more hideous acts of violence which the "special bodies of armed men" would perpetrate in the process of counter-revolution: against Coptic Christians and their allies, against protesters in Raba'a Square, against striking workers, on slum-dwellers and fishermen, on Shaima'a el-Sabbagh as she carried a wreath for the fallen martyrs of the revolution to Tahrir Square, against Sarah Hegazi and other LGBT+ people, and on all the thousands of the 'disappeared.' [76]

This summing up of the essential features of the state's violent apparatus is not simply how it behaves 'in extremis'— but rather what the revolutionary crisis reveals about its true character. This the nature of *all* states, not merely the more dysfunctional ones like Egypt in peripheral zones of the world economy. The sketch outlined above also holds true of the

---

76 Poet and activist Shaima'a el-Sabbagh was shot dead in Tahrir Square by armed police in 2015 as she took part in a procession to lay a wreath in memory of those who fell during the revolution. (Kirkpatrick, 2015). Sarah Hegazi was arrested and tortured after being photographed raising a rainbow Pride flag at a concert in Cairo in 2017. She died by suicide in exile in Canada in 2020 (Maurice, 2021).

'You became a whip in the hands of the powerful'

British state, the American state, the Chinese state, the Indian state, the French and German states—and when they are tested by revolution their "special bodies of armed men" will act in the same way. This, in a nutshell was the argument advanced by Lenin in his classic text, *The State and Revolution*.[77] Lenin's argument is elegant and simple—through a re-reading of Marx's writings on the Paris Commune and Engel's work on the *Origins of Class Society, the Family, Private Property and the State*,[78] he sets out a framework which analyses the capitalist state as a coercive instrument of class domination and proposes that the only way to achieve lasting revolutionary change for the vast majority in society is to smash it apart and build something else in its place.

Lenin's text was a sharp polemic against reformists such as Karl Kautsky, who argued that the state's violent and militaristic character could be tamed by the victory of socialist parties in parliament, opening up a route to a peaceful transition to socialism. By contrast, for Lenin, it was an expression of the need of the capitalist ruling class for a violent instrument to ensure the continuation and deepening of the extraction of surplus value through the exploitation of the working class.[79]

The relationship between the capitalist state's violence and its purpose as a mechanism for the perpetuation of the class rule of the bourgeoisie is crucial. As Hal Draper points out: "from Marx's standpoint, the state's task of class domination is not only basic but its specific reason for existence".[80] However, this does not mean that capitalist rule is sustained by the state alone. As John Molyneux notes, "neither Lenin nor Marx thought that state power was the only or even the main form of power in society. On the contrary, the essence of their theory was that state power, for all its relative autonomy, was ultimately an expression of class power the basis of which lay in control of the means and process of production".[81]

The social composition, training regimes and internal configuration of military institutions are therefore deeply revealing of the inner nature of the state across more than one

77 Lenin, 1917c.
78 Engels, 1884.
79 Lenin, 1916a.
80 Draper, 1977, p255.
81 Molyneux, 2017, p128.

Revolution is the choice of the people

dimension. In his polemic with reformist socialists, Lenin used the metaphor of "an instrument" when talking about how the ruling class uses the state's armed bodies of men to enforce and maintain its rule. He was clear that this "instrument" had a special character, which meant it could not be transferred from "from one hand to another" as Marx put it when discussing the lessons of the Paris Commune.[82] ".

It is easier to grasp the way in which the state's nature has consists of both 'instrumental' and 'relational' qualities if we think more deeply about the 'armed bodies of men' themselves.[83] These are largely composed of ordinary people (usually men) who allow *themselves* to be used as a weapon against other ordinary people. The most dangerous moment for any ruling class in revolutionary crises comes if the rank-and-file of its armed bodies start thinking of themselves as people with interests in common with others of their class and reject the social relations which transform them into instruments forged for purposes of maintaining the existing political and social order.

As German revolutionary Karl Liebknecht saw clearly at the turn of the 20th century, the stability of the whole military apparatus in modern, capitalist states rests on conditioning the rank-and-file of the army to accept their transformation into weapons:

> [Modern militarism] wants neither more nor less than the squaring of the circle; it arms the people against the people itself; it is insolent enough to force the workers... to become oppressors, enemies and murderers of their own class comrades and friends, of their parents, brothers, sisters and children, murderers of their own past and future. It wants to be at the same time democratic and despotic, enlightened and machine-like, at the same time to serve the nation and to be its enemy.[84]

The oppressive social relations inside military institutions—the abuse and fear which condition soldiers into the "discipline" which is necessary to make them do these unspeakable

---

82 Lenin, 1917b.
83 Molyneux, 2017, p128.
84 Liebknecht, 1907.

things—are thus inextricably linked to their function as defenders of the oppressive rule of a tiny minority over everyone else in society.

In early-twentieth century Germany the ruling class also had to contend with a mass socialist party, the SPD, which at least on the surface, presented 'proletarians in uniform' with a very different set of values to its own. It had passed numerous resolutions at party congresses affirming its commitment to revolution and opposition to militarism. While most of the party's leading figures—with the exception of Liebknecht himself—failed to stick to these principles when confronted by the test of the outbreak of the First World War, the fears of the German High Command about what might happen if army discipline broke down along class lines were highly prescient. Eleven years after the publication of Liebknecht's pamphlet, Germany was in the throes of a revolution which was partially driven by rebellions from below in the armed forces.[85]

While none of the regimes discussed in this book had to contend with the challenge of a mass social democratic party, they all had to grapple with the same basic set of dilemmas facing the German ruling class in Liebknecht's day. How to forge armed bodies of men which are effective against both external and internal enemies? How to balance the benefits and risks attached to relying on mass and elite military institutions in these two contexts (and when moving between them)? In fact, despite the caveats noted above about the differences between the colonial period and the form of imperialism which structured the militaries of the post-colonial states, some of the institutional mechanisms they favoured to insulate themselves against rebellions from below infecting the rank-and-file of the armed forces were directly inherited from their former colonial masters. The French colonial authorities in Syria deliberately favoured rural and sectarian recruitment to the *Troupes Spéciales du Levant* they relied on to complement their own military force in repressing the growing nationalist movement.[86]

This carried over into the relatively higher density of trainee officers from Alawite backgrounds in the Syrian military academy in the early years of independence, who in turn would resort to a version the same sectarian 'fix' for the

---

85 Mosler, 2013.
86 Van Dam, 1996, p26–7.

problem of how to maintain the rule of the Ba'thist regime in times of political and social rebellion from below.. When the Bahraini authorities placed adverts in March 2011 recruiting former soldiers from Pakistan for work with the Bahraini National Guard stating they immediately required "people with experience and qualifications as anti-riot instructors and security guards"[87] they were following in the footsteps of the British colonial authorities who recruited policemen from the same source in the 1960s in order to avoid the potential risks of integrating Shi'a Muslim Bahrainis into the rank and file or command structures of the military and security.[88]

The Israeli ruling class built its armed forces through a combination of ethnically and religiously segmented recruitment (by retaining the almost exclusively Jewish character of the armed forces despite the presence of a substantial minority of Palestinians as citizens). Within the Jewish population, the Israeli military has the character of a mass, "citizen army" which directly mobilises a exceptionally large proportion of adults. This is only sustainable in the long term because of two conditions. The first of these (and by far the most important) is the historic success of the Israeli ruling class in subsidising its economic and military activities through its services to the most powerful imperialist power in the region, the US. As noted previously this creates material privileges for the Jewish Israeli community in comparison to all Palestinian subjects of Israeli rule (whether they are formally citizens of Israel or live under Israeli occupation), which underpin the racist ideology of Jewish religious nationalism sustained and entrenched by the Israel military as an institution. The second condition is the continuation of the settler-colonial paradigm which has brought new waves of Jewish immigration to Israel, long after this model had collapsed elsewhere. These exceptional conditions interact with a third, which is the relative success of the ethnic cleansing of Palestine at the time of the Israeli state's foundation, transforming Jewish Israelis from a minority into a majority across historic Palestine.

However, viewed from a different perspective, the Israeli model of a large conscript army and substantial reserves complemented by a huge role for military institutions as direct

---

87 Deccan Herald, 2011.
88 Jones, 2013.

agents of capital accumulation and providers of state services was clearly cut from the same cloth as the military institutions of many of the other states of the region during the state capitalist era, including Egypt. The location of Egypt lower down the regional and global hierarchy of states means that the experience of Egyptian military conscripts looks on the surface quite different to their Israeli counterparts. Where Israeli soldiers have the chance to train for work in high-tech industries Egyptian conscripts are more likely end up working as slave labour on construction projects or toiling in food production for military-run companies.[89] Learning to fire guns was a laughably small aspect of the military training they received, a group of Egyptian conscripts told an *Al-Jazeera* documentary in 2016. One conscript said he had only fired three bullets during his entire service and that officers did not trust soldiers enough to leave them unsupervised with a loaded gun.[90] Behind nationalist slogans claiming that the armed forces are a "Factory of Men," lies the reality that the hundreds of thousands of Egyptians who go through conscription each year experience exploitation under military labour discipline which directly enriches their commanding officers both individually and as a class.[91]

The experience of conscription varies dramatically according to social class, as those with higher levels of educational qualifications can shorten their time in service. University graduates have the option of serving for three years as an officer or one year in the ranks, whereas those with only a high-school education must serve two years as conscripts, while those with lower levels of education have to serve for three years.[92] An even worse experience awaits those rejected for military service in the regular army who must serve in the ranks of the Central Security Forces, the paramilitary riot police who have acted as the regime's shock troops against internal dissent for decades.

> Of all army conscripts, CSF soldiers are drawn from the most disadvantaged social backgrounds. With no recourse to justice, they endure incessant humiliation

89 Sayigh, 2018.
90 Sakr, 2016.
91 Fayek, 2014; Salah & Al-Faruq, 2018.
92 Fayek, 2014.

and abuse in already bleak living conditions, as well as the risk of violence — and boredom — during missions outside camps that often involve standing in one place for hours on end.[93]

Ramy Essam's appeal to the young, brutalised country lads of the CSF's rank and file at the beginning of this chapter, pinpoints the acute contradiction between their interests and those of those who command them. Hopes that revolution would fracture the CSF from within were not just wishful thinking. In 2012, 'Hossam', a former CSF conscript recounted his experience of being sent to put down the demonstrations on 28 January 2011 to the *Egyptian Independent*.

"My friends and I went out together in the lorry and we were laughing and joking. We thought it would just be a normal protest," says the thin 22-year-old conscript, whose fingernails are chewed down to the quick. By that evening Hossam was running for his life—in his underwear. Abandoned by their commanding officers and surrounded by hordes of angry protesters, Hossam and other recruits tore off their uniforms in an attempt to escape identification. "My commanders, who always said to me, 'Be a man, be a man' ran away and left us," Hossam said. He eventually made his way home—before taking to the streets with his friends and joining the protesters.[94]

Conclusion

It is impossible to know how many CSF soldiers could recount anecdotes like 'Hossam's' from their experience in January 2011. What is clear, however, is that although the scale and ferocity of the popular uprising was enough to drive the CSF off the streets as its commanders withdrew the rank-and-file to their isolated camps on the edges of the major cities, there were no large-scale mutinies or a generalised breakdown of internal discipline (or at least none which lasted long enough for outsiders to hear about them).

It could be argued that the leaders of the armed forces also took effective preventative and evasive action to preserve

---

93 Adam, 2012.
94 Adam, 2012.

the internal coherence of the military machine when they manoeuvred Mubarak out of power on 11 February. There were certainly signs that the loyalty of the junior officers was fraying at the edges by then, with at least one, Major Ahmed Shouman announcing he was joining the revolution and appearing with the protesters in Tahrir Square on 10 February.[95] While some networks of dissident officers did emerge in the period after Mubarak's fall, their protests were quickly snuffed out by Military Intelligence. The Sudanese uprising in 2019 also saw the beginnings of similar fractures within the Armed Forces, with some junior officers and rank-and-file soldiers joining the protests.

Here the contrast between Lenin's strategy and a reformist approach becomes even more apparent. For all their rhetoric about asserting the dominance of the "civil" parts of the state over the military and reining in the violent and abusive behaviour of armed institutions with the aim of transforming them into genuine servants of "the nation", none of the reformist currents which entered the state as a result of the uprisings would even contemplate Lenin's alternative. They struggled at all costs to maintain the "thing-like" qualities of the rank-and-file of the armed bodies and their capacity to be used as a weapon. Instead, they concentrated efforts at reform on winning over the commanders instead, often working with them to reduce the pressure from the streets to hold the leaders of the armed forces and police accountable in court for their crimes during and before the revolutions, and promising them new resources and funding to rebuild themselves after the shock of the uprisings.

Yet the complicity of the entire interlocking complex of judicial, military and security institutions in torture, forced disappearances and extrajudicial killings at scale is not the result of officers or policemen "going rogue" or jumped-up bandits getting their hands on the levers of state power. It is an expression of that the *purpose* of the state in a capitalist society is to maintain the optimum conditions for the accumulation of capital—when that is disrupted by revolution, even if there is no explicitly anti-capitalist revolutionary movement, it is then the role of the military and security services to "restore order". Attempts to bargain with these people can lead only to tragedy.

---

95 Nassif, 2013.

Revolution is the choice of the people

The only viable road to victory over them lies in breaking their machinery of power, in smashing their state, and replacing it with something entirely different.

Although he did not have time to outline how the "smashing" of the military machine would proceed in *State and Revolution*, it is clear from the practice of the Bolsheviks that Lenin understood that "smashing" the social relations reproducing the alienation, hierarchy and violence of modern armies could not be achieved simply from "outside" the institutions themselves but required soldiers to dismantle them from within. A profound psychological change had to take place in the minds of soldiers, to undo the conditioning and discipline that they had internalised. The organisation of revolutionary soldiers and sailors in the lower ranks of the Russian army, and especially the creation of *soviets*, councils of elected delegates which mirrored the emergence of similar bodies composed of civilian workers was a crucial part of this process.

Only the rank-and-file soldiers' voluntary rejection of the authority of their commanders over them—including the "revolutionary" ones—and their self-conscious reorganisation into a new kind of armed force which is inseparable from the risen people itself can form the basis of a "real people's revolution".[96]

This also explains why it was forms of struggle which challenged and disrupted the power of that class at the point of production and across different circuits of capital accumulation were ultimately the most effective at constraining the military. The mass strikes and struggles in the workplaces were never simply another form of protest but rather had the potential to grow over into a revolutionary challenge on a new level. However, that process required the development of both broad-based and tightly-organised revolutionary organisations capable of working in combination to break apart the state.

---

96 Lenin, 1917b.

Chapter 13
'The permanent revolution' and the conditions for dual power

The last chapter analysed the limitations of seeing the fundamental problems for revolutionaries as tidying up the house of the state and persuading unruly 'snipers in the kitchen' to go back to their 'proper place'. We examined the fallacy of thinking that this 'tidying up' will be achieved by negotiation overseen by benevolent 'democratic' nations—usually the Western powers or their allies. In most case 'the snipers' have resolutely refused to budge, and started rampaging around shooting up the furniture, often taking out their reformist interlocutors in the process, and in some cases leaving the house and much of the surrounding neighbourhood in ruins.

Eventual retreat from implementing the hopes and expectations of radical political and social change raised by popular uprisings is inevitable so long as those challenging the old regime cannot see beyond the horizon of the existing state. But what if a different kind of revolution is possible? What if the intense crisis of state and society which is a precondition for the eruption of a revolution could open the door to a route from political to social revolution against not only the ruling regime, but against the state and the capitalist system itself? The idea that political struggles against a specific form of government could "grow over" as Trotsky often phrased it, into a generalised challenge to the entire ruling class and its social and economic system is not a new one. So this chapter will explore the relevance of theories from the classical Marxist tradition developed primarily by Marx, Lenin and Trotsky to understanding the possibilities for social revolution today.

The key elements in the theoretical framework sketched out here include firstly a method of analysing the *processes* of permanent revolution which proposes three axes along which the "growing over" from political to social revolution actually takes place. For the revolutionary crisis to develop and mature to a point where it becomes possible to implement decisions which will move society towards a social revolution against capital, there must be constant movement along these axes through processes of "reciprocal action" similar to the concept developed by Rosa Luxemburg to explain the relationship between the economic and political aspect of mass strikes.[97]

In addition to this back-and-forth motion between economics and politics, we will discuss how similar processes must also take place along an axis which lies between popular mobilisation to *disrupt* the old order, and mobilisation to *construct* a new one. A final axis of permanent revolution discussed here connects the multiple centres of the capitalist system with its peripheries. Although hard to grasp as an abstract concept, this axis runs from the "backward" to the "advanced" sectors of the economy and society at local, regional and global level and takes on different concrete, specific forms in each revolutionary context.

Secondly, I will discuss the role of those popular revolutionary institutions which emerge out of this dynamic of reciprocal action in order to guide and develop the mass revolutionary movement. In particular we are interested here in exploring the circumstances under which these institutions develop into embryonic forms of revolutionary self-government rooted in the movement from below. As Trotsky noted, questions of dual power arise in every revolution, but take a variety of forms, ranging from the development of parallel military commands and rebel governments-in-waiting which simply aim to replace the structures of the existing state, to radical experiments in democracy from below, such as the *soviets*, elected councils of workers and soldiers delegates which had first emerged in the failed Russian revolution of 1905.[98]

---

97 Luxemburg, 1964.
98 Trotsky, 1930.

'The Permanent Revolution': from Marx to Trotsky

In 1850, Marx wrote a long letter to the members of the small network of activists he had co-founded with Engels and other revolutionary socialists laying out a strategy for the coming years.[99] The shockwaves from upheavals of the 1848 Revolutions which had shaken the old political order across Europe were still reverberating, and the Central Committee of the Communist League, adopted Marx's proposals in the hope that their organisation could grow and develop. Although a whole generation would elapse before the next major revolutionary crisis in Europe, Marx's 1850 document remains a crucial starting point for developing the strategies required to build revolutionary organisation capable of leading the working class to political victory over its opponents.

The rousing call of the final sentence—"Their battle-cry must be: The Permanent Revolution"—was taken up by Trotsky, decades later, as he tried to make sense of the possibilities and challenges posed to revolutionaries in Russia in the wake of the 1905 revolution against the Tsarist autocracy. Expanded and developed over subsequent years of revolutionary experience, this version of the theory of 'Permanent Revolution' became in many ways the central axis of Trotsky's efforts to defend the core lessons of the unexpected success of the Bolshevik-led October Revolution in Russia. His antagonists would lead a counter-revolution which transformed the Soviet Union from the first national manifestation of a workers' state into the vehicle for accumulation by a new capitalist class under Stalin's leadership. His explanation of the paradox of the revolution's success in a country which appeared economically, politically and culturally 'backward' by the standards of the core of the global capitalist system also emphasized the counter-revolutionary nature of Stalin's imposition of the limits of 'national revolution' on the unfolding process of social revolution embodied in the 'growing over' from the battle for political emancipation from Tsarist autocracy to the struggle for liberation from the tyranny of exploitation.[100]

At first sight, Marx and Trotsky's versions of 'permanent revolution' appear antithetical. Marx emphasizes the need for "a

---

99 Marx & Engels 1850.
100 Trotsky, 1930; 1931.

protracted revolutionary development" so that workers can train themselves and build the independent organisations needed to exercise power. Imagining that democratic parties led by the petty bourgeoisie would take power, Marx envisaged a situation where workers would form their own parallel government of "revolutionary local councils", backed up by armed workers' militias. These independent workers' organisations would force the democratic government to take increasingly radical political and economic measures aimed at pushing state and society in the direction of socialism.[101] (In 1850 he still left open the possibility that this tension could be resolved by workers' organisations taking over at least some elements of the existing state apparatus, following the experience of the Paris Commune in 1871 he definitely revised his assessment, arguing that workers' power could only be realised by 'smashing' the bourgeois state).[102]

Trotsky, by contrast, was insistent on the possibility of "skipping" whole epochs of economic development in the course of a relatively short revolutionary process. Rather than limiting the democratic ambition of the workers' movement to accepting the role of loyal opposition in a bourgeois republic, Trotsky's strategy emphasized the possibility of moving straight from Tsarism to socialism in one "compressed" revolutionary process. In furious polemics with his antagonists as the leaders of 1917 attempted to come to terms with the revolution's isolation and defeat he insisted:

> One stage or another of the historical process can prove to be inevitable under certain conditions, although theoretically not inevitable. And conversely, theoretically 'inevitable' stages can be compressed to zero by the dynamics of development, especially during revolutions, which have not for nothing been called the locomotives of history.[103]

One of the main reasons why Trotsky's proposals about the possibility of 'permanent revolution' could be tested in practice was Vladimir Lenin's decision to make a public break with the political orthodoxy of the Bolshevik Party through the

---

101 Marx & Engels, 1850.
102 Marx, 1871.
103 Trotsky, 1931.

'The permanent revolution' and the conditions for dual power

declaration of his "April Theses" in 1917 on his return from exile. At the core of Lenin's new perspective lay the renunciation of a revolution limited to what was achievable within the framework of the existing bourgeois state. Like other Bolshevik leaders he had previously imagined that the revolution could go no further than establishing a democratic capitalist republic in place of the monarchy, but in the April Theses he argued that the actions of the organised working class in the revolution could open the road to the abolition of capitalism.[104] Lenin's reimagining of what could be achieved during the Russian Revolution was intimately bound up with a very concrete assessment of the significance and potential of the condition of "dual power" which resulted from the actions of the Soviet of Workers' and Soldiers' Deputies. Just two days after publishing the April Theses in Pravda, he identified the "entirely different kind of power" exercised by the Soviet as being "of *the same type* as the Paris Commune of 1871".[105]

A crucial difference between the situation in Russia in April 1917 and Paris in March-May 1871 lay in the prospects for translating the 'discovery' of the political form of power which would open the way towards a process of permanent revolution and provide the foundations for the new socialist order into action through the intervention of a revolutionary party. Lenin, unlike Marx, who could only dissect the achievements of the Paris Commune *after* its tragic defeat, had the opportunity to affect the course of events while they were still in motion. Another crucial lesson about revolutionary method lies in Lenin's ability to look at this form as both an insider and an outsider. As 'insiders', that is to say, as participants in the Russian revolutionary movement, Lenin and Trotsky both grasped the significance of the 'homegrown', 'local' form of popular revolutionary organisation which had been forged not by the revolutionary party, but by workers themselves, to lead their own struggles. But in order to see its potential, they both had to look beyond the politics of the people who dominated the actual soviets, and beyond its contradictory stance in relation to the Provisional Government and its confused conceptions of its own historic role, to make a case for what it could *become*. This required a perspective which was 'external' to a certain extent, not immersed in the narrow localism of the moment, capable of comparison with the experiences of other times and places.

---

104 Lenin, 1917a.
105 Lenin, 1917b.

It required also a theoretical approach which demanded rigorous assessment not only of the soviet as *organisational form* but also of its *class content* and *revolutionary context*. Looked at from the perspective of organisational form alone, a meeting of representatives of different workplaces could be a (distinctly non-revolutionary) local Trades Council in Britain, a Polish inter-factory strike committee, a regional committee of the UGTT union federation in Tunisia, or a council of workers' deputies such as the Russian soviet. Moreover, considering 'class content' as a static, sociological category, rather than as a shorthand for a dynamic process of making and self-transformation will fail to capture properly what's at stake. What working class people can achieve through this type of organisational form, when they are engaged in collective struggle which is causing the state to fracture, bears little relationship to the possibilities open to the very same people during 'normal' times.

The development of popular revolutionary organisations into organs of dual power is not a question of simply calculating the sum of their features, but rather the outcome a process similar to what Rosa Luxemburg called 'reciprocal action' (a mutually reinforcing dynamic of cause and effect) along several axes at once. Indeed, one way of thinking about the specific dual power forms which have the potential to open the road to socialist revolution is that these types of organisations are in fact *defined* by their capacity to intensify and accelerate this kind of cyclical motion.

Powers of the Paris Commune type

What were the features of the "special type of state" which Lenin identified with both the Paris Commune and the *soviets* of the Russian Revolutions of 1905 and 1917.

The fundamental characteristics of this type are:

(1) the source of power is not a law previously discussed and enacted by parliament, but the direct initiative of the people from below, in their local areas—direct "seizure", to use a current expression;

'The permanent revolution' and the conditions for dual power

(2) the replacement of the police and the army, which are institutions divorced from the people and set against the people, by the direct arming of the whole people; order in the state under such a power is maintained by the armed workers and peasants *themselves,* by the armed people *themselves*;

(3) officialdom, the bureaucracy, are either similarly replaced by the direct rule of the people themselves or at least placed under special control; they not only become elected officials, but are also *subject to recall* at the people's first demand; they are reduced to the position of simple agents; from a privileged group holding "*jobs*" remunerated on a high, bourgeois scale, they become workers of a special "arm of the service", whose remuneration *does not exceed* the ordinary pay of a competent worker.

This, and this *alone*, constitutes the *essence* of the Paris Commune as a special type of state.[106]

This essence underlies a set of features have appeared repeatedly in other democratic, popular bodies created by workers and the poor in later revolutionary crises. Many of them, as Donny Gluckstein points out, begin to germinate "wherever labour takes action on its own behalf".[107]

Lenin argued in *State and Revolution* that the embryonic state which emerged in the Paris Commune as the workers, artisans and poor of Paris took control of the besieged city in 1871 showed it was possible to replace the "armed bodies" of the capitalist state with a different model of "the people in arms". By undoing separation between those bearing arms and the rest of society, and by subjecting the exercise of violence against the revolution's enemies to strict democratic control from below the Commune had taken a giant step forward towards the development of a form of the state which workers could build on to create a different kind of society.

The Commune, therefore, appears to have replaced the

---

106 Lenin, 1917c
107 Gluckstein, p33.

Revolution is the choice of the people

smashed state machine "only" by fuller democracy: abolition of the standing army; all officials to be elected and subject to recall. But as a matter of fact this "only" signifies a gigantic replacement of certain institutions by other institutions of a fundamentally different type. This is exactly a case of "quantity being transformed into quality": democracy, introduced as fully and consistently as is at all conceivable, is transformed from bourgeois into proletarian democracy; from the state (a special force for the suppression of a particular class) into something which is no longer the state proper.[108]

A crucial feature of a fully-developed workers' council is its conscious opposition to both the *institutions* and the *form* of the existing state. As noted above, bodies which emerge from ordinary people's activities to fill in the gaps left by the *incapacity* of the existing state to serve their needs unless they also *mobilise against it* will not be able to break out of the system. This also points to why alternative governments which might emerge in a revolutionary crisis and make a bid to displace the previous regime - perhaps appealing for the loyalty of the army and police, or calling for diplomatic recognition by foreign states - differ fundamentally from workers' councils, even though there may be some common ground between these two types of 'dual power' forms of government. The common ground lies in the fact that both may set themselves up consciously as a 'counter-power' which poses a set of sharp questions to the majority in society - are you with them, or with us? Whose authority do you recognise - ours or theirs? But they are not an "anti-state" in the way that the Paris Commune or the Russian *soviets* turned out to be.

Workers councils and popular power after 1917

One of the distinctive arguments advanced by the political current within revolutionary Marxism in which this book stands is the insistence that revolutions in which the organised working class takes action as part of a broader clash between 'the people', the state and the capitalist ruling class will create

---

108   Lenin, 1917b.

'The permanent revolution' and the conditions for dual power

conditions for the *rediscovery* of versions of this same political form, even in contexts where there is no revolutionary party explicitly committed to its creation. Although nowhere since Russia in October 1917 has there been a successful seizure of state power in the name of a workers' council, the form itself has reappeared in large numbers of revolutionary crises.[109]

More precisely, political forms bearing the potential to *develop into* workers' councils or *create the conditions* for their emergence have been a feature of large numbers of revolutions since 1917. Likewise, some of the conditions necessary for a *situation of dual power* have repeatedly been met, although often it has been recognised by the antagonists of the popular revolutionary mobilisation in the state and the wider capitalist class, before the participants or leaders of the movement from below themselves.

In addition, it is important to recognise that *workers' councils* composed largely of delegates elected by workplaces or groups of workplaces are located within a broader family of popular institutions which emerge in revolutionary situations. This includes other kinds of revolutionary bodies which are organised on a geographical basis (such as neighbourhood committees). Some of the examples discussed here combined participation by delegates from specific areas with those representing workplaces, professions or trades. The broad family of popular revolutionary bodies also includes organisations which only contest the rule of the capitalist class in a specific domain rather than making a general claim to sovereignty and authority which challenges the capitalist state. Workplace or factory councils are an important example in this category and are in fact a necessary first stage in the development of a workers' council which aggregates decision-making by a group of workplace councils. In the context of mass strikes and popular mobilisations it is relatively common to find examples of expanding workers' control within individual workplaces or even across whole sectors of the economy. However, while the proliferation of such bodies does indicate that a "dual power situation" is ripening, they should not be confused with the more developed and mature forms of workers' councils.

The Russian revolution of 1917 saw such soviets composed of workers and soldiers' delegates spread across the Russian

---

109 Barker, 1987.

Revolution is the choice of the people

Empire. Simultaneously, the pressures of the World War on the societies of Western and Southern Europe was creating conditions for the emergence of similar bodies in Italy (factory councils) and Germany (workers' councils). In Russia the Bolshevik Party led an insurrection which transferred state power to the soviets, by contrast in Germany, the Executive Committee of the Arbeiterräte or workers' councils despite being in effective control of most of the country voted to accept the restoration of parliament acknowledging the political sovereignty of the existing state.[110] The defeat of the revolutionary wave elsewhere in Europe and the isolation of the new Soviet Republic despite military victory in the Civil War which followed, opened the door to a counter-revolution led by Stalin in the late 1920s. The implications of this counter-revolution were partially camouflaged by the fact that the Communist Party remained in power and bodies called 'soviets' continued to exist, but their content was fundamentally altered. Rather than expressing the will of ordinary people, mobilising them in struggle and acting as organs of revolutionary democracy, they transmitted the orders of the state executive and mobilised workers to increase production.[111]

Yet despite this defeat, Eastern Europe did witness a revival of the traditions of workers' democracy through struggle from below after World War Two, notably in the Hungarian uprising of 1956 and the mass strikes led by the independent union Solidarity in Poland in 1979-80. The Central Workers' Council of Budapest was formed in response to the Russian invasion of Hungary which had deposed reforming Prime Minister Imre Nagy. It brought together delegates from most major factories and presented political demands to the government in the name of the Budapest working class.[112] Repression led to the crushing of the Hungarian uprising, but twenty years later in Poland, workers again discovered the power of a very similar organisation, the Inter-Factory Committee (MKZ). The most important examples were created in Gdansk during the mass strikes which started at the Lenin shipyard. The scale of the strike movement in August 1980 led to a major crisis in the Polish state, forcing the government to negotiate with the leadership of

---

110 Harman, 2014; Broué, 2017.
111 Cliff, 1996.
112 See Nagy, 1964 for an account of its formation.

'The permanent revolution' and the conditions for dual power

the independent trade union Solidarity over political reforms.[113]

Europe has not been historically the only continent where workers and the poor have created revolutionary bodies which bear a family resemblance to workers' councils. The revolutionary crisis which developed in Chile between 1972-3 led to the birth of the *Cordón industrial* (industrial belt) a committee which linked workers across factories and sectors to coordinate resistance to the attempts by the Chilean ruling class to destabilise the Popular Unity government of Salvador Allende. Popular Unity's efforts to redistribute some wealth in society through nationalisations met with fierce opposition by Chile's bosses, who in October 1972 as Mike Gonzalez explains:

> ...declared themselves on strike against a government that was attempting to introduce social reforms. The lorry owners tried to disable the vehicles that carry most goods up and down the country. The response was immediate. Workers took over many factories, local people seized the lorries and made sure they went on running, and the communities reopened supermarkets and distributed food according to need. The organisations they built to coordinate the response of the majority were called cordones—joint committees of workers, farmers, local residents and others.[114]

A distinctive and important feature of the *cordones* was that they brought together working people across a wide variety of sectors, and included representatives of the unemployed, residents in the shanty-towns and sometimes student organisations, rather than only those in workplaces. They also included agricultural workers and farmers.[115] The *cordones* first emerged in support of the Popular Unity government, attempting to defend the gains its election promised for ordinary people from reversal by the Right and later through repeated attempted military coups (which would finally succeed in overthrowing Allende in September 1973). Yet, many of them were prepared to take much more radical positions than Allende—instead of negotiating with the armed forces, they

---

113 Barker & Weber, 1982.
114 Gonzalez, 2003.
115 Barker, 1987, p60.

organised the self-defence of workplaces and neighbourhoods, requisitioned food and organised essential services. The town of Constitucion provides an example. In February 1973 local people called a "Mass Assembly of the People" to collectively identify the problems faced by workers, people living in shanty towns and peasant farmers. This assembly put a series of demands to the regional governor, who refused to take action, so the assembly took over the town, erecting barricades, forming health committees and vigilance committees to keep order.[116] In the face of an attempted military coup in June 1973, the *cordones* across Chile swung quickly into action. Workers took over their factories, establishing 'joint commands' with other plants. They requisitioned materials and vehicles, set guards on the gates, and prepared to defend themselves against the military.

The cycle of revolt in Bolivia between 2000 and 2005 created another set of rich experiences in popular mobilisation and democracy. The "infrastructure of class struggle" in El Alto, the huge, impoverished neighbourhood overlooking Bolivia's capital, La Paz has been analysed in detail by Jeffrey R. Webber[117]. As Webber notes, the neighbourhood councils of El Alto reflect not only the experience of working class life in the city, but also the traditional structures of rural indigenous communities. This in turn reflects the importance of the struggle against racism in the Bolivian context, and the battles against a state which has marginalised and oppressed the country's indigenous people. The context for this explosion of popular organising was the struggle to secure access to basic services (for example in the Cochabamba 'Water War' of 2000 opposing water privatisation) and to assert social control over Bolivia's natural resources (such as the 'Gas War' of 2003). In El Alto the key bodies which organised mass mobilisation for protests and highway blockades in 2003 were the FEJUVE- El-Alto (a federation of neighbourhood committees) and COR-El-Alto (a coordinating committee of trade unions which includes both workers in formal workplaces and unions representing market traders. As Webber describes, in October 2003 as these organisations coordinated blockades of the highways in protest at the government's policies over the export of natural gas, they found themselves in control of the city".[118]

116 Barker, 1987, p72.
117 Webber, 2021.
118 Webber, 2021, p185.

'The permanent revolution' and the conditions for dual power

The Middle East has also seen notable experiments in popular, revolutionary democracy. Before the current Sudanese revolution, the deepest and most sustained example was probably that of the workplace *shoras* (councils) of the Iranian revolution of 1979. A popular uprising combined with mass strikes in the strategically important oil industry and a mutiny in the army led to the flight of the Shah in February 1979. Workers in many industries took over their workplaces, creating democratically elected committees.

"The councils by their executive committees were directly elected and were subject to recall at any time by the members. The committees were accountable to general assemblies, and their members were not paid any extra salary for their positions on the committee. Almost all workers in a unit would attend meetings in which heated debates would take place on issues concerning the running of the workplace".[119]

The political dominance of the Islamist current led by Ayatollah Khomeini in the revolutionary movement meant that many workers who created these *shoras* initially saw them as supporting the new Islamic government and the Islamic revolution. However, in places where the *shoras* developed into means for workers to exercise democratic control over their workplaces this quickly put them at odds with the new regime. The critically important oil industry, where mass strikes had played a vital role in the fall of the Shah, was a stronghold of the *shoras*. In April 1979, the "world's largest oil refinery" was "controlled by revolutionary workers dissatisfied with their own revolutionary government".[120] They demanded "redistribution of income, an end to foreign control of industry and the right to reject management appointees".[121]

The *shoras* in the factories were part of a much wider phenomenon which saw ordinary people extend the political revolution which was unfolding at the top of society into "the everyday" as Assef Bayat puts it:

> These actions were not simply anarchy or chaos—in there was little evidence of assaults on fellow citizens or property in pursuit of opportunistic self-interest.

---

119 Assef Bayat, quoted in Rose, 2020, p180.
120 Rose, 2020, p184.
121 Rose, 2019.

Rather, they reflected a powerful question for self-rule, redistribution of social goods, and establishment of an alternative in conditions where the old order had been tattered.[122]

In universities, students and staff established councils to make democratic decisions about the governance of the institution, with students demanding the right to "elect [university] presidents, participate in the design of the curriculum, and be part of the governance structure".[123] The poor shantytowns around Tehran saw the spectacular growth of neighbourhood committees which aimed to improve their areas with the participation of residents, while squatter movements took over apartments and hotels abandoned by the rich to solve the housing crisis. Peasant movements seized control of the land in some areas which were run by peasant *shoras*.[124]

The Khomeini's Islamist current, which had attained partial control over the apparatus of the state in the first phase of the revolution, was able to gradually assert its domination over these popular movements and the workplace *shoras*. Sometimes this involved direct repression, through the arrest and detention of activists, but it was also partially achieved by building its own movement which propagated the idea that activism at the base of society must be subordinated to the commands of the state. This could involve incorporation of the popular institutions into the bottom layers of the state apparatus, or their destruction. The role of the mosques as organising centres serving people's needs in the neighbourhoods played a role in this process while in the workplaces, "formal shora organisation was not so much dismantled but institutionalised" as John Rose puts it.[125]

A key difficulty faced by the workplace *shoras*, even the most well-organised, was their lack of connection with each other and with other initiatives for popular control of resources, housing and land. There were some examples of coordinating committees uniting *shoras* across different factories, such as the one which emerged in Tabriz in the winter of 1979-80.[126] But this took place

---

122 Bayat, 2017, p137.
123 Bayat, 2017, p51.
124 Bayat, 2017, p51.
125 Rose, 2020, p177.
126 Rose, 2020, p193.

in the context of increasing repression and following splits in the major left organisations as to whether to support the regime which disoriented leftist activists in the *shoras*.

There was also the challenge of how to relate the workplace *shora* organisational form which emerged in relatively large, formal workplaces to the experiences of workers in tiny workshops where production was still partially organised on artisanal lines or to the unemployed. The experience of the workplace *shoras* was therefore not directly analogous to that of *workers' councils* which coordinate between workplaces and pose a challenge to the sovereignty of the state at a more general level, beyond the realm of production and distribution.

In addition to the examples discussed above, self-organised councils or committees composed of workers or wider layers of the poor (residents in shanty-towns and informal urban neighbourhoods and sometimes small farmers or rural workers) appeared in Portugal during the revolution of 1974-5 and Argentina during the economic crisis of 2000..[127] To some degree, the popular committees (*al-lijan al-sha'abiyya*) of the Palestinian Intifada of 1987-88 crossed into the same territory, as they began to coordinate both the ongoing popular resistance to the Israeli occupation and starting to build alternative, popular institutions to deliver education and healthcare in opposition to the Israeli state.[128] The problem faced by the Palestinian popular movement however was that the exclusion of Palestinian workers from the strategically important centres of capital accumulation in the Israel economy meant that the uprising did not on its own generate a deep enough crisis to paralyse and disrupt the functioning of the Israeli state and open a period of revolutionary crisis across the whole of the territory it claimed as its own.[129]

Rupturing state power

If we return to the definition of revolution proposed by Lenin and Trotsky discussed in at the beginning of this book, another process of reciprocal action becomes visible. The transformation of the councils and committees created in the

---

127 Barker, 1987; Barker, Dale & Davidson, 2021.
128 Alexander, 2022.
129 Marshall, 1989.

heat of mass mobilisations into bodies capable of challenging the state's authority everywhere its tentacles reach requires its existing institutions and their personnel to *lose* some of that authority. But what about conditions where the cause of the state's incapacity is some other factor besides a popular movement? In fact, it is relatively common for a revolutionary situation to develop out of defeat in war or external intervention (such as the disastrous defeat of the French Empire which led to the revolution in Paris in 1871). The incapacity of the existing state in the face of climate or ecological disaster could in some circumstances be the initial factor in opening up the road to a revolutionary situation developing—but Lenin's point that governments never 'fall' but rather must be 'toppled' still holds true.[130] Nor is it sufficient to create *substitutes* for existing state functions on a more democratic, 'progressive' or equitable basis. Even at the height of a revolutionary crisis, it is not possible to simply side-step the problem of the existing state. New 'popular' institutions for delivering services and redistributing resources will inevitably either end up working in collaboration with a state of the same type as the old one (even if some of its personnel might be different), or face extinction through repression.

In a context where crisis has developed on a scale which makes carrying on within the bounds of 'normal politics' impossible for both rulers and ruled, *if* there is resistance at scale by 'the people' *and* existing modes of government are no longer capable of containing that self-activity (for example by diverting its energies towards electoral channels), then the kinds of organisations discussed in this chapter are likely to emerge. Specifically, there has to be a crisis *of the state apparatus* across its material, social and ideological dimensions. The state must be unable to control and distribute resources as it did previously. It must be riven by internal fractures as the people who staff its bottom layers at least fail to carry out its orders and are potentially themselves drawn into the struggle against it. An ideological rupture must emerge in its ability to stand 'above' society as impersonal, violent 'public' power.

Without such a rupture—or when the tears and cracks heal again—the forms we are talking about are only indications of possibility, intimations of unrealised futures, shimmering at the borders between imagination and reality.

---

130   Lenin, 1915.

'The permanent revolution' and the conditions for dual power

The crisis of the state apparatus must be felt in the realm of the everyday—not confined to a 'cabinet crisis' or a falling out among elites. It must also be generated by the activity of ordinary people and not just by 'external' factors. *They* must cause the rupture in the state so that they can see what lies beyond it. Of course, there is not a neat linear, mechanical relationship of causation here—but rather loops of reciprocal action between the fragmentation of the ideological manifestations of state power, the social relationships it embodies and the materiality of that power. The "swift, intense and passionate changes" in the psychology of millions of people which Trotsky argues "*directly* determine" the course of revolutionary events, only become possible when repeated waves of collective action from below are hammering the weak points in the state's armoury at a societal scale.

I remember sitting with Iman, an activist in the Egyptian tax collectors' union in April 2011 discussing her experience of the 18-day uprising which had toppled Mubarak two months before. One incident which stuck in her mind was the moment when she confronted a police officer in the middle of the clashes taking place in her own neighbourhood. The security forces had turned out and started shooting, right in the middle of the main street, killing not only some of the young people trying to organise a march, but a young girl watching on her balcony and passers-by. "I just told him. Told him to get out of here", she said. It was a small moment of rebellion, but the light in her eyes as she said it pointed towards a deeper change within, a breaking with the routines of acquiescence to state authority and a willingness to directly confront its agents which had not been there before.

Revolutionary situations are characterised by similar encounters taking place simultaneously across large parts of the country. 'Simultaneously' needs to understand somewhat expansively here—of course some people have to do it first. The story of every revolution (and in fact every mass, popular movement) is of multiple failures before the sparks of defiance (or even despair) catch in the imagination of millions. But the generalisation of those encounters, and their practical effects on the capacity of the state apparatus to function, especially its 'armed bodies of men' is a *necessary precondition* for the emergence of the political forms we are analysing here.

Three axes of permanent revolution

Yet there still remains a yawning gap between the eruption of popular mobilisations demanding the end of a specific political regime or calling for a shift to a different model of governance to removing the capitalist class from power. How can this gap be closed or at least narrowed enough to make the kind of "leap" from political to social revolution? The opening of a situation of dual power is an integral element in this process. As Trotsky noted, the social revolutions which established the rule of the bourgeoisie also contained multiple episodes of dual power and transitions between its various configurations were inevitably marked by civil war.[131] Moreover, as precondition of the splitting of the state apparatus in revolution, the rising revolutionary class had to have already:

> ... assumed a very independent attitude towards the official ruling class; moreover, it must have focused upon itself the hopes of intermediate classes and layers, dissatisfied with the existing state of affairs, but not capable of playing an independent rôle. The historic preparation of a revolution brings about, in the pre-revolutionary period, a situation in which the class which is called to realise the new social system, although not yet master of the country, has actually concentrated in its hands a significant share of the state power, while the official apparatus of the government is still in the hands of the old lords.[132]

In the case of the great bourgeois revolutions which Trotsky analyses it was certainly apt to talk about the rising bourgeoisie encroaching on state power before the revolution, even appropriating and transforming pre-existing institutions such as the English parliament to legitimise its bid for supremacy. The preparatory phase of the *coming* social revolution which overthrows the capitalist class will also require a period of "initial dual power", even if it is not yet realised at the level of the state. It will require forms of organisation and practice which foster "a very independent attitude to the official ruling class",

---

131 Trotsky, 1930.
132 Trotsky, 1930.

'The permanent revolution' and the conditions for dual power

create bodies capable of taking initiatives which start to tug at the loyalty of "intermediate classes and layers" pulling them away from their dependence on the old ruling class and hasten the polarisation of society into the two opposing camps which will meet in cataclysmic battle during the revolution itself. This is why amidst the rupture there must also be continuity, just as the green shoots break the crust of the earth in spring. It is also why these kinds of institutions are new and familiar at the same time, as they are rooted deep in the fundamental conflict in capitalist society between exploited and exploiters.

But what are the axes around which the political forms which open the road to the social revolution will take shape? The first is surely found between the poles of mobilisation against the existing order and the construction of alternative forms of government. The to-and-fro between disruption and construction is visible even in non-revolutionary contexts during mass strikes in the collective action machinery which delivers people and placards to picket lines, keeps them refreshed and fed and ensures they are not forced back to work early by hardship. Strikes which succeed in forcing a general shutdown of production and services pose much harder questions about responsibility for the impact of disruption on the vulnerable. Kamel Aissat, describing the general strike in the Algerian provincial capital Bejaia in December 2019 explains that in contrast to the much more spontaneous strike of March 2019, when "nothing was functioning at all":

> It was decided that the bakeries, pharmacies, health services must remain open because this is what would ensure confidence from society. In terms of the factories, it was the workers themselves with their trade unions and local committees, who decided which sections to shut down and which would be under minimal security, in particular for the dairy industry, for services such as gas, as we are dependent on bottled butane gas. So these services were assured.[133]

What is important here is not just that the form of collective action can create spaces for the prefigurative enactment of different, more egalitarian ways of living (as large protest

---

133   Aissat, 2019.

camps and occupations of public spaces often do), but that it starts to bring this process of disruption and construction inside the 'everyday' spaces of work in production and services resulting in startling shifts across the 'frontier of control' between management and workers.[134] This is likely to involve workers taking decisions themselves which would normally be reserved for management—such as the selection of a new director through an election or agreeing a consensus candidate among the workforce, or collectively deciding which goods and services to provide.

A similar process must also be at work in the other crucial 'everyday' spaces where ordinary people live, reflecting growing confidence among workers and the poor that their own actions can change their experience as consumers and householders for the better. The ratcheting up of economic crisis which follows political revolutions poses urgent questions for popular forms of revolutionary organisation—should a local neighbourhood committee just organise a demonstration against rising prices of bread and the theft of vital flour supplies from government bakeries by black marketeers connected with the security services or organise its own guards and inspectors to stop this happening? As we will see in the following chapter, when faced with this dilemma, several of the Sudanese Resistance Committees crossed the threshold from mobilisation against the existing state to partially replacing its functions by doing precisely that.

The role of confrontation with the state in acting as midwife to permanent revolution along this axis can be seen at work in Sudan between 2018 and 2022. The Resistance Committees evolved from being protest mobilisers to political actors courted by the established parties as potential allies and developed positions and demands on questions far beyond their original remit. At the time of writing this had not yet crossed the threshold of a self-conscious intervention into the realm of government, but some of the seeds from which such an intervention could grow had clearly been planted. What is notable here though is that this is not a linear process, but a back-and-forth motion of what Rosa Luxemburg called "reciprocal action" (a mutually reinforcing dynamic of cause and effect).

A second axis of permanent revolution can be conceptualised

---

134 Goodrich, 1920.

'The permanent revolution' and the conditions for dual power

as the reciprocal action between the 'political' and 'economic' aspects of the revolutionary process. It is important to note here that the 'interlacing' of the economic and political struggles characteristic of episodes of mass strikes and revolutions does not in itself guarantee the emergence of dual power forms but it is a necessary precondition of their development. Protest movements which remain in the realm of politics without raising questions about how the economy works, and who it works *for*, will always be containable within the boundaries set by the capitalist system. Conversely, movements which raise strictly 'economic' demands such as strikes over pay do not inevitably lead to confrontations with the state and thus to as least some of the strikers drawing conclusions that political change is necessary to meet their economic goals. In practice, however, when mass movements arise in either the realm of politics or economics so long as they involve ordinary people "acting on their own behalf" rather than being mobilised in the interests of the ruling class or reactionary forces from other classes, it becomes extremely difficult to stop economic struggles breaking through into the realm of politics and *vice versa.*

All of the revolutions and uprisings discussed in this book were the result of a degree of interlacing between political and economic struggles. But the subsequent trajectories of most of the revolutions underscores why the question of organisational forms matters in these discussions. Popular revolutionary movements require types of organisation capable of acting at the juncture between political and economic aspects of the crisis in order to unleash dynamics of permanent revolution, creating the conditions for the 'leaps' over 'historical stages' which Trotsky noted in the case of Russia. Organs of *workers'* power are particularly well-suited to this goal, more so than any other possible form of popular revolutionary organisation in a situation of dual power. This is because they mobilise workers *as workers* to take political action against the existing state and build alternatives to it, rather than mobilising them as engaged citizens, or part of 'the poor' or 'the 99 percent'. Working backwards into the pre-history of the uprisings, even trade unions often play a role which visibly accelerates and deepens the revolutionary crisis, provided there is a way to breach the normal separation between 'politics' and 'economics' which dominates their everyday existence and which is systematically upheld by the trade union bureaucracy.

Revolution is the choice of the people

The third axis of permanent revolution can be conceptualised as lying along scales of uneven and combined development from the centre to the periphery of the capitalist system. 'Scales' is in the plural here, because processes of permanent revolution necessarily develop around this axis simultaneously at several levels of the capitalist system, sparking off the frictions caused by the collisions between social and political formations which are characteristic of different stages of economic development interacting in the same space and time. Trotsky's theorisation of permanent revolution as a process which turned Russia's political and cultural 'backwardness' in capitalist terms to the advantage of revolutionaries is particularly relevant here. The uneven processes of economic development in Russia created concentrations of factory workers in a largely peasant country, and a ruling class which relied on the combination of political and religious institutions from the Middle Ages with elements of a modern authoritarian state resulted in a combustible mixture of social and political forms. Sparks from collective action at a moment of major crisis for the ruling class thus unleashed a revolution which leapt from the struggle for a capitalist democracy to socialism in the space of a few months.

Trotsky believed that the 'peculiarities' of Russia's national development had the potential to unravel the same international capitalist order which had co-produced them.[135] Against the emerging Stalinist orthodoxy during the 1920s, he set on the record the impossibility of 'socialism in one country' and insisted that without the victory of revolutionary movements elsewhere in Europe, the Bolshevik experiment could not survive. A crucial element in his theory was the idea that it was the weaknesses and vulnerabilities of capitalist development in countries such as Russia, which would create a breach through which revolution could travel from the periphery to the core of the system. 'Backward' Russia's 'leap' towards socialism would provide the example for the workers of 'advanced' Germany to follow. In contrast to Trotsky's emphasis on the *internationalist* nature of the revolutionary struggle within Russia, Stalin's counter-revolution was geared towards perfecting a new *national* state, led by a state capitalist ruling class, and engaged in fierce economic and military competition with other states

---

135 Trotsky, 1930.

'The permanent revolution' and the conditions for dual power

and capitals, not attempting to dismantle the capitalist system.[136]

Later waves of uprisings have borne out Trotsky's insight that revolutions rarely succeed or fail solely within national boundaries. The initial successes of uprisings in Tunisia, Libya and Egypt in 2011 fed into a region-wide revolutionary process. In the first heady months of 2011, as regimes trembled from Rabat to Manama and Aleppo to Aden, the internationalisation of the revolution seemed to be building a self-reinforcing dynamic where the fall of an autocrat in one country bolstered the chances of success for revolutionary mobilisations in another. Moreover, the revolutionary wave began in countries which were lagging behind their regional competitors compared to their potential economic power, such as Egypt, or where neoliberal reforms had dramatically widened social inequality between different regions such as Tunisia and Syria. The states overseeing relatively more dynamic centres of capital accumulation in the region—Turkey, Iran and the Gulf states—successfully contained and repressed popular movements for change before they developed revolutionary momentum, allowing them to pivot towards counter-revolutionary interventions across the region.

This axis of permanent revolution encompasses movement between the peripheries or the margins and the centres of economic and political power *within* existing nation states. In some cases this can be visualised through a sketch of the social geography of revolution, for example in Tunisia where the popular uprising began in the impoverished towns of the rural provinces, but political revolution was consummated in the capital and the industrial centres of the coast.

The effects of unevenness and combination do not only operate geographically, but also on social scales. They affect the relations between different classes among the people (and their relations with the variegated middle classes which wobble

---

136 In order for Stalinism to take hold and ultimately dominate both the Bolshevik Party and the Soviet state apparatus, revolution had to go into reverse across multiple scales of the capitalist system. The uprisings in Western Europe, in particular the revolution in Germany, were defeated. The victorious European powers invaded Russia hoping to strangle the new Soviet government and aid the internal counter-revolution, which bogged the Bolshevik-led state down in a brutal civil war which destroyed much of the country's social fabric, including the working class which had led the revolution of 1917.

socially and politically between the people and the ruling class). Unevenness shapes the internal composition of these classes, too, including the working class itself.

Uneven and combined economic development makes a revolutionary alliance between the organised working class and wider layers of the poor necessary. The general trajectory in capitalist development is towards the expansion of the working class, and globally the majority of humanity now depends on some form of waged labour to survive.[137] However, there are few contexts, especially in countries which are poorer and economically weaker than those at the core of the system, where waged workers could simply rely on their majority status as the basis for becoming a revolutionary class. This might be because waged workers and their dependents are not actually the majority in society, or because most waged workers are separated from each other in very small workplaces, or because waged work is combined with other ways of making a living (possibly seasonally with subsistence agriculture, or petty production, or state support through benefits) and does not necessarily appear as the overarching organiser of the lives of the majority.

Dual power institutions which arise in revolutions in these kinds of contexts must take account of both the differentiated structure of the working class and the shifting boundaries between the working class and other sections of the poor. One of the ways they can contribute to the deepening of permanent revolution along this particular axis is through the psychological, political and organisational transformation of relatively passive relationships between people who share common destinies within the capitalist system into bonds of solidarity, through collective struggle against the ruling class and its state. This transformation arises out of a movement of reciprocal action back-and-forth *along* different scales of uneven and combined development (between regions, sectors, neighbourhoods and social layers - sometimes between classes but also within them). It provides a mechanism to articulate a positive answer to Claire Ceruti's question: "Can a street

---

137 Chris Harman wrote a good survey of this process just over 20 years ago. See Harman, 2002. At the level of basic statistical indicators, the ILO estimates that waged and salaried workers make up just over 53 percent of all employment (see World Bank 2021)..

trader selling bubblegum develop a community of fate with a permanently employed machine operator?"[138]

Ceruti posed this question in the context of a discussion of the challenges to creating a "proletarian community of fate" between the employed and unemployed (and all the variegated categories of work and income generation in between) in contemporary Soweto, South Africa's largest township. As she points out, Sowetans are required to make themselves available for exploitation without being ever guaranteed a job. They are forced to rely on intergenerational and familial bonds within households to pool the resources needed to survive while they dip into and out of different worlds of work, rather than being structurally polarised between a permanent, better-off and more secure 'core' of waged workers, and an equally permanent layer of marginalised long-term unemployed who have been forced out of the capitalist labour market entirely. They often experience movement between more marginalised and more secure forms of work as a disciplining factor, a "whip" which encourages caution and fear of confrontation. Their "differentiated unity" functions as a "lever of accumulation" (by driving down wages or inhibiting collective organisation for example). A significant feature of recent revolutionary crises (and some of the moments which have perhaps been less than fully-realised revolutionary crises but where levels of contestation between popular movements and the state have approached that threshold), is that they have begun to throw up the conditions for the emergence of dual power forms which could conceivably turn the "differentiated unity" of the working class and wider layers of the poor into a "lever of revolution".

In a sense, the core of Trotsky's vision of "permanent revolution" was precisely that. He proposed that the working class and its allies could make use of the hybrid, contradictory mess of social and political forms which characterised capitalist development in countries such as Russia to short-circuit the revolutionary process by leaping straight from the incomplete bourgeois (democratic) revolution to the socialist. Crucially, this would reverse the trick performed by the Russian ruling class, which wanted electric lights in its palaces, and advanced battleships patrolling its shores, without conceding a more democratic style of government.

---

138 Ceruti, 2010.

Revolution is the choice of the people

The ideological dimension of the struggles around this axis is also critically important.. In particular, such forms must be able to actively withstand the ideological pressures of whatever forms of oppression arise in their specific national or regional context out of the processes of uneven development (for example based on language, religion or culture). The longest-lasting and most intractable of these processes of uneven development (such as the predatory relationship between the military and economic institutions of riverine centre and the pastoral peripheries of Sudan, or the differential treatment of the Kabyle region by the French colonial power in Algeria) can become vulnerabilities which derail the revolutionary process and send it into reverse.

This is why the counterpart of the political 'leap' from political to social revolution against the ruling class within any given national state, demands not just internationalist politics in the general sense, but the creation of real and practical forms of international solidarity between movements engaged in revolutionary struggles against their 'own' state. In a world where the representatives of capitalist states and corporations dominate the international arena it can be hard to imagine how popular and revolutionary movements of workers and the poor could also shape what happens there.

Yet the power of such organisations to act across borders is no illusion. Somewhat paradoxically, the *national* struggle of the Palestinian people has from time to time provided concrete examples of this process at work, even if the main Palestinian nationalist movements have persistently undermined both its internationalist and revolutionary potential. The long tradition of Egyptian activist groups mobilising caravans of solidarity across the Sinai peninsula in an effort to break the siege on Gaza is a case in point. In December 2004, the bus loads of activists only got as far as the edge of Sinai governorate before being stopped by the security forces. Just under eight years later, in November 2012, there was a real possibility that similar mobilisations would not just deepen the crisis of the Egyptian state as the Muslim Brotherhood-led government temporarily opened the border while Israeli missiles pounded Gaza once again. It doesn't take a great leap of the imagination to see how a call and response between Egyptian solidarity protests and a Palestinian general strike similar to the 'Unity Intifada' of 2021 might have begun to put into practice a kind of internationalism from below, even if it was framed in terms of solidarity with a people facing national oppression. Unlocking the powers of the third axis of permanent revolution requires a conscious break with nationalism. It must forge horizontal connections between workers and the poor that strengthen their revolutionary movements by reaching beyond the prison walls of the national state.

Conclusion

Interdependence between mass collective action by ordinary people against the ruling class and its state, and democratic self-organisation in the context of revolutionary crisis lies at the root of the historical experiences of revolutionary organisation discussed briefly here. These experiences of building organs of workers' and popular power provide the necessary starting point for analysis of the last decade. However, these comparisons have to be sensitive to variations in composition and structure of the working class itself in different historical periods. The historical experience of the Russian working class in creating the only example of organs of workers' power which did (albeit temporarily) provide the foundations for a new form of state power at a national level remains an essential reference point for these discussions. But it is through distilling the lessons of that experience at the level of general principles and practices that ensures its continued relevance for revolutionaries today. At the core of the approach taken by Lenin and by Trotsky (whose identification of the *soviet* with a strategy of permanent revolution in the Russian context preceded Lenin's by a decade) was a recognition that ordinary people could *themselves* discover the political form necessary to open the horizons of revolutionary action beyond a change in the personnel or style of government towards the overthrow of capitalism.

Revolution is the choice of the people

Chapter 14
Egypt, Syria and Sudan: results and prospects

Were there experiences during the two waves of uprisings discussed here which could be compared to the historical examples outlined in the previous chapter? Do any of the revolutionary councils and popular committees thrown up in the heat of these revolutions merit comparison with the Chilean *cordones*, the Iranian *shoras*, the Polish Inter-Factory Strike Committees or the Russian *soviets*? In this chapter we will discuss three contrasting case studies from Egypt, Syria and Sudan, examining examples of independent unions which exercised workers' control to some workplaces and the neighbourhood Popular Committees in Egypt, the Local Coordinating Committees and Revolutionary Councils in Syria and Sudan's Resistance Committees in the revolutionary process.

These bodies all emerged out of revolutionary mobilisation from below, and like their predecessors discussed in the previous chapter, all showed some potential to develop along the axes of permanent revolution, moving back and forth from mobilising for disruption to the construction of political and social alternatives, crossing the porous membrane separating the spheres of 'economics' and 'politics', and transforming unevenness in the social formation and class structure into levers of revolution. But this potential was only ever partially realised.

In Egypt, examples of workers' control were restricted to small numbers of workplaces without forging strong connections with the mass movement in the streets, and the efforts to build neighbourhood-based revolutionary committees which could mobilise to defend the revolution fizzled out after a few months.

From one perspective, the local revolutionary councils which governed Syria's rebel municipalities presented a far more politically developed challenge to the existing state. These were instances of rebel government under siege from the old regime, holes in the fabric of the state's claim to sovereignty. However, these civilian bodies had to negotiate power with armed forces on the rebel side which were at best indifferent - and often actively hostile—to any form of democratic and popular control from below.

Moreover, seen from a different vantage point the Syrian experience of revolutionary democracy was strikingly *underdeveloped* compared to the experience of Egypt and Sudan. Unlike its counterparts there, the Ba'athist state in Syria was able to stop workers in key public services, transport networks, government ministries and major industrial workplaces developing a democratic challenge to its authority from below *inside* these institutions.

The Sudanese Resistance Committees, which are rooted in mobilising committees at neighbourhood level, have begun to articulate visions of radical reforms to the existing state,[139] but by the time of writing had not been able to break down the internal structures of its armed core.

In fact, that goal did not even figure in the discussions of most Sudanese activists about revolutionary strategy, where instead the emphasis was laid on taming the existing national army and the state's militias.[140] Nevertheless, the Resistance Committees demonstrated that it was possible to combine effective mobilisation in the streets with an enlargement of the space for popular democracy and a form of revolutionary leadership which clearly articulated an alternative to the reformist opposition parties hoping to negotiate their way back into power with the generals.

---

139 Alneel, 2022
140 Alneel & Abdelrahman 2022.

Egypt, Syria and Sudan: results and prospects

Egypt: separating economics and politics

The experience of Egypt in 2011 and 2012 showed the promise and the limits of many 'spontaneous' forms of popular organisation during a revolutionary crisis. It demonstrated the difference that the intervention of organised revolutionaries makes in a revolutionary crisis, but also the problem of generalising from examples without sufficient numbers. Perhaps above all it illustrated how the separation between "economic" forms of struggle and the political dynamics of the revolution reasserts itself, even in the midst of surges of strikes. The popular uprising of 2011 built on years of interlaced social and political struggles, including waves of mass strikes which had broadened the organisational experience of millions of working class Egyptians. However, the relative inexperience of activists and organisers combined with the political dominance of conservative reformist forces (especially the opposition Islamist parties) proved a huge obstacle to the development of forms of popular revolutionary organisation in the workplaces and neighbourhoods which could have stopped or at least challenged the slide towards counter-revolution.

The major sit-ins in Tahrir Square and other iconic locations in city centres showed some of the possibilities for self-organisation by ordinary people—with the establishment of their pavement pharmacies, makeshift field hospitals and clean-up squads (who piled up bags of rubbish and put a sign on top saying "National Democratic Party HQ" in a corner of the square overlooked by the burnt-out hulk of the real NDP building).[141] There were security teams and volunteer checkpoints at the entrances to the sit-in, and a widely attested absence of violence or abuse between protesters inside, at least at the height of the 18-day long uprising. Tahrir Square was the scene of extraordinary displays of solidarity between Muslim and Christian Egyptians, particularly on 'Revolution Sunday', 6 February 2011.[142] Graffiti of the symbol of the 1919 Revolution showing the crescent embracing the cross appeared in chalk

---

141 This and other examples cited here are taken from my own observations of Tahrir Square when I was there between 5-6 February 2011.
142 Alexander, 2011b.

Revolution is the choice of the people

around the square and Muslim protesters kept watch while Christians celebrated public prayers.

However, the internal organisation of the sit-ins did not generate new forms of popular revolutionary organisation. In Tahrir Square, the organisation of the perimeter security and the setting up of stages and tents did not evolve much beyond tacit cooperation between existing opposition organisations, or rather between specific sections of existing organisations, sometimes acting in defiance of their national leadership. This was the case during the early phase of the 18-day uprising, when Muslim Brotherhood youth activists were clearly an organised presence in Tahrir Square, in opposition to the leadership of the Brotherhood's insistence that the organisation was not supporting the protests.

The Square was an important space for more plebiscitary forms of popular democracy where organisations and individuals could test the mood of the crowds through call and response from the stages with chants and slogans. The crowds in the Square could thus shape events and sometimes force reformist leaders to respond to demands which gained traction among the crowds.[143] But using the sit-ins as a space for collective deliberation and discussion which could result in actual decisions and establish expectations of democratic accountability proved difficult. One reason for this was that in contrast to the Sudanese experience, the sit-ins in Egypt were relatively short-lived. The first wave of sit-ins ended with the fall of Mubarak in February, and longer-term protest encampments were not re-established until November that year.

Moreover, mobilisation for protests in the squares relied heavily on social media, especially Facebook pages and events, which sometimes substituted for 'offline' forms of popular organisation. Although Facebook pages did exhibit some similar characteristics to the physical squares themselves in

---

143 The Muslim Brotherhood's leadership found this out to its cost when it entered negotiations with Mubarak's vice-president Omar Soleiman on 6 February 2011, only to be decried for betraying the revolution by activists in Tahrir Square and other sit-ins. The exit strategy for the regime which emerged from these talks turned out to be a dead-end, however, largely thanks to the escalation of the revolutionary crisis through the mass strikes beginning around the same moment. See Al Jazeera, 2011 for a contemporary report.

Egypt, Syria and Sudan: results and prospects

terms of providing spaces to test out slogans and demands (with 'likes' and comments providing rough metrics for those looking to use this method to gauge the popular mood), their centralised and opaque administration systems made this method of mobilisation harder to subject to democratic control from below.[144]

The difficulties in creating 'new' forms of popular revolutionary organisation in the squares need to be considered in relation to the development of these forms in neighbourhoods and workplaces. During the 18-day uprising in January 2011 there was an organic relationship between some poor, working class and lower-middle class urban districts and the creation of 'the squares' as revolutionary spaces.

Mass mobilisation from these districts, organised through interventions by activists in mosques and churches and through marches to turn out crowds to join the uprising was critical in tipping the balance in favour of the protesters and driving the security forces off the streets of major cities.[145] In some cases, this involved actively redirecting the energies of protesters in poor and working class districts away from localised confrontations with the police (such as besieging or burning down police stations) towards the symbolic contest over control of the streets in the city centre and the taking of the main public square.[146]

The combination of a large number of attacks on police stations with the failure of the Central Security Forces to stop crowds of protesters taking control of Tahrir Square during the 'Friday of Anger', 28 January 2011 led to a shift in tactics by the regime, Ahmed Ezzat argues:

> The police completely fragmented and the state was paralysed as its attempts to stop the protests had failed. The police had been defeated but the state's rhetoric now changed to raise fears of a security vacuum through propaganda about how crime would increase.[147]

Across all social classes the response by ordinary people

---

144 Alexander, 2011a; Aouragh & Alexander, 2011.
145 Shenker, 2016, p217-8
146 Alexander & Bassiouny, 2014.
147 Alexander, 2021b.

was to organise themselves to fill the security gap, protect property and people from attack and secure food supplies for vulnerable people. Vigilance committees, makeshift barricades and checkpoints and neighbourhood security appeared across residential districts during the 18-day uprising. Often called 'Popular Committees', these bodies focussed on attempting to protect local residents and businesses following the withdrawal of the police. As Ezzat notes, while the committees appeared because of the developing revolutionary crisis, they were not formed to mobilise support *for* the revolution, even if in some cases (especially in poor and working class areas) residents were organising to protect themselves from the return of the police, who they expected to engage in looting and violence to discredit the revolution.[148] Rather they reflected the uncertainty experienced by ordinary people in the midst of strange and often frightening events.

Later, in some cases they intervened in issues such as cooking gas distribution, attempted to force the expansion or provision of basic services such as water and power, and sometimes went on to challenge the power and violence of the local police, corrupt businessmen and political figures.[149]

As Asya el-Meehy points out, they were not necessarily democratic, and in fact as time passed, tended towards a range of models of unaccountable, top-down intervention in politics—being transformed into NGOs, or GONGOs (Government sponsored NGOs) either through direct state funding or patronage, or through reliance on donations from Islamist charities. In the countryside, popular committees tended to be formed by appointment and provided a route for the reconfiguration of traditional politics, even creating spaces for the rehabilitation of members of the old ruling party.[150]

By contrast, the formation of Popular Committees for the Defence of the Revolution was an overtly political attempt by the revolutionary left to connect the neighbourhoods and the protests in the squares. Ezzat and other activists from the Revolutionary Socialists hoped to nurture popular revolutionary organisation rooted in poor and working class areas which could connect these areas to the growing

---

148 Alexander, 2021b.
149 El-Meehy, 2013.
150 El-Meehy, 2013.

Egypt, Syria and Sudan: results and prospects

revolutionary movement. The initiative was inspired by reports reaching activists in the sit-in of the spontaneous formation of popular committees but began in Tahrir Square itself a few days before the fall of Mubarak, with activists inviting individuals and groups from different neighbourhoods to help set up a network of Popular Committees.

Within a short while there were around 20 active committees across Greater Cairo, Fayyoum, Alexandria and some of the provinces. A four-page bulletin, *Revolutionary Egypt*, listed active groups and provided phone numbers for anyone wanting to contact their local committee. Donations paid for the publication and the activists could barely keep up with the demand: "we distributed 30,000 copies in a single day", remembers Ezzat.[151] After the fall of Mubarak the focus shifted towards more activities and campaigns in the neighbourhoods, including information stands and meetings to spread the word about the revolution's demands and agitation over local issues.

The Revolutionary Socialists were at first practically alone in attempting to connect revolutionary organisation at neighbourhood level with mobilisation for the major street protests and sit-ins. A large part of the problem was simply one of scale, but the embryonic network of revolutionary Popular Committees was hampered by the fact that its opponents in the state were far better organised. "The problem was—and this was an issue with the revolution as a whole - we weren't ready to develop the movement, but the state was ready," notes Ezzat.[152] And as the stakes rose and the tempo of confrontations with the military increased, the gap between the task of mobilisation and the available resources to do it widened. "Events were faster and stronger than us on every level—organisationally, politically and in terms of propaganda. We had no means to get the message out. We couldn't recruit enough people".[153]

However, the other reason for the difficulties in incubating popular revolutionary organisation at neighbourhood level was that this political space had been monopolised by Islamist movements during the pre-revolutionary decades. This was primarily the Muslim Brotherhood which sustained a formidable base of electoral and charitable organisation across

---

151 Alexander, 2021b.
152 Alexander, 2021b.
153 Alexander, 2021b.

Egypt following its revival in the 1970s after the repression of the Nasserist era. The Brotherhood's main competitors were drawn from Salafist currents, rather than the Left. There were plenty of examples of localised social and political struggles which were to some extent organised independently of the Islamist currents. These included battles over housing issues, over police violence and torture, over access to utilities, or over pollution.[154] But these campaigns lacked connections to each other and were usually isolated from the national political arena, unless they sparked wide-scale repression.

By contrast, the ground for building popular revolutionary organisations in the workplaces appeared much more hospitable. There was a fresh residue of organisation for collective action through strikes and workers' protests which had convulsed most sectors of the economy since the mid-2000s. In a small number of cases this had broken through into independent union organisation, but the conditions for the explosive growth of workers' organisations and their potential radicalisation in the context of the revolution were clearly evident. Moreover, the Brotherhood's strategy in relation to building in the workplaces left much greater space for activists from other political currents to organise. Although the Brotherhood had many worker members and made some efforts to get leading figures elected to positions in the official trade union federation, its activists were discouraged from organising workers to use their class power directly—through strikes, workplace occupations or protests. Instead, the Brotherhood broadly related to workplaces as vote banks for its candidates.[155]

The potential of the workplaces to act as incubators for popular revolutionary organisation was not simply a question of the presence or absence of particular political currents, however. Strike organisation maps directly onto some of the axes of permanent revolution outlined earlier in this chapter in ways that are more difficult to replicate in other settings. This is visible in the way that strikes moved from disruption (stopping production and services) to the construction of alternatives (even if this was limited in the pre-revolutionary period to

---

154 The long running battle over Qursaya Island in the Nile which pitted its poor residents against military-led efforts to redevelop it is one example. See Ali Eddin, 2013.
155 Alexander, 2021a.

building the strikers' *own* organisational capacity, for example through arranging logistics and food for workers' sit-ins, organising security at occupied workplaces, developing their own communications infrastructure). Strike organisation had demonstrably breached the walls separating 'economics' from 'politics' before the 2011 revolution on some occasions, winning *de facto* recognition for the independent union created by the Property Tax Collectors from a hostile state, and fragmenting the regime's apparatus of political control over the workplaces. This had political implications beyond the workplaces themselves, as the ruling party's electoral apparatus was partially rooted in the workplaces with the state trade union federation playing a crucial role in mobilising voters for the NDP's candidates. In addition, larger and longer strikes did create spaces for discussion and deliberation through mass meetings, as well as opportunities for rank-and-file members to exercise some control over the conduct of negotiations and the outcome of disputes.[156]

The strike wave which erupted after the revolutionary uprising had begun, generalised and expanded these experiences to much wider layers of society. 'Independent unions' mushroomed and the numbers of strikes and workers' protests soared. Revolutionary struggles in the workplaces began to breach the limits of trade unionism and in a minority of cases created conditions for workers' control. What set this process in motion was the battle for *tathir* (cleansing) of public institutions from managers loyal to the old ruling party and the regime. This took the form of strikes and protests by workers demanding the removal of *feloul al-nidham* (remnants of the regime).

There are many documented cases of workers forcibly removing their bosses themselves—for example by ejecting them from the building as the journalists at state-run magazine Rose el-Youssef did during the 18-day uprising, or by locking them in a cupboard as the staff of the Workers' University, the regime's trade union training centre did. Striking workers at Manshiet el-Bakry General Hospital agreed that the security guards (all members of the newly-founded independent hospital union) should be instructed to escort the hospital director off the premises after he refused to resign. Workers at Cairo Airport organised strikes and blockades of the airport

---

156 Alexander & Bassiouny, 2014, p157-191

access roads to force the Ministry of Civil Aviation to appoint a new civilian director for the first time in the Airport's history in July 2011.[157]

There were several ways in which *tathir* worked along the axes of permanent revolution outlined earlier. Firstly, the removal of *feloul* (remnants) of the ruling party immediately posed questions of whether to stop work in the absence of the boss or to self-manage. It also raised the question of who should replace him, and through which mechanism should the replacement be chosen, moving seamlessly from the tactics of disruption to questions of construction. In a small number of documented cases this included direct intervention by workers in both of these questions, not simply the 'vetting' of candidates proposed by higher levels of the state. The independent hospital union at Manshiet al-Bakry organised an election for a replacement to the old director, with hustings for candidates and ballot boxes supervised by bus drivers from the independent union at the Public Transport Authority. Council workers in one of the municipalities of Alexandria were reported to have to also elected a council worker to replace the general who had previously occupied the post of director.[158]

Movement between the political and economic aspects of the revolutionary process was deeply embedded in struggles for *tathir*. The demand to remove members of the ruling party from positions of power was clearly a political question, but it could not be separated from economic demands for several reasons. These included the fact that striking workers inevitably raised a whole host of other demands alongside their call to remove the *feloul*, including better pay, more secure jobs and the right to organise independent unions. Moreover, the strike wave which persisted and expanded in the immediate aftermath of Mubarak's fall was a direct challenge to those among opposition activists and the emerging revolutionary movement who argued that now the dictator had gone, everyone should "get back to work" and wait for constitutional change and elections to bring about change.

The bodies which developed inside workplaces to carry out tasks along the axes of permanent revolution included strike committees and independent unions. The loosening of state

---

157 Bassiouny & Alexander, 2021.
158 Alexander & Bassiouny, 2014.

control over the workplaces and the early successes of *tathir* created conditions for experimentation with forms of organising which had been previously extremely difficult to carry out. In some cases, this process was shaped by the democratic impulses of workers' collective action, through mass meetings and workers' conferences which elected committee members for new independent unions.

There are some examples where the comparison with the workplace councils of the Iranian revolution are clearly apt. The degree of democratic control exercised by the hospital workers in Manshiyet al-Bakri general hospital over their workplace, the clear relationship with the basic processes of the revolution and the transformation of service delivery and patient care all point to this. There were a number of deliberate choices made by the organisers of the independent union in the hospital which worked at the micro level to deepen these processes. One of the most important was the levelling of professional hierarchies by creating a single hospital union representing all grades of staff, careful attention to democratic internal organisation and the partial extension of those principles to the management of the hospital.[159]

However, the label 'independent union' was also applied to new bodies which lacked firm roots in the struggle—sometimes set up opportunistically, without setting up mechanisms for democratic accountability and in isolation from strikes and collective action.[160] The loosening of the regime's control over the workplaces not only created the conditions for deeper and more radical struggles, it also paradoxically made reformist strategies for solving to workers' problems appear more realistic and achievable. Tendencies towards bureaucratic models of trade union organising in the independent unions were already visible even in the short period between the emergence of the first independent union in 2008 and the eruption of revolution in 2011. Some these pressures were inherent in trade unionism itself, which by its nature seeks to negotiate the amelioration of workers' conditions of exploitation through a combination of negotiation and the pressure of collective action. There were also specific forms of bureaucratisation driven both by pressures towards NGOisation and by intervention from the international

---

159 Ibrahim, 2012; Alexander & Bassiouny, 2014.
160 Bassiouny & Alexander, 2021.

trade union bureaucracy (especially the ITUC), which worked closely with the leaders of the Property Tax Collectors' Union.[161]

One of the key absences in the experience of the independent unions both before and during the revolution was in cross-sectoral or geographically-coordinated strike action. The federations of independent unions which were set up during the revolution never became effective *strike organising* bodies, instead they usually functioned more like pressure groups or campaigns for workers' rights. They often focussed specifically on winning concessions from the state over questions which mattered more to the emerging trade union bureaucracy such as the right to organise and legal recognition for the independent unions, rather than coordinating action on the core problems faced by rank-and-file workers. The independent union movement was also beset by bureaucratic competition partially driven by personal rivalries and not only by matters of political principle or differences in practice.

The approach of leading figures in the independent unions to the relationship between economic and political struggles in the context of the revolution was complex.[162] It was not the case that they simply eschewed 'politics' and argued that trade unions should stick to 'economic' questions or distance themselves from the revolutionary movement (although there were certainly some who began to push for a more 'professionalised' and 'apolitical' approach to trade unionism). There was some suspicion of 'party politics' (*hizbiyya* in Arabic), but the party allegiances of activists in the independent unions were quite heterogenous. These included not only well-known figures in the Nasserist opposition Dignity Party such as Kamal Abu-Aita, the first president of the Egyptian Federation of Independent Trade Unions, but even members of Salafist political parties such as Al-Nour and Al-Hadaf. When I asked him how he dealt with possible contradictions between his role as a political activist and his role as trade union leader, Abu-Aita told me that he kept "two shirts" in his cupboard, a "political shirt" for engagement in electoral or party political activities and a "trade union shirt" for his role in EFITU.

When it came to the question of whether trade union activists

---

161 Alexander & Bassiouny, 2014, p83–7.
162 This section is based on the author's discussions with leading Egyptian independent trade union activists during 2011-2

could participate *as organised workers* not in party politics, but in the revolutionary mobilisations in the streets and squares, such neat distinctions were hard to maintain. EFITU was in fact formed in Tahrir Square at a meeting held during the 18-day uprising which launched the revolution, and EFITU's leadership did attempt to build an organised presence for the independent unions in the Square at various points. This included organising a May Day march and celebration in the Square in 2011, setting up a tent during the sit-in which re-occupied Tahrir in November 2011 and attempting to organise a trade union march a few days later. Independent trade unions were also present in the Square in December 2012 during the mass protests against the new constitution following the Muslim Brotherhood's election victory in June 2012. EFITU's leaders made statements calling on workers to strike in support of the November 2011 sit-in and backed the call by a coalition of revolutionary movements for a general strike on 11 February 2012.

The problem was that none of these efforts did in fact mobilise large enough numbers to embed the independent unions (or any other kinds of workers' organisations) as a component element within a revolutionary movement, let alone as part of its leadership. Workers' struggles took place *in parallel* with the mass mobilisations in the streets in the early stages of the revolution, and although they accelerated the dynamics of the revolutionary process as they *interlaced* with street protests and sit-ins, the separation between its political and economic aspects was never really overcome. Unlike in Sudan in 2019, political general strikes did not emerge as an effective weapon in the struggle against dictatorship, either on a local or national level. The revolutionary movement which developed during 2011 firstly castigated workers for 'selfish' strike action in the wake of Mubarak's fall, then largely ignored the workplaces as a possible space for revolutionary mobilisation for the rest of the year.

The weakness of the organisational connections between collective action in the workplaces and continuing revolutionary mobilisations in the streets helps to explain why the shift towards agitation for a general strike in February 2012 on the anniversary of the fall of Mubarak did not produce the results which revolutionary activists hoped for. However, it was unlikely to have been the only reason. The cycle of parliamentary and

Revolution is the choice of the people

presidential elections in 2011 and 2012 meant that there appeared to be a choice between the ballot box on the one hand, and street protests or strikes on the other as means to bring about further political and economic change.

The Muslim Brotherhood and its allies certainly counterposed voting to collective action when campaigning against the February 2012 general strike call.[163] Millions of Egyptians who had known only the ritual of the sham elections which returned the ruling party to office every few years were prepared to give the former opposition party a chance in government. Meanwhile, the mood among the revolutionary youth currents was strongly for a boycott of the elections. Electoral abstentionism also affected the nascent Democratic Workers' Party, an initiative involving the revolutionary left and key trade unionists.[164]

Between 2012 and 2013, the implications of the economic and political struggles in the workplaces and streets for the development of the revolutionary process began to diverge, rather than simply running along parallel tracks in broadly the same direction. The movement in the streets confronted a government which was led by the Muslim Brotherhood following Mohamed Morsi's narrow victory in the presidential elections of June 2012. Over the course of the following year, the politics of the National Salvation Front, a coalition of parties which included Liberal, Arab Nationalist, Stalinist organisations and figures from the old ruling party came to dominate the mass mobilisations on the streets.

Meanwhile, battles in the workplaces continued over issues of pay, working conditions and the right to organise, but started to take on a defensive character as employers went on the offensive against the gains made by the workers' movement during the first year of the revolution.[165] The focus of the NSF's demands on fighting the "Brotherhoodisation" of the state and its open alliance with a key component of the old regime, the judiciary (even if this was often cloaked in liberal rhetoric about the "separation of powers" and "judicial independence") began to feed back into the workplaces. In the Civil Aviation sector, for example, this language was used to rehabilitate

---

163 Alexander, 2021a.
164 Alexander, 2021a.
165 Alexander & Bassiouny 2014, p221-3.

the appointment of military figures as a bulwark against a Brotherhood takeover.[166]

The pivot around which the cycle of revolution and counter-revolution turned was the events of 30 June 2013 the massive protests against Morsi which provided the backdrop to the military coup of 3 July. Could things have played out differently with the development of different kinds of popular revolutionary organisation? Asking this question is no mere indulgence in counterfactual fantasy, but a necessary part of debating strategies for the future. One problem which the experience of the mass movement in the streets during 2012-3 exposed was the over-reliance on mobilisation through social and mass media channels and their lack of roots in spaces where ordinary people could debate through the demands and slogans being raised, propose alternatives or additions or seek to change the movement's direction.

In the case of Sudan, where the Resistance Committees often developed genuine, democratic roots in neighbourhoods where their leadership was known to local people, and where they could be held accountable over their choice of demands and slogans in forums they deliberately created to build a popular base for the revolutionary movement. The contrast with the plebiscitary broadcasts of the key Facebook pages mobilising the movement against the Muslim Brotherhood government in Egypt especially during the run-up to the 30 June demonstrations is stark.[167]

Yet why did organisations in Egyptian workplaces not provide this kind of alternative leadership for the revolutionary movement? Here the tragedy was that despite extremely high levels of strikes and protests, trade unionism as model for workers' organisation was not able to reconnect the severed social and political souls of the revolutionary process. For that to happen, a much larger layer of activists in the workplaces needed to adopt an explicitly revolutionary agenda.

---

166 Alexander & Bassiouny 2014, p317.
167 One of the key youth movements which called for the 30 June protests and played a major role in mobilising against Morsi was Tamarod (Rebellion). Unverified recordings which leaked in 2015 suggest that the Egyptian army and the UAE funded Tamarod's campaign against Morsi. See Kirkpatrick, 2015.

Revolution is the choice of the people

The tragedy of Syria's revolutionary communes

The Syrian experience provides the clearest examples of instances of revolutionary government which in some cases did emerge out of the self-organisation of ordinary people as they mobilised to confront the Ba'thist state. Ghayath Naisse argues:

> In many places there were elections for representatives of the population for the first time. Although this did not happen everywhere, there are many examples of elections of councils to manage people's lives in 2011 and 2012. They oversaw sanitation and waste disposal, organised bread for people to eat and provided education. The popular classes created their own organs of self-organisation that were at the same time coordinating the development of the revolution.[168]

These "organs of self-organisation" included the revolutionary councils which sprang up following the retreat of regime forces from Idlib and Aleppo provinces by mid-2012. As Abdesalam Dallal and Julie Hearn note:

> Civilian revolutionary organisation stepped in with the formation, initially, of revolutionary councils or *al-Majalis al-thawriyyah*, later known as local councils (*al-Majalis al-Mahalliyah*). These often sprang from the local coordination committees (LCCs, *Lijan Attanseeq al-Mahalliyyah "al-Tansiqiyat"*), which had been set up to organise and document the initial pro-democracy protests. Revolutionaries now saw their attention focused on meeting the emergency needs of a village or town under attack.[169]

The first instance where revolutionary activists created a local revolutionary council was in the town of al-Zabadani in the Rif Dimashq province close to the Lebanese border in January 2012.[170] The political inspiration for this experiment reportedly came from Syrian anarchist Omar Aziz, who was involved

---

168 Alexander, 2021a.
169 Hearn & Dallal, 2019a.
170 Hearn & Dallal, 2019a.

Egypt, Syria and Sudan: results and prospects

directly in the council's formation. Aziz's 2011 article arguing for the creation of revolutionary organs of local government to take over from the local authorities of the Ba'thist regime was widely circulated.[171] Other rebellious suburbs of the capital also witnessed the formation of revolutionary councils, including in Barzeh, Darayya and Douma. Anand Gopal's detailed account of the formation and development of the Local Council in Saraqib between 2012 and 2017, provides a compelling narrative of the major challenges faced by Syrian revolutionary activists.[172] This "melancholy one-post-office town" in Idlib province with a population of around 30,000 was in many ways an unlikely incubator for experiments in democratic self-government. As in much of the rest of the country there were few prior experiences that activists could draw on to guide them in developing any kind of political organisation, let alone institutions of self-government. Before the revolution "there was no point in thinking about politics, because we felt like the regime was everywhere—even in the bedroom," Hossein, one of the leaders of the Local Council told Gopal. These young university students, farmers and labourers had "no clear idea of what should replace the government".

> None of them besides Hossein had ever read a political tract or attended a party meeting. The regime had so impoverished civic life that the activists' unity was based entirely on what they opposed: corruption, the rising cost of bread, the daily degradations of dictatorship.[173]

Hossein argued against armed resistance but emerged after a spell in prison to find that his friends, "once mere teachers and construction workers, were now armed, each a master of his own brigade". In the autumn of 2012, it seemed that these fighters, mainly local men who had taken up arms to defend themselves against the state, had been vindicated. Across the country, the Syrian army was rapidly losing ground to the hydra-headed armed rebellion. The remaining government forces were expelled from the town in November, leaving the revolutionary activists with the question of how to keep the lights on and ensure people would be fed. They formed a

---

171 Al-Shami, 2021.
172 Gopal, 2018.
173 Gopal, 2018.

Revolution is the choice of the people

12-member local council to govern the town and named Hossein its first president.

The Saraqib Local Council clearly enjoyed a much deeper popular mandate than the institutions of dictatorship which had ruled for the previous fifty years. Local residents repeatedly risked their lives to defend its "civil" authority against attempts by armed Islamist groups (first Ahrar al-Sham and later the al-Qa'idah affiliated Jabhat al-Nusra) to seize control of the town and its resources. They confronted the gunmen with mass protests and several times forced them to withdraw. They created a flourishing culture of democratic discussion in an active local media scene and mobilised a successful campaign for an election which was eventually held in 2017, despite Jabhat al-Nusra storming the town at the conclusion of the vote.

The conditions of war and siege created intense pressures on the fragile growth of democracy from below, however. Survival was often the most urgent task, and Hossein was well aware that success in the struggle to keep the lights on and flour arriving in the town bakery was key to the Local Council's authority. Unlike many in the region, Saraqib's council managed to do both, at one point securing continued supplies of flour by threatening the governor in regime-controlled provincial capital Idlib that revolutionaries would blow up the main electricity line which ran through the town.

In Manbij, close to the Turkish border, the "politics of bread" also illuminate the limitations on the authority of the Local Council which ruled the town of 200,000 as a miniature city-state between July 2012 and January 2014. As Yasser Munif notes, the origins of the Local Council in Manbij were directly rooted in the popular movement opposing the Assad regime which mobilised at a neighbourhood level through protests and "creative peaceful actions".[174]

> The revolutionary council and activist groups in the city also began a process of de-Ba'thification, deploying a combination of traditional knowledge and decolonial practices. The experimental legal system that the city assembled in 2012–13 is one such example. It was based on the Unified Arab Law, tribal customs, vernacular knowledge, and articles debated at the

---

174 Munif, 2021.

revolutionary trustee council's monthly meetings.[175]

Manbij's flour mill is one of the largest in northern Syriaand can process enough wheat to feed 1 million people a day, far beyond the needs of the city itself. Even after withdrawing from Manbij, the Assad regime continued to supply the mill with wheat and to pay the mill manger and staff, hoping to bolster its base of support within the city and stage a rapid reconquest with support from inside.

> In 2013, the director and his employees threatened to leave, due to repeated disputes with various powerful actors in the city. As a result, the revolutionary council created a team of volunteers to shadow the mill's technicians and engineers, in order to gain the necessary skills to operate the mill independently. In this way, the revolutionary council sought to strengthen the city's autonomy.[176]

The Ba'thist regime's retention of a degree of leverage over the operation of essential manufacturing, production and service sectors in Manbij was not an isolated case. It negotiated with ISIS to keep the lights on in Damascus by continuing to employ the workers operating the oil refinery at Palmyra despite losing military control of the area to the jihadist group.[177] The regime also continued to pay the wages of teachers and other state employees in areas which fell to rebel control, although often using this leverage as a form of remote control to reward loyalists and punish teachers active in the opposition.[178]

The case of the Manbij flour mill demonstrates how when the Ba'thist state's control over the lives of Syria's people began to fragment it often did not evaporate all at once, producing fully "liberated territories" where new revolutionary institutions could begin to exercise authority (even if this was contained within small, besieged enclaves). Rather, it often created conditions for layered, competing sovereignty with multiple bodies jostling for power in different spheres of life.

---

175 Munif, 2021.
176 Munif ,2021.
177 Solomon, 2015.
178 Khaddour, 2015, p7.

Revolution is the choice of the people

By the time that the local revolutionary movements were able to exercise any degree of local control over public affairs and service delivery, the fragmentation of forces opposed to the regime were already well under way.

A part of this story is the rise of armed Islamist currents deeply hostile to the democratic and "civil" impulses of the wave of popular mobilisations which had launched the revolutionary process. As Saraqib's experience illustrates, local s had to first contend with the challenges of working with (and sometimes against) local armed brigades which labelled themselves part of the Free Syrian Army (FSA) but lacked any kind of coherent national command structure. Islamist armed factions, whose military rise was fuelled by funding from the Gulf and the influx of commanders who had gained experience fighting in Iraq, Afghanistan and elsewhere in the international jihadist conflict circuit, proved even more difficult to deal with. This was not only because they were more efficient fighters and better funded, but because their political vision directly competed with the civilian revolutionary groups in areas such as the creation of alternative justice systems and service delivery.[179]

In addition, the local councils had to contend with the pressures of co-optation by Western governments, especially the US and its allies, as the latter attempted to divert the trajectory of the revolution in a direction which suited their goals. The US and other Western governments recognised and provided diplomatic and financial support to exiled opposition parties, hoping to weld them together into something which could ultimately replace the Assad regime.

> The United States and its donor partners viewed the Syrian opposition's fragmentation as a major weakness in its potential to emerge as a viable counterstate. Consequently, they devised local projects to build up a more cohesive, broader political opposition body to the Assad regime. The scores of local councils that surfaced early in the uprising had clear revolutionary credentials and grassroots energy, but donors believed that these activists needed to cohere into a larger "political mass" to counterbalance the regime.[180]

179 Alexander, 2015
180 Brown, 2018.

"Politically oriented assistance" to local councils in rebel held areas provided by the US and other Western donors between 2011 and 2018 included more than $1 billion worth of funding for interventions to support democracy and participation, build legitimacy and popular support for the local councils, improve their administration and service provision in areas such as water, sanitation, waste removal, bakery operation and power generation.[181] Meanwhile, the civilian revolutionary movements were also subject to intense pressures of 'NGOisation' as Julie Hearn and Abdulsalam Dallal have noted, as the relatively small amounts of Western aid which did find its way to these local bodies was made contingent on the professionalisation of 'service delivery', turning "revolution into a "humanitarian crisis" and transforming the consciousness of the young revolutionaries who came to work for them into that of "neutral humanitarians".[182]

In order to understand why the local councils and other popular revolutionary bodies ended up trapped in this situation, we have to go back to the specific ways in which they formed in in relation to the axes of permanent revolution mapped out in the previous chapter. The shift from disrupting the state to constructing the foundations of alternative local governments was clear to see in the relationship between the activist Coordinating Committees and the Local Councils in many areas of the country. The revolution was also in many ways a uprising of Syria's multiple peripheries: Dera'a in the south where the revolution began, to the rebellious working class and poor suburbs on the semi-rural fringe of Damascus, to Deir el-Zor and Raqqa and the northern governorates. The problem for the popular movement was that the regime was largely successful in preventing revolution reaching the public squares and workplaces of the major urban centres during its first year.

"The lessons from Egypt and Tunisia were to prevent people from gathering in major city squares. At all costs they had to prevent this," explains Ghayath Naisse.[183] On the rare occasions when protesters did manage to break through in large numbers, the regime's response was unspeakably violent".[184] The regime's

---

181 Brown, 2018.
182 Hearn & Dallal, 2019.
183 Alexander, 2021a.
184 Alexander, 2021a.

ideological grip on public sector institutions had not broken down, argues Salam Ahmad:

> Whoever was planning to strike to demand their rights would be informed upon by their colleagues, and they would be detained and tortured. Society was atomised through these associations. People would proudly claim to be part of the trade unions or the teachers' syndicates; but these organisations were controlled by the Ba'ath Party and the security and intelligence services.[185]

Even one year into the revolution, the regime could still mobilise tens of thousands of workers from public services and state institutions to fill the streets with crowds cheering for the dictator. Activists like Salam were forced to join these rallies, mouthing slogans of praise for the regime during the day, while at night they would secretly organise protests in support of the revolution.

> One day, I was called by the head of the school to submit my identity papers, and he took my details and gave them to the Ba'ath Party branch in the nearest town. They would send us a minibus to go to Aleppo and show our support for the leader, and if I didn't go, the regime would come and get me. It was full. The main square of Aleppo, Saadallah al-Jabri Square, was full. University students, university lecturers, university staff, school teachers, school students. All the state institutions were gathering there, and the helicopter was, of course, livestreaming the rally. If you watched the television it was saying, "The people of Aleppo came together to show their support for the Assad regime. They came to support their support for the leader, confirm their willingness to stop the conspiracy and show their love to their home".[186]

The capacity of workers *inside* the state machinery to repurpose it to aid mobilisation for their own demands was one of the major differences between the uprisings in Tunisia, Egypt,

---

185 Alexander, 2021a.
186 Alexander, 2021a.

Sudan and Algeria, and those such as Syria and Libya. Coupled with strikes in critical industries and infrastructure such as transport, communications, and financial services—both those in private and public ownership—the rebellion of public service workers temporarily disrupted the circuits of state power at critical points in the uprisings.

The absence of the working class not just as a political actor, but even as an economic one had a significant impact on the trajectory of the revolution as the revolutionary mobilisations were unable to paralyse key state institutions or effectively shut down the major cities such as the capital Damascus and Aleppo during the initial phase of the uprising. This in turn allowed the regime to isolate rebellious districts through sieges and bombardment, accelerating the militarisation of the popular resistance as local men defected from the Syrian army to defend their families and neighbourhoods. The character of the organisations which came to dominate the armed struggle proved a powerful counterweight to the initial relatively democratic, egalitarian and anti-sectarian impulses of the popular movement.[187]

The absence of precursor class struggles *inside* a public sector spanning key industries such as food processing, power, water and telecoms infrastructure and nationwide public services, including the health and education systems, came back to haunt the activists of the popular revolutionary movements even *after* the regime's military withdrawal as we saw in the case of Manbij. Why was the director of the flour mill able to continue acting in the regime's interests unconstrained by resistance from among the mill employees? Why was the revolutionary council not able to persuade any of them to switch allegiance and isolate him? The plan formulated to 'shadow' existing employees suggests that part of the problem lay in the regime's ideological hold over people in technical and professional roles, rather than being simply about the failure of manual workers at the mill to support the revolution. Munif's account of this conflict emphasises the resilience of the Ba'thist bureaucracy but does not ask why it proved more effective than similar authoritarian ruling parties in the region at suppressing the internal class tensions between those at the bottom and middle layers of the employment hierarchy in the public sector who were coerced into party

---

[187] Alexander & Bouharoun, 2016.

membership but had much more to gain from the success of the revolution than their senior managers.

The regime's ability to maintain an indirect presence in many of the liberated areas shows how questions of democracy in revolutions are never solely resolved in the realm of politics but will be inevitably posed in relation to the issue of 'who controls the workplaces?'. In order to properly break the hold of those Ba'thist bureaucrats over the mass of manual and white-collar workers inside the public sector both in the areas controlled by the regime and in the liberated territories, it was not enough to present an alternative model of revolutionary government. The school teachers, civil servants, nurses, doctors, transport workers, oil workers and flour mill workers who formed the backbone of the public sector also had to liberate *themselves*, through their own collective action against their party bosses.

The problem of whether revolution could be achieved *without* this process of self-liberation from below underlay the dilemmas faced by the form of autonomous government created by the Kurdish PYD party and affiliated militias in Rojava, the Kurdish name given to the three districts of Afrin, Kobani and Cizîrê (or Afrin, Ayn al-Arab and Jazīrat Ibn 'Umar in Arabic). There is not space here to do justice to the complexity of the political, social and military struggles over these territories and their relationship to the wider conflicts which engulfed the region.

However, some key points can still be distilled which are important to the questions discussed in this chapter, namely whether the communes or local assemblies of Rojava were another instance of popular revolutionary bodies akin to experiments in revolutionary democracy outlined in the previous chapter.

David Graeber, writing after visiting Rojava in 2014, argued that these autonomous areas were experiencing a situation of "dual power".

> On the one hand, there is the democratic self-administration, which looks very much like a government, replete with ministries, parliament, and higher courts. If you simply read the formal constitution of the Rojava cantons you would have very little sign this was anything other than an enlightened social

Egypt, Syria and Sudan: results and prospects

democratic, or perhaps at most democratic socialist, state. It includes numerous political parties but was largely set up by the PYD. On the other there's the bottom-up structures, organized by TEV-DEM, the Movement for a Democratic Society, many of whose members are also PYD or former PYD, where initiative flows entirely from popular assemblies.[188]

However, unlike situations where "dual power" was formed through contestation between *rival* authorities,

The unique thing is that this seems to be the only known case of a dual power situation where both sides are not just in alliance, as in Bolivia, but were actually set up by the same movement, even, in some cases, the same individuals.[189]

Cihad Hammy provides an account of the formation of the commune in Kobani which emphasizes that the initiative in creating these democratic bodies came directly from Abdullah Ocalan, the imprisoned leader of the PYD, rather than being born out of the self-activity of ordinary people.

The Canton system does not entirely follow my vision. Communes must be built," a PYD member read Abdullah Ocalan's letter from Imrali among a few other members of PYD in the Kobane canton in 2014. The member paused for a bit after closing Ocalan's letter and addressed his friends, "We have a new task to do, friends". ... After Ocalan's call for establishing communes in Rojava, some members of PYD and other civil people came to gather to initiate the first commune in Kobane. The group was comprised of 10 people—4 women and 6 men—varying in terms of age and social status.[190]

As Hammy and Jeff Miley point out, the way in which the PYD and its military forces established actual authority over the territories which would later become Rojava, differed

---

188 Knapp, Flach & Ayboğa, 2016.
189 Knapp, Flach & Ayboğa, 2016.
190 Hammy, 2018.

substantially from the vision of direct democracy articulated by the anarchist writer Murray Bookchin, whose work has been influential in shaping Ocalan's political programme for the creation of "Democratic Confederalism".[191]

> The circumstances in which the revolutionary forces came to power thus differ quite substantially from the scenario of dual power envisioned by Bookchin. For Bookchin foresaw a grassroots movement gaining momentum, growing from the bottom up, progressively raising the consciousness of the citizenry, provoking a conflict with the state. What happened in Rojava, by contrast, was more of a military achievement than anything else, accomplished by cohesive and well-trained armed groups, affiliated with the PYD, who proved able to take advantage of a vacuum of power triggered by a civil war. A civil war, we should add, that it did not provoke, and towards which it did its best to maintain a posture of neutrality.[192]

A further problem was that the opening of a "third path" for the PYD, allowing it to continue "siding neither with the increasingly Islamized and armed [Syrian] opposition, nor with the Baath regime,"[193] was conditional on a particular conjuncture in the geopolitical conflicts in the region. Specifically, it required that the US, because it desired to enlist PYD military forces in order to halt the growth of ISIS, the jihadist movement which had seized power in Raqqa and Mosul, would put pressure on its longstanding ally Turkey to tolerate the existence of a PYD-administered Kurdish entity on its borders, despite the decades-long war by the Turkish authorities against the PYD's sister party the PKK (which counted Ocalan as its founder).

For a short while this compromise did in fact hold, as the result of a variety of factors, including a relative relaxation of repression against Kurdish parties and political activity inside Turkey allowing for example, the pro-Kurdish Peoples' Democratic Party (HDP) to win substantial votes in parliamentary elections and mobilise large protests in solidarity

---

191 Ocalan, 2011.
192 Hammy & Miley, 2022.
193 Hammy & Miley, 2022.

with Rojava.[194] However, there was a sharp shift in the policies of the Turkish government, as Recep Tayyip Erdogan's AKP party reignited the war with the PKK in 2015 and embarked on a vicious crackdown against anyone arguing for Kurdish rights inside Turkey, which led to the arrest and dismissal of hundreds of academics and state employees.[195] The tragedy of Syria's communes thus was repeated in a variant form across Rojava. The establishment of "revolutionary" municipal authorities as a by-product of armed conflict, without the simultaneous expansion of workers' power in the workplaces (especially in strategically important industries and services on which the state relied to carry out its functions) meant that visions of alternatives to the state remained at best aspirations and at worst ideological cover for distinctly undemocratic military and bureaucratic forms of rule.[196]

Sudan: All power to the Resistance Committees?

Sudan's Resistance Committees are clearly much more advanced in terms of their scale and political development than the embryonic popular bodies of the Egyptian revolution and have created deeper and richer forms of popular democracy than was possible in the Syrian context. Yet at the time of writing, they were still grappling with the problem of not having overcome the military regime which seized power in October 2021. Although the Resistance Committees' work in developing popular charters and visions for radical political reform, often envisaged this process as being genuinely democratic and bottom-up, only a tiny minority of Sudanese revolutionary activists were prepared to raise the idea of building something which was an alternative form of state power.

Following the military coup of 25 October, which forcibly ended the "partnership" between the military and militia generals and civilian opposition parties in the Transitional Government, the Resistance Committees have emerged as a real and effective leadership of a mass popular movement committed to resisting the restoration of military rule through

---

194 Margulies, 2018.
195 Kaya, 2018.
196 Hammy & Miley, 2022.

protests, strikes and various forms of civil disobedience. The resurgence of the revolutionary movement from below has been accompanied by intense activity at a local level, which at the time of writing was engaging hundreds of thousands of people in political debates and discussions over the future course of the revolution.

Despite having confidently disposed of their civilian 'partners' in the Transitional Government the generals found themselves unable to calm the streets. Abdalla Hamdok, the Prime Minister who negotiated his way back out of house arrest by agreeing to most of the military's demands in a widely-decried deal backed by Western government and the counter-revolutionary quartet of regional powers (Saudi Arabia, UAE, Egypt and Israel) on 21 November finally resigned on 2 January 2022. The upsurge in the popular movement did not benefit the civilian parties who had been kicked out power, however. As Muzan Alneel noted in March 2022,

> Activists have joked that the slogan of "The Three Nos" (no negotiations, no partnership, no legitimacy) adopted by the resistance committees has reversed the job description of these civilian parties. After the overthrow of the El Bashir regime, the entire purpose of these parties was to carry out negotiations, seek partnership with the military and provide them with legitimacy. This slogan has cancelled the role of these parties. They are as much in crisis as the military are.[197]

The same could be said of the Sudanese Professionals Association, which played an important role in the 2019 uprising against Umar al-Bashir, but split into two factions and was also tarnished by the failures of the Transitional Government its leaders helped to create.

Organised through district-wide 'Coordinations' (*tansiqiyyat* in Arabic), the committees now command a formidable machinery of collective action. The infrastructure of protest has come a long way since the first gatherings of desperate people in December 2018 shouting for bread and cooking gas on street corners. Their Facebook pages count 'likes' in the tens of thousands, they have their own media teams, press officers

---

197   Alneel & Abdelrahman, 2022e.

and networks to gather intelligence on the location of the police and adjust the location of barricades or the route of marches. They are not simply a product of the dynamics of revolutionary contestation in the capital. A report by the Carter Center based on a large-scale survey carried out in March 2021 mapped 5289 Resistance Committees across Sudan—the researchers found committees were a nation-wide phenomenon.[198]

Resistance Committees distributed by province[1]

Province	Number of Resistance Committees mapped
Blue Nile	338
South and West Kordofan	199
Eastern Sudan	705
Greater Darfur	809
White Nile & Greater Kordofan	601
Central Sudan	1,173
North Sudan	650
Khartoum	814
Total	5,289

During the period the Transitional Government was in office some Resistance Committees were already intervening in matters of everyday life in their areas, such as ensuring the supply of flour to bakeries and the distribution of bread and cooking gas. At the beginning of the Covid-19 pandemic some sent out teams of activists to spread public health messages and distribute face masks and sanitiser.199 In many areas, a formal division of labour emerged between the neighbourhood political leadership embodied in the Resistance Committee and a Change and Services Committee which brings together revolutionary activists working specifically on improving the delivery of services. Often this division of labour maps onto a generational divide, with younger activists leading the Resistance Committee. Since the October 2021 coup more ambitious plans have been published by some committees. In a video posted on Facebook on 29 March 2022, the Resistance

---

198 Carter Center, 2021.
199 Alexander and Bak, 2020

Committee in Burri al-Diraysa, a district of Khartoum, outlined local goals including the establishment of local productive and consumer cooperatives to "ease the burden of living and increase the income of the population", drafting a local government law in coordination with other Resistance Committees, taking initiatives in collaboration with the local Change and Services Committee to develop policies for local development projects and services in areas such as health and education, public libraries, green spaces and tourist facilities.[200]

The video connects this participatory experiment in re-imagining local government with the idea of "Basic Construction" (*al-bina'a al-qa'idi*). Initially this was a process which involved refreshing or setting up their internal structures on a more democratic basis through convening general assemblies and electing new leadership bodies, begun in the months before the coup of October 2021 by some Resistance Committees in the capital city and other major centres including Gadaref and Port Sudan. Some unions and workplace-based networks of activists including university teachers, pharmacists, media workers were reported to be undergoing similar processes. According to activist Khalid al-Sheikh on Facebook, Resistance Committees in the district of Khartoum Bahri launched a campaign of basic construction following the failed attempt at a military coup on 21 September 2021. The committees in Um Duwwan Ban, a small town 40 km south of Khartoum declared basic construction was the "real coup" against the military's "state of the ghouls".[201]

The political crisis of the Forces of Freedom and Change and the deepening split between the civilian parties willing to negotiate with the military and the mood on the streets and neighbourhoods pushed the Resistance Committees towards the development of a series of political declarations or charters. As with the process of 'Basic Construction', the charters were developed through a process involving widespread consultation and discussion with local residents through surveys, mass meetings and debates.[202] The scope of the charters showed that activists in the Resistance Committees now wanted to address the challenges facing the revolutionary movement at a national

200 Thuwar, 2022.
201 Alexander, 2022a.
202 Alneel & Abdelrahman, 2022.

level, by posing direct alternatives to existing state policies and institutions. Sami Muhammad Abd-al-Halim, official spokesperson for the Coordinations of Resistance Committees in Khartoum announced in December 2021 that the charter developed by the capital city's Resistance Committees would address "the economy, reform of the military and security apparatus, national borders and foreign relations and living conditions".[203] The document was eventually published in February 2022, under the title "Charter for the Establishment of the People's Authority".[204]

One of the first political charters to be published was, however, authored by the Resistance Committees in Wad Madani, the capital of Al Jazirah province in Central Sudan, and later revised and adopted by Resistance Committees in seven Sudanese states as "The Revolutionary Charter for People's Power".[205] As Muzan Alneel notes, the Madani RC's document proposed a more radical vision of a reformed Sudanese state than the Khartoum charter.

Many voices reject the road map for government formation proposed by the Khartoum resistance committees, which calls for appointing the prime minister first, and then the national assembly, state-level assemblies and legislative bodies. The prior publication of alternative proposals by the Madani resistance committees and others has boosted the voices of those who see the flaws in the Khartoum resistance committees' proposal. It is frequently argued that the Madani proposal is closer to implementing "people's power" because its road map starts from the local assemblies then goes to the state level and national assembly, which appoints the prime minister. The process of the different proposals being shared and discussed publicly is adding to the depth of the debates taking place.[206]

The charters point to the ambiguity which surrounds the highly participatory forms of democracy created by the Resistance Committees. Are they building the institutions of a new state, or refreshing the bottom layers of the old one? Mohamed Abdelrahman points out:

"Basic construction" is a plausible experiment, but we

---

203   Ayin Network, 2021.
204   MENA Solidarity, 2022b.
205   Alneel & Abdelrahman, 2022.
206   Alneel & Abdelrahman, 2022.

should keep in mind that it can be hijacked by the state and absorbed into its bureaucracy. For instance, one view on basic construction suggests electing different representatives from the neighbourhoods through different geographical levels and all the way up to parliament. Yet, if basic construction is understood in this way, then its work has to be done within the legislative framework of the state.[207]

The scale and scope of the democratic experiment led by the Resistance Committees strongly underscores the argument that the emergence of such popular revolutionary bodies is related to the development of the process of permanent revolution along the three axes outlined earlier in this chapter. The connection between *disruption* of the military regime through protests, strikes and civil disobedience and the *construction* of alternatives is clear from the examples discussed above. Moreover, as the Resistance Committees moved from protest mobilisation and logistical support into the political leadership of the mass movement as a response to the coup of October 2021, the constructive aspect of their role became more apparent, growing in scope from building their internal democratic processes, to issuing political charters and consciously intervening to reshape local government, production and services in their image.

In contrast to Syria, movement along the second axis from political to economic struggles and back again was much clearer in the case of Sudan, although the development of popular revolutionary bodies in the workplaces lagged behind those in the neighbourhoods. The initial stage of this process preceded the eruption of revolution in December 2018, through strikes in the health and education sector led by junior doctors and teachers which built the independent union networks and laid the basis for the formation of the Sudanese Professionals Association. Health workers led the way in using the weapon of strike action, as opposed to protests, as the uprising grew in the last weeks of 2018. The rising profile of the SPA in the popular movement by the spring opened the door to the use of political general strikes as a tactic to increase pressure on the regime, especially after the fall of El Bashir in the face of manoeuvres by the military and militia leaders of the Transitional Military Council to retain political power for themselves.

---

207 Alneel & Abdelrahman, 2022.

Egypt, Syria and Sudan: results and prospects

Although these general strikes were in a sense called 'from above', by the political leadership of the mass movement, rather than being led by workers' organisations rooted in the workplaces, they were widely supported, mobilising new layers of people in support of the revolution's demands, and clearly caused a crisis for the TMC. The general strike of 28-29 May was followed by the forced clearance of the protest sit-in outside the Army General Command in Khartoum and the massacre of over 100 protesters on 3 June. This was turning point for the revolutionary movement, and the context for the first intimations that the Resistance Committees could move towards political independence from the SPA and the FFC parties. As Magdi el-Gizouli recounts, the fury in some neighbourhoods after the 3 June massacre was channelled through the Resistance Committees as activists confronted the SPA leaders demanding they refuse backroom negotiations with the military and continue the struggle for civilian rule.

Representatives of the SPA and FFC were hard pressed to explain their choices to angry young women and men around the capital in political rallies organized by the neighbourhood committees. The Burri Lions, champions of Khartoum's epicentre of protest, were hard to convince and shouted down one speaker after another. Only the SPA star, Mohamed Naji al-Assam, an able communicator, could manage their disappointment with the compromise that the SPA and its allies were about to make with the establishment. Nobody showed up to soothe the anger of Kalakla.[208]

Another general strike 9-11 June further increased the pressure on the generals and paved the way for the signing of the agreement which established the Transitional Government in August 2019.

As in Egypt in 2011, there were signs that the political progress of the revolutionary movement could open the door to both waves of economic struggles and an upsurge in workers' self-organisation. During the years of the Transitional Government, independent union bodies began to grow and there were some important strikes, including one by workers at the Kenana Sugar Company, one of Sudan's largest agro-processing facilities.[209] However, the SPA's support for the Transitional

---
208 El-Gizouli, 2020a, p5.
209 Civil Disobedience in Sudan, 2019.

Government, and the opportunities for workplace organisers to work with, rather than against the new regime in sectors such as education and health meant that there was no spontaneous wave of strikes combining demands for economic gains and *tathir* on the same scale as the one in Egypt in the wake of Mubarak's fall. The relative weakness of the strike movement also reflected the different class structures of the two countries. Sudan lacks Egypt's public sector industrial base and a smaller segment of the population are working in formal employment at all. In addition, the precursor strike waves in Egypt were also stronger and more widespread than in Sudan.

The deepening economic crisis which engulfed the Transitional Government in its final year, combined with the political crisis resulting from the military's preparations for the coup, did not immediately translate into a revival of strikes and workplace-based organising in the Autumn of 2021. The huge political general strikes which played a vital role in the first phase of the revolution in Spring 2019 were not repeated, with the Resistance Committees mobilising street protests and days of "total civil disobedience" instead. However, the failure of the coup leaders to form a government and the political rise of the Resistance Committees did open the door to a revival of major sectoral strikes in early 2022. These included important strikes by court workers, financial sector workers, doctors, nurses and pharmacists and a major teachers' strike called by the Sudanese Teachers' Committee in March 2022.[210] Significantly, most of these articulated both 'economic' and 'political' demands, and some were directly supported by some Resistance Committees which mobilised solidarity demonstrations, and sent activists to visit picket lines and sit-ins. The teachers' strike, however, raised a dilemma for revolutionary activists, as it was driven by largely economic goals, including the implementation of promised reforms to the pay and grading system that the military regime had refused to enact in the midst of a spiralling cost-of-living crisis. The strike was powerful enough to force the government to negotiate directly with the teachers' union leadership and won some concessions. However, this in turn provoked recriminations from some activists who argued that the STC's leaders were giving the military regime legitimacy by sitting down for talks with Al-Burhan's government over their

---

210 MENA Solidarity, 2022d.

demands.[211] What about the 'third axis' of permanent revolution: the movement along the different scales of unevenness between the system's centres and their peripheries? As Magdi el-Gizouli and Edward Thomas note, underlying Sudan's current political crisis is a long-term social one which has been structured into the fabric of Sudanese society throughout the country's modern history.[212] This takes the form of predatory and extractive state policies rooted in serving the interests of the 'centre' (meaning the river valley around Khartoum and its fertile agricultural lands) towards the 'peripheries' (such as the plains of the West and South which support valuable livestock farming and are rich in mineral resources including oil in the South and gold in the Jebel Amer area in North Darfur). Urban revolutionaries, whose bread is baked from imported wheat paid for through the livestock and gold exports from the peripheries, ignore the lessons of the co-option of the rural militias at their peril, el-Gizouli and Thomas argue. The question of peace, the supply of bread and the issue of who controls the land and its resources are intimately connected.

Could the Resistance Committees offer an alternative to the long history of pillage and plunder connecting the centre and periphery in Sudan? At a political level there is hope that they might—the fact that Hemedti's paramilitary forces continue to terrorise and kill in both Darfur and the major cities has helped to create a sense of unity. The anti-racist slogan—"The whole country is Darfur"—was revived again in December 2021, after government forces raped and assaulted women protesters during demonstrations at the Republican Palace. Building a stable political alliance between the poor of the towns and the countryside will pose much greater challenges. One of the conditions for such an alliance to develop must surely be for the revolutionary movement in the towns to develop forms of self-organisation which cross the threshold from demands *on* those in power to the execution of those demands under their own authority. Could this open the door to feeding the cities without leaving the countryside hungry? How could the machinery which currently generates profits for Gulf investors and their Sudanese cronies through agricultural and mineral exports be altered by such democratic, revolutionary authorities to meet

---

211 MENA Solidarity, 2022f.
212 Thomas & El-Gizouli, 2021.

the needs of ordinary people?

A glimpse of both the potential and challenges of intervention by the Resistance Committees along this axis could be seen in responses to the mass movement by farmers in Northern State, who erected barricades across the highway to Egypt, cutting the flow of agricultural exports by road to protest over a huge rise in electricity prices. The farmers' movement mobilised support from Resistance Committees the capital, who sent delegations to join the barricades.[213]

However, some activists from the urban resistance committees had a tendency to ignore the original social demands raised by the farmers, instead focussing on the barricades as a way to damage the Egyptian economy and hit back at Egyptian president Abdelfattah al-Sisi, who has been one of the strongest regional supporters of the military coup. As Muzan Alneel notes, "There is a tendency for urban demands to simply take over, unless there is an organisation capable of putting out an analysis that goes to the root of the situation so that the urban and rural masses can come together".[214] There is also the question of how the Resistance Committees relate to the class composition of the neighbourhoods they represent. Within the tripartite capital city (Khartoum, Omdurman and Bahri) for example, there are huge social differences between areas. Magdi el-Gizouli highlighted the differing aspirations of the Resistance Committees of middle-class areas such as Riyadh and those like impoverished Kalakla during the first phase of the revolution in 2019.[215] In the wake of the signing of the agreement which led to the creation of the Transitional Government it seemed as if the well-heeled activists of Riyadh might slam the doors of power shut on the young men from Kalakla who had risked their lives on the barricades. But the Resistance Committees continued to build support for the revolution in the poorest areas of the capital—Kalakla, Janub al-Hizam —giving residents of some of these areas political organisation of their own and amplifying their demands on a national stage.

This underscores of course that processes of political differentiation are taking place between Resistance Committees (as we saw above around the different revolutionary charters)

---

213 Alneel & Abdelrahman, 2022.
214 Alneel & Abdelrahman, 2022.
215 El-Gizouli, 2020a.

Egypt, Syria and Sudan: results and prospects

and raises the question of which version of 'the people' do they represent? Is it everyone except the very top layers of the old regime? Or is it "the mass of the people, their majority, the very lowest social groups, crushed by oppression and exploitation", as Lenin put it?[216]. *Some* Resistance Committees have acted as a vehicle for demands from the bottom of Sudanese society to shape the revolutionary process, but as the example of the Greater Khartoum political charter illustrates, city-wide coordination leads towards compromise in order to find a degree of cross-class consensus between the urban poor and workers on one hand, and those elements of the middle class which are supporting political revolution against the generals' regime on the other.

There is also the question which the Sudanese revolutionary movement has so far sidestepped—whether it is possible to really defeat the states special bodies of armed men, without the people taking arms to confront them? The belief that an armed vanguard can bring about political or national revolution from above was the preferred model for rebel movements against the Sudanese state in the previous generation. In many ways it was a step forward to turn away from this strategy, creating space for the emergence of the Resistance Committees themselves. However, as Mohamed Abdelrahman comments, a situation of dual power in Sudan will require both a split in the Armed Forces, RSF and militias along class lines, and the emergence of the people in arms as an alternative to the standing army.

"This is simply not discussed publicly at the moment. Actually, the discourse of "peaceful" revolution, combined with the need to "build a national army" representing the national interest rather than the interests of corrupt generals, is dominant. The closest the Sudanese Revolution came to breaking the state's monopoly on rifles was from 7 to 11 April 2019, when El Bashir fell. In those few days, soldiers and junior officers sided with the revolutionaries and fired at the security forces that tried to disperse them".[217]

For all the progress they have made, the Resistance Committees are running up against obstacles which they are unlikely to overcome alone. As Muzan Alneel notes

---

216 Alneel & Abdelrahman, 2022.
217 Alneel & Abdelrahman, 2022.

"We may be reaching the limits of the resistance committees' role as the sole revolutionary leadership. It will serve everyone much better if there was a clear revolutionary voice, supporting the revolutionary inclinations within existing resistance committees and providing sharp analysis. Without a revolutionary organisation we are at the mercy of individuals and social media algorithms".[218]

The challenges of building such a revolutionary party will be the focus of the concluding chapter.

---

218 Alneel & Abdelrahman, 2022.

Conclusion:

The revolutionary party

On Sunday 6 February 2011 I encountered my first revolutionary barricade. It was stretched across Champollion Street, somewhere between a restaurant famous for *koshary* (a cheap dish of pasta, rice, fried onions and spicy sauce) and the entrance to Tahrir Square nearest to the looming red bulk of the Egyptian Museum. The barricade was no longer actively defended, but my feet crunched on the debris littering the approach: a reminder of the battles fought out during the previous week between protesters in the Square and a mob of *baltagiyya* (thugs) mobilised by the security forces in an attempt to snuff out the revolution. Just over a decade later scrolling through messages on my phone from my friend Marwa I can see barricades again, this time bisecting the streets of Khartoum. Flashing me a dazzling smile, she is posing with a spent tear gas canister in front of one of the many barricades erected by the Resistance Committees during protests against the military coup.

In the popular imagination, the barricaded streets are likely to remain the most prominent stage for the revolutionary dramas which have unfolded from Tunis to Khartoum over the last decade. This is an image of revolution as a heroic rising of the people, complete with insurrectionary technologies which sometimes seem to have been lifted straight from the streets of the rebellious faubourgs of Paris in 1848. This book has attempted to widen the lens to uncover deeper processes which led to crisis at the top and bottom of society and opened equally important fields of battle in neighbourhoods and workplaces. As we have seen, the presence of organised workers engaged in mass strikes often proved decisive in shaking loose the grip of authoritarianism enough to open a period of political reforms, or at least creating conditions for ordinary people to take some of their democratic rights to assemble, strike and organise by storm. Conversely, the absence of the organised working class from the field of battle with the regimes generally correlated with the early militarisation of the counter-revolution and a rapid descent into civil war.

This is one indication that although none of the slogans or demands of the uprisings targeted the capitalist system directly, they were all "revolutions of the common people," as Yassin al-Haj Saleh described the Syrian uprising.[219] But how close did they come to the model of a "real people's revolution" that Lenin identified with his experience of the Russian Revolution of 1905?

Here, the picture is more confused. The common people certainly rose, but generally lacked politically independent organisations of their own in order to shape the course of the revolutions. Organised workers, as the most cohesive and powerful sections of the poor majority in all these societies, were obvious candidates to play a leading role in this process. However, despite making great strides in developing independent trade unionism, workers' organisations were rarely effective in the domain of politics. Or rather, they were rarely effective at achieving the kind of political and social changes which would have benefitted their own members, let alone wider layers of the poor. In the case of Tunisia, the UGTT union federation brokered a democratic transition, but seemed completely powerless to impose any alternative to further neoliberal economic reforms which turned the screws tighter on those sections of Tunisian society which had risen in revolt in 2011. In Sudan, the SPA, representing a series of independent trade unions and professional associations, was a party to the negotiations setting up a Transitional Government led by an economist obsessed with proving to the "international community" that the new government would conform their expectations of prudence and fiscal discipline.

The Sudanese revolution did show, however, that neighbourhood-based revolutionary organisation could begin

219 Saleh, 2017.

The revolutionary party

to articulate the voice of some sections of the poor in national politics. But the geographical form of the Resistance Committees contained an inbuilt tendency to dilute their class content, as the demands of working class and poor districts were inevitably counterbalanced by the different goals of middle class districts. As Mohamed Abdelrahman put it in February 2022:

Right now in Sudan there's a general feeling of yearning for social justice. There is a "spectre" haunting Sudan. But this needs to be captured and transformed into a political programme with clear and specific goals that can inspire millions of workers all across the country. All these tasks require a vantage point that only a political party can attain.[220]

This clarity of perspective can translate into the ability to respond swiftly to the abrupt twists and turns of the unfolding revolutionary process. In contrast to the broader, more politically heterogenous popular revolutionary bodies which form along the axes of permanent revolution, a revolutionary party is defined by a much firmer commitment to a defined set of political principles and practices. This tightness and cohesion must complement the differentiated unity of the councils and committees organised by workers and the poor to drive the revolution forward. In fact, as the experience of revolution since 1917 illustrates, these broader revolutionary bodies will not transform into the basis for an alternative government of their own accord.

Although the experience of revolutions (and the ones discussed in this book are no exception) is rich in experiments with alternatives to the existing political and social order, breaking the ideological barriers which trap ordinary people in continued submission to the capitalist state requires more than imagination. It demands a centralised, cohesive, well-organised force which is rooted in the one social class capable of shattering not just the state but replacing the capitalist ruling class and its economic system.

A 'party' in this sense, simply means an organised group of people who are able to think like the state they want to beat but are also at the same time committed to breaking its power for good. Thinking 'like the state' in this case means anticipating their antagonists' manoeuvres and countering them with organised forces of their own.

---

220 Alneel & Abdelrahman, 2022.

Revolution is the choice of the people

Here it is worth taking a short diversion to try and further demystify the phrase "revolutionary party". Many of the revolutions and uprisings discussed here have gone through phases where large numbers of their participants found the idea that these were "leaderless" mobilisations which were partially against parties or party politics (or certainly against the ones which actually existed at the time whether in power or in opposition). Yet the experience of the mass popular mobilisations of the decade has demonstrated time and time again that social media algorithms are no substitute for popular and democratic organisation rooted in the everyday and real life spaces of ordinary people's lives—which is to say in the places where they live and work. Simply sustaining mass mobilisations in the streets on the scale to withstand the full spectrum counterattack which those who have the most to lose from the revolution inevitably mount once the regime's unlucky figurehead has fallen, demands this level of organisation.

Popular revolutionary bodies—usually labelled as some kind of revolutionary council or committee—are likely to start forming along the different axes of permanent revolution once masses of ordinary people are pulled into action by the revolutionary crisis. These councils and committees seek to draw in wide layers of the working class and the poor under their authority, the party sets tougher conditions for membership and demands tighter agreement from its cadres. All genuine workers' or popular revolutionary councils will include among their members a spectrum of political opinion. Their members will disagree often on quite basic issues such as what the goals of the revolution should be and may even have as members people who want to end the revolution and hand over power to parliament.

By contrast a revolutionary *party* in the sense the term is meant here is an organised body committed to permanent revolution. It is an instrument designed to speed up the revolutionary process, its purpose is to engineer conditions for the leap from political to social revolution through the breaking of the capitalist state which squats across the tracks, blocking our way to a socialist future. Moreover, we need revolutionary parties *before* the revolution makes the broader, popular bodies possible. Lenin was right of course that revolutionaries do not will revolutions in being, but they can change the terrain

The revolutionary party

on which they take place. Even before the revolution begins, members of a party committed to permanent revolution will be trying to push along its axes far as they can. That might mean organising a strike committee which is independent of the union officials and is open and accountable to all strikers with daily meetings on the picket line. It might mean not ducking the harder arguments which erupt around fissures and divisions in the working class in order to assert a principled politics opposing all forms of oppression. Every time revolutionary activists show in practice that we do not only have the power to disrupt the flow of profits, we can also construct a new world, they sow seeds for the future.

The intervention of revolutionary parties into the 'everyday' struggles of ordinary people beyond the revolutionary crisis itself is thus qualitatively different to action by reformist organisations, even if they are on the surface doing similar things and raising the same kind of demands. Every spark of resistance, every flicker of a flame in the embers of rebellion should be important to a revolutionary party, even in the most difficult circumstances.

What does it mean to internalise that kind of politics? A revolutionary party provides a means to achieve that, creating a bond and forging a community between people who share those ideas. Members of a party committed to permanent revolution should not need their leaders to write them a letter urging them to set up organs of revolutionary democracy, this ought to have been the lodestar of their political practice from the start. Beyond ideas, the structures and processes of party organisation matter as well. Without effective and democratic organisation, the ideas of the party will remain untested. Its members have to be able to take decisions, disagree with one another yet remain united in action. They will need to trust each other enough to respect decisions that not everyone agrees with, as well as trusting each other enough to delegate responsibility and authority.

And as the experience of the last decade has repeatedly demonstrated, such a party if it is going to match up to the power of the state, needs to be well-rooted in the working class. As Hossam el-Hamalawy points out, creating revolutionary socialist organisation demands that workers who join internalise its politics:

Revolution is the choice of the people

> We have had factory workers who joined and became part of the organisation for several years. They played an instrumental role in the strikes, but I don't think we managed to turn them into Marxist cadres. We made trade unionists out of them, basically. This also meant that when it came to political initiatives, we were not that successful in mobilising those factories.[221]

Does this mean that somehow the efforts by the small forces of revolutionary left in Egypt and elsewhere in the region were in vain or pointless? Far from it. One of the most important lessons of the experience of the revolutions discussed in this book is that even in the most difficult circumstances it is possible to build and grow, winning new generations to revolutionary socialism in the process. The Egyptian Revolutionary Socialists' website, media and other publications has introduced hundreds of thousands, perhaps millions of people to socialist ideas, for example. This is not about clever social media tactics or good design on their own, but rather reflects the way in which the 'fit' between the ideas relayed by the site and the experience of revolution boosted the audience for a politics which had previously been a very minor strand in the opposition. In almost all of the revolutions discussed in this book, where revolutionary left groups existed before the revolution, they saw their audience and influence grow when it erupted.

Getting right how to relate to reformist currents whether in the trade unions, on the left or those of other political traditions (principally Arab nationalism and Islamism) was often more difficult. Maintaining independence involved steering a course which avoided falling into the trap of resorting to abstract propaganda on one side, or simply acting as radical cheerleaders for reformist organisations on the other. In most of the countries discussed here, the left in the broader sense was largely absent from society, and this did shape the politics and outcomes of the revolutions. The betrayals and compromises of the past still weighed heavily on the present in countries where the 'old' Stalinist left had hitched itself to the nationalist regimes, leaving the field of opposition largely in the hands of the Islamists. This does not mean that those who argued that Islamism was one reactionary mass of "fundamentalist" ideas were correct.

---

221 Alexander, 2021a.

The revolutionary party

Rather, the drama of revolution revealed that the compromises made by reformist leaders to save the system from collapse looked remarkably similar whether the politicians in question were trade union bureaucrats in Tunisia, Muslim Brotherhood figures in Egypt, or Sudanese technocrats.

The problem facing all of us is finding a way to break through that cycle of compromise and repression. Without a revolutionary party capable of playing that role the awe-inspiring power of the risen people who have "chosen revolution" will not be enough. The creativity and democratic invention flowering in the squares and neighbourhoods will not be enough. The mass strikes and the extension of workers control will not be enough.

Someone will have to both ask and answer the question: not just how will we break their state but what will replace it?

Meanwhile the crisis at the heart of the capitalist system deepens. It was never 'just' political, but now encompasses the prospect of the breakdown not just of the social order but of the planet's ecology (or at least the destruction of an ecology which can sustain human life as we know it). The four horsemen of the apocalypse—death, famine, pestilence and war—are reeling through the lives of billions in a deadly *danse macabre*, arm-in-arm with our corrupt and brutal ruling class.Out of all of this, the catastrophe engulfing humanity and millions of other species because of capitalism's addiction to fossil fuels is the most urgent. On this score alone the success and failure of popular revolutions in the Middle East and North Africa has planetary significance. The Middle East as a region is the location for already-financed new projects which will produce 32.8 billion barrels of oil and gas in the near and medium future. These 'carbon bombs' will blow a hole in any chance of halting or even slowing down the slide into climate chaos.[222] The prime culprits in this crime are the counter-revolutionary and reactionary monarchies of the Gulf, aided and abetted by the US (which is itself the largest fossil fuel polluter on the planet).

Do we have time to stop them? The experience of the last decades of campaigning underlines what the climate movement can learn from the uprisings discussed here about how revolutions expand time, making shifts in the consciousness and self-organisation of millions finally possible. 'Revolution time' is different to the frozen time of everyday life in the apocalypse.

---

222   Carrington & Taylor, 2022.

Revolution is the choice of the people

It is what happens when millions of people start really living, releasing the power and potential which has been locked up and repressed. This is what compresses whole epochs into the leaps between historical stages that Trotsky described.

What about the problem of organisation? Is the gap between hope and expectation too large? The small and scattered forces of the revolutionary left would barely fill one Tahrir Square. They are just a drop in the ocean of 8 billion people: a laughably tiny number compared to the armed might of the states which confront us. Yet the record of the revolutions analysed here is that organised revolutionaries do make a difference wherever they are. Hundreds can shift the ideas of tens of thousands and thousands can reach hundreds of thousands or even millions.

In the end we know we are still making a wager of hope.

But that is not the real choice.

The only real choice is yours—will you join us?

Revolution is the choice of the people

Bibliography

Abbas, Reem, 2019, "How an illegal Sudanese union became the biggest threat to Omar Al Bashir's 29-year reign", *The National (Abu Dhabi)* (28 January), thenationalnews.com/world/africa/how-an-illegal-sudanese-union-became-the-biggest-threat-to-omar-al-bashir-s-29-year-reign-1.819159

Abbass, Samia, 2010, "Sudanese Students, Workers Bring down Numeiri Dictatorship, 1985", *Global Nonviolent Action Database* (31 October). nvdatabase.swarthmore.edu/content/sudanese-students-workers-bring-down-numeiri-dictatorship-1985

Abdelnasser, Gamal, 2004 'Egypt: Succession Politics', in *Arab Elites: Negotiating the Politics of Change*, ed Volker Perthes, Lynne Rienner, Boulder, Colorado.

Abdullah, Khaled & Ghobari, Mohammed, 2011, "Thousands March in Yemen to Demand Change of Government", *Reuters* (27 January) reuters.com/article/us-yemen-protests-idUSTRE70Q23620110127.

Abu Moghli, Mai & Qato, Mezna, 2018, "A Brief History of a Teacher's Strike" *Middle East Research and Information Project:* merip.org/2018/06/a-brief-history-of-a-teachers-strike/

Abul-Magd, Zeinab, 2012, "Egypt's Politics of Hidden Business Empires: The Brotherhood Versus the Army", Atlantic Council website (5 October) atlanticcouncil.org/blogs/menasource/egypt-s-politics-of-hidden-business-empires-the-brotherhood-versus-the-army/

Abu Sneineh, Mustaf, 2021, "Who was Nizar Banat, the outspoken critic who died in Palestinian Authority custody?", *Middle East Eye*, 24 June 2021 middleeasteye.net/news/palestine-nizar-banat-who-critic-palestinian-authority

Achcar, Gilbert, 2013, *The People Want: A Radical Exploration of the Arab Uprising* (Verso).

Adam, M. 2012. "Brute Force: Inside the Central Security Forces." *Egypt Independent*, November 11. egyptindependent.com/brute-force-inside-central-security-forces

AFP (Agence France-Press), 2019, "Iraq's Mosul Strains to Revive Manufacturing Past", *France 24*, (22 October). france24.com/en/20191022-iraq-s-mosul-strains-to-revive-manufacturing-past.

AFP (Agence France-Presse in Cairo), 2020, "Egypt arrests young women who posted clips on TikTok", *The Guardian*, (11 June). theguardian.com/world/2020/jun/11/egypt-arrests-young-women-who-posted-clips-on-tiktok

Ahmed, Yasmine Moataz, 2019, "The Social Life of Wheat and Grapes: Domestic Land-Grabbing as Accumulation by Dispossession in Rural Egypt", *Review of African Political Economy* 46: 162 (2 October): 567–81. doi.org/10.1080/03056244.2019.1688486

Aissat, Kamel, 2019, "How Grassroots Democracy Powered Béjaia's General Strike against Algerian Presidential Election", *Middle East Solidarity* (31 December) menasolidaritynetwork.com/2019/12/31/how-grassroots-democracy-powered-bejaias-general-strike-against-algerias-presidential-election

Al Jazeera, 2019, "Sudan Protest Leaders, Military Sign Transitional Government Deal", *Al Jazeera* (17 August) aljazeera.com/news/2019/08/sudan-protest-leaders-military-sign-transitional-government-deal-190817122225172.html

Al Jazeera, 2020a, "Iraq forms new government after six months of uncertainty", *Al Jazeera* (7 May), aljazeera.com/news/2020/5/7/iraq-forms-new-government-after-six-months-of-uncertainty

Al Jazeera, 2020b, "'Countdown to Catastrophe' in Yemen as UN Again Warns of Famine", *Al Jazeera* (5 December) aljazeera.com/news/2020/11/12/yemen-faces-looming-famine-needs-millions-un-food-chief.

Al Jazeera, 2011, "Muslim Brotherhood in Egypt talks", Al Jazeera website, (6 February) www.aljazeera.com/news/2011/2/6/muslim-brotherhood-in-egypt-talks

Al Jazeera, 2011a, "Thousands Rally across Yemen", *Al Jazeera* (14 February) aljazeera.com/news/2011/2/14/thousands-rally-across-yemen.

Al Jazeera, 2011b, "Top Army Commanders Defect in Yemen", *Al Jazeera* (21 March) aljazeera.com/news/2011/3/21/top-army-commanders-defect-in-yemen

Al-Ali, Nadje, 2014 "Reflections on (Counter) Revolutionary Processes in Egypt", *Feminist Review* 106: 1 (February): 122–28. doi.org/10.1057/fr.2013.35.

Al-Anani, Khalil, 2020, "Devout Neoliberalism?! Explaining Egypt's Muslim Brotherhood's Socio-economic Perspective and Policies", Politics and Religion, Vol 13, No. 4, (December), cambridge.org/core/journals/politics-and-religion/article/devout-neoliberalism-explaining-egypts-muslim-

brotherhoods-socioeconomic-perspective-and-policies/688
C459D5BC8448C16B7BF7BF6D27C28

Al-Khalil, Samir, 1990, *Republic of Fear: The Inside Story of Saddam's Iraq* (New York, Pantheon)

Al-Ishtaraki, 2019, "Five Lessons from Sudan and Algeria", *Al-Ishtaraki* (9 March), global.revsoc.me/2019/03/five-lessons-from-sudan-and-algeria

Al-Mahkama al-Dusturiyya al-Uliya, "Dustur 1964". hccourt.gov.eg, 2012. hccourt.gov.eg/Constitutions/Constitution64.asp.

Al-Rasheed, Madawi, 2010, *A History of Saudi Arabia*, 2nd edition (Cambridge: Cambridge University Press): 14–15.

Al-Shamahi, Abubakr, 2012, "Yemen Rises up against Its Mini-Dictators". *The Guardian*, (5 January) theguardian.com/commentisfree/2012/jan/05/yemen-mini-dictators-parallel-revolution

Al-Shami, Leila, 2021. "Building Alternative Futures in the Present: The Case of Syria's Communes." *The Funambulist Magazine*, (2 March). thefunambulist.net/magazine/the-paris-commune-and-the-world/building-alternative-futures-in-the-present-the-case-of-syrias-communes

Alexander, Anne, 2005, *Nasser* (London: Haus).

Alexander, Anne, 2011a. "Digital Generation", in Sardar, Ziauddin & Yassin-Kassab, Robin (eds) *Critical Muslim 1: The Arabs Are Alive* (London: C Hurst & Co Publishers).

Alexander, Anne, 2011b, "Egypt's Muslims and Christians Join Hands in Protest", *BBC News* (10 February), bbc.co.uk/news/world-middle-east-12407793.

Alexander, Anne, 2015, "ISIS and counter-revolution: towards a Marxist analysis", International Socialism Journal (January), isj.org.uk/isis-and-counter-revolution-towards-a-marxist-analysis/

Alexander, Anne, 2016, "ISIS, Imperialism and the War in Syria", *International Socialism,* 2: 149 (Spring). isj.org.uk/isis-imperialism-and-the-war-in-syria

Alexander, Anne, 2019, "'We're Organising the Revolution'—Eyewitness from the Sudanese Sit-Ins", *Socialist Worker (Britain)*, (12 May) socialistworker.co.uk/art/48327/Were+organising+the+revolution+eyewitness+from+the+Sudanese+sit+ins

Alexander, Anne, 2020. "Class, Power and Revolution in Sudan", *International socialism* (166) (March). isj.org.uk/class-power-and-revolution-in-sudan

Alexander, Anne, 2021a. "Ten Years since the Arab Revolutions: Voices from a Rebellious Decade." *International Socialism* (April 6). isj.org.uk/rebellious-decade

Alexander, Anne, 2021b. "Interview with Ahmed Ezzat." Zoom recording.

Alexander, Anne, 2022a. "All Power to Sudan's Resistance Committees?" *Socialist Worker*, (8 January). socialistworker.co.uk/long-reads/all-power-to-sudans-resistance-committees

Alexander, Anne, 2022b, "Ending apartheid in Palestine: the case for a revolutionary strategy", *International Socialism*, 2: 175 (Spring).

Alexander, Anne & Assaf, Simon, 2005, "Iraq: The Rise of the Resistance", *International Socialism,* 2: 105. isj.org.uk/iraq-the-rise-of-the-resistance/ (Spring).

Alexander, Anne & Assaf, Simon, 2005, "The Elections in Iraq". *International Socialism,* 2: 106 (Summer). isj.org.uk/the-elections-and-the-resistance-in-iraq/

Alexander, Anne & Bak, Irang, "Filling the gap when the state fails", Middle East Solidarity, (17 April) menasolidaritynetwork.com/2020/04/17/sudan-filling-the-gap-when-the-state-fails/

Alexander, Anne & Bassiouny, Mostafa, 2014, *Bread, Freedom, Social Justice: Workers and the Egyptian Revolution* (London: Zed Books).

Alexander, Anne, & Bouharoun, Jad, 2016, *Syria: Revolution, Counter-Revolution and War* (London: Socialist Workers Party).

Alexander, Anne & Koubaissy, Farah, 2008, "Women Were Braver than a Hundred Men." *Socialist Review*, (1 January). socialistreview.org.uk/321/women-were-braver-hundred-men.

Alexander, Anne, Rose, John, Hickey, Tom & Marfleet, Phil, 2018, *Palestine–Resistance, revolution and the struggle for freedom* (London: Socialist Workers Party).

Alexander, Christopher, 2000, "Opportunities, organizations, and ideas: Islamists and workers in Tunisia and Algeria", *International Journal of Middle East Studies* 32: 4 (November): 465–90. doi.org/10.1017/S0020743800021176.

Ali, Nasma, 2010, "'Ai'sha: La Nuhtag Ila Maqa'id al-'ummal Idha Indamagu Fi al-Ahzab," (12 October), *Al-Masry Al-Youm*, almasryalyoum.com/node/268280

Ali Eddin, Mohamed, 2013, "The battle over Qursaya Island", Mada Masr, www.madamasr.com/en/2013/01/20/panorama/u/the-battle-over-qursaya-island-by-mohamed-ali-eddin/

Alnasrawi, Abbas, 1992, "Iraq: Economic Consequences of the 1991 Gulf War and Future Outlook". *Third World Quarterly* 13: 2 (January): 335–52. doi.org/10.1080/01436599208420280

Alneel, Muzan, & Abdelrahman, Mohamed, 2022. "Interview: Prospects for Revolutionaries in Sudan." *International Socialism* 2: 174 (April). isj.org.uk/interview-revolutionaries-in-sudan

Alneel, Muzan, 2022, "The Charters of Sudan's Political Landscape", The Tahrir Institute for Middle East Policy website, (26 April) timep.org/commentary/analysis/the-charters-of-sudans-political-landscape/

Alsaafin, Linah, 2021, "Palestinian protests in Israel showcase 'unprecedented' unity", *Al Jazeera* (16 May), aljazeera.com/news/2021/5/16/palestinian-protests-in-israel-showcase-unprecedented-unity

Amin, Mohamed, 2019, "Strikes, Protests and a Massacre: The Port in the Sudanese Storm", *Middle East Eye* (6 February). middleeasteye.net/news/strikes-protests-and-massacre-port-sudanese-storm.

Amin, Mohamed, 2020, "Cries of Censorship in Sudan as Media Outlets Linked to Old Regime Closed | Middle East Eye", *Middle East Eye* (20 January), middleeasteye.net/news/fears-over-freedom-speech-sudan-following-closure-several-media-outlets.

Amnesty International, 2020, "The Yemen Conflict Shows No Real Signs of Abating as It Enters Its Fifth Year", *Amnesty International* (24 March). amnesty.org/en/latest/news/2015/09/yemen-the-forgotten-war

Angus, Ian, 2016, *Facing the Anthropocene: Fossil Capitalism and the Crisis of the Earth System* (New York, Monthly Review Foundation).

ANHRI, 2012, *Duwa Fi Darb Al-Hurriya: Shuhada Thawrat 25 Yanayir,* (Cairo: The Arabic Network for Human Rights Information). anhri.net/wp-content/uploads/2012/05/book-2.pdf

Aouragh, Miriyam & Alexander, Anne, 2011. "The Egyptian Experience: Sense and Nonsense of the Internet Revolution", *International Journal of Communication* 5 (January): 1344-1358. researchgate.net/publication/268384780_The_Egyptian_Experience_Sense_and_Nonsense_of_the_Internet_Revolution

Arab Republic of Egypt, 1956, "Constitution, Arab Republic of Egypt", *ConstitutionNet,* constitutionnet.org/sites/default/files/constitution_of_1956-arabic.pdf.

Arraf, Jane, 2020, "Iraq's Protests Shook the Government. Now The Movement Is Nearly Crushed", *National Public Radio* (21 February), npr.org/2020/02/21/807725624/iraqs-powerful-protests-forced-political-change-now-they-re-nearly-crushed?t=1654961727236

Armitage, Jim, 2018, "Libya Sinks into Poverty as the Oil Money Disappears into Foreign Bank Accounts", *The Independent* (18 July). independent.co.uk/news/business/analysis-and-features/libya-poverty-corruption-a8451826.html.

Assaf, Simon, 2012, "Libya at the Crossroads", *International Socialism,* 2: 133 (Spring). isj.org.uk/libya-at-the-crossroads/

Ashour, Omar, 2012. *From Bad Cop to Good Cop: The Challenge of Security Sector Reform in Egypt.* Brookings Doha Center, Stanford University "Project on Arab Transitions" Paper, *Brookings Institute* (November). brookings.edu/research/from-bad-cop-to-good-cop-the-challenge-of-security-sector-reform-in-egypt

Awad, Marwa, 2012, "Islamist businessmen challenge Egypt's old money", Reuters, (17 October) reuters.com/article/egypt-economy-brotherhood-idUSL6E8L9NQ420121017

Awad, Sumaya & Their, Daphna, 2021, "In Israel, Zionism Prevents Working-Class Solidarity" *Jacobin* (4 April). jacobin.com/2021/04/israel-zionism-palestine-unions-workers

Ayeb, Habib, 2011, "Social and Political Geography of the Tunisian Revolution: The Alfa Grass Revolution." *Review of African Political Economy* 38: 129 (September): 467–79. doi.org/10.1080/03056244.2011.604250.

Ayeb, Habib & Bush, Ray, 2019, *Food Insecurity and Revolution in the Middle East and North Africa: Agrarian Questions in Egypt and Tunisia* (London: Anthem Press). doi.org/10.2307/j.ctvpr7r45

Ayin Network, 2021, "Al-mutqawama al-sudaniyya tabta'ad 'an al-ahzab wa tataa'hab litarh iyalan siyaysi." *Ayin network.* 3ayin.com/sudanese-resistance

Ayubi, Nazih N, 2006, *Over-Stating the Arab State: Politics and Society in the Middle East* (London: I.B. Tauris).

Azhari, Timour, 2019, "Lebanese protesters celebrate Hariri resignation, but want more", *Al Jazeera* (30 October).

Barker, Colin, 1978, "A Note on the Theory of Capitalist States", *Capital & Class* 2: 1 (Spring): 118–26. marxists.org/history/etol/

writers/barker-c/1978/xx/capstates.htm

Barker, Colin, 1987, *Revolutionary Rehearsals* (London: Bookmarks).

Barker, Colin, Dale, Gareth & Davidson, Neil, 2021, *Revolutionary Rehearsals in the Neoliberal Age: 1989-2019* (Chicago: Haymarket).

Barker, Colin & Weber, Kara, 1982, "Solidarność: From Gdansk to Military Repression", *International Socialism* 2: 15 (Winter): 1–154. marxists.org/history/etol/writers/barker-c/1982/solidarnosc/

Baron, Adam, Al-Madhaji, Maged & Alharari, Waleed, 2017, "The Destabilizing Legacy of US Military Aid and Counterterrorism Efforts in Yemen", *Sana'a Centre For Strategic Studies* (4 August) sanaacenter.org/publications/analysis/4517.

Bassam, Laila & Osseiran, Dala 2019, "Lebanon Business Group Urges General Strike to Push for End to Crisis", *Reuters* (25 November), reuters.com/article/us-lebanon-protests-idUSKBN1XZ1YI

Bassiouny, Mostafa & Alexander, Anne, 2021, "The Workers' Movement, Revolution and Counter-Revolution in Egypt",*Transnational Institute* (October). longreads.tni.org/the-workers-movement-revolution-and-counter-revolution-in-egypt.

Bassiouny, Mostafa & Said, Omar, 2007, *Raiyyat al-idirab fi sama' masr: haraka 'ummaliyya gadida 2007,* (Cairo: Markaz al-dirasat al-ishtarakiyya).

Batatu, Hanna, 1978, *The Old Social Classes and the Revolutionary Movements of Iraq: A Study of Iraq's Old Landed and Commercial Classes and of Its Communists, Ba'thists, and Free Officers* (New Jersey, Princeton University Press).

Batatu, Hanna, 1982, "Syria's Muslim Brethren", *Middle East Report*, 110 (December).

Bayat, Assef, 2017, *Revolution without Revolutionaries: Making Sense of the Arab Spring*, (Redwod, California: Stanford University Press).

BBC News, 2018b. "Algeria Seizes 700kg of Cocaine on Container Ship", *BBC News* (30 May) bbc.com/news/world-africa-44305875

BBC News, 2018c, "Algeria's Powerful Police Chief Gen Abdelghani Hamel Sacked." *BBC News*, (27 June) bbc.com/news/world-africa-44629079.

BBC News, 2019a, "How Algeria's Army Sacrificed a President to Keep Power", *BBC News*, (6 April), bbc.com/news/world-africa-47821980.

BBC News, 2019b, "Khalifa Haftar: The Libyan general with big ambitions", (8 April) bbc.co.uk/news/world-africa-27492354

BBC News, 2019c, "Algeria Jails Two Former Prime Ministers Ahead of Election", (10 December) bbc.com/news/world-africa-50728562.

BBC News, 2020, "Female Iraqi activist killed in Basra as gunmen target protesters", BBC News (20 August) bbc.co.uk/news/world-middle-east-53847648

Beinin, Joel, 2010, *The Struggle for Worker Rights in Egypt*, (Washington DC, Solidarity Center).

Beinin, Joel, 2016, *Workers and Thieves: Labor Movements and Popular Uprisings in Tunisia and Egypt*, (Stanford University Press).

Bellin, Eva Rana, 2002, *Stalled Democracy: Capital, Labor, and the Paradox of State-Sponsored Development* (Ithaca: Cornell University Press).

Bennoune, Mahfou, 1979, "Primary Capital Accumulation in Colonial Tunisia". *Dialectical Anthropology* 4: 2 (July). doi.org/10.1007/BF00264988.

Bensaïd, Daniel, 2002, "'Leaps, Leaps, Leaps': Lenin and Politics", *International Socialism 2:* 95 (Summer) marxists.org/archive/bensaid/2002/07/leaps.htm

Berridge, Willow, 2014, "50 Years on: Remembering Sudan's October Revolution." *African Arguments* blog, (20 October). africanarguments.org/2014/10/20/50-years-on-remembering-sudans-october-revolution-by-willow-berridge

Berridge, Willow, De Waal, Alex & Lynch, Justin, 2022, *Sudan's Unfinished Democracy: The Promise and Betrayal of a People's Revolution* (London: C Hurst & Co).

Birchall, Ian, 1979. "Social Democracy and the Portuguese 'Revolution.'" *International Socialism* 2: 6 (Autumn). marxists.org/history/etol/writers/birchall/1979/xx/portrev.html.

Bouhlel, Chaima, 2019, "Hundreds of Thousands Strike in Tunisia over Public Sector Pay Freeze." *Middle East Eye* (17 January). middleeasteye.net/news/hundreds-thousands-strike-tunisia-over-public-sector-pay-freeze.

BP, 2020, "Statistical Review of World Energy 2020". bp.com/en/global/corporate/energy-economics/statistical-review-of-world-energy.html.

Broué, Pierre, 2017, *The German Revolution 1917-1923* (Chicago: Haymarket Books).

Brown, Frances, 2018, *Dilemmas of Stabilization Assistance: The Case of Syria*. Carnegie Middle East Center. Carnegie Endowment for International Peace. carnegieendowment.org/2018/10/26/dilemmas-of-stabilization-assistance-case-of-syria-pub-77574.

Bsoul, Janan, 2017, "Janan Bsoul Rips Into Israel's New Bill Stripping Arabic of Official Status", *Haaretz* (11 May).

Bukharin, Nikolaĭ, 1967, *Imperialism and World Economy* (New York: H Fertig).

Burchfield, Emily, 2017, "PYD Governance in Northeastern Syria." *Atlantic Council* (February) atlanticcouncil.org/blogs/syriasource/pyd-governance-in-northeastern-syria

Caldwell, Sue, 2019, "From Civil Resistance to Revolution", Socialist Review, (5 November), socialistworker.co.uk/socialist-review-archive/civil-resistance-revolution/

Callinicos, Alex, 1988, "An Imperialist Peace?" *Socialist Worker Review* 112 (September) marxisme.dk/arkiv/callinic/1988/09/iraniraq.htm.

Callinicos, Alex, 2009, *Imperialism and Global Political Economy* (Cambridge, UK; Malden, MA: Polity Press).

Callinicos, Alex & Harman, Chris, 1987, *The Changing Working Class: Essays on Class Structure Today* (London: Bookmarks).

Cammett, Melani, 1999/2000, "International Exposure, Domestic Response: Financiers, Weavers, and Garment Manufactures in Morocco and Tunisia". *Arab Studies Journal* 7/8: 2/1 (Fall, Spring).

Carrington, Damian, & Taylor, Matthew, 2022, "Revealed: The 'Carbon Bombs' Set to Trigger Catastrophic Climate Breakdown", *The Guardian* (11 May). theguardian.com/environment/ng-interactive/2022/may/11/fossil-fuel-carbon-bombs-climate-breakdown-oil-gas

Carter Center, 2021, *Sudan's Youth and the Transition: Priorities, Perceptions and Attitudes*. Carter Center (Atlanta & Khartoum). cartercenter.org/resources/pdfs/news/peace_publications/conflict_resolution/sudan-youth-survey-report-en.pdf.

Chalcraft, John, 2010, "Monarchy, Migration and Hegemony in the Arabian Peninsula," *LSE Global Governance Working Paper*, eprints.lse.ac.uk/32556/1/Monarchy,_migration_and_hegemony_%28working_paper%29.pdf

Ceruti, C. 2010. "One class or two? The labour reserve and 'surplus population' in Marx and contemporary Soweto." *South African Review of Sociology* 41: 2 (June):77–103. doi:10.1080/21528586.2010.490386.

Charrad, Mounira M & Zarrugh, Amina, 2014, "Equal or Complementary?

Women in the New Tunisian Constitution after the Arab Spring", *The Journal of North African Studies* 19: 2 (15 March): 230–43. doi.org/10.1080/13629387.2013.857276

Chenoweth, Erica, 2021, *Civil Resistance: What Everyone Needs to Know*. (Oxford, Oxford University Press USA)

Choonara, Joseph, 2018, "Class and the Classical Marxist Tradition" in O'Neill, Deirdre

& Wayne, Mike, *Considering Class: Theory, Culture and Media in the 21st Century* (Chicago: Brill).

Chulov, Martin, 2011, "Bahrain Destroys Pearl Roundabout", *Guardian*, (18 March) theguardian.com/world/2011/mar/18/bahrain-destroys-pearl-roundabout.

CIMI & PIBA, 2016, *Labor Migration to Israel*, (Jerusalem: Center for International Migration and Integration & Population and Immigration Authority).

Civil Disobedience in Sudan, 2019 "Initsar Tarikhi Lil Ammilin Bisharikat Sukkar Kenana", *Facebook* (11 May), facebook.com/CivildisobedienceinSudan/posts/324457271569382

Civil Society Knowledge Centre, 2014, "EDL Workers", *Civil Society Knowledge Centre* (3 September). civilsociety-centre.org/party/edl-workers

Cliff, Tony, 1957, 'The Economic Roots of Reformism', reprinted in Cliff, Tony, *Neither Washington nor Moscow* (Bookmarks, London, 1982).

Cliff, Tony, 1963, *Deflected Permanent Revolution,* marxists.org/archive/cliff/works/1963/xx/permrev.htm

Cliff, Tony, 1985, "Patterns of mass strike", *International Socialism* 2: 29 (Summer): 3–61. marxists.org/archive/cliff/works/1985/patterns/index.htm

Cliff, Tony & Gluckstein, Donny, 1986, *Marxism and Trade Union Struggle: The General Strike of 1926* (London: Bookmarks).

Cliff, Tony, 1996, *State Capitalism in Russia* (London & Chicago: Bookmarks).

Cookman, Liz, 2019. "Algeria's Year of Protest: How the 'Revolution of Smiles' Remained Peaceful against Impunity", *The National* (30 December). thenationalnews.com/world/mena/algerias-year-of-protest-how-the-revolution-of-smiles-remained-peaceful-against-impunity-1.957306

Dabla-Norris, Era & Kochhar, Kalpana, 2019, "The Economic Benefits of Bringing More Women into the Labor Force Are Greater than Previously Thought", *IMF* (March 2019).

Daher, Joseph, 2016, *Hezbollah: The Political Economy of Lebanon's*

Party of God (London, Pluto Press).

Daher, Joseph, 2018, *Révolution and Counter-Revolution in Syria, origins and developments*, Phd Thesis, (University of Lausanne). serval.unil.ch/resource/serval:BIB_27632B4295FC.P001/REF

Daher, Joseph, 2020, "Between Control and Repression: The Plight of the Syrian Labour Force", *European University Institute*, cadmus.eui.eu/handle/1814/67858

Daou, Walid, 2017, "What Are the Possible Strategies for the Emergence of a Democratic and Revolutionary Labour Movement in Lebanon?" in Lazar, Sian (ed) *Where Are the Unions?* (London: Zed Books).

Daoudy, Marwa, 2020, *The Origins of the Syrian Conflict: Climate Change and Human Security*. 1st edition, (Cambridge: Cambridge University Press). doi.org/10.1017/9781108567053

Darlington, Ralph & Upchurch, Martin, 2012, "A Reappraisal of the Rank-and-File versus Bureaucracy Debate", *Capital & Class* 36: 1 (February 1, 2012): 77–95. doi.org/10.1177/0309816811430369

Daw, Mohamed A, El-Bouzedi, Abdallah & Dau, Aghnaya A, (2015) "Libyan Armed Conflict 2011: Mortality, Injury and Population Displacement", *African Journal of Emergency Medicine,* Vol 5, No 3 (1 September), pp101–7, doi.org/10.1016/j.afjem.2015.02.002

Deccan Herald, 2011, "Bahrain National Guard to Recruit Former Soldiers from Pak." *Deccan Herald* (11 March) deccanherald.com/content/144961/bahrain-national-guard-recruit-former.html

Del Panta, Gianni, 2017, "Does Workers' Rebellion Herald Algeria's Coming Storm?" *Middle East Solidarity* (2 October). menasolidaritynetwork.com/2017/10/02/archive-does-workers-rebellion-herald-algerias-coming-storm/

Del Panta, Gianni, 2019, "Cross-Class and Cross-Ideological Convergences over Time: Insights from the Tunisian and Egyptian Revolutionary Uprisings", *Government and Opposition* (17 January): 1–19. doi.org/10.1017/gov.2018.52

Del Panta, Gianni, 2020, "From Uneven and Combined Development to Revolution: The Roots of Algeria's Crisis", *International Socialism 2:* 166 (Spring). isj.org.uk/roots-of-algerias-crisis

Disney, Nigel, 1978, "The Working Class Revolt in Tunisia", *MERIP*

Reports, 67 (May). doi.org/10.2307/3011401.

Donnelly, Richard, 2020, "Iraq's Climate Crisis: War, Water and Resistance", *Socialist Review* (March). socialistreview.org.uk/455/iraqs-climate-crisis-war-water-and-resistance.

Dougherty, George M, 2020, "Accelerating Military Innovation Lessons from China and Israel", Joint Force Quarterly 98, (Autumn).

Draper, Hal, 1966, *The Two Souls of Socialism,* www.marxists.org/archive/draper/1966/twosouls/

Draper, Hal, 1977, *Karl Marx's Theory of Revolution Vol I—State and Bureaucracy* (New York: Monthly Review Press)

Draper, Hal, 1978, *Karl Marx's Theory of Revolution Volume II—The Politics of Social Classes* (New York: Monthly Review Press)

Drew, Allison, 2014, *We Are No Longer in France: Communists in Colonial Algeria* (Manchester University Press). manchester.universitypressscholarship.com/view/10.7228/manchester/9780719090240.001.0001/upso-9780719090240

Dumenil, Gerard & Levy, Dominique, 2005, "The Neoliberal (Counter-)Revolution", in Saad-Filho, Alfredo & Johnston, Deborah (eds) *Neoliberalism: A Critical Reader:* 5–19. (London & Ann Arbor, MI: Pluto Press).

Economist, 2010, "Beyond the start-up nation: Israel has become a high-tech superpower over the past two decades. Can the good news last?" The Economist Business report (29 December). economist.com/business/2010/12/29/beyond-the-start-up-nation

Economist, 2017, "Startup nation or left-behind nation? Israel's economy is a study in contrasts, *The Economist Special Report* (18 May).

El Dahan, Maha & Raya, Jalabi, 2018, "Special Report: How Iraq's Agricultural Heartland Is Dying of Thirst". *Reuters*, (25 July 25). reuters.com/article/us-iraq-water-nineveh-special-report-idUSKBN1KF1C2.

El-Ghobashy, Mona, 2005 "The Metamorphosis of the Egyptian Muslim Brothers." *International Journal of Middle East Studies* 37: 3 (August): 373–95. doi.org/10.1017/S0020743805052128.

El-Gizouli, Magdi, 2019a, "Sudan's Revolutionary Crisis: Markets, the Quran and Army Officers", *Review of African Political Economy* blog (5 March). roape.net/2019/03/05/sudans-revolutionary-crisis-markets-the-quran-and-army-officers/

El-Gizouli, Magdi, 2019b, "The Fall of Al-Bashir: Mapping

Contestation Forces in Sudan". *Arab Reform Initiative* (blog), (12 April). arab-reform.net/publication/the-fall-of-al-bashir-mapping-contestation-forces-in-sudan

El-Gizouli, Magdi, 2020a, *Mobilization and Resistance in Sudan's Uprising*. Briefing Paper, Rift Valley Institute (January). riftvalley.net/publication/mobilization-and-resistance-sudans-uprising

El-Gizouli, Magdi, 2020b, "Grooming a Dictator: Al-Burhan Calls on Netanyahu". *StillSUDAN* (blog), (13 February). stillsudan.blogspot.com/2020/02/grooming-dictator-al-burhan-calls-on.html.

El Gizouli, Magdi, 2020c, "Wa jihaz al-dawla: hal man hal wasat?", *StillSUDAN* (February), stillsudan.blogspot.com/2020/02/blog-post_25.html

El-Meehy, Asya, 2012, "Egypt's Popular Committees", *Middle East Research and Information Project*, 265 (Winter). merip.org/2013/01/egypts-popular-committees

Empson, Martin, 2020, "Non-Violence, Social Change and Revolution", *International Socialism* 2: 165 (Spring). isj.org.uk/non-violence-social-change-and-revolution

Enab Baladi, 2019, "Sudanese Kandaka Alaa Saleh on the Walls of Idlib", *Enab Baladi* (11 April) english.enabbaladi.net/archives/2019/04/sudanese-kandaka-alaa-saleh-on-the-walls-of-idlib/

Engels, Friedrich, 1845, "Labour Movements" in *The Condition of the Working Class in England*, marxists.org/archive/marx/works/1845/condition-working-class/ch10.htm

Engels, Friedrich, 1884, *The Origin of the Family, Private Property and the State*. Marxists Internet Archive. marxists.org/archive/marx/works/1884/origin-family/index.htm

Evans, Martin, 2012, "Contextualising Contemporary Algeria: June 1965 and October 1988". *OpenDemocracy* (25 May). opendemocracy.net/en/contextualising-contemporary-algeria-june-1965-and-october-1988

Farraj, Lamees & Dana, Tariq, 2021, "The Politicization of Public Sector Employment and Salaries in the West Bank and Gaza", *Al Shabaka* (14 March). al-shabaka.org/summaries/the-politicization-of-public-sector-employment-and-salaries-in-the-west-bank-and-gaza/

Fathi, Yasmine, 2012, "Egypt's 'Battle of the Camel': The Day the Tide Turned", *Ahram Online* (2 February) english.ahram.org.eg/News/33470.aspx

Fanon, Frantz, Philcox, Richard, Sartre, Jean-Paul & Bhabha, Homi K,

2001, *The Wretched of the Earth*, (London, Penguin).

Fattah, Khaled, 2011, "Yemen: A Social Intifada in a Republic of Sheikhs", *Middle East Policy,* 18: 3 (Fall), dx.doi.org/10.1111/j.1475-4967.2011.00499.x

Fassihian, Dokhi, 2018. *Democratic Backsliding in Tunisia: The Case for Renewed International Attention*, Freedom House, Policy Brief. freedomhouse.org/report/policy-brief/2018/democratic-backsliding-tunisia-case-renewed-international-attention.

Fayek, Mina, 2014k. "Welcome to the 'Factory of Men'", *OpenDemocracy* (20 May). opendemocracy.net/en/north-africa-west-asia/welcome-to-factory-of-men/

Feltrin, Lorenzo, 2019, "Labour and Democracy in the Maghreb: The Moroccan and Tunisian Trade Unions in the 2011 Arab Uprisings", *Economic and Industrial Democracy* 40: 1 (February): 42–64. doi.org/10.1177/0143831X18780316

Financial Times, 2020, "Bankrupt Lebanon's Turn to IMF Is Overdue", *Financial Times: Editorial* (4 May) ft.com/content/ae2484c4-8bc1-11ea-a01c-a28a3e3fbd33.

Finn, Tom, 2011, "Yemen's Southern Rebels Emerge from the Shadows", *The Guardian*, (11 November) theguardian.com/world/2011/nov/11/yemen-southern-rebels-hirak-secession.

Finden, Alice, 2015, "LGBT Lives in Egypt and Lebanon: Surviving Moral Panics and State Homophobia." *Middle East Solidarity* 2 (Autumn).

Foreign Relations of the United States: *Diplomatic Papers, 1943, The Near East and Africa, Volume IV* (Madison, University of Wisconsin). history.state.gov/historicaldocuments/frus1943v04/d893.

Forces of Freedom and Change, 2019, "Declaration of Freedom and Change", *Radio Dabanga* (1 January) dabangasudan.org/uploads/media/5cf94b02b2055.pdf

Fouad, Hisham, 2004, "Qiraa Awliyya Fi Al-Ihtigagat al-Ummaliyya al-Rahina." e-socialists.net, (8 November). e-socialists.net/node/1425

Fowler, Gary L, 1973, "Decolonization of rural Libya", *Annals of the Association of American Geographers* 63: 4 (December): 490–506. doi.org/10.1111/j.1467-8306.1973.tb00943.x

Freedom House, 2010, "The Global State of Workers' Rights - Sudan", *Freedom House*, (31 August). refworld.org/docid/4d4fc7f42.html

George, Alan, 2003, *Syria: Neither Bread nor Freedom* (London, New York: Zed Books).

Ghanem Yazbeck, Dalia, 2017, "Challenging Fieldwork Researching Large-Scale Massacres in Algeria", *Anthropology Matters*, 17: 2, anthropologymatters.com/index.php/anth_matters/article/view/466

Ghanem-Yazbeck, Dalia, 2018, "Limiting Change through Change: The Key to the Algerian Regime's Longevity", *Carnegie Endowment for International Peace* (April) carnegieendowment.org/files/CMEC_70_Yazbeck_Algeria_Final.pdf.

Glanz, James, 2007, "Bechtel Meets Goals on Fewer Than Half of Its Iraq Rebuilding Projects, U.S. Study Finds", *New York Times*, (26 July). nytimes.com/2007/07/26/world/middleeast/26reconstruct.html.

Gliech, Oliver, 2020, "Petroleum" in *International Encyclopedia of the First World War Online*. encyclopedia.1914-1918-online.net/article/petroleum

Globalfirepower.com, 2022, Annual Defense Review 2022 globalfirepower.com/

Gobe, Eric, 2010, "The Gafsa Mining Basin between Riots and a Social Movement: Meaning and Significance of a Protest Movement in Ben Ali's Tunisia", *HAL Open Science, Working Paper*. halshs.archives-ouvertes.fr/halshs-00557826

Goodrich, Carter, 1920, *The Frontier of Control: A Study in British Workshop Politics* (New York: Harcourt, Brace and Howe). archive.org/details/frontierofcontro00gooduoft.

Gopal, Anand, 2018, "Syria's Last Bastion of Freedom", *The New Yorker* (3 December). newyorker.com/magazine/2018/12/10/syrias-last-bastion-of-freedom.

Grewal, Sharan, 2016, "A Quiet Revolution: The Tunisian Military After Ben Ali." *Carnegie Endowment for International Peace* (24 February) carnegieendowment.org/2016/02/24/quiet-revolution-tunisian-military-after-ben-ali-pub-62780.

Habani, Amal, 2015, "Arrested and Beaten for Wearing Trousers: Stop the Public Flogging of Women in Sudan!" *Human Rights Now* blog (31 March). blog.amnestyusa.org/africa/arrested-and-beaten-for-wearing-trousers-stop-the-public-flogging-of-women-in-sudan

Haddad, Fanar, 2020, "The Iraqi people will pay the price for Iran-US rivalry, again: One of the early victims of the US escalation against Iran is Iraq's unprecedented protest movement", *Al Jazeera* (9 January), aljazeera.com/opinions/2020/1/9/

the-iraqi-people-will-pay-the-price-for-iran-us-rivalry-again

Haddour, Azzedine. "Torture Unveiled." *Theory, Culture & Society* 27, 7–8 (December 2010): 66–90. doi.org/10.1177/0263276410383710.

Halper, Jeff, nd, "The Matrix of Control", ICAHD website, icahd.org/get-the-facts/matrix-control/

Hammy, Cihad, 2018, "The First Commune in Kobane: Construction and Challenges." *OpenDemocracy*, (3 September). opendemocracy.net/en/north-africa-west-asia/first-commune-in-kobane-construction-and-challenges

Hammy, Cihad & Miley, Thomas J, 2022, "Lessons from Rojava for the Paradigm of Social Ecology", *Frontiers in Political Science* 3 (January). frontiersin.org/articles/10.3389/fpos.2021.815338/full

Hanieh, Adam, 2011, *Capitalism and Class in the Gulf States* (Palgrave Macmillan).

Hanieh, Adam, 2013 *Lineages of Revolt: Issues of Contemporary Capitalism in the Middle East* (Haymarket)

Hanieh, Adam, 2018, *Money, Markets, and Monarchies: The Gulf Cooperation Council and the Political Economy of the Contemporary Middle East* (Cambridge University Press).

Harman, Chris, 1994, "The Prophet and the Proletariat", *International Socialism 2:* 64 (Autumn). marxists.org/archive/harman/1994/xx/islam.htm.

Harman, Chris, 1991, "The State and Capitalism Today", *International Socialism* 2: 51 (Summer) isj.org.uk/the-state-and-capitalism-today/

Harman, Chris, 2002, "The workers of the world", *International Socialism* **2: 96** (Autumn) marxists.org/archive/harman/2002/xx/workers.htm

Harman, Chris, 2010, *Zombie Capitalism: Global Crisis and the Relevance of Marx* (Chicago: Haymarket Books).

Harman, Chris, 2014, *The Lost Revolution* (London: Bookmarks).

Hashemi, Nader, 2015, *The ISIS Crisis and the Broken Politics of the Middle East*, University of Denver, bu.edu/cura/files/2016/12/hashemi-paper1.pdf.

Hashmat, Dina, 2011, "Ahlan bikum fi midan al-tahrir ... gumhuriyya al-ahlam al-mumkina", *Al-Akhbar*, (8 February)Hassan, Budour, 2021, "Palestine's uprising and the actuality of liberation", *Mada Masr* (24 May), madamasr.com/en/2021/05/24/opinion/u/palestines-uprising-and-the-actuality-of-liberation/

Hearn, Julie & Dallal, Abdulsalam, 2019, "The 'NGOisation' of the Syrian Revolution." *International Socialism* 2: 164 (Winter). isj.org.uk/the-ngoisation-of-the-syrian-revolution/

Herring, Eric & Rangwala, Glen, 2006, *Iraq in Fragments: The Occupation and Its Legacy* (London: Hurst).

Hiltermann, Joost, 1993, *Behind the Intifada: Labor and Women's Movements in the Occupied Territories* (Princeton, NJ: Princeton University Press).

Hinnebusch, Raymond, 2006 "Authoritarian persistence, democratization theory and the Middle East: An overview and critique", Democratization, 13:3, 373-395

Hirschauge, Orr, 2015, "Israeli Army Builds a Desert Outpost—Tech Firms Follow", *Wall Street Journal,* (5 June) wsj.com/articles/israeli-army-builds-a-desert-posttech-firms-follow-1433525715

Hirst, David, 2003, *The Gun and the Olive Branch: The Roots of Violence in the Middle East* (London: Faber).

Historical Materialism, 2019, "The Lebanese October Revolution against Sectarian Realism and Neoliberal Authoritarianism", *Historical Materialism blog*, (November), historicalmaterialism.org/interviews/lebanese-october-revolution-against-sectarian-realism-and-neoliberal-authoritarianism.

Hmed, Choukri, & Raillard, Sarah-Louise, 2012, "Abeyance Networks, Contingency and Structures: History and Origins of the Tunisian Revolution". *Revue Française de Science Politique (English)* 62, No 5: 31, doi.org/10.3917/rfspe.625.0031

Human Rights Watch, 2011, "Egypt: Retry or Free 12,000 After Unfair Military Trials | Human Rights Watch", hrw.org/news/2011/09/10/egypt-retry-or-free-12000-after-unfair-military-trials.

Human Rights Watch, 2015, "'Men With No Mercy' | Rapid Support Forces Attacks against Civilians in Darfur, Sudan." *Human Rights Watch*. hrw.org/report/2015/09/09/men-no-mercy/rapid-support-forces-attacks-against-civilians-darfur-sudan

Human Rights Watch, 2016, "'We Feel We Are Cursed,'" (18 May), hrw.org/report/2016/05/18/we-feel-we-are-cursed/life-under-isis-sirte-libya.

Human Rights Watch, 2018, "World Report 2019: Rights Trends in Syria", (17 December) hrw.org/world-report/2019/country-chapters/syria

Human Rights Watch, 2021, "Tunisia: Police Use Violent Tactics to Quash Protests." *Human Rights Watch*. hrw.org/news/2021/02/05/tunisia-police-use-violent-tactics-quash-protests.

Hummaida, Abdelrazig S & Dousa, Khalid M, 2019, "Sudan's Doctors Treating the Political Ailments of the Nation," *Africa Is A Country* (3 February) africasacountry.com/2019/03/sudans-doctors-and-treating-the-political-ailments-of-the-nation.

Hyman, Richard, 1975, *Industrial Relations: A Marxist Introduction* (London: Macmillan).

Ibrahim, Arwa, 2015, "Head of Egypt's Council for Women Slams Detained Female Activists", *Middle East Eye* (13 February). middleeasteye.net/news/head-egypts-council-women-slams-detained-female-activists.

Ibrahim, Mohammed Shafiq, 2012. "A Revolution in an Egyptian Hospital," *British Medical Journal (BMJ)* 344 (1 February). bmj.com/content/344/bmj.e576

ICG, 2001, "Algeria's Economy: The Vicious Circle of Oil and Violence", *International Crisis Group* (26 October). crisisgroup.org/middle-east-north-africa/north-africa/algeria/algerias-economy-vicious-circle-oil-and-violence

ICG, 2017, "How the Islamic State Rose, Fell and Could Rise Again in the Maghreb", *International Crisis Group* (24 July). crisisgroup.org/middle-east-north-africa/north-africa/178-how-islamic-state-rose-fell-and-could-rise-again-maghreb.

ICG, 2018, "Breaking Algeria's Economic Paralysis", *International Crisis Group* (19 October). crisisgroup.org/middle-east-north-africa/north-africa/algeria/192-breaking-algerias-economic-paralysis

ILOSTAT, 2022, "ILO Data Explorer", *International Labour Organisation* (ILO) website, ilostat.ilo.org/data/

IMF, 2013, "World Economic Outlook", *International Monetary Fund Research Department, World Economic and Financial Surveys* (April). imf.org/en/Publications/WEO/Issues/2016/12/31/World-Economic-Outlook-April-2013-Hopes-Realities-Risks-40201

IMF, 2016, "Historical Public Debt Database". *International Monetary Fund, Historical Public Debt Database*. data.imf.org/?sk=806ED027-520D-497F-9052-63EC199F5E63.

Israel Central Bureau of Statistics, nd, 'Total Immigration to Israel from the Former Soviet Union', *Jewish Virtual Library*, jewishvirtuallibrary.org/total-immigration-to-israel-from-former-soviet-union

Israeli Ministry of Foreign Affairs, 1950, 'Law of Return', MFA website, mfa.gov.il/MFA/MFA-Archive/1950-1959/Pages/Law%20 of%20Return%205710-1950.aspx

Jafari, Peyman, 2009, "Rupture and Revolt in Iran", *International Socialism* 2: 124 (Autumn) isj.org.uk/rupture-and-revolt-in-iran

Jalal, Marwa, 2019. "Outsourcing Fortress Europe: The Khartoum Process and the Rebranding of Sudan's Brutal Militia." *MENA Solidarity Network*, October 27. menasolidaritynetwork.com/2019/10/27/outsourcing-fortress-europe-the-khartoum-process-and-the-rebranding-of-sudans-brutal-militia

Joda, Fatima, 2019, 'We are no longer scared of death', *Middle East Solidarity* magazine, (17 March).

Johnson, Angella, 2013, "Freedom in Egypt? It Just Gave Men the Freedom to Rape Me in Tahrir Square: As Violence Erupts in Cairo, Woman Attacked by a Gang in Demonstration Recounts Her Ordeal", *Daily Mail* (7 July). dailymail.co.uk/news/article-2357633/Freedom-Egypt-It-just-gave-men-freedom-rape-Tahrir-Square.html

Jones, Marc O, 2013, "The History of British Involvement in Bahrain's Internal Security." *OpenDemocracy* (8 August). opendemocracy.net/en/opensecurity/history-of-british-involvement-in-bahrains-internal-security

Kabbani, Nader, 2019, "Youth Employment in the Middle East and North Africa: Revisiting and Reframing the Challenge." *Brookings* blog (26 February). brookings.edu/research/youth-employment-in-the-middle-east-and-north-africa-revisiting-and-reframing-the-challenge/

Karouny, Mariam, 2013b. "Shi'ite Fighters Rally to Defend Damascus Shrine", *Reuters*, (3 March) reuters.com/article/us-syria-crisis-shiites-idUSBRE92202X20130303.

Katouzian, Homa, 1998, "The Campaign against the Anglo-Iranian Agreement of 1919", *British Journal of Middle Eastern Studies,* 25:1 (May).

Kaya, Muzaffer, 2018. "Turkey's Purge of Critical Academia." *Middle East Research and Information project (MERIP)*, (15 December). merip.org/2018/12/turkeys-purge-of-critical-academia

Kellier, Peter, 2012, "Ghosts of Syria: Diehard Militias Who Kill in the Name of Assad", *The Guardian* (31 May). theguardian.com/world/2012/may/31/ghosts-syria-regime-shabiha-militias.

Khaddour, Kheder, 2015, *The Assad Regime's Hold on the Syrian State*, Carnegie Middle East Center, Carnegie Endowment for

International Peace (July). carnegieendowment.org/files/syrian_state1.pdf.

Khalil, Andrea, 2014a, "Tunisia's Women: Partners in Revolution", *The Journal of North African Studies* 19: 2 (15 March): 186–99. doi.org/10.1080/13629387.2013.870424.

Khalil, Andrea, 2014b, "Gender paradoxes of the Arab Spring", *The Journal of North African Studies*, Volume 19:2, (27 March): 131-136

Kienle, Eberhard, 2000, *A Grand Delusion: Democracy and Economic Reform in Egypt* (London: I.B. Tauris).

King, Stephen J, 2003, *Liberalization Against Democracy: The Local Politics of Economic Reform in Tunisia* (Bloomington: Indiana University Press). ebookcentral.proquest.com/lib/cam/detail.action?docID=157821.

King, Stephen J, 2017, "6. Informalized Government Workers in Tunisia" in Eaton, Adrienne E, Schurman, Susan J & Chan, Martha A (eds) *Informal Workers and Collective Action: A Global Perspective* (Ithaca, NY: Cornell University Press):141-156. doi.org/10.7591/9781501707964-008

Kingsley, Patrick & Nazzal, Rami, 2021, In Show of Unity, Palestinians Strike Across West Bank, Gaza and Israel", *New York Times* (18 May), nytimes.com/2021/05/18/world/middleeast/palestine-strike.html

Kirkpatrick, David, 2015, "Coming to mourn Tahrir Square's Dead and Joining Them Instead, New York Times (3 February) nytimes.com/2015/02/04/world/middleeast/shaimaa-el-sabbagh-tahrir-square-killing-angers-egyptians.html

Kirkpatrick, David D, 2015, "Recordings Suggest Emirates and Egyptian Military Pushed Ousting of Morsi", *The New York Times* (2 March). nytimes.com/2015/03/02/world/middleeast/recordings-suggest-emirates-and-egyptian-military-pushed-ousting-of-morsi.html.

Knapp, Michael, Flach, Amja & Ayboğa, Ercan, 2016, *Revolution in Rojava: Democratic Autonomy and Women's Liberation in Syrian Kurdistan,* The Anarchist Library, theanarchistlibrary.org/library/michael-knapp-anja-flach-and-ercan-ayboga-revolution-in-rojava

Knecht, Eric & Ellen, Francis, 2020, "Starved of Dollars and Drowning in Debt, Lebanon's Economy Sinks Fast", *Reuters* (12 March), reuters.com/article/us-lebanon-crisis-economy-insight-idUSKBN20Z1FC.

Koach LaOvdim, nd, "Who Are We?", *Koach LaOvdim* website, workers.org.il/?lang=en

Kristianasen, Wendy. "Truth & Justice after a Brutal Civil War: Algeria: The Women Speak." *Review of African Political Economy*, 33: 108 (2006): 346–51. jstor.org/stable/4007174.

Larabi, Samir, Smith, Shelagh & Hamouchene, Hamza, 2020, "Trade Unions and the Algerian Uprising", *MENA Solidarity Network* (April). menasolidaritynetwork.files.wordpress.com/2020/05/tradeunions_algerianuprising_0520_web-1.pdf.

Laura & Charan, 2021, "Report on the general strike in Palestine // an interview with Riya Al'Sanah", *Notes from Below* (26 May), notesfrombelow.org/article/report-general-strike-palestine

Lawson, Fred, 1982, "Social Bases for the Hama Revolt", *Middle East Research and Information Project Reports*, 110 (November).

Lawson, Fred, 2018, "The Political Economy of the Syrian Uprising", in Hinnebusch, Raymond A & Imady, Omar (eds) *The Syria Uprising: Domestic Origins and Early Trajectory* (London: Routledge).

Layachi, Azzedine, 2019, "Algeria—Economic Austerity, Political Stagnation and the Gathering Storm" in *The Lure of Authoritarianism: The Maghreb after the Arab Spring*. (Bloomington: Indiana University Press). ebookcentral.proquest.com/lib/cam/detail.action?docID=5744489.

Lellis, Francesco de, 2019, "Peasants, Dispossession and Resistance in Egypt: An Analysis of Protest Movements and Organisations before and after the 2011 Uprising", *Review of African Political Economy* 46: 162 (2 October): 582–98. doi.org/10.1080/03056244.2019.1688487.

Lenin, Vladimir, 1899, "On Strikes", marxists.org/archive/lenin/works/1899/dec/strikes.htm.

Lenin, Vladimir, 1915, *The Collapse of the Second International*, marxists.org/archive/lenin/works/1915/csi/ii.htm.

Lenin, Vladimir, 1916a, *Imperialism, the Highest Stage of Capitalism*, (January-June) marxists.org/archive/lenin/works/1916/imp-hsc

Lenin, Vladimir, 1916b, *The Discussion On Self-Determination Summed Up*, (July) marxists.org/archive/lenin/works/1916/jul/x01.htm

Lenin, Vladimir, 1917a. "The Tasks of the Proletariat in the Present Revolution (a.k.a. the April Theses)", *Pravda* (7 April). marxists.org/archive/lenin/works/1917/apr/04.htm.

Lenin, Vladimir, 1917b. "The Dual Power", *Pravda*, (9 April), marxists.org/archive/lenin/works/1917/apr/09.htm.

Lenin, Vladimir, 1917c, *The State and Revolution,* marxists.org/archive/lenin/works/1917/staterev

Lenin, Vladimir, nd, "Kautsky, 1914 and 1915 (On Imperialism, War and Social-Democracy)", marxists.org/archive/lenin/works/1916/ni-delta/kautsky.htm#v39pp76-264.

Lieberman, Aviva, 2018, " Immigrants from the Former Soviet Union: A Snapshot of their Situation in the Israeli Labor Market", *Adva Center website*, (26 June) adva.org/post-soviet-aliyah-laborforce/

Liebknecht, Karl, 1907, *Militarism & Anti-Militarism*, marxists.org/archive/liebknecht-k/works/1907/militarism-antimilitarism/index.htm.

Long, Scott, 2017, "Egypt's Wipe-Out-the-Queers Bill", *A Paper Bird* blog, (30 October). paper-bird.net/2017/10/30/egypts-wipe-out-the-queers-bill

Loveluck, Louisa & Salim, Mustafa, 2020, "How powerful cleric Moqtada al-Sadr could snuff out Iraq's mass street protests", *Washington Post* (4 March), washingtonpost.com/world/middle_east/how-mercurial-cleric-moqtada-al-sadr-could-snuff-out-iraqs-mass-street-protests/2020/03/03/a9172c56-4dc4-11ea-967b-e074d302c7d4_story.html

Lumley-Sapanski, Audrey, Schwarz, Katarina & Valverde-Ca, Ana, 2021, "The Khartoum Process and Human Trafficking", Forced Migration Review, 68 (November). fmreview.org/externalisation/lumleysapanski-schwarz-valverdecano

Luxemburg, Rosa, 1900, "The Consequences of Social Reformism and General Nature of Reformism", Reform or Revolution. Marxists Internet Archive www.marxists.org/archive/luxemburg/1900/reform-revolution/ch05.htm

Luxemburg, Rosa, 1913, *The Accumulation of Capital,* marxists.org/archive/luxemburg/1913/accumulation-capital/

Luxemburg, Rosa, 1906, *The Mass Strike, the Political Party and the Trade Unions,* marxists.org/archive/luxemburg/1906/mass-strike/

Mabro, Robert & Radwan, Samir Muhammad, 1976, *The Industrialization of Egypt, 1939-1973: Policy and Performance* (Oxford: Clarendon Press).

MacLeod, Arlene E, 1993, *Accommodating Protest: Working Women, the New Veiling, and Change in Cairo* (New York: Columbia University Press).

Mada Masr, 2019, "Al-Sudan fil idrab", *Mada Masr* (7 March), madamasr.com/ar/2019/03/07/feature

Maiberg, Emmanuel, 2021, "Israeli mob organized destruction of Arab [Palestinian] business on WhatsApp", *Vice*, (19 May), vice.com/en/article/jg8myx/israeli-mob-organized-destruction-of-arab-business-on-whatsapp

Makdisi, Ussama Samir, 2000, *The Culture of Sectarianism: Community, History, and Violence in Nineteenth-Century Ottoman Lebanon* (Berkeley: University of California Press).

Majed, Rima, 2019, "Lebanon's 'October Revolution' Must Go On!" *OpenDemocracy*, (20 October). opendemocracy.net/en/north-africa-west-asia/lebanons-october-revolution-must-go-on

Makara, Michael, 2013, "Coup-Proofing, Military Defection, and the Arab Spring." *Democracy and Security* 9: 4 (September): 334–59. doi:10.1080/17419166.2013.802983

Malm, Andreas, 2017, *Fossil Capital: The Rise of Steam Power and the Roots of Global Warming*. (London; New York: Verso).

Maloney, Suzanne, 2015, *Iran's Political Economy since the Revolution* (Cambridge: Cambridge University Press).

Margulies, Ron, 2016, "What are we to do with Islam? The case of Turkey", *International Socialism* 2:151 (Summer) isj.org.uk/what-are-we-to-do-with-islam/

Margulies, Ron, 2018, "Why Turkish Troops Are in Syria", *International Socialism* 2:158 (11 April). isj.org.uk/why-turkish-troops-are-in-syria

Marfleet, Philip, 2014, "Egypt: After the Coup", *International Socialism* 2: 142 (2 April). isj.org.uk/egypt-after-the-coup

Marfleet, Philip, 2017, "Neoliberalism, the state and revolution: the case of Egypt", International Socialism Journal, Vol 2, no. 155, (29 June) isj.org.uk/neoliberalism-the-state-and-revolution-the-case-of-egypt/

Marfleet, Philip, 2019, "Iraq: What Happened Next...", *International Socialism* 2: 161 (Spring). isj.org.uk/iraq-what-happened-next

Markaz Awlad al-Ard, 2010, "Hasad al-harakah al-ummaliyya fi am 2010." ecesr.com.

Marsawa, Lubna & Abu Sneineh, Mustafa, 2020, "Palestinian citizens of Israel protest against land grab in Negev desert", *Middle East Eye* (22 June)   middleeasteye.net/news/israel-palestinian-bedouin-negev-protest-land-grab

Marshall, Phil, 1989, *Intifada: Zionism, Imperialism and Palestinian Resistance* (London: Bookmarks).

Marshall, Shana & Stacher, Joshua, 2012, "Egypt's Generals and Transnational Capital", *Middle East Report*, 262 (Spring). merip.org/mer/mer262/egypts-generals-transnational-capital.

Marx, Karl & Engels, Frederick, 1848, *The Manifesto of the Communist Party*. marxists.org/archive/marx/works/1848/communist-manifesto.

Marx, Karl, 1871, *The Civil War in France*, marxists.org/archive/marx/works/1871/civil-war-france/ch05.htm.

Marx, Karl & Engels, Friedrich,1850. "Address of the Central Committee to the Communist League by Marx and Engels", marxists.org. marxists.org/archive/marx/works/1847/communist-league/1850-ad1.htm.

Masmoudi, Radwan A, 2021, "Keep Tunisia's Military Out of Politics." *Foreign Policy* (2 September). foreignpolicy.com/2021/09/02/unisia-kais-saied-constitution-coup-parliament-suspension-military-apolitical

Matthiesen, Toby, 2013, *Sectarian Gulf: Bahrain, Saudi Arabia, and the Arab Spring That Wasn't* (Redwood, California: Stanford University Press).

Maurice, Emma Powys, 2021, "Poignant tributes for Sara Hegazy, the Egyptian activist tortured for flying a Pride flag, one year after her tragic death", Pink News (14 June) pinknews.co.uk/2021/06/14/sara-hegazy-egyptian-lgbt-activist-died-suicide-anniversary/

McGregor, Sheila, 2018, "Social Reproduction Theory: Back to (Which) Marx?" *International Socialism* 160 (16 October). isj.org.uk/social-reproduction-theory/

McKernan, Bethan & Akoush, Hussein, 2020, "Exclusive: 2,000 Syrian Fighters Deployed to Libya to Support Government", *The Guardian*, (15 January) theguardian.com/world/2020/jan/15/exclusive-2000-syrian-troops-deployed-to-libya-to-support-regime.

McLarney, Ellen, 2013, "Women's Rights in the Egyptian Constitution: (Neo)Liberalism's Family Values." *Jadaliyya* blog (22 May). jadaliyya.com/Details/28666.

MENA Solidarity, 2011, "Egypt: Teachers Tell Generals 'Meet Our Demands ... or No School This Year.'" *MENA Solidarity Network* blog, (13 September). menasolidaritynetwork.com/2011/09/13/egypt-teachers-tell-generals-meet-our-demands-or-no-school-this-year

MENA Solidarity Network, 2012, "Egypt: Women Workers Speak out—Teachers' Unions Build Unity from below," *Middle East Solidarity,* (13 March). menasolidaritynetwork.com/

egyptwomen4

MENA Solidarity Network, 2013, "Egypt: Bread Distribution Workers Speak Out", *Middle East Solidarity* (11 June). menasolidaritynetwork.com/2013/06/11/egypt_bread_distribution_workers

MENA Solidarity, 2019a, "'This Is Not Just Protests over Bread and Fuel, It Is a Revolution—Sudanese Doctor Speaks Out", *MENA Solidarity Network* blog, (3 February). menasolidaritynetwork.com/2019/02/03/this-is-not-just-protests-over-bread-and-fuel-it-is-a-revolution-sudanese-doctor-speaks-out

MENA Solidarity, 2019b, "Sudan's General Strike Sends a Message to General Hemeti: 'We Want Civilian Rule Now'", *MENA Solidarity Network* blog, (28 May) menasolidaritynetwork.com/2019/05/28/sudans-general-strike-sends-a-message-to-general-hemeti-we-want-civilian-rule-now

MENA Solidarity Network, 2019c, "Algeria: The Storm Breaks," *Middle East Solidarity,* (8 July). menasolidaritynetwork.com/2019/07/08/algeria-the-storm-breaks-2

MENA Solidarity, 2020, "'This Is the Ministry of Corruption, Fraud and Plunder' Lebanese Protesters Occupy Government Buildings as Army Uses Live Ammunition against Demonstrations for Justice", *MENA Solidarity Network* (9 August). menasolidaritynetwork.com/2020/08/09/this-is-the-ministry-of-corruption-fraud-and-plunder-lebanese-protesters-occupy-government-buildings-as-army-uses-live-ammunition-against-demonstrations-for-justice

MENA Solidarity Network, 2019, "Not My President, Say Algerians, as Army's Candidate Claims Electoral Victory despite Massive Poll Boycott and Continuing Protests", *MENA Solidarity Network* (15 December), menasolidaritynetwork.com/2019/12/15/not-my-president-say-algerians-as-armys-candidate-claims-electoral-victory-despite-massive-poll-boycott-and-continuing-protests

MENA Solidarity, 2021, "Updated: More Arrests of Sudanese Teachers as Generals Try to Tighten Grip on the State", *MENA Solidarity Network.* menasolidaritynetwork.com/2021/11/11/more-arrests-of-sudanese-teachers-as-generals-try-to-tighten-grip-on-the-state

MENA Solidarity, 2022b. "Sudan Update: Resistance Committees Call for Formation of 'People's Authority' to Overthrow Coup Regime." *MENA Solidarity Network.* menasolidaritynetwork.

com/2022/03/01/sudan-update-resistance-committees-call-for-formation-of-peoples-authority-to-overthrow-coup-regime

MENA Solidarity, 2022d. "Conference Report: Report on the Sudanese Teachers' Strike." *MENA Solidarity Network*. menasolidaritynetwork.com/2022/04/01/conference-report-report-on-the-sudanese-teachers-strike

MENA Solidarity, 2022f. "Sudan Teachers' Strike and Exam Boycott Forces Concessions from Generals' Regime." *MENA Solidarity Network*. menasolidaritynetwork.com/2022/04/27/sudan-teachers-strike-and-exam-boycott-forces-concessions-from-generals-regime

Middle East Eye, 2019, "Sudan: The Names of 100 People Killed in a Week of Deadly Violence" *Middle East Eye* (12 June), middleeasteye.net/news/sudan-names-100-killed-deadly-week

Middle East Eye, 2020, "Sudan's Transitional Government Appoints Civilian Rulers to States", *Middle East Eye* (23 July). middleeasteye.net/news/sudan-transitional-government-appoints-civilian-rulers-states

Ministry of Education, 2007, "National Strategic Plan For Pre-University Education Reform in Egypt 2007/8—2011/2," *UNESCO*. planipolis.iiep.unesco.org/upload/Egypt/EgyptStrategicPlanPre-universityEducation.pdf

Mitchell, Timothy, 2013, *Carbon Democracy: Political Power in the Age of Oil* (London: Verso).

Molyneux, John, 2017, *Lenin for Today* (London: Bookmarks).

Monedero, Juan Carlos, 2019, "Snipers in the Kitchen: State Theory and Latin America's Left Cycle", *New Left Review* 120 (December). newleftreview.org/issues/II120/articles/snipers-in-the-kitchen.

Mosler, Volkhard, 2013, "An Army in Revolt: Germany 1918-9", in Gonzale, Mike and Barekat, Houman (eds) *Arms and the People Popular Movements and the Military from the Paris Commune to the Arab Spring* (London: Pluto Press).

Munif, Yasser, 2021b. "The Syrian Revolt and the Politics of Bread." *TNI Website*. longreads.tni.org/the-syrian-revolt-and-the-politics-of-bread.

Murray, Rebecca, 2013, "Land Disputes Threaten South Yemen Stability", *Al Jazerra* (13 April) aljazeera.com/features/2013/4/13/land-disputes-threaten-south-yemen-stability

Naguib, Sameh, 2006, *Al-Ikhwan al-Muslimun: Ru'iya Ishtarakiyya*.

Markaz al-dirasat al-ishtarakiyya, (Cairo: Centre for Socialist Studies).

Naguib, Sameh, 2011a, "None of us in our wildest dreams could have imagined wheat happened that day", *Socialist Worker* (28 June) socialistworker.co.uk/features/egyptian-revolution-none-of-us-in-our-wildest-dreams-could-have-imagined-what-happened-that-day/

Naguib, Sameh, 2011b, *The Egyptian Revolution* (London: Bookmarks).

Nagy, Balázs, 1964, "Budapest 1956: The Central Workers' Council", *International Socialism* 1:18, (Autumn): 24-31, marxists.org/history/etol/newspape/isj/1964/no018/nagy.htm

Nassif, Hicham Bou, 2013, "Why the Egyptian Army Didn't Shoot." *Middle East Research & Information Project (MERIP)*, (2 January). merip.org/2013/01/why-the-egyptian-army-didnt-shoot

Nassif, Hicham Bou, 2022, "Why the Military Abandoned Democracy", *Journal of Democracy* 33: 1 (January):27–39. muse.jhu.edu/issue/47135

Niblock, Tim, 1987, *Class and Power in Sudan: The Dynamics of Sudanese Politics, 1898-1985*. (Albany: State University of New York Press).

Nixon, Ron, 2011, "US Groups Helped Nurture Arab Uprisings", *The New York Times*, (14 April) nytimes.com/2011/04/15/world/15aid.html.

Nur Duz, Zehra, & Geldi, Mahmut, 2020, "Material Damage from Beirut Blast Surpasses $15 Billion", *Anadolu Agency* (12 August), aa.com.tr/en/middle-east/material-damage-from-beirut-blast-surpasses-15-billion/1939886

Ocalan, Abdullah, 2011, *Democratic Confederalism* (London: Transmedia Publishers).

OPEC, nd, "OPEC : Member Countries", *Organisation of the Petroleum Exporting Countries*, website. opec.org/opec_web/en/about_us/25.htm

Osborn, Larence E, 1971, *Cotton in Iran*, (Washington: US Department of Agriculture, Foreign Agricultural Service).

Palumbo, Michael, 1990, *Imperial Israel: The History of the Occupation of the West Bank & Gaza* (London: Bloomsbury).

Pappe, Ilan, 2015, *The Ethnic Cleansing of Palestine* (London: Oneworld).

PCPSR, 2021, Poll, *Palestinian Center for Policy and Survey Research website* (14 December), pcpsr.org/sites/default/files/

Poll%2082%20English%20full%20text%20DEC2021.pdf

Peterkin, Tom, 2018, "New Book Traces Story of Secretive Highlands Oil Agreement", *The Scotsman*, (6 January). scotsman.com/business/new-book-traces-story-secretive-highlands-oil-agreement-1434003

Petran, Tabitha, 1987, *The Struggle over Lebanon* (New York: Monthly Review Press).

Physicians for Human Rights, 2020, "'Chaos and Fire'—An Analysis of Sudan's 3 June 2019 Khartoum Massacre—Sudan," (5 March), reliefweb.int/report/sudan/chaos-and-fire-analysis-sudan-s-june-3-2019-khartoum-massacre.

Pierret, Thomas, 2013, *Religion and State in Syria: The Sunni Ulama from Coup to Revolution*, (Cambridge: Cambridge Middle East Studies).

Poya, Maryam, 2010, *Women, Work and Islamism: Ideology and Resistance in Iran* (London: Zed Books).

Purfield, Catriona; Finger, Harald; Ongley, Karen; Baduel, Benedicte; Castellanos, Carolina; Pierre, Gaelle; Stepanyan, Vahram & Roos, Erik, 2018, "Opportunity for All : Promoting Growth and Inclusiveness in the Middle East and North Africa." International Monetary Fund (IMF), (12 July). imf.org/en/Publications/Departmental-Papers-Policy-Papers/Issues/2018/07/10/Opportunity-for-All-Promoting-Growth-and-Inclusiveness-in-the-Middle-East-and-North-Africa-45981.

Radio Dabanga, 2016, "Sudan: Doctors At 65 Sudanese Hospitals Now On Strike". *Radio Dabanga (Amsterdam)*, (9 October) allafrica.com/stories/201610090021.html.

Radio Dabanga, 2018, "Strike by 20,000+ Cargo Workers Paralyses Port Sudan", *Radio Dabanga*, (2 May). dabangasudan.org/en/all-news/article/strike-by-20-000-cargo-workers-paralyses-port-sudan.

Radio Dabanga, 2019, "Sudan Junta 'Retires' 98 Senior NISS Officers". Radio Dabanga, (11 June). dabangasudan.org/en/all-news/article/sudan-junta-retires-98-senior-niss-officers

Radio Dabanga, 2019b, "El Burhan: 'Rapid Support Forces Are an Integral Part of the Sudanese Army'", *Radio Dabanga* (23 December). dabangasudan.org/en/all-news/article/el-burhan-rapid-support-forces-are-an-integral-part-of-the-sudanese-army.

Radio Dabanga, 2020a, "Central Bank of Sudan Orders 47 Al Bashir Regime Leaders' Accounts Frozen". *Radio Dabanga*, (14 February). dabangasudan.org/en/all-news/article/central-bank-of-sudan-orders-47-al-bashir-regime-leaders-accounts-frozen.

Radio Dabanga, 2020b, "Police Violence at Sudan Demonstrations". *Radio Dabanga*, (21 February). dabangasudan.org/en/all-news/article/police-violence-at-sudan-demonstrations.

Radio Dabanga, 2022a. "Protest in El Geneina Demands Stop to West Darfur Violence." *Radio Dabanga*, March 14. dabangasudan.org/en/all-news/article/protest-in-el-geneina-demands-stop-to-west-darfur-violence.

Radio Dabanga, 2022b. "West Darfur: At Least 168 Dead, 110 Injured in 'tribal' Massacre." *Radio Dabanga*, April 26. dabangasudan.org/en/all-news/article/west-darfur-at-least-168-dead-110-injured-in-tribal-massacre.

Radio Dabanga, 2022c, "West Darfur Violence Leaves 200+ Dead— 'Cautious Calm' as Hospitals, Markets Stay Closed." *Radio Dabanga*, April 27. dabangasudan.org/en/all-news/article/west-darfur-violence-leaves-200-dead-cautious-calm-as-hospitals-markets-stay-closed.

Rafiq, Mehdi, 2019, "Moroccan Teachers Fight Back against Repression as Water Cannons Used to Disperse Protest." *MENA Solidarity Network* blog (30 March). menasolidaritynetwork.com/2019/03/30/moroccan-teachers-fight-back-against-repression-as-water-cannons-used-to-disperse-protest/

Raje, Manar, Shukhaidem, Haya & Challen Flynn, Oisin, 2020, "'You can't liberate the land without liberating women'", *Middle East Solidarity* (15 April) menasolidaritynetwork.com/2020/04/15/you-cant-liberate-the-land-without-liberating-women/

Ramdani, Nabila, 2012, "Fifty Years after Algeria's Independence, France Is Still in Denial", *The Guardian* (5 July). theguardian.com/commentisfree/2012/jul/05/50-years-algeria-independence-france-denial.

Raslan, Sarah, 2011, "Cairo Bus Drivers Partially Suspend Strike after 18 Days", *Ahram Online*, (4 October). english.ahram.org.eg/NewsContent/1/64/23343/Egypt/Politics-/Cairo-bus-drivers-partially-suspend-strike-after--.aspx.

Reuters, 2019a, "Egypt Kills Hundreds of Suspected Militants in Disputed Gun Battles", *Reuters* (15 April) reuters.com/investigates/special-report/egypt-killings/

Reuters, 2019b, "Sudan Forms 11-Member Sovereign Council, Headed by Military Leader", *Reuters* (20 August) uk.reuters.com/article/uk-sudan-politics/sudan-forms-11-member-sovereign-council-headed-by-military-leader-idUKKCN1VA26F.

Reuters, 2020, "Sudan Quells Revolt of Former Spy Service Men after Clashes", *Reuters* (14 January) reuters.com/article/us-sudan-security-idUSKBN1ZD19F.

Richards, Alan & Waterbury, John, 2008, *A Political Economy of the Middle East* (Boulder, Colorado: Westview Press).

Richter, Frederik, 2011, "Bahrain Promises Government Jobs, Protests Continue", *Reuters*, (6 March). uk.reuters.com/article/uk-bahrain-jobs-idUKTRE72513420110306.

Roberts, Hugh, 2003, *The Battlefield: Algeria 1988-2002* (London: Verso).

Roberts, Michael, 2020, "A World Rate of Profit: A New Approach", *Michael Roberts Blog*, (25 July). thenextrecession.wordpress.com/2020/07/25/a-world-rate-of-profit-a-new-approach/

Rose, John, 2019, "Iran 1979: an opportunity squandered, *Socialist Review* (4 February), socialistworker.co.uk/socialist-review-archive/iran-1979-opportunity-squandered/

Rose, John, 2020, "Workers' Power and the Failure of Communism", PhD thesis, Kings College London, kclpure.kcl.ac.uk/portal/files/129644633/2020_Rose_John_1641033_ethesis_version_for_Pure_upload.pdf

Roser, Max, 2014, "Fertility Rate", *Our World in Data* (19 February). ourworldindata.org/fertility-rate.

Roy, Sara, 1987, "The Gaza Strip: A Case of Economic De-Development", *Journal of Palestine Studies,* 17:1: 56–88. doi.org/10.2307/2536651

Rubin, Lawrence, 2015, "Why Israel Outlawed the Northern Branch of the Islamic Movement." *Brookings* (blog), (30 November). brookings.edu/blog/markaz/2015/12/07/why-israel-outlawed-the-northern-branch-of-the-islamic-movement

Russia Today, 2020, "Is the US Trying to Hijack the Iraq Protests to Install a Puppet Dictatorship?", *Going Underground* (YouTube), youtube.com/watch?v=2ap1C3-cYsM

Sabella, Bernard, 1993, " Russian Jewish Immigration and the Future of the Israeli-Palestinian Conflict", *Middle East Report* (May/June), merip.org/1993/05/russian-jewish-immigration-and-the-future-of-the-israeli-palestinian-conflict/

Sadiki, Larbi & Saleh, Layla, 2021, "Tunisia's Presidential Power-Grab Is a Test for Its Democracy", *OpenDemocracy* (28 July). opendemocracy.net/en/north-africa-west-asia/tunisias-presidential-power-grab-is-a-test-for-its-democracy/

Sakr, Taha, 2016. "Conscript Labour in Civil Projects a Necessity to Deal with Economic Difficulties: Military Expert", *Daily News Egypt* (28 November). dailynewsegypt.com/2016/11/28/conscript-labour-civil-projects-necessity-deal-economic-difficulties-military-expert

Salah, Mohamed & Al-Faruq, Samia, 2018, "Mudir Al-Kulliya al-Harbiyya: Nahnu Masna' al-Rigal Wa 'arayn al-Abtal", *Al-Wafd*, (7 December). alwafd.news/2137266

Saleh, Yasmine, 2014, "Egypt's Sisi Tells Interior Minister to Fight Sexual Harassment." *Reuters* (10 June). uk.reuters.com/article/egypt-sisi-harassment-idINKBN0EL27N20140610.

Saleh, Yassin al-Haj, 2017, *The Impossible Revolution. Making Sense of the Syrian Tragedy* (London: Hurst & Co).

Salhab, Akram & al-Ghoul, Dahoud, 2021, "Jerusalem Youth at the Forefront of 2021's Unity Intifada", *Middle East Research and Information Project* (10 November), merip.org/2021/11/jerusalem-youth-at-the-forefront-of-2021s-unity-intifada/

Salhi, Zahia Smail, 2003, "Algerian Women, Citizenship, and the 'Family Code'", *Gender and Development*, 11: 3 (November).

Salloukh, Bassel F, 2019, "Taif and the Lebanese State: The Political Economy of a Very Sectarian Public Sector", *Nationalism and Ethnic Politics* 25: 1 (January). doi.org/10.1080/13537113.2019.1565177.

Sampson, Anthony, 1981, *The Seven Sisters: The Great Oil Companies and the World They Made*, Fifth edition (London: Coronet).

Savage, Jesse D & Caverley, Jonathon, 2017a, "When Human Capital Threatens the Capitol: Foreign Aid in the Form of Military Training and Coups", *Journal of Peace Research* 54 (4) (July): 542–57. doi:10.1177/0022343317713557.

Savage, Jesse D & Caverley, Jonathon, 2017b, "Training the Man on Horseback: US Training and Military Coups." *War on the Rocks* (August). warontherocks.com/2017/08/training-the-man-on-horseback-the-connection-between-u-s-training-and-military-coups

Sayigh, Rosemary, 1984, *The Palestinians: From Peasants to Revolutionaries* (London: Zed Books).

Sayigh, Yezid, 2012, *Above the State: The Officers' Republic in Egypt*. Carnegie Endowment for International Peace. carnegieendowment.org/files/officers_republic1.pdf

Sayigh, Yezid, 2018, "Mapping the Formal Military Economy Part 2: We Build Egypt, We Feed Egypt, We Are Egypt", in *Owners of the Republic: An Anatomy of Egypt's Military Economy*. Carnegie Endowment, carnegie-mec.org/2019/11/18/mapping-formal-military-economy-part-2-we-build-egypt-we-feed-egypt-we-are-egypt-pub-80335

Sekaily, Sherene, 2013, "The Meaning of Revolution: On Samira Ibrahim", *Jadaliyya*blog), (28 January). jadaliyya.com/

Details/27915.

Sen, Kasturi, & al Faisal, Waleed, 2012, "Syria Neoliberal Reforms in Health Sector Financing: Embedding Unequal Access?", *Social Medicine* 6: 3 (15 April): 171–82.

Sghaeir Saihi, Mohamed, 2012, *Interview* (12 November).

Shafiq, Mohammed, 2011, "'The Union Is a Shield and Our Sword Is the Strike'", *Socialist Review* (December). socialistreview.org.uk/article.php?articlenumber=11845

Sharp, Gene, 1973. *The Politics of Nonviolent Action* (Boston: Porter Sargent Publishers).

Sharp, Gene, 2008, *From Dictatorship to Democracy: A Conceptual Framework for Liberation*, 3rd US edition (Boston, MA: Albert Einstein Institution).

Sharp, Jeremy N, 2022, *US Foreign Aid to Israel* (Washington: US Congressional Research Service). sgp.fas.org/crs/mideast/RL33222.pdf

Shenker, Jack, 2016, *The Egyptians*, Allen Lane

Shiblak, Abbas, 1996, "Residency Status and Civil Rights of Palestinian Refugees in Arab Countries. *Journal of Palestine Studies*, 25: 3, 36–45. doi.org/10.2307/2538257

Singer, Peter W, 2004, "Warriors for hire in Iraq", *Salon* (15 April). salon.com/2004/04/15/warriors/

Sirag-al-Din, Isra'a, 2019, "Qa'idat Bayanat al-Fa'iliyyat al-Ihtigagiyya Fil Sudan Khilal 3 Ashur", *Revolutionary Socialists, Egypt*, revsoc.me.

SIPRI, 2021, "Trends in world military expenditure", Stockholm International Peace Research Institute website, (4 April) sipri.org/sites/default/files/2021-04/fs_2104_milex_0.pdf

Sohrabi, Nader, 1995, "Historicizing Revolutions: Constitutional Revolutions in the Ottoman Empire, Iran, and Russia, 1905-1908", *American Journal of Sociology* 100: 6 (May): 1383–1447. doi.org/10.1086/230667.

Soliman, Samer 2011, *The Autumn of Dictatorship: Fiscal Crisis and Political Change in Egypt under Mubarak* (Stanford: Stanford University ress).

Solomon, Erica, 2015, "Isis Inc: Syria's 'Mafia-Style' Gas Deals with Jihadis." *Financial Times* (15 October). .ft.com/cms/s/0/92f4e036-6b69-11e5-aca9-d87542bf8673.html#axzz3trkhNslB.

Solomon, Shoshanna, 2021, "Israel cybersecurity firms raise record $3.4b, 41% of global sector investment", *Times of Israel*, timesofisrael.com/israel-cybersecurity-firms-raise-record-3-4b-41-of-global-sector-investment/

Sonneveld, Nadia, 2018, "The Case of Women's Unilateral Divorce Rights in Egypt: Revolution and Counterrevolution?" in Gray, Doris H & Sonneveld, Nadia, (eds) *Women and Social Change in North Africa* (Cambridge: Cambridge University Press): 331–52. doi.org/10.1017/9781108303415.016.

Sonneveld, Nadia & Lindbekk, Monika, 2015, "A Revolution in Muslim Family Law? Egypt's Pre- and Post-Revolutionary Period 2011-2013, Compared" in *New Middle Eastern Studies* 5 (20 May). doi.org/10.29311/nmes.v5i0.2666.

Soto, Hernando de, 2011, "The Free Market Secret of the Arab Revolutions", *Financial Times* (8 November). ft.com/content/653fab0e-0a00-11e1-85ca-00144feabdc0.

Springborg, Robert, 1989, *Mubarak's Egypt: Fragmentation of the Political Order* (Boulder, Colorado: Westview Press).

Springborg, Robert & Williams, F C. "Pink", 2019, The Egyptian Military: A Slumbering Giant Awakes." *Carnegie Middle East Center*. carnegie-mec.org/2019/02/28/egyptian-military-slumbering-giant-awakes-pub-78238

Stelter, Brian, 2011, "CBS Reporter Recounts a 'Merciless' Assault", *The New York Times* (28 April), nytimes.com/2011/04/29/business/media/29logan.html

Stewart, Phil, 2013. "Insight: In Small American Town, a Window into Egyptian General's Past", *Reuters*, (23 August). reuters.com/article/us-usa-egypt-sisi-insight-idUSBRE97M01920130823.

Stubbington, Tommy & Cornish, Chloe, 2020, "Lebanon's Creditors Face 70% Hit from Debt Restructuring", *Financial Times* (9 April), ft.com/content/12747deb-f4e8-4cad-8b64-c271411c30a3.

Sudam, Mohamed & Ghobari, Mohammed, 2011, "aleh Refuses to Sign Yemen Deal despite Pressure", *Reuters*, (22 May).

Sudan in the News, 2019, "The Rapid Support Forces: A Comprehensive Profile". *Sudan in the News* (29 October). sudaninthenews.com/the-rapid-support-forces-a-comprehensive-profile.

Sudam, Mohamed & Ghobari, Mohammed, 2011, "Svaleh refuses to sign Yemen deal despite pressure", *Reuters* (22 May). reuters.com/article/us-yemen-idUSTRE73L1PP20110522.

Sudanese Professionals Association, nd, "About Us". Sudanese Professionals Association.

Stalin, J V, 1931, "The Tasks of Business Executives", *Pravda* (4 February). marxists.org/reference/archive/stalin/works/1931/02/04.htm.

Streitfield, David, 2006, "Bechtel Calls It Quits after More than 3 Years in Iraq, *Los Angeles Times*, (3 November). latimes.com/archives/la-xpm-2006-nov-03-fi-bechtel3-story.html.

Swirski, Shlomo, Konor-Attias, Etty &Lieberman, Aviva, 2020, *Israel: a social report 2020*, Adva Center, (March), adva.org/wp-content/uploads/2020/02/social-2020-ENG.pdf

SyriaUntold, 2016, "Cities in Revolution." cities.syriauntold.com/

Tadros, Mariz, 2013, "Why Does the World Ignore Violence against Arab Women in Public Spaces?" *Guardian* (2 December) theguardian.com/global-development/poverty-matters/2013/dec/02/world-ignore-violence-against-arab-women.

Talaat, Hala, 2012, Interview, (5 April).

Tayeb, Sami, 2019, "The Palestinian McCity in the Neoliberal Era", *Middle East Research and Information Project* 290 (Spring). merip.org/2019/07/the-palestinian-mccity-in-the-neoliberal-era/

Thiollet, Hélène, 2016, "Managing migrant labour in the Gulf: Transnational dynamics of migration politics since the 1930s", *HAL Open Science, Working Paper.* hal.archives-ouvertes.fr/hal-01346366

Tiryakioglu, Muhsin Baris, 2018, "Iran keeps top position as crude oil exporter to Turkey", *Anadolu Agency* (30 May), aa.com.tr/en/economy/iran-keeps-top-position-as-crude-oil-exporter-to-turkey/1160729

Thomas, Edward, 2017, "Patterns of growth and inequality in Sudan, 1977-2017", *Durham Middle East Papers* (November), dro.dur.ac.uk/23578/1/23578.pdf

Thomas, Edward & El-Gizouli, Magdi, 2021, "Creatures of the Deposed: Connecting Sudan's Rural and Urban Struggles." *African Arguments* (November). //africanarguments.org/2021/11/creatures-of-the-deposed-connecting-sudans-rural-and-urban-struggles/

Thomas, Peter D, 2009. *The Gramscian Moment: Philosophy, Hegemony and Marxism* (Boston: Brill).

Thuwar, Burri al-Diraissa. 2022, *Nahnu Fi Lajna Muqawama Burri Al-Diraissa*. facebook.com/watch/?v=945701439751135

Traboulsi, Fawwaz, 2012, "The Bloody Death of the Muqata`ji System (1842–1861)" in *A History of Modern Lebanon* (London: Pluto Press). doi.org/10.2307/j.ctt183p4f5.8.

Trotsky, Leon, 1930, *The History of the Russian Revolution,* marxists.org/archive/trotsky/1930/hrr/ch00.htm

Trotsky, Leon, 1931, *The Permanent Revolution*. marxists.org/archive/trotsky/1931/tpr/prre.htm.

Truman, Harry, 1952, "Special Message to the Congress on the Mutual Security Program", *The Truman Libary, Public Papers*. trumanlibrary.gov/library/public-papers/55/special-message-congress-mutual-security-program

UNESCO Office, Iraq, 2019, "Assessment of the Labour Market & Skills Analysis: Iraq and Kurdistan Region-Iraq: Construction", *United Nations Educational, Scientific and Cultural Organisation website*. unesdoc.unesco.org/ark:/48223/pf0 000371371?posInSet=3&queryId=01b89835-23c0-4ab3-a0c9-62d83157d17a.

UN Habitat, 2011, "Cairo—a City in Transition", *UN Habitat*. unhabitat.org/sites/default/files/download-manager-files/Cairo%20-%20a%20City%20in%20Transition.pdf.

United Nations, 2021, "As Plight of Syrians Worsens, Hunger Reaches Record High, International Community Must Fully Commit to Ending Decade-Old War, Secretary-General Tells General Assembly", *United Nations*, (30 March) un.org/press/en/2021/sgsm20664.doc.htm.

United Nations Organisation for the Coordination of Humanitarian Affairs (UN OCHA), 2019, "Assessing the Impact of War on Development in Yemen—Yemen", *Reliefweb* (April) reliefweb.int/report/yemen/assessing-impact-war-development-yemen.

US Department of Defense, 2019a, *Foreign Military Training Report, Fiscal Years 2018 and 2019, Joint Report to Congress Volume I*. state.gov/wp-content/uploads/2019/12/FMT_Volume-I_FY2018_2019.pdf.

US Department of Defense, 2019b, *Foreign Military Training Fiscal Years 2016-17 Joint Report to Congress Volume 1*. state.gov/wp-content/uploads/2019/04/fmt_vol1_16_17.pdf.

US State Department, nd(a), "The Red Line Agreement, 1928", *US State Department, Office of the Historian, Milestones: 1921-1936*, history.state.gov/milestones/1921-1936/red-line

US State Department, nd(b), "The Truman Doctrine, 1947", *US State Department, Office of the Historian, Milestones: 1945–1952*, history.state.gov/milestones/1945-1952/truman-doctrine.

US State Department, 1969, "The Fall of the Libyan Monarchy," (9 September). cia.gov/library/readingroom/docs/LOC-HAK-287-1-4-8.pdf

Uwaydah, Gamal, 2008, *Mulahma 'itisam Muwadhfi al-Dara'ib al-'aqariyya*. Markaz al-dirasat al-ishtarakiyya, (Cairo, Centre for Socialist Studies).

Van Dam, Nickolaos, 1996, *The Struggle for Power in Syria: Politics and Society under Asad and the Ba`th Party* (London: Tauris).

Vandewalle, Dirk, 2006, *A History of Modern Libya* (Cambridge: Cambridge University Press). doi.org/10.1017/CBO9780511986246

Vogel, Lise, 1987, *Marxism and the Oppression of Women: Toward a Unitary Theory* (New Brunswick, NJ: Rutgers University Press)

Webber, Jeffery R, 2021, 'Bolivia's cycle of revolt: Left-Indigenous struggle 2000-5', in Barker, Colin, Dale, Gareth & Davidson, Neil (eds) *Revolutionary rehearsals in the Neoliberal Age*: 181-2.

WAC-MAAN, 2020, "Following MAAN's petition, Israeli Interior Ministry's Payments Section has stopped deducting service fees from the wages of Palestinian workers", WAC-MAAN website, (8 December) eng.wac-maan.org.il/?p=2495

Wahdat al-Dirasat, 1999, "Tahawwulat Al-Iqtisad al-Misri (Muladhat Awliyya)", *Al-Tariq al-Ishtaraki*, 1: 5–51.

Waterbury, John, 1985, "The 'Soft State' and the Open Door: Egypt's Experience with Economic Liberalization, 1974-1984", *Comparative Politics* 18: 1 (October): 65–83. doi.org/10.2307/421658.

Watling, Jack, 2016, 'The Shia Militias of Iraq', *The Atlantic* (December 22) theatlantic.com/international/archive/2016/12/shia-militias-iraq-isis/510938/

Webber, Jeffery R, 2021, 'Bolivia's cycle of revolt: Left-Indigenous struggle 2000-5', in Barker, Colin, Dale, Gareth & Davidson, Neil (eds) *Revolutionary rehearsals in the Neoliberal Age*: 181-2.

Wedeen, Lisa, 1999, *Ambiguities of Domination Politics, Rhetoric, and Symbols in Contemporary Syria* (Chicago: University of Chicago Press).

Wickham, Carrie Rosefsky, 2015, *The Muslim Brotherhood: Evolution of an Islamist Movement* (New Jersey, Princeton University Press).

Wills, Matthew, 2017, "The Turkish Origins of the 'Deep State.'" *JSTOR Daily* (10 April) daily.jstor.org/the-unacknowledged-origins-of-the-deep-state/

World Bank, 2008, "Arab Republic of Egypt Urban Sector Update", (June). documents1.worldbank.org/curated/en/749891468023382999/pdf/411780v10REVIS1Box0327393B01PUBLIC1.pdf.

World Bank, 2020, "The Fallout of War: The Regional Consequences of the Conflict in Syria", *World Bank,* worldbank.org/en/region/mena/publication/fallout-of-war-in-syria.

World Bank, 2021, *Open Data*, data.worldbank.org/

Vandewalle, Dirk, 2012, *A History of Modern Libya: Second Edition* (Cambridge: Cambridge University Press).

Vitalis, Robert, 1986, "Egypt's Infitah Bourgeoisie," *Middle East Research and Information Project* (September/October). merip.org/1986/09/egypts-infitah-bourgeoisie/

Yassin-Kassab, Robin & Al-Shami, Leila, 2018, *Burning Country: Syrians in Revolution and War* (London: Pluto Press).

Yousfi, Hèla, 2018, *Trade Unions and Arab Revolutions: The Tunisian Case of UGTT* (London: Routledge).

Zetkin, Clara, 1896, "Proletarian Woman and Socialism", marxists.org/archive/zetkin/1896/10/women.htm.

Ziv, Oren, 2021, Lydd's Palestinians are leading a new uprising, *+972 Magazine* (20 May), 972mag.com/lydd-police-settlers-palestinians/

Data sources

Much of the data used in this book is from publicly accessible sources including:
World Bank Open Data https://data.worldbank.org/
Our World in Data project https://ourworldindata.org/
ILO Labour Statistics https://ilostat.ilo.org/
SIPRI (Stockholm International Peace Research Institute) databases (https://www.sipri.org/databases) especially the Military Expenditure database https://milex.sipri.org/sipri
Only some of the analysis made it into the final book in graphical form. More will be published along with more detailed discussion of the methods of analysis, in the accompanying website: revolutionisthepeopleschoice.wordpress.com.

Note On Transliteration Of Arabic

Arabic contains a number of letters which are not easy to render exactly in roman script for English readers. These are often indicated by an apostrophe which stands in for the letter 'ayn and the hamza (a glottal stop). This book uses a simplified transliteration system for Arabic words which are not well-known in English, however in the case of proper nouns which have established English spellings I have adopted versions which are likely to be familiar to English readers. Where possible I have adopted the English spelling of individual names preferred by the person concerned. Names of people and places from Morocco, Tunisia and Algeria have generally been transliterated following the French system, however.

The prefix al- signifies the definite article in Arabic. The word al (meaning family/clan) is sometimes confused with this, especially at the beginning of English sentences. In this index, you will find Arabic nouns (such as place names) where the definite article is commonly included (such as the industrial city of al-Mahalla al-Kubra in Egypt) indexed under the first letter of the word itself, so al-Mahalla will be found listed under M. Al- can also be rendered el- but I've tried to stick to al- for consistency. Some proper names which usually include the al- in Arabic, but where it is commonly dropped in English usage have been index have been indexed without the al- (for example Muhammad Anwar al-Sadat will be found index as Anwar Sadat).

Inevitably in a book of this size there will be errors and I hope that readers will be indulgent if they find any.

Index

A

Abd-Al-Qadir Amir 230
Abdelgalil Sara 230
Abd-Rabbo Hadi 230
Abu-Aita, Kamil 230
Achcar Gilbert 211, 230
Achnacarry Agreement 66, 67, 230
Aden 30, 34, 40, 185, 230
Afghanistan 198, 230
AFL-CIO 74, 230
Africa 7, 9, 12, 39, 50, 56–58, 60, 61, 63, 65–67, 70, 71, 79, 80, 106, 137, 154, 166, 210, 211, 214, 218–20, 225, 227, 230, 238
Afrin 200, 230
Agribusiness 84, 107, 230
Agriculture 61, 66, 73, 74, 76, 81, 82, 84, 85, 89, 102, 105–8, 116, 129, 131, 186, 225, 230
Ahrar al-Sham 33, 197, 230
Aid 30, 33, 40, 63, 64, 67, 69, 87, 131, 140, 161, 167, 185, 198, 199, 214, 226, 227, 230
Aircraft 68, 127, 230
Airport 44, 45, 192, 230
Aissat Kamel 212, 230
Alawite 95, 158, 171, 230
Al-Binaa Al-Qaidi 230
Aleppo 31, 96, 105, 108, 185, 196, 199, 230
Alexandria 8, 23, 60, 110, 125, 147, 191, 193
Algeria 5, 7, 12, 13, 20, 37, 42, 46, 48, 52, 53, 59–62, 67, 68, 70, 71, 75, 93–97, 99, 102, 103, 107, 115–17, 119–26, 129, 140, 144, 154, 155, 157–59, 161, 165, 166, 168, 187, 199, 212, 213, 215, 217, 218, 220, 221, 223, 226
Allotment state 100, 101
Amazigh 9, 47, 53
America 12, 154, 164
Anarchist 196, 201, 221
Anglo-Egyptian Condominium 60
Ankara 85
Antalya 8
Anti-capitalist 173, 230
Anti-colonial revolutions 15, 20, 69, 71, 78, 169, 230
Anti-imperialism 77, 230
Anti-Zionist 8, 230
Aoun, Michel 230
Apartheid 50–53, 88, 89, 100, 117, 131, 132, 213, 230
Apotex 93, 230
April Theses 176, 222, 230
Arab 4, 9, 26, 29, 31, 35, 37, 50, 68, 71, 73, 74, 76, 82, 84, 86, 91, 92, 96, 118, 120, 125, 127, 138, 195, 197, 209, 211, 213–18, 221–24, 227–30, 240
Arabia 12, 22, 27–30, 39–41, 45, 53, 57, 59, 62–64, 67, 68, 85, 97, 100, 101, 138, 161, 165, 166, 168, 169, 202, 212, 223, 230, 238
Arabic-Speaking 9, 230
Arabism 9, 230
Arab Socialist Union ASU 230

Arafat, Yasser 230
Aramco 67, 117, 230
Argentina 181, 230
Armaments 63, 230
Arms 32-34, 59, 63, 64, 74, 87, 88, 123, 161, 162, 164, 166-68, 171, 177, 196, 206, 224, 230
Army 16, 24, 29, 31-33, 35, 40-42, 44-46, 48, 53, 60, 73, 76, 80, 87, 92, 93, 97, 110, 121, 134, 136, 143, 145, 154, 157-59, 162-64, 166, 168, 170-72, 174, 177, 178, 180, 189, 195, 196, 198, 199, 204, 206, 211, 212, 215, 217, 219, 223-25, 230
Artisans 73, 177, 230
Ashura 49, 230
Askari 35, 230
Askary 155, 156, 163, 230
Atbara 111
Authoritarianism 92, 94, 152, 162, 207, 219, 221
Autocracy 15, 175
Autogestion 72
Axes of Permanent Revolution 183, 188, 192, 193, 198, 208

B

Baghdad 48, 49, 69, 77, 144
Bahrain 12, 20, 26-28, 34, 39, 42, 71, 78, 91, 115, 119, 139, 154, 158, 159, 166, 168, 216, 223, 226, 231
Bahri 203, 206, 231
Bakeries 142, 183, 184, 202, 231
Baltagiyya 207, 231
Banat, Nizar 231
Bandits 173, 231
Bangladesh 84, 231
Baniyas 31, 231
Banks 44, 45, 48, 73, 76, 82, 84, 101, 192, 231
Barracks 23, 164, 231
Bashir, Umar al- 231
Basic Construction 203, 204, 231
Basra 49, 215, 231
Beersheva 88, 231
Beidh Ali, al- 231
Beirut 48, 53, 64, 101, 102, 117, 224, 231
Beja 43, 231
Bejaia 183, 231
Bekaa 101, 231
Belaid 37, 231
Benghazi 25, 26, 40, 231
Ben Gurion, David 231
Benjedid, Chadli 231
Bensalah 47, 231
Bensallal 47
Berber 47, 52, 53
Berber-Speaking 99
Bint Al-Bomban 143
Bizerte 124, 127
Blackwater 169
Bolivia 180, 200
Bolshevik 176, 179, 185
Boumediene, Houari 231
Bourgeois 72, 100, 109, 135, 176-78, 183, 186, 231
Bourgeoisie 14-16, 58, 72-74, 80-83, 86, 91-93, 95, 96, 98-103, 109, 112, 161, 169, 170, 176, 183, 229, 231
Bourguiba, Habib 231
Bouteflika, Abdelaziz 231
Britain 14, 16, 58, 62-65, 67-69, 85, 136, 137, 161, 177, 213, 231
British Petroleum BP 231

Budapest 179, 224, 231
Bukharin, Nicolai 231
Burhan Abdelfattah al- 231
Burri 111, 143, 203, 204, 228, 231
Burri, al-Diraysa 203, 231

C

Cairo 11, 23, 24, 68, 105, 109, 110, 123, 133, 140, 141, 145, 170, 191, 192, 212, 214, 220, 222, 224, 225, 228, 229, 231
Capitalism 8, 9, 14, 15, 56–58, 60, 63, 65, 66, 71, 72, 74, 78–81, 85, 86, 89, 112, 115, 116, 120, 125, 135–37, 148, 161, 169, 176, 187, 213, 216, 219, 222, 231, 239
Central Security Forces Egypt 231
Chile 179, 180, 231
China 71, 84, 165, 217, 231
Christians 12, 24, 142, 170, 190, 212, 231
CIA 229, 231
Civilian 13, 18, 35, 42–45, 154, 155, 158–61, 163, 164, 166–68, 174, 189, 193, 196, 198, 201–4, 223, 224, 231
Class 8, 13–17, 19–21, 28, 30–32, 34, 36, 49, 52–54, 58–60, 63, 64, 67, 69–89, 91–94, 96–101, 103, 105, 106, 109–18, 121, 125, 126, 128–32, 134–40, 144, 148, 149, 152–54, 156, 157, 161, 164, 167, 169–72, 174–80, 183–92, 198, 199, 205–10, 213–17, 219, 224, 231
Cliff, Tony 216, 231
Clinton, Bill 231

Coal-Mining 65
Cochabamba 180
Collectives 53
Colonialism 12, 21, 57, 58, 60, 72, 81, 127, 132, 149, 169
Communist Party 69, 77, 78, 131, 179
Constitucion 180
Constitution 22, 25, 26, 38, 40, 46, 47, 94, 95, 138, 147, 148, 159, 164, 194, 200, 214, 216, 223
Containerisation 117
Cooperatives 74, 76, 77, 203
Cordones 179, 180, 188, 232
Cossack 15, 232
Counter-revolution 3, 10, 12, 13, 18, 19, 21, 25, 31, 34, 36, 37, 39, 41, 42, 56, 63, 81, 83, 90, 106, 146, 152, 154, 160, 162, 164, 170, 175, 179, 185, 189, 195, 207, 212, 214, 216, 232
Countryside 16, 71, 96, 105–8, 112, 129, 130, 191, 205, 232
Coups 75, 154, 160, 161, 168, 179, 226, 232
Covid-19 48, 49, 52, 118, 202, 232
Crisis 3, 5, 13, 14, 16–18, 21, 27, 29, 32, 34, 37–39, 41, 42, 45–49, 52–54, 56, 58, 67, 68, 73, 75, 77–79, 81, 82, 89, 95–97, 103, 105, 106, 108, 112, 113, 116, 118, 120–22, 124, 126, 129, 132, 136, 144, 150, 152–54, 157–59, 162, 164, 170, 174, 175, 178, 179, 181, 182, 184, 185, 187, 189–91, 198, 202–5, 207–10, 213, 214, 217, 219, 220, 227, 232

Crony capitalists 92, 232
Cross-Class 153, 206, 217, 232
Cuba 71, 232
Cyber-Security 87, 232

D

Dagalo, Mohamed Hemedti 232
Damanhour 140, 232
Damascus 31, 32, 41, 50, 92, 96, 108, 110, 133, 197–99, 220, 232
Daniel, Mina 232
Darfur/Darfuris 232
Dawla al-Muhassasa 232
Dayan, Moshe 232
De-collectivisation 232
Decolonisation 60, 71, 232
Deir-Ez-Zor 108, 110, 133, 232
Democracy 47, 91, 126, 135, 141, 142, 152, 154–56, 159, 161, 163, 168, 175, 178–80, 185, 189, 190, 197, 198, 200, 201, 203, 209, 212, 215, 218, 221, 222, 224, 226, 227
Democratic Confederalism 201, 224
Derna 41
Destourian 92
Disappearances 38, 173
Dongola 111
Dual Power 3, 5, 174, 176–78, 183, 184, 186, 200, 201, 206, 222, 232

E

Economic Reform and Structural Adjustment Programme ERSAP 232

Education 31, 39, 59, 75, 88, 95, 96, 100, 101, 108, 112–16, 118, 119, 121–23, 126, 127, 135–38, 143, 168, 172, 181, 196, 199, 203–5, 224, 232
Egypt 3, 5, 7–9, 11, 12, 20, 23, 25, 26, 30, 33–35, 37, 38, 40–42, 45, 59, 60, 68, 70, 71, 73–75, 78, 82–84, 86, 87, 89, 91–95, 97, 99, 106–9, 111, 113, 114, 116, 117, 119–21, 123–26, 129, 130, 132, 133, 137–40, 144, 146, 147, 154, 155, 157–61, 166–68, 170, 172, 185, 188–92, 195, 198, 199, 202, 204–6, 209–12, 214, 215, 218–27, 229, 231, 232, 236, 240
Egyptian Federation of Independent Trade Unions EFITU 232
Egyptian Trade Union Federation ETUF 94, 232
Engels, Friedrich 223, 232
Engineers 44, 68, 97, 113, 122, 197, 232
England/English 232
Ennadha 23, 25, 37, 38, 147, 232
Erbil 85, 232
Erdogan, Recep Tayyip 232
Ettadhamoun 109, 232
Ettakatol 23, 232
Europe 7, 12, 14, 16, 58–63, 65, 77, 79, 86, 91, 136, 153, 166, 168, 169, 175, 179, 185, 220, 232
European Union EU 232
Execution 77, 205, 232
Exploitation 11, 34, 57, 74, 135–38, 149, 164, 170, 172, 175, 186, 193, 206, 232

Export-led Export-Oriented industrialisation 232
Exxon 66, 232
Ezzat, Ahmed 232

F

Facebook 18, 23, 44, 139, 143, 162, 190, 195, 202, 203, 216, 228, 232
Factory 58, 110, 124, 125, 140, 141, 172, 178, 179, 185, 209, 218, 232
Farmers 61, 71, 72, 74, 75, 80, 81, 94, 107, 108, 179–81, 196, 206
Fascist 76, 153, 154
Fatah 51, 100, 131
Faustian bargain 152, 161
Fayyoum 191
Feloul, al-Nidham 192
Financialisation 84
Food-Processing 93
France 14, 58, 61, 63, 64, 67, 68, 75, 81, 165, 212, 217, 223, 225
Front Islamique du Salut (FIS) 96, 233

G

Gadaref 111, 203, 233
Gafsa 22, 109, 128, 218, 233
Gaid, Saleh 157, 233
Gaza 50, 52, 68, 69, 100, 111, 117, 168, 187, 218, 221, 225, 226, 233
Gdansk 179, 214, 233
General Federation of Bahraini Trade Unions (GFBTU) 233
Germany 16, 63, 65, 165, 171, 179, 185, 224, 233

Ghannouchi, Rachid al- 233
Giza 123, 126, 133, 233
Gizouli, Magdi el- 233
Gluckstein, Ygael 233
Golan Heights 69, 75, 83, 233
Gongos 191, 233
Gonzalez, Mike 179, 233
Gopal 196, 218, 233
Government 11, 13, 14, 18, 22–26, 30, 34, 35, 37–49, 52, 53, 60–63, 69, 74–78, 81, 84, 85, 87, 88, 91–93, 96, 97, 99, 100, 103, 108, 110–12, 116–18, 122, 125–27, 133, 141, 146, 147, 152, 154, 157, 160–62, 164, 165, 174, 176, 178–80, 182–87, 189, 191, 195, 196, 200–208, 211, 212, 214, 217, 221, 223, 224, 226, 233
Governments-In-Waiting 175, 233
Graeber, David 233
Grain 48, 60, 106, 233
Greece 69, 233
Gulf Cooperation Council GCC 20, 233

H

Hadaf al- 233
Haifa 50, 51
Hama 31, 32, 96, 108, 221
Hamas 100, 133
Hanieh, Adam 219
Harman, Chris 215, 219, 233
Hashemite Monarchy 69, 233
HDP party (Turkey) 233
Healthworkers 44, 117, 122, 123, 233
Hebron 50, 233
Hegazi, Sarah 233

Helwan 133, 233
Hemedti 42, 44, 45, 53, 157, 160, 167, 232, 233
Hemedti, Mohamed Dagalo 233
Hezbollah 33, 41, 99, 169, 216, 233
Hilla 49, 233
Hirak 46–48, 52, 155, 233
Histadrut 233
Hizbiyya 194, 233
Homophobia 146, 218, 233
Homosexuality 146, 233
Homs 31, 133, 233
Hospital 21, 102, 110, 113, 141–43, 192, 193, 220, 233
Humanitarian 39, 198, 228, 233
Human Rights 23, 29, 39, 41, 44, 108, 146, 155, 156, 159, 162, 166, 214, 219, 220, 225, 233
Hungary 179, 233
Hussein, Saddam 233
Huthis 40, 233
Hydrocarbon 76, 124, 125
Hyperinflation 87

I

ICT 88
Ideologies 35, 60, 152, 153, 156, 161
Idlib 134, 196, 197, 217
IMET 168
IMF 76, 97, 108, 118, 134, 216, 218, 220, 225
Imperialism 8, 16, 57, 60, 63, 64, 149, 167, 168, 171, 212, 215, 222, 223
Import-Substitution Industrialisation 71, 73, 79, 80
India 62, 84, 165
Indonesia 67
Industrialisation 61, 63, 66, 68, 71–76, 79, 80, 136, 232, 234
Industries 30, 43, 59, 61, 64, 73, 74, 76, 80, 82, 83, 87, 88, 97, 115, 124, 125, 128, 137, 167, 172, 180, 199, 201, 234
Infitah 75, 82, 91, 99, 100, 229, 234
Instagram 134, 234
Insubordination 133, 234
Insurgency 72, 85, 101, 234
Insurrection 35, 96, 120, 179, 234
Inter-Factory Strike Committee Poland 234
Internationalism
Internationalist 234
Intifada 29, 50, 89, 95, 97, 112, 118, 130, 155, 181, 187, 218, 219, 223, 226, 234
Iran 9, 21, 27, 28, 39, 41, 49, 53, 57, 59, 62, 64, 67–69, 79, 80, 83, 85, 86, 89, 92, 96, 137–39, 166, 168, 185, 219, 220, 225–28, 234, 238
Iraq 12, 13, 37, 39, 41, 42, 48–50, 52, 53, 66–69, 75, 77, 83, 85–87, 91, 94, 95, 100–103, 107, 115, 116, 119, 144, 154, 158, 161, 162, 165, 166, 168, 169, 198, 212–14, 218, 219, 222, 226–29, 234
Iraq Petroleum Company IPC 67, 234
Ishtaraki, al- 234
Islah, al- 234
Islambouli, Khalid al- 234
Islamic State of Iraq and Syria ISIS 234

Islam Islamic 234
Islamism Islamist 234
Israel Israeli Israelis 234
ISROR Tunisia 234
Istanbul 85, 234
Italian Italy 234

J

Jabhat al-Nusra 33, 197, 234
Janjaweed 44, 158, 165, 166
Janub, al-Hizam 206
Jarrah 50
Jenin 50
Jerusalem 50, 51, 131, 216, 226
Jisr al-Shughour 32
Jordan 12, 42, 117, 123, 165, 168, 234
Journalist 29, 145, 234
Judges/Judicial/Judiciary 234
Jumlukiyya 102, 234
Justice and Development Party (AKP) Turkey 234

K

Kabyle, Kabylia 234
Kafr, al-Dawwar 125, 234
Kalakla 44, 111, 204, 206, 234
Karman 29, 234
Karman, Tawakkul 234
Kasbah 22, 234
Kasserine 21, 22, 109, 162, 234
Kautsky, Karl 234
Kemal 62, 234
Kenana 43, 204, 216, 234
Kerbala 49, 234
Khaldoun 109, 234
Khartoum 44, 45, 105, 108, 111, 112, 134, 140, 143, 160, 169, 202–7, 215, 220, 222, 225, 234
Khawa 50, 51, 234
Khawalid 27, 234
Khenchala 46, 234
Kherrata 46, 234
Khomeini, Ayatollah Ruhollah al- 234
Khul 140
Kirkuk 85
Kobani 200
Kordofan 44, 202
Koshary 207
Kuwait 12, 67, 92, 118, 165, 168

L

Labour 8, 17, 21, 27, 38, 48, 52, 57–60, 82, 84, 88, 89, 94, 102, 107, 108, 111, 112, 115–19, 122, 125, 127, 129–31, 133, 135–37, 140, 143, 144, 148, 166, 172, 177, 186, 202, 216–18, 220, 226, 228
Land-grab 59, 61, 235
Landlord Landlords
Landowner Landowners
Landownership Landowning 235
Latakia 31, 235
Lawyers 235
Leaders Leadership
Leaderships 235
Lebanese Lebanon 235
Lecturers 100, 199, 235
Left-Nasserists 38, 235
Left-Wing Leftist 235
Legislation 95, 126, 235
Lend-Lease 235
Lenin, Vladimir, 13-14, 21,

24-25, 31, 110, 114, 122, 177, 325, 335, 337, 339, 344, 346, 349, 350, 351, 352, 354, 359, 360, 371, 409, 411, 413
Levant 235
LGBT 146, 170, 218, 235
Libya 235
Liebknecht, Karl 235
Local Coordinating Committees (Syria) 235
London 3, 60, 212–26, 228, 229, 235
Luxemburg, Rosa, 13-14, 32, 34, 122, 262, 312, 346, 350
Lydd 51, 235

M

Mada Masr 43, 219, 222, 235
Madaniyy Madaniyya Madany 235
Mahalla, al-Kubra al- 235
Malls, shopping 235
Malnutrition 39, 108
Manama 27, 28, 185
Manbij 197, 199
Manifesto 16, 223
Mansoura-Espana 141
Manufacturing 57, 73–76, 79, 80, 82, 85, 93, 99, 102, 116, 117, 124, 126, 129, 133, 138, 197, 212
Maoist 153
Martyrs 110, 170
Marxism 7, 178, 216, 228, 229, 235
Marx Karl 223, 235
Massacre 25, 38, 43–45, 160, 161, 204, 213, 225, 235
Memorandum of Understanding MOU 235
Mercenaries 169, 235

Merchants 59, 73, 74, 235
Messouci, Samira 235
Mexico 66, 235
Midan al-Taghir 235
Midan al-Tahrir 11, 219, 235
Migration 27, 87, 89, 98, 107, 108, 113, 117, 118, 129, 136, 169, 216, 222, 228, 235
Militarisation 167, 169, 199, 207, 235
Military-Bureaucratic machine 13, 164, 169, 235
Military-Industrial-Service complex 235
Militia 33, 40, 42, 44, 45, 49, 108, 157, 160, 161, 165, 201, 204, 220, 235
Minawi, Minni 235
Misogynist Misogyny 235
Misr al-Thawriyya 235
Misrata 26, 235
MKZ see Inter-Factory Strike Committee 235
Mobilisation 12, 27, 29, 30, 34, 35, 39, 44–51, 72, 86, 89, 97, 109–11, 113, 121, 122, 126, 128, 129, 133, 140, 153, 154, 157, 158, 175, 178, 180, 183, 184, 188–91, 194, 195, 199, 204, 235
Modernisation 61, 62, 117, 235
Modes of production 235
Monarch Monarchical Monarchies Monarchy 235
Monastir 124
Monopolies 65
Morocco 12, 42, 123, 129, 168, 215
Moscow 78, 216
Mosque 28, 50, 51, 91, 95, 110
Mosul 85, 87, 162, 201, 212

467

Movement 3, 4, 14, 16, 17, 21–24, 26–33, 37–40, 42–49, 51–53, 60, 61, 69–73, 76–78, 94–100, 103, 109–12, 116, 119–23, 127, 129–32, 138, 140, 143, 144, 147, 148, 153–62, 171, 173, 175, 176, 178–82, 185, 186, 189, 191, 193–95, 197–206, 210, 214, 216, 218, 219, 226, 229
Movement-Building 120
Muhassasa al- 236
Multinationals 101, 102, 236
Municipalities 189, 193, 236
Muslim Brotherhood 23, 25, 38, 93, 97, 100, 109, 113, 140, 141, 147, 148, 159, 190, 191, 195, 210, 212, 229, 236
Mutinies 32, 161, 173, 236
Muwazzafin 122, 236

N

Nahr, al-Bared 236
Naisse, Ghayath 236
Najaf, al- 236
Najd, al- 236
Nakba, al- 236
Naqab, al- 236
Nasser, Gamal Abdel 236
Nasserist 25, 73, 91, 95, 98, 130, 192, 194, 236
Nasserists 98, 236
National Democratic Party (NDP) Egypt 236
Nationalisation 68, 69, 74–77, 95, 236
Nationalism 236
National Salvation Front (NSF) 147, 195, 236
NATO 25, 26, 40, 69, 236
Nedaa, Tounes 236

Negev 88, 223, 236
Neoliberalism 3, 71, 75, 76, 79–81, 83, 86, 89, 93, 94, 101, 102, 106, 114–16, 118–20, 122, 212, 217, 222
Nepotism 113
Ngoisation 193, 198, 219
NGOs 156, 191
Nubians 9
Nyala 108, 111, 236

O

Obama, Barack 236
Ocalan, Abdullah 230, 236
Occupation 37, 41, 49, 60, 61, 69, 71, 88, 92, 101–3, 110, 117, 131, 132, 141, 154, 162, 169, 172, 181, 219, 225, 236
Oceania 166, 236
October Revolution 48, 175, 215, 219, 222, 236
Oil 20, 26, 27, 30, 33, 40, 41, 46, 57, 62–69, 71, 75–80, 82–85, 91, 115, 117, 118, 125, 129, 167, 180, 197, 200, 205, 210, 214, 220, 224, 226, 228, 236
Olive 57, 61, 219, 236
Oman 165, 168, 236
Omdurman 206, 236
Opposition Opposition
Oppositions 236
Organisation of Petroleum Exporting Countries OPEC 236
Orthodox Orthodoxy 236
Oslo Accord 118, 236

P

Pakistan 165, 172, 236
Palestine 8, 12, 42, 50, 52,

59–62, 69, 88, 98, 100, 111, 112, 117, 118, 162, 172, 213, 221, 225–27, 236, 237
Palestine Liberation Organisation PLO 236
Palmyra 197, 236
Pan-Arab 37, 236
Pandemic 39, 48, 49, 52, 53, 83, 118, 154, 202, 236
Parallel Revolution 29, 30, 236
Paramilitarisation 169, 236
Paramilitary 26, 42, 49, 52, 87, 102, 154, 163–68, 172, 205, 236
Paris 60, 164, 170, 171, 176–78, 182, 207, 224, 236
Paris Commune 164, 170, 171, 176–78, 236
Participatory 122, 126, 203
Party 17, 22–24, 28, 30, 31, 37, 38, 46, 60, 66, 69, 72, 73, 75, 77, 78, 81, 82, 85, 91–97, 99–102, 107, 109–11, 126–29, 131, 140, 147, 152–54, 165, 171, 176, 178, 179, 185, 189, 191–96, 199–201, 207–10, 213, 216, 222, 223, 229, 233, 234, 236
Paypal 88
Pearling 57, 62
Pearl Roundabout 27, 28, 216
People-Trafficking 165
Permanent Revolution 3, 14, 15, 71, 150, 174–76, 183–88, 192, 193, 198, 205, 208, 209, 216, 228, 237
Persia 62
Petrochemicals 84
Petrodollars 84, 237
Petroleum 67, 218, 224, 231, 234, 236, 237
Pharmaceutical 93, 237

Pharmacies Pharmacists 237
Pharmalliance 93, 237
Piety 91, 95, 99, 237
Planned Planning 237
Plantation 59, 60, 80, 237
Plebiscitary 190, 195, 237
Poland 77, 179, 234, 237
Polar Classes 16, 237
Polarisation 35, 37, 38, 41, 82, 101, 146, 147, 155, 183, 237
Police 12, 14, 21, 23, 27, 31, 47, 51, 80, 89, 109, 110, 124, 138, 140, 143–46, 157, 159, 160, 162, 166, 170, 172, 173, 177, 178, 182, 190–92, 202, 215, 220, 225, 237
Political revolution 9, 14, 28, 42, 79, 122, 185, 206, 237
Polluter 210, 237
Popular Front the Liberation of Palestine PFLP 237
Port 22, 30, 41–43, 48, 53, 77, 111, 117, 122, 125, 203, 213, 225, 237
Portugal 154, 181, 237
Post-Colonial 52, 60, 161, 171, 237
Poverty 16, 23, 27, 39, 40, 46, 49, 52, 73, 82, 85, 88, 97, 101, 107, 110, 214, 228, 237
Power 3, 5, 9, 12–15, 17, 18, 24, 25, 29, 30, 32, 35, 37–40, 42, 44–46, 48–50, 58, 59, 62, 63, 65, 67–78, 80, 82, 83, 85, 86, 88, 92–94, 96, 98–103, 107, 109, 112, 115, 122, 129, 131, 135–40, 143, 146, 147, 153–58, 162, 164, 167–70, 172–79, 181–87, 189, 191–93, 197–206, 208–10, 213, 215, 222, 224, 226, 229, 232, 237
Power-Sharing 92, 100, 160,

Pravda 176, 222, 228
Pre-Capitalist 15, 57, 58, 60, 62, 84, 96
Precarious 46, 105, 111, 112, 122, 141
Privatisation 38, 43, 81, 83, 84, 93, 97, 101, 114, 117, 122, 141, 180
Professionals 18, 21, 42, 43, 52, 103, 110, 113, 114, 123, 152, 161, 202, 204, 228, 239
Proletarianisation 114, 117
Propaganda 28, 33, 162, 190, 191, 209
Protest 9, 17, 19–24, 26–31, 39, 42–53, 71, 79, 82, 94, 97, 111, 112, 124, 127, 128, 131, 133, 142, 143, 145, 147, 154, 155, 158, 159, 165, 168, 170, 173, 174, 180, 183, 184, 190, 202, 204, 206, 212, 216, 218, 219, 221–23, 225
Public Sector 30, 44, 46, 74, 75, 81–83, 87, 93, 94, 96, 97, 101, 113, 116–18, 120, 121, 125, 128–31, 137, 199, 200, 205, 215, 226

Q

Qatar 33, 40, 67, 68, 165, 168, 237
Qualitative Military Edge QME 87, 237

R

Rabat 185, 237
Racism 9, 12, 132, 136, 143, 144, 180, 237
Radiologists 43, 237
Railworkers 77, 237
Rainbow flag 237
Ramallah 50, 131, 237
Rape 44, 139, 145, 220, 237
Rapid Support Forces RSF 237
Raqqa 108, 162, 198, 201, 237
Reciprocal Action 175, 177, 181, 182, 184, 186, 237
Refineries 43, 237
Reformism 90, 97, 98, 102, 120, 152, 153, 156, 216, 222, 237
Regime 12, 13, 19–21, 23–35, 37–45, 47–50, 52, 53, 59, 61, 62, 68, 73–76, 78, 80, 82, 83, 85–87, 89, 92–103, 107, 109–13, 124, 127–30, 132, 133, 139, 140, 142, 143, 146, 147, 152, 154, 156–62, 172, 174, 178, 180, 181, 183, 189, 190, 192, 195–202, 204–6, 213, 224, 225, 237
Religiosity 94, 139, 237
Resistance Committees 4, 45, 160, 184, 188, 189, 195, 201–8, 224, 237
Resource-Extraction 61, 237
Revolt 3, 9, 13, 17, 20, 22, 26, 29, 34, 35, 42, 46, 49, 53, 60, 73, 80, 82, 83, 95, 96, 105, 109, 110, 119, 121, 122, 124, 125, 128, 129, 133, 137, 162, 164, 180, 207, 217, 219–21, 224, 226, 229, 237
Revolution 1–24, 26–40, 42, 44, 45, 48, 49, 53, 55–57, 61, 62, 65, 68, 69, 71, 72, 74–79, 83, 86, 89, 90, 94, 96, 103, 106–13, 118–20, 122, 128, 129, 132–35, 137–39, 141–45,

150, 151, 153–55, 157, 158, 160–64, 166, 170, 171, 173–96, 198–202, 204–10, 213–29, 236, 237, 239
Revolutionary party 176, 178, 207–10
Revolutionary Socialists (Egypt), 378-9, 415
Revolution Sunday 142, 189
Rif ,Dimashq 196
Riyadh 28, 206
Roadblocks 48, 108
Rojava 200, 201, 219, 221
Rouiba 46
Royalist 69
Rulership 13, 238
Ruling-class 96, 238
Rumaila 67, 238
Rural 17, 32, 61, 72, 73, 86, 105–11, 117, 129, 139, 161, 171, 180, 181, 185, 205, 206, 212, 218, 228, 238
Russia 15, 16, 40, 41, 49, 63, 71, 73, 84, 165, 166, 175, 176, 178, 179, 184–86, 216, 227, 238

S

Saadallah 199, 238
Sabahi, Hamdeen 238
Sadat,, Anwar 238
Sadr Muqtada al- 238
Sahwa, al- 238
Saied, Kais 238
Sailors 174, 238
Salafist 33, 34, 40, 41, 140, 146, 147, 192, 194, 238
Sanctions 26, 41, 49, 83, 86, 87, 92, 95, 101, 102, 116, 238
Saraqib 196, 197, 238
Saudi Arabia 12, 22, 27–30, 39–41, 45, 53, 59, 62, 64, 67, 68, 85, 97, 100, 101, 138, 161, 165, 166, 168, 169, 202, 212, 223, 238
Sawiris, Naguib 238
Sayga Flour Mills 43, 238
School 12, 21, 22, 31, 108, 110–12, 122, 126–28, 137, 147, 199, 200, 223, 238
Scramble For Africa 61, 238
Sectarianism 28, 35, 41, 91, 94, 100, 101, 222
Secular 23, 34, 35, 37, 38, 74, 91, 97, 134, 144, 146–49, 153, 155, 159, 238
Security 23–32, 35, 38, 43, 45, 47–49, 51, 69, 80, 88, 93, 102, 105, 106, 108–11, 118, 127, 130, 132, 137, 139, 142–44, 154, 155, 157–59, 162, 164–69, 172, 173, 182–84, 187, 189–92, 199, 203, 206, 207, 212, 214, 216, 220, 222, 228, 231
Self-determination 155, 222
Self-employment 115
Self-government 175, 196
Self-management 72
Self-organisation 51, 115–17, 120, 124, 126, 153, 187, 189, 196, 204, 210
Sellal 47
Settlements 112, 131
Settler-Colonialism 52
Settlers 51, 59, 61, 131
Seven Sisters the 226
Sexism 24, 142–45, 149
Sexual assault 238
Sexual harassment 51, 138, 139, 144, 146, 226, 238
Sfax 22, 124, 127, 238
Shabiha 32, 35, 165, 238

Shafiq, Ahmad 238
Shah of Iran 64, 238
Shantytowns 181, 238
Sheikhdoms 62, 238
Shell 66, 238
Shibin, al-Kom 125, 238
Shora 181, 238
Shouman, Major Ahmed 238
Shura Council 147, 238
Sidi Bouzid 21, 107, 162, 238
Siege 32, 48, 50, 100, 110, 112, 187, 189, 197, 238
Silmiyy 155, 238
Sinai 69, 187, 238
Sirte 26, 41, 238
Sit-in 22, 24, 25, 44, 49, 126, 133, 134, 143, 144, 160, 189, 191, 194, 204, 238
SNVI 46, 117, 124, 128, 238
Socal 67
Social Democratic 127, 153, 171
Socialisation 135
Socialism 5, 16, 72, 74, 76, 77, 79, 96, 153, 170, 176, 185, 209, 212–17, 219, 220, 222–24, 229
Socialists 63, 164, 171, 175, 191, 209, 227
Social Revolution 14, 16, 174, 175, 183, 187, 208
Societal revolution 14
Soldiers 15, 31, 32, 45, 60, 61, 145, 162, 166, 167, 171–76, 178, 206, 216
Solidarity 4, 5, 22, 24, 34, 35, 37, 38, 43, 44, 47–49, 53, 77, 109, 114, 115, 123, 126–28, 131–33, 142–45, 160, 179, 186, 187, 189, 201, 203, 205, 212–16, 218, 220, 221, 223–25

Sonatrach 46, 125, 239
Sonelgaz 125, 239
Soviet Union 63–70, 72, 74, 78, 79, 87, 91, 118, 167, 175, 220, 222, 239
Soweto 186, 216, 239
Stalinism 239
State and Revolution (Lenin) 239
State capitalism 66, 71, 74, 86, 89, 216, 239
State feminism 239
State-formation 62, 239
State-owned 30, 66, 125, 239
Steel 15, 74, 75, 84, 92, 102, 124, 133, 167, 239
Steelworkers 17, 239
Stevedores 122, 125, 239
Strikes 12, 17, 22, 24, 26, 29, 30, 34–38, 40, 42–48, 50, 52, 53, 68, 71, 73, 77, 78, 94, 96, 99, 103, 120–27, 129–34, 140–42, 149, 152, 155, 158–61, 165, 174, 175, 178–80, 183, 184, 189, 190, 192–95, 199, 202, 204, 205, 207, 209, 210, 213, 221, 239
Sub-contracting 95, 122, 239
Sub-imperial 64, 86, 239
Subsidies 38, 59, 62, 83, 107, 137, 239
Subsistence farming 239
Succession 15, 93, 157, 211, 239
Sudanese Professionals Association SPA 239
Suez 68, 133, 142, 239
Sufi 61
Sugar 43, 204
Sunni 27, 28, 35, 36, 41, 83, 92, 101, 158, 225
Supermarkets 179

Superpowers 65, 68, 79
Supremacist 51
Syria 3, 9, 12, 20, 31–35, 37, 39, 41, 42, 68, 70, 73–75, 78, 83, 85, 87, 89, 92, 94–97, 99, 101, 102, 106–8, 110, 119, 122, 129, 130, 133, 154, 158, 162, 165, 166, 168, 169, 171, 185, 188, 189, 199, 204, 212, 213, 215, 216, 218, 220–22, 225, 227, 229, 234, 235

T

Tabriz 181
Tahrir Square 23, 29, 49, 109, 110, 133, 142, 144–46, 170, 173, 189–91, 194, 210, 220, 239
Talpiot 88, 239
Tamarod 38, 195, 239
Tansiqiyyat 202, 239
Tathir 192, 193, 205, 239
Teachers 21, 22, 32, 44, 46, 72, 100, 110, 113, 114, 118, 122, 123, 126–29, 131, 141, 196, 197, 199, 200, 203–5, 223–25, 239
Teargas 31, 143, 239
Tebboune 47, 239
Technical 66, 199, 239
Technocrats 42, 161, 210, 239
Technologies 15, 58, 60, 88, 167, 207, 239
Teenagers 31, 239
Tehran 181, 239
Telecoms 43, 44, 81, 133, 199, 239
Temperatures 53, 239
Terbil 25, 239
Terbil Fethi 239
Terrorism 35, 239

Tev-Dem 200, 239
Texas 66, 239
Textiles 57, 80, 93, 133, 239
Thala 21, 22, 109, 239
Torture 12, 31, 38, 77, 146, 152, 160, 164, 173, 192, 219
Trade unions 24, 27, 34, 38, 43, 74, 77, 94, 98, 113, 122, 128, 129, 131, 140, 144, 158, 159, 183, 184, 194, 199, 207, 209, 218, 222, 229, 232, 233
Transport 32, 44, 52, 61, 65, 71, 82, 115, 117, 121, 124, 125, 129, 133, 136–38, 140, 167, 189, 193, 199, 200
Tripoli 26, 40
Trotsky, Leon, 13, 25, 26-29, 33, 138-139, 309, 335, 345, 346-9, 361-2, 365-6, 371, 417
Trotskyist 8
Trotsky, Leon 228
Truman Harry 228
Tsarism 176, 240
Tuk-Tuk 117, 240
Tunis 22, 109, 207, 240
Tunisia 12, 20, 21, 23, 25, 26, 30, 34, 35, 37, 38, 42, 59–61, 70–75, 81, 82, 89, 92, 94, 99, 106–9, 111, 115, 116, 119–21, 124–27, 129, 133, 139, 140, 146–48, 154, 157–59, 162, 168, 177, 185, 198, 199, 207, 210, 213–15, 217, 218, 220, 221, 234, 240
Turabi, Hassan al- 240
Turkey 8, 9, 32, 33, 39–41, 53, 57, 59, 62, 67, 69, 80, 83, 85, 86, 99, 103, 166, 169, 185, 201, 222, 228, 233, 234, 240
TV 38, 240
Twitter 134, 240

U

UK 3, 138, 166, 212–17, 219, 220, 222–24, 226–28, 240
Umm al-Fahm 50, 51, 240
UN 26, 39, 101, 108, 212, 228, 240
Unemployed Unemployment 240
Union of Property Tax Collectors RETAU Egypt 240
Union of Soviet Socialist Republics USSR 240
Union Unionism 240
United Arab Emirates UAE 240
United Arab Republic UAR 73, 240
United States US 240
Universities 46, 119, 133, 148, 181
Uprising 4, 5, 11, 20–22, 24–27, 29, 30, 32–35, 37, 38, 40, 42–44, 50–53, 60, 77, 92, 97, 98, 108–11, 113, 116, 117, 121, 122, 124, 127–30, 132–34, 141–43, 145, 152–55, 158, 163, 173, 179–82, 185, 189–92, 194, 198, 199, 202, 204, 207, 211, 217, 219, 221, 229
Urban 21, 59, 60, 71–75, 80, 82, 83, 86, 96, 105–9, 111, 112, 117, 120, 130, 138, 139, 148, 161, 181, 190, 198, 205, 206, 228, 229
Urbanisation 106
Utilities 124, 192

V

Vanguard 70, 97, 161, 206

Venezuela 66, 67

W

WAC-Maan 132, 229
Wage-workers 114
Wahhabism 62, 240
War 8, 12, 16, 20, 25, 26, 30–34, 36, 37, 39–42, 48, 58, 60, 62–65, 67–73, 75, 76, 78, 80, 83, 86, 87, 92, 93, 97, 99–103, 107, 108, 110, 115, 116, 118, 121, 128, 129, 132, 154, 155, 158, 161, 162, 167–69, 171, 179, 180, 182, 183, 185, 197, 201, 207, 210, 212, 213, 217, 218, 221–23, 226, 228, 229, 240
Warlord 102, 240
Wataniyy Wataniyya Watany 240
Water 31, 32, 65, 107, 112, 117, 122, 124, 131, 180, 191, 198, 199, 217, 225, 240
Wealth 12, 15, 46, 56, 62, 68, 77, 82–84, 93, 96, 100, 101, 105, 113, 179, 240
Weapon 17, 156, 171, 173, 194, 204, 240
Western governments 118, 152, 161, 198, 240
Whatsapp 48, 51, 52, 143, 222, 240
Wildfires 53, 240
Women 3, 12, 24, 29, 34–36, 44, 49, 51, 53, 93, 95, 105, 107, 108, 115, 116, 126, 134–49, 166, 169, 170, 200, 204, 205, 213, 216, 219–23, 225–29, 240
Workers 3, 8, 15, 17, 24, 27, 28, 30, 32, 34, 37, 38, 41–44,

46, 48, 52, 57–60, 65, 68,
71–75, 77, 78, 84, 85, 89,
93–96, 100, 110–18, 120–33,
135–38, 140–43, 153, 154,
156, 158, 159, 170, 171,
174–81, 183–89, 192–97,
199–201, 203–11, 213–16,
218, 219, 221, 223–26, 229,
239, 240
Working-class 78, 94, 109,
136, 240
Workplace 46, 116, 122,
126–28, 131, 135–37, 140,
142, 148, 178, 180, 181, 192,
193, 203, 205, 240
Workplace-Based 205, 240

X

Xenophobia 35, 36, 240

Y

Yemen 12, 29, 30, 34, 37,
39–42, 71, 106, 107, 115,
116, 154, 162, 166, 168, 169,
211–14, 218, 224, 227, 228,
240
Youssef 146, 240
Youth 21, 22, 25–28, 38, 46,
50, 118, 119, 128, 190, 195,
215, 220, 226, 240

Z

Zionism 61, 132, 214, 223
Zombie parties 91